DUEL FOR THE SKY

DUEL FOR THE SKY

CHRISTOPHER SHORES

Doubleday & Company, Inc.

Garden City, New York
1985

Duel for the Sky was edited, designed and produced by Grub Street, London

Library of Congress Cataloging in Publication Data

Shores, Christopher
  Duel for the sky.

  Includes index.
  1. World War, 1939–1945—Aerial operations.   2. Air
  warfare—History. I. Title.
  D785.S455 1985   940.54′4   85-4380

  ISBN 0-385-19917-1

Printed in Great Britain by
Blantyre Printing & Binding Ltd.,
London and Glasgow.

CONTENTS

INTRODUCTION 6

GLOSSARY 8

ACKNOWLEDGEMENTS 12

CHAPTER ONE

BLITZKRIEG ON POLAND
13

CHAPTER TWO

THE BATTLE OF BRITAIN
29

CHAPTER THREE

INVASION OF THE PHILIPPINES
61

CHAPTER FOUR

THE LONG STRUGGLE FOR MALTA
77

CHAPTER FIVE

THE BATTLE FOR GUADALCANAL
93

CHAPTER SIX

BREAKING THE MARETH LINE
121

CHAPTER SEVEN

FIERCE CLASHES AT KURSK
137

CHAPTER EIGHT

THE NIGHT BOMBER OFFENSIVE
153

CHAPTER NINE

THE DAYLIGHT BOMBER OFFENSIVE
169

CHAPTER TEN

THE GREAT MARIANAS 'TURKEY SHOOT'
189

INDEX 206

INTRODUCTION

This is a book about air battles — crucial air battles — and specifically those which occurred 40 or more years ago during World War II. Battles are one of the major facets of wars, and wars are one of mankind's oldest forms of activity. Wars are intricate, with inter-relating causes, and similarly battles are not events in isolation; the degrees of planning leading up to them can vary considerably, but they occur in the main as a direct result of politico-geographical imperatives.

Air battles particularly take place as a direct result of what is happening — or is about to happen — on the surface of the globe below, and cannot be understood without reference to such factors. For this reason a background to each battle has been provided in the text, together with a map of the area over which it was to occur.

Fighting in the air is but an infant compared with the more traditional forms of military and naval action, yet it has transformed the face of war totally. Setting aside the ultimate use of air power to deliver thermo-nuclear devices, whereby war, civilization, and indeed probably life itself ceases in any recognizable form, air power alone cannot win wars. Yet without control of the skies, the battle on land or sea probably can no longer be won. Bear in mind too that by the mid 1980s the world had had some 70 years' experience of the military use of the sky, gained in numerous wars of greater or lesser importance. Time and experience now provide a fairly comprehensive appreciation of what can and cannot be achieved by air power.

In 1939 much less than half this time had expired; theories abounded — many of which greatly overestimated the effects of action from the air and underestimated man's ability to adapt to and resist this new threat — but experience was lacking. Rapid technological change appeared to have rendered many of the early lessons learned during World War I already outdated. Generally, this was not to be the case, but it is a common human failing to overrate new developments and underrate the lessons of history.

Writings of the leading visionaries and thinkers such as America's 'Billy' Mitchell and Italy's General Guilio Douhet tended to overstate the effectiveness of the bomber, but Douhet gave tongue to one truism which was to stand the test of time: 'He who seeks to control the battlefield must first control the air above it.'

It will be seen in the accounts of the battles to come that the instrument of air superiority is the fighter aircraft, while the instrument of air power is the bomber. However, early theories giving great predominance to the bomber tended to downgrade the fighter as a mainly defensive weapon. Defensive weapons can prevent wars being lost, but cannot by their nature win them; that is the function of the offensive weapon. Since resources are always restricted, governments and military establishments favor those weapons which can win the war or, even better, have a dual function. In consequence, fighter aviation had, in general, been somewhat neglected prior to 1939, because its function and need was not fully understood. This proved an expensive lesson to learn.

Much controversy has surrounded the mounting of sustained bombing offensives against the Axis powers by the Western Allies, the results achieved for the effort invested being the subject of frequent dispute. Let it be clear that this was not the result of long planned strategy. True, certain air force commanders in Britain and the United States believed that air power alone could bring an enemy nation to its knees, and lost no opportunity to press these convictions on any politician who would listen. Only the naive, however, would believe that governments were convinced of this.

Quite simply, the expulsion of the Western Allies from the main European and Asian land masses by the early superiority of the Axis forces prevented the initial weight of effort being thrown into major land battles. So great is the preponderance of strength and resources necessary to mount a seaborne invasion as a preliminary to such land battles, that it had to be some years before the greater productive capacity of the West could overtake the opposition.

In the meantime, the launching of air bombardment campaigns on a massive scale appeared to be the most cost-effective way of maintaining some form of action against the enemy in the interim. It was hoped that this would divert from the Eastern Front at least some proportion of Germany's resources for home defense, to allow a degree of support to the hard-pressed Soviets — the only members of the Allies who were involved in truly major land warfare.

The role of an air force

It should not be forgotten that the first military function of aviation was reconnaissance, and while often overlooked, this remains one of the most important tasks of any air force. To know what the opponent is going to do before he does it grants an inestimable advantage to any commander.

The roles of an air force therefore may be summed up as follows:-

1 Strategic Reconnaissance.
   In effect, the ability to fly over the opponent's back garden and see what he plans to do before he does it.
2 Air Defense.
   The ability to defend one's own back garden from hostile reconnaissance or bombing attack, allowing forces to be marshalled for action and weapons to be produced.
3 Counter-Air.
   The destruction of the opponent's air force over the chosen battlefield and/or over his own back garden to allow one's own reconnaissance, bombing and ground-support aircraft to operate with impunity either in support of the ground forces or against the opponent's sources of production. The objective is to gain at least superiority, and preferably, supremacy over the chosen area.
4 The Exercise of Air Superiority/Supremacy.

The employment of bombing and ground-support aircraft in direct support of the forces on the ground by attacking the opponent's defensive positions, troop concentrations, supply convoys, etc. Tactical reconnaissance to see where he is marshalling his reserves, bringing forward or pulling back units, etc. The use of transport aircraft to carry up supplies and reinforcements, evacuate casualties, etc; and bombing the opponent's communications with his home base, and his sources of production there.

Number 3 can take two major forms. Essentially, it is a battle to control the air between the fighter aircraft of the opposing sides. Against a small, or unprepared opponent, the 'pre-emptive strike' can be highly effective, whereby at one fell swoop his aircraft are destroyed on the ground in a surprise attack. This is not so effective against a major industrial nation, since only the aircraft are destroyed, and these can be relatively easily and quickly replaced from production. Effective pilots take over a year to produce however, and in this case 'counter-air' must take the form of a series of air battles of attrition in order that sufficient of the opponent's experienced pilots may be rendered non-effective (by killing, wounding or capturing) to make it impossible for his fighter force to provide the necessary protection against attack on his other aircraft, his land forces, and his production facilities.

Selection of battles

All these various roles will appear in the battles to be related. These were of widely different duration, size, and effect, but all marked a particular milestone in the development of air warfare. They were by no means the only crucial engagements of World War II, but have been selected to provide an insight into the similarities and differences of the various theaters of war, and of the interaction between them. In selecting them, I have sought to identify those which either had a major effect on the course of the war as a whole, or introduced some important new role or tactic in the development of air power. Several of the battles dealt with are well-known, but not all.

Consideration has also been given to providing the widest possible diversity of geographical location, air forces, aircraft types and circumstances in order not to confront the reader with too many battles of a repetitive nature. Efforts have also been made to show the general changes occurring in the air over the six-year period of hostilities.

'Blitzkrieg' on Poland was selected as it introduced air support to modern armored armies on the ground in a manner which had only been a theorist's concept before. The Battle of Britain is probably the most famous air battle of all, and was a classic situation in that its conclusion was a pre-condition to any other action by land, sea or air. Its repercussions were far reaching in the long term, while its implementation introduced many new facets to aerial warfare. For this reason it is given particularly substantial coverage, although the reader will soon discover that this author questions the degree of decisiveness attributed to its events then and now.

The long defense of Malta was chosen to illustrate a truly heroic series of actions which had a marked effect on the fighting in North Africa, and subsequently in the Mediterranean area as a whole. The Japanese destruction of US air power in the Philippines demonstrates one of the fastest and most complete aerial victories of the war. At Guadalcanal the efforts of the US Marine and Navy air units were critical to the American hold on this island, the securing of which was undoubtedly one of the turning points of the war. It started the haemorrhage of the Japanese Naval Air Force in the Solomons which resulted directly in the overwhelming US naval victories of 1944.

Mareth was not a battle of major import in the strategic sense. However, it was a watershed in the Allied application of tactical air power. For the first time Allied air units intervened directly in the air battle, as the Luftwaffe had been doing since 1939. Such an intervention proved decisive on this first occasion and paved the way for victories such as that at Avranches in Normandy against a German armored thrust in August 1944.

Kursk warranted inclusion for two reasons. Firstly, it marked the large-scale introduction of really effective anti-tank aircraft by both sides. Secondly, the scale of victories claimed made its opening day the greatest day of aerial combat the world has ever seen, and one unlikely to be repeated. The land actions which these aerial activities supported were undoubtedly the major turning point of the European war.

The Anglo-American day and night bomber offensives were the true manifestation of all the theories and hopes for the exercise of independent air power as a war-winning element in its own right. As such both warrant consideration as to their successes and failures. Taking place with massive forces over vast areas and during the course of several years, these were campaigns rather than battles. Therefore, each campaign is sketched in as background, with a particular battle picked out in detail to demonstrate typical events in more depth.

'Big Week' has been chosen for the daylight campaign as it marked the start of an offensive against the Luftwaffe fighter force which, while not decisive at the time, marked the beginning of its destruction and therefore was to have repercussions throughout every aspect of the rest of the European war. The Leipzig raid represents one of the two hardest and most costly battles ever fought by Bomber Command. In terms of cost it was second only to the Nuremburg attack which has already been the subject of thorough investigation.

Finally, the Marianas carrier battle gave the Americans a far greater victory at much lower cost than they could have anticipated. It demonstrated suddenly the total eclipse of the Imperial Japanese Navy and the relative invulnerability of the new US Fast Carrier Task Forces; it was truly the beginning of the end of the Pacific War.

Despite the conscious attempt to ensure variety, several threads run through the book — most especially the interaction of one battle on another far away; and the appearance of certain units and personnel again and again in widely different areas and situations. For instance, the great German fighter pilot Heinz Bär appears briefly in the Battle of Britain, and then over Malta, Mareth, and finally during the 'Big Week' fighting of the day-bomber offensive. Japan's Saburo Sakai features in every Pacific battle to some extent, and there are other such linking elements, the Polish pilot Stanislaw Skalski being another example.

There are many battles which could have been included instead — Midway and the destruction of the Red Air Force during Operation *Barbarossa* in June 1941 being just two. Indeed, there are many endless permutations, but at the end of the day, choice must always be subjective and the following ten battles most faithfully represent the criteria I outlined above.

GLOSSARY

In order that the reader may appreciate some of the terms, abbreviations and designations used within the text, a synopsis is provided below of the basic unit, rank and command structures of the air forces involved in the various chapters, together with an explanation of some of the technical or semi-technical terms used in the text.

United States Army Air Force (USAAF)

The basic command unit was the Group, which was usually composed of a Headquarters flight and three squadrons. During the course of the war most bomber groups were increased in size by the addition of a fourth squadron. Normal strength in aircraft and pilots of each squadron was sufficient to allow 12 fighters or nine bombers to be operated regularly. As the war progressed this number was frequently increased to 16 and 12 respectively. Except in the Pacific war zone, it was rare for squadrons to operate individually — they operated as a part of the group. Command of a squadron would normally be in the hands of a Major, though it was not uncommon for fighter squadrons to be commanded by Captains — or even by 1st Lieutenants in the early months of the war. Commander of the group was usually a Lieutenant Colonel, who had a second officer of this rank, or a senior Major as his Group Operations officer.

For administrative purposes a number of groups would be formed into a Combat Wing in the larger US theater air forces, a separate air force being formed for each war zone initially, while later the more important war zones would have two air forces, one for independent strategic operations and one for tactical activities in support of ground armies. Only in the very large 8th Air Force were Combat Wings gathered into Air Divisions. In other air forces the Wings came under the direct command of the air force headquarters.

Aircrew ranks in diminishing order of seniority were:

Brigadier General	(Brig Gen)
Colonel	(Col)
Lieutenant-Colonel	(Lt Col)
Major	(Maj)
Captain	(Capt)
1st Lieutenant	(1/Lt)
2nd Lieutenant	(2/Lt)

A few pilots also served in the non-commissioned rank of Flight Officer (Flt Off), basically a Warrant Officer grade. In bomber units gunners were generally enlisted men of a variety of non-commissioned ranks, while navigators, bomb-aimers, pilots and radio operators were generally commissioned officers.

United States Navy (USN)

US Navy air units were normally formed into Air Groups, each aircraft carrier having an air group allocated to it. For the large Fleet carriers, the group usually comprised a fighter squadron (VF), bomber squadron (VB), scouting squadron (VS) and torpedo-bomber squadron (VT): each squadron usually carried the same suffix number as the air group. On the smaller light carriers, the air group tended to comprise only a fighter squadron and a bomber or torpedo-bomber squadron. Escort carriers carried single composite squadrons (VC), containing both fighter and bomber aircraft. The aircraft strength of a squadron varied with the size of carrier, but in some of the Fleet carriers, fighter squadrons particularly could be almost the size of a USAAF group, while on light carriers they would be nearer the size of a standard USAAF squadron.

Air groups were generally led by a Commander or Lieutenant Commander, while squadrons were usually in the hands of a Lieutenant Commander. Apart from a few rare exceptions early in the war, all US Navy pilots were commissioned officers, though gunners were frequently of non-commissioned rank.

Pilot ranks were:

Commander	(Cdr)
Lieutenant Commander	(Lt Cdr)
Lieutenant	(Lt)
Lieutenant (junior grade)	(Lt (jg))
Ensign	(Ens)

United States Marine Corps (USMC)

Marine squadrons were generally land-based and were comparable in size to USAAF squadrons. They were formed into Marine Air Groups (MAG) which usually administered four–six squadrons divided equally between fighter (VMF) and bomber (VMSB) units, which carried three figure unit numbers related to the MAG number. Squadrons operated as independent units in action in the majority of cases. Squadron commanders were generally Majors, MAG commanders being Lieutenant Colonels or senior Majors. Like the USN, pilots were generally commissioned officers after the early months of the war, while gunners were often NCOs. Ranks were similar to those in the USAAF.

Royal Air Force (RAF)

The RAF basic unit was the squadron, structures above this level being much less formal and less structured than in most other air forces. Squadrons were generally of a size to be able to operate at least 12 aircraft on a regular basis, though frequently this strength was increased later in the war. After 1940 all aircrew were of at least Sergeant rank; gunners had been volunteers from other duties down to the lowest rank of Aircraftsmen 2nd Class (AC2) prior to this, but pilots too could be of NCO rank.

Squadrons were subdivided into Flights, but these usually operated only as a part of the squadron. Initially Flight Lieutenants held flight commander posts and Squadron Leaders headed squadrons. At an early date the ranks in units equipped with multi-engined aircraft were increased to Squadron Leader and Wing Commander respectively, since the numbers of personnel commanded were much larger than in the single-engined (usually fighter) squadrons. For operational purposes RAF components overseas grouped squadrons into Wings of three–six squadrons, but squadrons were interchangeable between Wings. Such Wings were usually commanded by a Group Captain and led by a Wing Leader of Wing Commander rank. Wings were grouped administratively into Groups, each group serving a command and supply function, rather than a direct operational function.

In the United Kingdom squadrons operated within groups which were both geographical and by function. Thus a Fighter Group, Bomber Group and Coastal Group might all operate in the same geographical area, but two Fighter Groups would not. The size of groups was flexible, and they were generally commanded by an Air Vice-Marshall (AVM). Squadrons were based at airfields, which were administered by a Group Captain; there would usually be one or two squadrons at a bomber or coastal airfield, while a fighter airfield in the operational zone would have at least three squadrons. At the latter there would also be a Sweep or Wing Leader of Wing Commander rank to lead the units in the air.

RAF aircrew ranks were:

Group Captain	(Gp Capt)
Wing Commander	(Wg Cdr)
Squadron Leader	(Sqn Ldr)
Flight Lieutenant	(Flt Lt)
Flying Officer	(Flg Off)
Pilot Officer	(Plt Off)
Warrant Officer	(Wt Off)
Flight Sergeant	(F/Sgt)
Sergeant	(Sgt)

Polish Air Force

The basic command unit was the Dyon (abbreviation of Dywizjona), or Wing, each of which contained two Eskadry (squadrons) of approximately the size of a Luftwaffe Staffel, rather than a British or US squadron. Until just before the outbreak of war, Dyons were allocated to Air Regiments which were geographically based to support the various ground armies. Hence 2nd Air Regiment, Kracow supported Army Kracow; 3rd Air Regiment, Poznan supported Army Poznan; 4th Air Regiment, Torun supported Army Pomorze, and so on, 1st Air Regiment being based on Warsaw.

Dyons were allocated Roman numerals as a prefix to the Arabic numeral of the Air Regiment to which they were allocated, and usually I and II Dyons were equipped with reconnaissance or light bombing aircraft, III Dyon with fighters. Only 1st Air Regiment had more than three Dyons. Thus III Fighter Dyon of the 6th Air Regiment would be identified as III/6 Dyon.

Eskadry within Dyons were given a double number identification, the first numeral identifying the Air Regiment. Thus the 4th Eskadra in the 3rd Air Regiment would be 34 Eskadra, forming one half of a separately numbered Dyon — for instance II/3 Dyon. The fighter eskadry were an exception to the rule. For historic reasons, having all originally been in one special Fighter Regiment, they carried three figure numbers; the last two numerals identified them in the same way as did those of the two-

numeral eskadry, but were prefixed with a 1. Hence the fighter eskadry of III/6 Dyon were numbered 161 and 162. Fighter eskadry were generally numbered 1 and 2 in an Air Regiment, light bomber and reconnaissance units taking up the numbers from 3 to 6.

When the first medium bomber eskadry were formed, new high-number special Dyons were created within the 1st Air Regiment, and the eskadry were given three figure numbers similar to the fighters, but prefixed with a 2. However it was intended that bombers should have their own independent range of numbers so that, for instance, the eskadry of the new Bomber Dyon X/1 were numbered 211 and 212.

Just before the outbreak of war a new independent Dispositional Air Force under the direct command of the Commander-in-Chief, Armed Forces, was formed from 1st Air Regiment. It contained a Pursuit Brigade for the defense of Warsaw with five eskadry, and a Bomber Brigade with nine eskadry. The fighters comprised the two Dyons already forming part of the Regiment, III/1 and IV/1, together with one independent unit. The Bomber Brigade included the two new medium bomber Dyons and two moved from the other Air Regiments, but which retained their Regimental Dyon and eskadra numbers. While the other Air Regiments were disbanded and the units they had controlled were attached directly to the geographical armies, the fighter Dyons retained their original designations.

However, because of the reduction in the number of light bomber units available to the armies due to the transfer of five to the Bomber Brigade, the remaining I and II Dyons with each army were disbanded and these eskadry operated independently, although still retaining their original numbers. A glance at the Order of Battle of the Polish Air Force (see page 20) will help unravel this rather complex chain of events.

Aircrew ranks were from Corporal to Colonel, the rank being followed by the function in abbreviated form — pil (pilot) or obs (observer). In the book ranks have been transposed into their English equivalent, as in the original Polish they tend to be somewhat 'tongue-twisting' for Anglo-Saxon pronunciation.

Aircrew ranks, with abbreviations and translation:

Pulkownik (plk)	Colonel
Podpulkownik (Pplk)	2nd Colonel
Major (Mjr)	Major
Kapitan (Kap)	Captain
Porucznik (Por)	Lieutenant
Podporucznik (Ppor)	2nd Lieutenant
Starszy Sierzant (St Sierz)	Sergeant Major
Plutonowy (Plut)	Staff Sergeant
Kapral (Kpr)	Sergeant
Starszy Szeregowiec (St Szer)	Corporal

Soviet Air Force

In May 1942 the Red Air Force was re-organized into a series of mobile Air Armies (Vozdushnaya Armiya); there would eventually be 18 of these. An Air Army usually comprised 5–8 (on occasion up to 13) Air Divisions. An Air Division (Avatsionnaya Diviziya) incorporated three Air

Regiments and was roughly comparable with a Luftwaffe Geschwader in size. An Air Regiment (Aviatsionnaya Pulk) incorporated three Squadrons. Nominal strength of a fighter or ground-attack regiment was 40 aircraft, while a bomber regiment had a strength of 32 aircraft. An air regiment was thus roughly equivalent to a Luftwaffe Gruppe.

A Squadron (Eskadrilya) was the basic unit, equivalent to a Luftwaffe Staffel. Fighter and ground-attack squadrons had a strength of 12 aircraft and bomber squadrons of nine aircraft, squadrons being divided into flights (Zveno) of three-four aircraft. Thus a Fighter Air Division would field 124 aircraft, and a Bomber Air Division 98 aircraft. The largest flying unit within an Air Army was an Air Corps (Aviatsionnyi Korpus) which would be made up of two or three Air Divisions.

German Air Force (Luftwaffe)

The basic unit of the German Luftwaffe was the Geschwader. A Geschwader normally comprised a Stabs-staffel (Headquarters Staffel) and three Gruppen (sometimes four later in the war). Each Gruppe comprised a Stabs-skette (headquarters flight) and three Staffeln (sometimes four later). The structure was thus in many ways comparable with the USAAF Group, although units were not directly comparable. A Staffel was larger than an RAF Flight, but smaller than a British or American squadron, usually allowing for an operational strength of 9–12 fighters or dive-bombers, or 6–9 bombers. Staffeln rarely operated independently, but Gruppen frequently did.

The Geschwader normally carried the basic function indication as a prefix, fighter (Jagd [JG]), bomber (Kampf [KG]), dive-bomber (Stuka [StG]), ground-attack (Schlacht [SchG]), heavy fighter (Zerstörer [ZG]), night fighter (Nachtjagd [NJG]), coastal (Küstenflieger [KflGr]), or reconnaissance (Aufklärüngs [AufGr]). This was followed by a unit number. Gruppen were identified by a Roman numeral I to IV, while Staffeln carried Arabic numerals 1 to 12 (occasionally higher). Thus structure was generally:

	I Gruppe	1, 2, 3 Staffeln
Geschwader	II Gruppe	4, 5, 6 Staffeln
	III Gruppe	7, 8, 9 Staffeln

Thus the second Gruppe of Kampfgeschwader 30 would be identified as II/KG30; however, 8 Staffel in III Gruppe was referred to as 8/KG30. For operational purposes in offensive operations, units were gathered into Luftflotten (Air Fleets) which were arranged geographically. The larger Luftflotten could be subdivided for administrative and command convenience into Fliegerkorps (Flying Corps) which could include a variety of types of units, or units of one type, such as the specialized dive-bomber and ground-attack VIII Fliegerkorps.

Aircrew ranks (with English translations) were:

Oberst	(Obst)	Colonel
Oberstleutnant	(Obstlt)	Lieutenant Colonel
Major	(Maj)	Major
Hauptmann	(Hpt)	Captain
Oberleutnant	(Oblt)	1st Lieutenant
Leutnant	(Lt)	2nd Lieutenant
Fahnenjünkeroffizier	(Fhnjr)	Officer Cadet
Hauptfeldwebel	(Hptfw)	Sergeant Major
Oberfeldwebel	(Ofw)	Flight Sergeant
Feldwebel	(Fw)	Sergeant
Unteroffizier	(Uffz)	Corporal
Flieger	(Flg)	Aircraftsman

The Luftwaffe had a fixed establishment of officer ranks, not necessarily a specific rank for each post. Considerable command responsibility was given to officers of quite junior rank. A Staffel therefore might be commanded by a Lt or Oblt, a Gruppe by an Oblt, Hpt or Maj, and a Geschwader by a Maj, Obstlt, or Obst.

Italian Air Force (Regia Aeronautica)

The basic Italian unit was the Gruppo, which comprised three Squadriglie. In size the Squadriglia was similar to a Luftwaffe Staffel, and the Gruppo to a Gruppe. Gruppi were frequently formed into Stormi, although they could operate independently, indicated by the word Autonomo (Aut) appended to the designation. The Stormo was smaller than a Geschwader, however, comprising only two gruppi. Flexible numbers of Stormi formed Squadra Aerea, similar to RAF Groups, which were organized geographically.

Each unit — squadriglia, gruppo or stormo — carried two letters after the designation to indicate function and type of base. The second letter was generally a T (Terrestre) for land-based, or M (Marittimo) for water-based floatplanes or flyingboats. The first letter indicated function (ie:-

C (Caccia)	Fighter
B (Bombardamento)	Bomber
B a'T (Bombardamento a Tuffo)	Dive Bomber

Exceptions to the rule were some of the more specialist units, where the two letters both related to function:-

OA (Osservazione Aerea)	Air Reconnaissance
AS (Aerosiluranti)	Torpedo Bomber
CN (Caccia Notturno)	Night Fighter

As in the RAF, Italian pilots were of at least Sergente rank. However, amongst other aircrew, gunners, radio operators and flight engineers were frequently of more junior rank.

Pilot ranks were:

Colonello	(Col)	Colonel
Tenente Colonello	(Ten Col)	Lieutenant Colonel
Maggiore	(Magg)	Major
Capitano	(Cap)	Captain
Tenente	(Ten)	1st Lieutenant
Sotto Tenenente	(S Ten)	2nd Lieutenant

Maresciallo	(Mar)	Warrant Officer
Sergente Maggiore	(Serg Magg)	Flight Sergeant
Sergente	(Serg)	Sergeant

Imperial Japanese Naval Air Force

The Naval Air Force was divided between carrier-based and land-based units. The basic land-based unit was the Kokutai (Ku), which was comparable in size and composition to a Luftwaffe Gruppe, containing three Chutai (Chu). A flexible number of Kokutais formed an Air Flotilla, several Air Flotillas making up an Air Fleet, which was organized geographically. While generally composed of one class of aircraft, it was not unusual for some Kokutais to have a mixed complement of fighters and bombers at certain times. Fighter Kokutais often also included a small number of reconnaissance aircraft to provide a navigational function on long flights.

During the first half of the war each aircraft carrier had its own air group, comprising fighter, dive-bomber, torpedo-bomber and reconnaissance aircraft. Later, these were formed into large Kokutai which then provided the air groups for one or more carriers. Officer ranks were similar to those of the USN, but Japanese units had only a small number of officers, most pilots and other aircrew being NCOs. There was a complex and highly-graded NCO structure which has no direct comparison in other air forces. These were, with appropriate translations:-

Warrant Officer	Chief Petty Officer	
NAP 1/C	Petty Officer	1st Class
NAP 2/C	Petty Officer	2nd Class
NAP 3/C	Petty Officer	3rd Class
NA 1/C	Naval Airman	1st Class
NA 2/C	Naval Airman	2nd Class
NA 3/C	Naval Airman	3rd Class

Imperial Japanese Army Air Force

The basic Army unit was the Hiko Sentai (Flying Squadron). This was similar to the Navy's Kokutai, and was subdivided into three Chutais. Several Hiko Sentais formed a Hikodan (Flying Battalion), while a number of Hikodans formed a geographically based Hikoshidan (Air Army). Ranks for aircrew were similar to USAAF ranks, but included NCO pilots down to the rank of Corporal.

ACKNOWLEDGEMENTS

It had been intended to include a Bibliography, but space failed to allow this. During the preparation of this work, many authoritative books and articles were consulted — those who have good libraries and those who wrote these works will soon be aware which these were. My general thanks therefore to the latter group of fellow writers for providing such excellent reference material. Specifically, tremendous help and support was received from my old friend and colleague, John 'Jack' Foreman in the preparation of the chapter on the Night Bomber Offensive, and the illustrations for it, while timely aid with the Kursk chapter came from Tomas Polak in Czechoslovakia.

A reliable group of good friends as always came up with a variety of photographic material, Col Ray Toliver and Yasuho Izawa particularly performing in their usual marvellous fashion with the US/Japanese chapters. Thanks here also go to Jerry Scutts, Malcolm Passingham, Jerzy Cynk and John Batchelor.

Delivery of the manuscript ran very late, and in the last minute rush several people stepped in to help out with the typing — no less than eight of us 'pounded the keys' in the end! Special thanks here to my wife Marion, to ex-colleagues and dear friends Jo Levy and Dilys de la Rue, to present colleague Rhonda Andreucetti, and to Grub Street for doing more than their share to meet the deadlines! Thanks to my old collaborator from the days of 'Profiles' glory, Terry Hadler, for undertaking the paintings, to James Goulding for the maps, and to John Batchelor for preparing the aircraft sideviews.

CFS
Hendon, April, 1985.

BLITZKRIEG ON POLAND

SEPTEMBER 1939

Overleaf

A Messerschmitt Bf109D fighter of I/ZG2 shoots down a PZL
P.11C fighter from Dyon III/6 of the Army Lodz as it attempts to intercept Junkers Ju87B dive-
bombers of Stukageschwader 2, on 4 September, 1939.

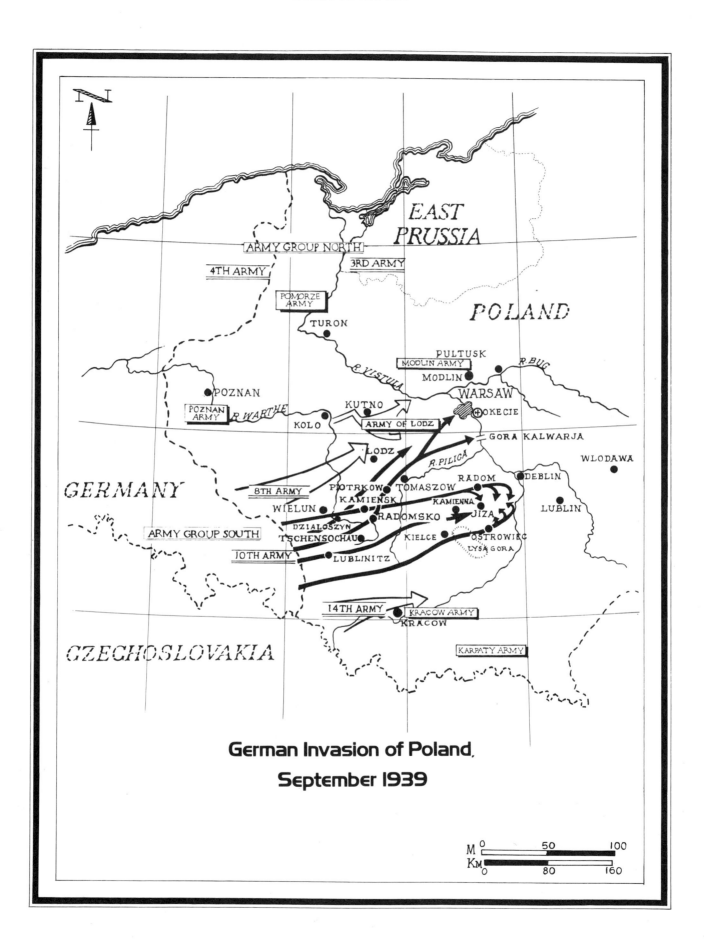

German Invasion of Poland, September 1939

The dawn was barely up and the early September mist clearing when bombs from 60 Heinkels began crashing down on airfields around Kracow. From their well-camouflaged 'campaign' landing ground, the little gull-wing PZL P.11c fighters of III/2 Fighter Dyon of the Polish Air Force, attached to the Army Kracow, clawed their way into the sky. Suddenly, before sufficient height had been gained for safety, ugly, cranked-wing dive-bombers appeared behind them and before they could react, the Poles saw their commanding officer, Captain Mieczyslaw Medwecki, plunging to his death. Evading the attack of the intruders, Lieutenant Wladyslaw Gnys turned on one of the 'Stukas' — for such they were — and shot it down; the first aerial victories of World War II had been gained, and the first of tens of thousands of aircraft which would be destroyed during the next six years had fallen in combat! The dive-bombers were Junkers Ju87Bs of I Gruppe, Stukageschwader 2 (I/StG2), and the day was Friday, 1 September, 1939.

The war had not been unexpected — indeed, it had become almost a matter of *when*, rather than *if*. Despite his renunciation of further territorial ambitions following the Munich crisis of 1938, it had been clear to most who wanted to see that Adolf Hitler was not prepared to leave the 'Polish Question' unresolved. His recent Non-Aggression Treaty with Josef Stalin's Soviet Union had put the final seal on the fate of the Poles. In fact, Hitler had initially ordered Operation *Ostmarkflug* (the solution of the question by violence) for 26 August, but this had been postponed. On 31 August came 'War Directive No 1', ordering the forces massed on the border to strike at 0445 hours on 1 September following a fabricated border incident. The world waited with bated breath for news of terrible aerial bombardments of the Polish cities; none came, initially. Dr Goebbels' Propaganda Ministry trumpeted triumphantly that the Luftwaffe had destroyed the Polish Air Force on the ground at its airfields on the first day; it was not true.

Such annihilation would come eventually, but the true lesson of the assault on Poland was the terrible, morale-shattering efficacy of Germany's fast-moving, aggressively-handled armored columns — the Panzers — closely supported by dive-bombers acting as mobile assault artillery for them to blast a way through all opposition. A new word of violence entered the world's vocabulary — *Blitzkrieg* (the lightning war).

The disparity in numbers between the two air forces was not as great as has often been stated (see the comparative Orders of Battle, page 18). True, the Luftwaffe had a total of over 1000 aircraft available, but a very substantial proportion of these had to be maintained in the West and in Central Germany in case the French and British fulfilled their guarantee to come to Poland's aid — which they did, in half-hearted fashion, two days later. German equipment was generally considerably more modern, however, the initiative was theirs, and the tactics employed were more effective. The Poles had recently re-organized their air force, concentrating a large part of their available fighters in a centrally-controlled Pursuit Brigade for the defense of Warsaw against major bombing attacks. A proportion of the bomber force had also been so concentrated, including the only truly modern aircraft available, the P.37 Los bombers. The rest of the bombers were still attached in individual units to the various land armies, the commanders of which were to display an almost total ignorance of the best ways to employ them.

POLISH AND GERMAN COMPARATIVE STRENGTHS, 1 SEPTEMBER 1939

POLISH

	WITH UNITS	RESERVE	IN REPAIR	TRAINING SCHOOLS
Fighters	161	15	55	40
Medium Bombers	36	25	5	10
Light Bomber/Reconnaissance	110	10	45	30
Army Co-operation	85	52	45	30
Liaison	49			
	441	102	150	110

LUFTWAFFE

	IN EAST	TOTAL (ALL FIGURES WITH OPERATIONAL UNITS)
Fighters	568	1179 (1053)
Medium Bombers	812	1108 (1008)
Dive Bombers & Ground Attack	351	406 (355)
Long-Range Reconnaissance	173	262 (235)
Army Co-operation	237	342 (294)
Coastal	116 approx	240 (214)
Transport	—	552 (540)
	2257	4089 (3699 serviceable)

THE AIRCRAFT IN THE EAST WERE AVAILABLE AS FOLLOWS:

	LUFTFLOTTE 1	LUFTFLOTTE 4	ARMIES	COASTAL	TOTAL
Long-Range Reconnaissance	57	36	80	—	173
Medium Bombers	507	305	—	—	812
Dive Bombers & Ground Attack	155	196	—	12	363
Fighters (Front)	219	75	—	—	294
Fighters (Home Defense)	125	149	—	24	298
Army Co-operation	—	—	237	—	237
Floatplanes/Flyingboats				80 approx	80 approx
	1063	761	317	116	2257

LUFTWAFFE ORDER OF BATTLE, 1 SEPTEMBER 1939

UNIT AND COMMANDER	BASE	AIRCRAFT

LUFTFLOTTE I HENNINGSHOLM/STETTIN
GENERAL DER FLIEGER ALBERT KESSELRING

UNIT AND COMMANDER	BASE	AIRCRAFT
Fernaufklarüngsgruppe 121 (under direct control)	Prenzlau	
1(F)/121	Prenzlau	11 Dornier Do17P
3(F)/121	Prenzlau	12 Dornier Do17P
Fliegerdivision I Generalleutnant Grauert	Crossinsee	
I/ZG1	Muhlen	32 Messerschmitt Bf110 B & C
II/StG2	Stolp/Reitz	38 Junkers Ju87B
III/StG2	Stolp/West	40 Junkers Ju87B
I(Jagd)/LG2	Lottin/Malzkow	36 Messerschmitt Bf109E
2(F)/121	Schönfeld/Crossinsee	10 Dornier Do17P
Kampfgeschwader 1 Oberst Kessler	Kolberg	
Stab	Kolberg	7 Heinkel He111E
I/KG1	Kolberg	37 Heinkel He111E
I/KG152	Pinnow	38 Heinkel He11H
IV(Stuka)/LG1	Stolp/Reitz	39 Junkers Ju87B
Kampfgeschwader 26 Oberst Siburg	Gabbert	
Stab	Gabbert	8 Heinkel He111H
II/KG26	Gabbert	35 Heinkel He111H
I/KG53	Schönfeld	32 Heinkel He111H
Kampfgeschwader 27 Oberst Behrendt	Werneuchen	
Stab	Werneuchen	6 Heinkel He111P
I/KG27	Werneuchen	34 Heinkel He111P
II/KG27	Neubrandenburg	26 Heinkel He111P
III/KG27	Königsberg/Nm	28 Heinkel He111P
Luftwaffenkommando Ostpreussen Generalleutnant Wimmer	Königsberg	
(under direct control)		
1(F)/120	Neuhausen	13 Dornier Do17P
I/StG1	Insterburg/Elbing	38 Junkers Ju87B
I/JG1	Jesau	54 Messerschmitt Bf109E
I/JG21	Elbing	29 Messerschmitt Bf109C,E
II/ZG1(JGr 101)	Fürstenwalde	36 Messerschmitt Bf109B,D
Kampfgeschwader 2 Oberst Fink	Cottbus	
Stab	Cottbus	9 Dornier Do17Z
I/KG2	Cottbus	37 Dornier Do17E
II/KG2	Liegnitz	35 Dornier Do17E,Z
Kampfgeschwader 3 Oberst von Charnier Gliszinski	Heiligenbeil	
Stab	Heiligenbeil	9 Dornier Do17Z
II/KG3	Heiligenbeil	36 Dornier Do17Z
III/KG3	Heiligenbeil	39 Dornier Do17Z
Luftwaffen-Lehrdivision Generalleutnant Foerster	Jesau	
(under direct control)		
4(F)/121	Jesau	11 Dornier Do17P
Lehrgeschwader 1 Oberst Bülowius	Powunden	
Stab	Powunden	10 Heinkel He111H
II(K)/LG1	Powunden	41 Heinkel He111H
III(K)/LG1	Powunden	40 Heinkel He111H
I(Z)/LG1	Elbing	32 Messerschmitt Bf110B,C

UNIT AND COMMANDER	BASE	AIRCRAFT
Luftgaukommando III Generalleutnant Weise	Berlin	
Stab/JG2 Oberst von Massow	Berlin/Döberitz	
I/JG2	Berlin/Döberitz	42 Messerschmitt Bf109E
I/JG3	Zerbst	48 Messerschmitt Bf109E
I/JG20	Straussberg	21 Messerschmitt Bf109E
10(N)/JG2	Berlin/Döberitz	9 Messerschmitt Bf109C
11(N)/LG2	Greifswald	9 Messerschmitt Bf109D

LUFTFLOTTE 4 Reichenback/Schlesien General der Flieger Alexander Löhr

UNIT AND COMMANDER	BASE	AIRCRAFT
(under direct control)		
3(F)/123	Breslau	13 Dornier Do17P
Wekusta 76	Breslau	3 Heinkel He111J
Fliegerdivision 2 Generalmajor Bruno Loerzer	Neisse	
2(F)/122	Neisse	12 Dornier Do17P
Kampfgeschwader 4 Oberst Fiebig	Oels	
Stab	Oels	6 Heinkel He111P
I/KG4	Langenau	31 Heinkel He111P
II/KG4	Oels	32 Heinkel He111P
III/KG4	Langenau	33 Heinkel He111P
Kampfgeschwader 76 Oberstleutnant Fröhlich	Zipser Neudorf	
Stab	Zipser Neudorf	9 Dornier Do17Z
I/KG76	Zipser Neudorf	36 Dornier Do17Z
III/KG76	Vienna	39 Dornier Do17E
Kampfgeschwader 77	Grottkau	
Stab	Grottkau	9 Dornier Do17Z
I/KG77	Brieg	37 Dornier Do17Z
II/KG77	Grottkau	39 Dornier Do17Z
III/KG77	Brieg	34 Dornier Do17Z
Fliegerfuhrer zbV Generalmajor Freiherr Wolfram von Richthofen	Schönau/Schleisen	
1(F)/124	Ohlau	11 Dornier Do17P
Lehrgeschwader 2 Oberst Baier	Nieder Ellguth	
II(Schlacht)/LG2	Altsiedel	40 Henschel Hs123
I/StG76	Nieder Ellguth	39 Junkers Ju87B
Stukageschwader 77 Oberst Schwartzkopf	Neudorf	
Stab	Neudorf	3 Junkers Ju87B
I/StG77	Neudorf	37 Junkers Ju87B
II/StG77	Neudorf	39 Junkers Ju87B
I/StG2	Nieder Ellguth	38 Junkers Ju87B
I/ZG2 (JGr102)	Gross Stein	44 Messerschmitt Bf109D
I/ZG76	Ohlau	31 Messerschmitt Bf110B,C
Luftgaukommando VIII Generalmajor Deuckelmann	Breslau	
I/JG77	Breslau	50 Messerschmitt Bf109E
II/JG77	Pilsen	50 Messerschmitt Bf109E

UNIT AND COMMANDER	BASE	AIRCRAFT
Luftgaukommando XVII Generalmajor Hirshauer	Vienna	
I/JG76	Vienna/Aspen	45 Messerschmitt Bf109E

BEFEHLSHABER DER HEERESFLIEGERVERBÄNDE Berlin
Generalmajor Bogatsch
(Army Co-operation Aviation)

UNIT AND COMMANDER	BASE	AIRCRAFT
Einsätz Ost/Polen Attached Army Unit		
Heeresgruppe Nord Koluft – Aufklärungsgeschwader 13 Generalmajor Krocker		
3(F)/11	Grossenhain	10 Dornier Do17F
10 PzDiv (Res) 1(H)/11	Grossenhain	9 Henschel Hs126 3 Heinkel He46
3 Armee Koluft – Aufklärungsgruppe 10 Oberst Zoch		
3(F)/10 1 Armeekorps	Neuhausen	12 Dornier Do17F
1(H)/10 XXI Armeekorps	Neuhausen	12 Henschel He126
2(H)/10	Neuhausen	12 Henschel Hs126
4 Armee Koluft – Aufklärungsgruppe 21 Oberst Keiper		
4(Γ)/11 XIX Armeekorps Mot	Grossenhain	11 Dornier Do17F
3(H)/21 3 PzDiv	Stargard 9 Henschel Hs126	11 Henschel Hs126
9(H)/LG2 II Armeekorps	Jüterborg	2 Heinkel He46
1(H)/21 III Armeekorps	Stargard	12 Henschel Hs126
2(H)/21	Stargard	12 Henschel Hs126
Heeresgruppe Sud Koluft – Aufklärungsgeschwader 41 Generalmajor Julius Schulz		
2(F)/11 VII Armeekorps (Res)	Grossenhain	12 Dornier Do17F
2(H)/13	Göppingen	11 Henschel Hs126
8 Armee Koluft – Aufklärungsgruppe 41 Oberst von Gerlach		
3(F)/31 X Armeekorps	Brieg	12 Dornier Do17F
1(H)/12 XIII Armeekorps	Munster	12 Henschel Hs126 9 Heinkel He45
5(H)/13	Göppingen	3 Heinkel He46
10 Armee Koluft – Stab III (Auflärungsgruppe)/LG2 Oberstleutnant G Lohmann		
7(F)/LG2 XIV Armeekorps Mot	Jüterborg	12 Dornier Do17F
3(H)/41 (Part) XI Armeekorps	Reichenberg	9 Henschel Hs126
3(H)/12 XVI Armeekorps Mot	Munster	9 Henschel Hs126
2(H)/41 4 PzDiv	Reichenberg	11 Henschel Hs126
4(H)/13 1 PzDiv	Göppingen	9 Heinkel He46 and Henschel Hs126
2(H)/23 IV Armeekorps	Göppingen	12 Heinkel He46 and Henschel Hs126
1(H)/41 XV Armeekorps Mot	Reichenberg	12 Henschel Hs126
4(H)/31 3 LeiDiv	Brieg	9 Heinkel He45 and He46
3(H)/41 (Part)	Reichenberg	See above

UNIT AND COMMANDER	BASE	AIRCRAFT
14 Armee Koluft – Aufklärungsgruppe 14 Oberst Pistorias		
4(F)/14 VIII Armeekorps	Bad Voslau	11 Dornier Do17F
1(H)/31 5 PzDiv	Brieg	9 Henschel Hs126
2(H)/31 XVI Armeekorps	Brieg	8 Heinkel He46 and Henschel Hs126
3(H)/14 XVIII Armeekorps	Bad Voslau	9 Henschel Hs126
2(H)/14 2 PzDiv	Bad Voslau	12 Henschel Hs126 9 Heinkel He46
1(H)/14	Bad Voslau	3 Henschel Hs126

FUHRER DER SEELUFTSTREITKRÄFTE OST
Kiel Generalmajor Bruch
(Marine Aviation)

UNIT AND COMMANDER	BASE	AIRCRAFT
Küstenfliegergruppe 306	Dievenow	
1/KFlGr 306	Dievenow	Heinkel He60
2/KFlGr 306	Dievenow	Dornier Do18
Küstenfliegergruppe 506	Pillau	
3/KFlGr 506	Pillau	Heinkel He59
1/KFlGr 506	Pillau	Heinkel He60
2/KFlGr 506	Kamp	Dornier Do18
3/KFlGr 706	Dievenow	Heinkel He59
Küstenfliegergruppe 706	Kamp	
2/KFlGr 606	Kamp	Dornier Do18
1/KFlGr 706	Nest	Heinkel He60
Stab II/Trägergruppe 186		
4(Stuka)/TrGr 186	Stolp	12 Junkers Ju87B
5(Jagd)/TrGr 186	Brüsterort	12 Messerschmitt Bf109C,D
6(Jagd)/TrGr 186	Brüsterort	12 Messerschmitt Bf109C,D
5/Bordflieger 196	Kiel/Holtenau	Heinkel He60

Yet had things gone according to plan, the formation of the Pursuit Brigade would have been immediately vindicated. Along the Polish border five German armies were ready for the attack. From north to south these were the 3rd, 4th, 8th, 10th and 14th Armies; it was the 10th which was to spearhead the main drive for Warsaw with its 1st and 4th Panzer Divisions. To support these forces were Luftflotte 1 to the north in East Prussia, and Luftflotte 4 to the south in Silesia and Czechoslovakia. Operation *Seebad* (Seaside) had been planned for the bombers of Luftflotte 1 — a massive attack on the Polish capital on the first morning of war — while Luftflotte 4 dealt with airfields in the way of the advance.

German tactics change

Fog on the morning of 1 September was so heavy in Luftflotte 1's area that only four bomber Gruppen were able to get into the air, followed by two more later in the morning. *Seaside* was at once postponed, and attacks ordered instead on airfields, naval installations along the Baltic coast, and in support of the armies. One raid did go according to plan, however: at 0400 hours, before the fighting had officially started, Ju87s of I/StG1 led by Oblt Bruno Dilley bombed the area of two rail bridges over the Vistula river in a pin-point attack designed to destroy not the bridges, but strong points from where demolition charges could be fired by the Poles. Their attack was

POLISH AIR FORCE ORDER OF BATTLE, 1 SEPTEMBER 1939

UNIT AND COMMANDER	BASE	AIRCRAFT
TACTICAL AIR FORCE		
Pursuit Brigade Col Stefan Pawlikowski		
Dyon III/1 (111 and 112 Squadron)	Warsaw – Okecie	23 PZL P.11c
Dyon IV/1 (113 and 114 Squadron)	Warsaw – Okecie	22 PZL P.11c
Dyon III/2 (123 Squadron)	Kracow	10 PZL P.7
Liaison Flight		3 RWD 8
Bomber Brigade Col Wladyslaw Heller		
Dyon X/1 (211 and 212 Squadron)	Warsaw – Okecie	18 PZL P.37 Los
Dyon XV/1 (216 and 217 Squadron)	Warswa – Okecie	18 PZL P.37 Los
Dyon II/2 (21 and 22 Squadron)	Kracow	20 PZL P.23 Karas
Dyon VI/6 (64 and 65 Squadron)	Lvov	20 PZL P.23 Karas
55 Squadron	Lida	10 PZL P.23 Karas
Liaison		
16 Squadron		7 Lublin R XIIID
		1 RWD 8
1, 2, 4, and 12 Liaison Flights		12 RWD 8
Transport Group		9 Fokker FVII/3m
Army Lodz Col Waslaw Iwaszkiewicz		
Dyon III/6 (161 and 162 Squadron)	Widzew	10 PZL P.11c
		2 PZL P.11a
		10 PZL P.7
32 Squadron	Sokolniki	10 PZL P.23 Karas
		1 RWD 8
63 and 66 Squadron	Lublinek	7 Lublin R XIIIF
		7 RWD 14 Lzupla
10 Liaison Flight		3 RWD 8
Army Kracow Col Stefan Sznuk		
Dyon III/2 (121 and 122 Squadron)	Igolomie	20 PZL P.11c
		1 RWD 8
24 Squadron	Klimontow	10 PZL P.23 Karas
		1 RWD 8
23 and 26 Squadron	Palczowice (23)	7 RWD 14 Czapla
	Zareleice (26)	7 Lublin R XIIIF
		3 RWD 8
		3 RWD 8
3 Liaison Flight		1 Lublin R XIIIF
Army Karpatz 2nd Col Olgierd Tuskiewicz		
31 Squadron	Werynian	10 PZL P.23 Karas
		1 RWD 8
52 Squadron	Mrowla	7 Lublin R XIIIF
		2 RWD 8
5 Liaison Flight		3 RWD 8

UNIT AND COMMANDER	BASE	AIRCRAFT
ARMY SUPPORT AIR FORCE		
Army Modlin Col Tadensz Prauss		
Dyon III/5 (152 Squadron)	Szpondowo	1 PZL P.11a
		9 PZL P.11c
		1 RWD 8
41 Squadron	Zdunowo	10 PZL P.23 Karas
53 Squadron	Sokolowek	7 RWD 14 Czapla
		2 RWD 8
11 Liaison Flight		3 RWD 8
Army Pomorze Col Boleslaw Stachon		
Dyon III/4 (141 and 142 Squadron)	Markowo	22 PZL P.11c
42 Squadron	Zduny	10 PZL P.23 Karas
43 and 46 Squadron	Niedzwielz (43)	14 Lublin R XIII D
	Balice Nowe (46)	
7 and 8 Liaison Flights		6 RWD 8
Army Poznan Col Stanislaw Kuzminski		
Dyon III/3 (131 and 132 Squadron)	Dzieznica	22 PZL P.11a and P.11c
34 Squadron	Mierzewo	10 PZL P.23 Karas
33 and 36 Squadron	Sielec (33)	14 Lublin R VIII D
	Gwiazdowo (36)	
6 Liaison Flight		3 RWD 8
Independent Army Group Narew 2nd Col Stanislaw Nazarkeiwicz	Biel	
Dyon III/5 (151 Squadron)	Zalesie	10 PZL P.7
51 Squadron	Wierzbowo	10 PZL P.23 Karas
13 Squadron		7 RWD 14 Czapla
9 Liaison Flight		3 RWD 8

followed by a level bombing raid by Dornier Do17Zs of III/KG3, but the ground forces were slow to follow up, and the Poles were able to repair some of the facilities and blow one of the bridges.

Only one raid got near Warsaw during the day, when Heinkel He111Hs from II (Kampf) Gruppe of Lehrgeschwader 1 attempted to attack the Okecie airfield. Fighters from several of the Pursuit Brigade's squadrons intercepted and, in a running fight, six Heinkels were lost, the first falling in flames to Lieutenant Aleksander Gabszewicz. Further P.11s from the Army Modlin unit joined in, but escorting Messerschmitt Bf110 'destroyers' from I(Z)/LG1 came to the bombers' aid, shooting down two elderly P.7s of 123 Squadron, while return fire from the Heinkels shot down two P.11s, and many others were damaged. In fighting back, the Poles were able to wound the commanding officer of I/(Z)/LG1, seven-victory Spanish Civil War veteran, Walter Grabmann.

Fog had not been as severe in Luftflotte 4's sector, allowing attacks to be mounted on airfields in the Kracow area after reconnaissance aircraft had seen Polish machines on the ground. Sixty He111s from I and III/KG4, escorted by Bf110s of I/ZG76 attacked, dropping 48 tons of bombs. They were followed by the Ju87s of I/StG2 which fought the combat with Army Kracow fighters already recorded, and by Do17Zs of KG77. Arriving to find their target shrouded in smoke and dust, III/KG77 attacked at only 150 feet altitude, many bombers being damaged by splinters from their own bombs as a result.

Many airfields in the area were attacked during the day but most operational aircraft had been dispersed to well-hidden airstrips in the countryside before operations began, and little damage was done. Only at Rakowice was any real success gained, but the 28 aircraft destroyed here were all elderly training or liaison machines. Indeed, the few Polish aircraft seen at all led the Germans to believe that they must have been successful in their task.

While most of Luftflotte 1's attacks had been launched against targets in the coastal area, during the afternoon LG1 again approached Warsaw. Simultaneously the whole of KG27 from Luftflotte 2 approached the same area to drop bombs after a 470-mile flight before flying back to join Luftflotte 1 on attachment. Only three of their He111s actually neared Warsaw just after LG1's attack, and as Ju87s of I/StG1 were dive-bombing radio stations at Babia and Locy, Pursuit Brigade P.11s were again scrambled — 30 of them this time — and these became involved in a hard fight with escorting Bf110s (I(Z)/LG1 again) and Bf109s.

The former escorts claimed five victories against the Poles, but suffered heavy losses, while the latter lost one Bf109 when 2nd Col Leopold Pamula, who had already claimed one He111 and one Ju87 shot down, rammed one of the German fighters and then baled out. Lt Gabszewicz, the Brigade's first victor of the morning, was shot down and baled out, reporting being attacked while parachuting down, as was Lt Szyszko, who received 17 bullet wounds in his leg from a Bf109.

The defense had been a complete success however, the bombers being scattered with not a single bomb falling on Warsaw. Together the Pursuit Brigade and Army Modlin Squadron had claimed 17 German aircraft shot down (Luftflotte 1 actually lost 14) for the loss of ten of their own, with 24 more damaged. By 1800 hours fog had again descended over the northern area, preventing further German raids from this zone. Further south perhaps the most important sorties of the day had been flown by GeneralMajor Wolfram von Richthofen's special Fliegerführer zbV ground support command.

His units were in the air from first light supporting 10th Army Panzers as they struck across the border towards Wielun and Panki. Radio vans manned by Luftwaffe personnel, accompanied the spearheads — a development which Richthofen had personally initiated in Spain — and these were able to call in direct support at short notice. Early in the day 1/StG76 Ju87s attacked defenses at Wielun while the little biplane Hs123s of II(Schlacht)/LG2 dropped 'Flambos' (percussion fused light incendiary bombs) in support of the attack on Panki, some of the pilots flying up to ten sorties before darkness fell. During the afternoon the Ju87s of I/StG2 dive-bombed a concentration of Polish cavalry at Wielun, followed by I/StG77, and then by Do17Zs of I/KG77. In 90 sorties, the cavalry brigade was shattered and ceased to exist as a fighting unit.

Against unprepared troops the Stuka was a truly terrifying and demoralizing weapon. The ugly bomber with its gull-shaped wing and spatted, fixed undercarriage, was fitted with drive brakes which allowed it to dive almost vertically onto its target — a form of attack allowing great accuracy of bombing. The howling of the engine as it descended was augmented by a siren, fitted to increase the general terror-inspiring effect. The result was to induce a paralyzing feeling of impotence in the face of an apparently extremely personal attack, which culminated in a cacophony of noise often inducing complete panic amongst those on the receiving end.

On 2 September as German intentions became clearer, Polish bomber aircraft were in action for the first time. At

THE BUSINESS END OF A MESSERSCHMITT BF110C OF I/ZG76, THE MOST SUCCESSFUL FIGHTING AIRCRAFT OF THE POLISH CAMPAIGN.

the southernmost part of the front, six P.23 Karas aircraft attacked armored columns of the 14th Army, while 18 more Karas from the Bomber Brigade's VI/6 Dyon were out after similar targets, making low attacks in six flights of three aircraft each; four were shot down by German Flak guns, one by Polish troops in error, and two more force-landed due to damage. The commander of the Army Pomorze requested his fighters to strafe tanks and infantry — a most unsuitable task for the little P.11, but 141 Squadron carried out the order, losing four aircraft and three pilots as a result, including their commanding officer, Captain Florian Laskowski. It was, however, the aircraft of this Army which gained the greatest air combat successes during the day with claims for nine victories — two of them by Lt Stanislaw Skalski of 142 Squadron. Indeed, all 21 Polish victories on this date were claimed 'in the field' by the Army fighter squadrons, the Pursuit Brigade not being called upon.

Deblin's three airfields were major targets for Luftflotte 4 bombers on this date, 88 He111s of KG4 attacking here, escorted by I/ZG76 Bf110s, which strafed, claiming 11 aircraft destroyed on the ground. Although two combat airfields were amongst those attacked, no operational aircraft were lost at these, the casualties again relating to a quantity of training machines. During the afternoon, six P.11s from Army Lodz's III/6 Dyon engaged Bf110s of I/ZG76 over the Lodz region, and in a fight with up to a dozen of the big aircraft, claimed two shot down for the loss of two of their own; the German unit lost a total of three Bf110s during its various sorties on this date, but was able to claim in all nine PZL fighters shot down, although only three of these appear to have been confirmed.

Richthofen's units were again active, I/StG2 and I/StG76 destroying a railway station at Piotrkow, and attacking troops detraining here, while StG77 attacked columns near Radomsko, which was becoming the focus of attack for 10th Army's XVI Corps. It was here early on 3 September, that the Bomber Brigade's Karas's were again thrown into the fray. Three times II/2 Dyon struck during the day, the independent 55 Squadron also joining the

MAIN AIRCRAFT TYPES EMPLOYED DURING THE POLISH CAMPAIGN

GERMAN

Messerschmitt Bf109
This was the classic German single-engined fighter which was employed in Poland in two main versions. The early models (B, C and D) which equipped some of the Zerstörergruppen were powered by Junkers Jumo 210G in-line engines of 640 hp which gave a top speed of around 290 mph, a service ceiling of 27 560 ft, and a range of 405 miles. Armament comprised four 7.9 mm MG 17 machine guns, two in the nose and one in each wing. The Bf109E featured a Daimler-Benz DB 601A engine of 1100 hp which increased top speed to 354 mph and ceiling to 36 000 ft. Initially armed with four 7.9 mm guns like the earlier models, the first examples with the wing guns replaced by 20 mm FF cannon were just entering service at the time of the outbreak of war.

Messerschmitt Bf110
A twin-engined heavy fighter, or 'destroyer', designed for long-range escort to bomber formations and interception of hostile bombers. Much was hoped for these aircraft, but they proved incapable of matching the performance of single-engined fighters when met by an effective defense force. The Bf110, the B and C versions of which were available in 1939, was very successful in Poland. Powered by two DB 601A engines of 1100 hp each, the low-wing, twin-tailed monoplane had a top speed of 349 mph, a ceiling of 32 000 ft and a range of 565 miles. It was heavily armed with two 20 mm MG FF cannon and four 7.9 mm machine guns in the nose, plus one flexible rearward-firing 7.9 mm for the gunner in the rear cockpit.

Heinkel He111
The main Luftwaffe twin-engined low-wing monoplane medium bomber, the He111 was operated over Poland in its E, H and P models. The determined Polish fighter defense proved the aircraft to be deficient in defensive armor and armament, efforts being made to improve these faults before the next campaign. Comparative performances of the three main types employed were:-

	He111E	He111H	He111P
Engines	Two Junkers Jumo 211A	Two Jumo 211A	Two DB 601A
Max Speed	261 mph	258 mph	247 mph
Range	932 miles	1740 miles	1224 miles
Ceiling	23 620 ft	25 500 ft	26 250 ft
Bombload	4410 lb	5510 lb	3908 lb
Armament	Three 7.9 mm	Three 7.9 mm	Three 7.9 mm

Dornier Do17
The Luftwaffe's second main medium bomber, smaller than the He111. Earlier models of the aircraft also equipped the long-range reconnaissance units — F models with the Army Support Air Force and P models with the Luftflotten. The older E model

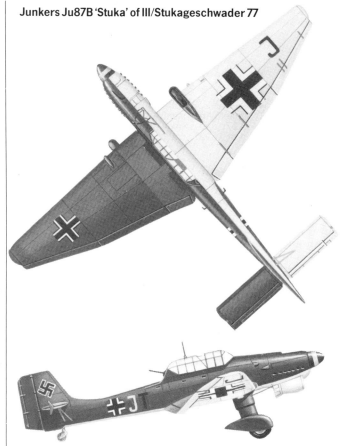

Junkers Ju87B 'Stuka' of III/Stukageschwader 77

was still in use as a bomber in 1939, though being supplanted by the more effective Z model which featured a completely redesigned cockpit area. The Do17 was a well streamlined monoplane of shoulder-wing design, featuring a twin fin and rudder tail assembly. Comparable performance figures for the four models used over Poland were:

	Do17E and F	Do17P	Do17Z
Engines	Two BMW VI in-line engines of 750 hp each	Two BMW 132N radial engines of 865 hp each	Two Bramo Fafnir 323P radial engines of 1000 hp each
Max Speed	220 mph	255 mph	255 mph
Range	932 miles	1367 miles	720 miles
Ceiling	16 730 ft	20 340 ft	22 965 ft
Bombload	1650 lb	2205 lb	2205 lb
Armament	Two 7.9 mm	Three 7.9 mm	Three 7.9 mm

attack. The cost was heavy, five bombers being shot down while seven more were so damaged that they crashed on landing. Despite these attacks, 10th Army's columns pressed on, LG2 Ju87s bombing Dzialoszyn in support of XI Corps to such good effect that the city fell.

Still the Los bombers had not entered action, and when the Dyons of the Bomber Brigade were ordered to change airfields on 3 September, following the Luftwaffe attack on their bases on the previous day, crews requested that they be allowed to detour to bomb Koenigsberg en route. Refusal of this request brought them almost to the edge of mutiny, but ensured that for the third day no Los sorties were flown. A raid on Malaszewicze, the fitting-out depot for the Los, resulted in the destruction of installations here, and of several bombers held as replacements.

On 3 September, Warsaw was again attacked, 40 Pursuit Brigade fighters rising to give battle, but gaining only three victories in return for equal losses. Again, the Bf110s of

Junkers Ju87B

The infamous 'Stuka' dive-bomber featured an inverted gull, or cranked wing, and a fixed undercarriage covered by heavy streamlined 'spats'. Of relatively low performance, the Ju87B fell easy victim to determined fighter attack, but could deliver its bombload with pinpoint accuracy on very small targets, making it a much more effective battlefield weapon than the larger medium bombers. A low-wing, two-seat monoplane, it was powered by a single Junkers Jumo 211Da engine of 1200 hp which gave a top speed of 238 mph, a service ceiling of 26 250 ft and a range of 370 miles. Armament comprised two fixed, wing-mounted 7.9 mm MG 17s and a single flexible gun for rear defense; a bombload of 1102 lb could be carried beneath the fuselage and wings.

Henschel Hs123A

A single-seat biplane, originally designed as a dive-bomber, but employed in 1939 for low-flying ground attack, the HS123A was powered by an 880 hp BMW 132Dc radial engine which gave a maximum speed of 207 mph, a ceiling of 29 525 ft and a range of 534 miles. Bombload totalled 440 lb and armament was two 7.9 mm MG 17 machine guns mounted in the nose.

Henschel Hs126

An army co-operation monoplane with a high-mounted wing and fixed undercarriage, the two-seater Hs126 was designed for operation from small, rough landing grounds in direct support of the army, ie for reconnaissance, gun spotting, etc. Range was unimportant, duration more so, the 850 hp Bramo Fafnir 323A radial engine allowing the aircraft to remain in the air for 2 hours 15 minutes. Top speed was 221 mph, and a small bomb-load of 220 lb could be carried. Armament comprised one fixed and one flexible MG 17.

POLISH

PZL P.11c

A small high-wing monoplane fighter with open cockpit and fixed undercarriage. Although thoroughly outdated by modern German fighters in 1939, the P.11c and its earlier develop-ments, the P.7 and P.11a, were robust, manoeuvreable aircraft, well-loved by their pilots, and gave a good account of themselves. The P.11c was powered by a PZL-built Bristol Mercury VIS radial engine of 645 hp; its top speed was 243 mph and its service ceiling an excellent 36 080 ft. Range was 503 miles and armament four 7.7 mm machine guns, two in the nose and one in each wing.

PZL P.37B Los

A twin-engined medium bomber monoplane of mid-wing design, with twin fins and rudders, the Los was the most modern air-craft in service with the Polish Air Force in 1939. It was comparable with the best of its contemporaries. Powered by two 918 hp PZL-built Bristol Pegasus XX radial engines, it could carry a 5688 lb bombload to a range of 1615 miles. Top speed was 276 mph and service ceiling was 30 350 ft. It carried a defensive armament of three 7.7 mm machine guns.

PZL P.23B Karas

The most numerous bombing aircraft available to the Poles, the Karas was a single-engined low-wing monoplane with fixed undercarriage. Obsolescent, and of rather low performance, it

was nonetheless a tough aircraft, and gave considerable service in the light bombing and reconnaissance role. It was powered by a PZL-built Bristol Pegasus VIII of 680 hp and had a maximum speed of 198 mph, a service ceiling of 23 949 ft and a range of 782 miles. Bombload comprised 1543 lb, and armament a single fixed 7.7 mm machine gun and two flexible weapons of similar calibre for upper and lower rear defense.

Lublin R.XIII

A two-seat high-wing monoplane built for reconnaissance and army co-operation duties, the R.XIII was directly comparable with the Luftwaffe's Hs126, but was a considerably older design. Powered by either a Skoda-built Wright J.5 Whirlwind radial of 220 hp (D model) or a more powerful PZL G.1620A Mars radial of 340-240 hp, the aircraft featured a top speed (dependent on which engine was fitted) of around 121 mph, a service ceiling of 14 600 ft and a range of 375 miles. It was armed with one or two flexible 7.7 mm machine guns in the rear cockpit for defense.

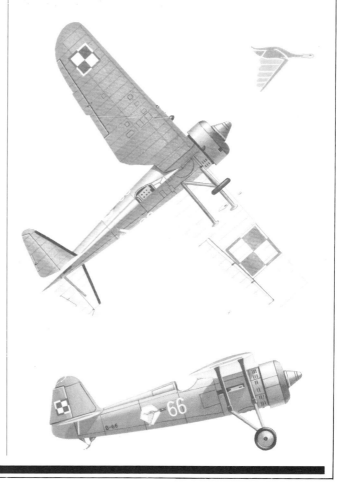

PZL P.11c of 142 Squadron, Dyon 111/4

I(Z)/LG1 were involved, claiming five for one loss against the Poles. Elsewhere, the armies' fighters added a dozen more successes, taking quite a toll of the tactical recon-naissance Henschel Hs126 units operating over the front. A major German achievement, however, was the completion of the near-annihilation of the Polish Navy. Eleven Ju87s of 4/186, a unit originally formed to serve aboard the first German aircraft carrier (which was never completed) hit and damaged the mine layer *Gryf*, the most modern ship in

the navy. Returning in the afternoon, *Gryf* was hit again while Oblt Rummel and Lt Lion sank the destroyer *Wichr*; *Gryf* was later sunk by a Heinkel He59 floatplane from the coastal unit 3/206.

There was heavy fighting over the Army Pomorze and Lodz areas on 4 September. In the former region 13 P.11s engaged Ju87s and Bf109s, claiming three of the dive bombers and one fighter for the loss of the 142 Squadron commander, Capt Miroslaw Lesniewski, who was badly

wounded, two more P.11s being badly damaged. One of the Ju87s was credited to Stanislaw Skalski for his fourth individual victory. Half of the ten available Lodz fighters were on patrol around noon when two were spotted and attacked by nine Bf109D fighters of I/ZG2, one being shot down. The aircraft crash-landed at Widzew, giving away the location of this field to the Germans, who at once strafed and destroyed three more P.11s on the ground before shooting down a further fighter.

The Poles fight hard

Meanwhile, the Bomber Brigade was making a maximum effort, and at last, the Los units were involved, five raids being made against the Panzers in the Radomsko-Piotrkow area. Twenty-seven Los were out during the morning, one flight of three being encountered by the I/ZG2 Bf109Ds returning from their fight with the Army Lodz fighters: the Messerschmitts swiftly shot down two of the bombers. Two more raids, each by five Los, were made in the afternoon, while in the evening Dyon VI/6 sent out six Karas to attack spearheads in the Pultusk area. Here very heavy casualties were inflicted, particularly on the 4th Panzer Division which suffered 28 per cent losses and thereby had its advance delayed by 48 hours. However, the X/1 Los Dyon's airfield at Kucing was discovered and twice bombed during the afternoon, but while nine Los (actually taking off when the second raid began) escaped damage, two parked aircraft were destroyed. By the end of the day, the Bomber Brigade had lost eight Los and two Karas to all causes. Warsaw was again attacked but on this occasion defending fighters were able to claim only one bomber shot down and could not prevent considerable damage being inflicted on the city.

During the first four days of fighting, Polish resistance had been strong and German progress generally slow, but now as resistance in the center around Radomsko and Piotrkow began to crumble, the Germans began to break

ABOVE: PZL P.23B KARAS LIGHT BOMBER-RECONNAISSANCE AIRCRAFT OF 41 SQUADRON, ATTACHED TO THE ARMY MODLIN.

ABOVE RIGHT: PZL P.37B LOS MEDIUM BOMBERS OF THE POLISH AIR FORCE'S BOMBER BRIGADE ARE PREPARED FOR A SORTIE. THESE WERE THE MOST MODERN AIRCRAFT AVAILABLE TO THE POLES IN 1939.

RIGHT: THIS P.37B LOS BOMBER (FOREGROUND) IS FLANKED BY PZL P.11C FIGHTERS OF THE PURSUIT BRIGADE'S DYON III/1. THE CLOSEST OF THESE AIRCRAFT IS FROM III 'KOSCIUSZKO' SQUADRON, WHILE THAT IMMEDIATELY BEYOND IS FROM 112 'FIGHTING COCKS' SQUADRON.

through and the tempo of 10th Army's advance started to increase. Six Los of XV/1 Dyon were over Radomsko again on 5 September, but fewer other sorties were made by them as they had to get on the move again to more secure bases. Over Warsaw on this date, Pursuit Brigade P.11s were twice in action, claiming nine victories including two Ju87s and two Bf110s. By dawn on 6 September the Pursuit Brigade was down to 21 serviceable fighters, but continued to operate with success, several early sorties bringing three more victories. At 1000 hours the Commander-in-Chief, Armed Forces, ordered the Brigade to sortie in force over the Lodz-Kielce region. Surprised by an order which seemed at variance with the Brigade's role as defenders of Warsaw, the pilots were then deeply shocked by what they saw of the German advance.

Early in the afternoon, 19 were off again to sweep over the battle area south and west of Warsaw. Large numbers of Do17s were met and then some 30 Ju87s. By the time they returned to base, the Brigade's pilots had raised their claims for the day to 15 and four probables, while the army fighters added nine more to make this the most successful day since

1 September, in terms of victories gained. Four of these went to Pomorze's 142 Squadron, which intercepted 14 Ju87s near the Vistula bridge at Torun, forcing them to jettison their bombs short of the target and claiming three shot down for the loss of one P.11.

The Bomber Brigade was also active, six Los of XV/1 Dyon being sent out in two sections. One of these fell foul of Bf109s, which sent all three bombers down in flames. As night fell the Polish fighters were reorganized, since so many of their bases were now threatened. The Brigade itself was ordered to the Lublin area where it was now to be brought back to strength by the addition of the army units, withdrawn from their regions. Army Poznan, defending Warsaw, protested vigorously and was allowed to retain their III/3 Dyon, but all others moved to Lublin.

Considering the odds and the obsolescence of their equipment, the Polish fighter pilots had achieved miracles. In six days, 105 victories had been claimed, 63 by the army units and 42 by the Pursuit Brigade. Losses had been heavy though, totalling 79 fighters, 38 of them Brigade aircraft. Amongst the army units, Pomorze's III/4 Dyon had been most successful with 21 victories for the loss of nine P.11s, their successes including six Ju87s and six He126s. Now in the new location, the Brigade's two Dyons had 16 aircraft available, III/4 adding 13 more, while III/6 from Lodz added another five, and Modlin's 152 Squadron a further six for a total of 40 — still quite a formidable force.

A degree of confusion then ensued on 8 September; 152 Squadron was despatched to Warsaw again, but two days later it returned, joined by III/2 Dyon from Army Krakow with another 13 P.11s. Now, however, with the retreat towards Warsaw in full spate, the early warning system broke down and the well-organized back-up supplying the chain of airstrips collapsed. The Brigade managed just three more victories in two days (7 and 8 September) but then achieved nothing more — virtually all the rest of the air fighting during the final ten days of operations was

ACES OF THE POLISH CAMPAIGN

Each nation produced a leading fighter pilot during the brief campaign, the scores of these two top protagonists being closely comparable. The Poles considered the Messerschmitt Bf110 to be a more dangerous opponent than the single-engined Bf109 — a view out of line with that subsequently formed by other allied fighter pilots. But this was because in Poland the Bf109s usually encountered were the older B, C and D models, the more potent Es being retained in the main for home defense.

Lieutenant Stanislaw Skalski flew with 142 Squadron in the Army Pomorze's Dyon III/4. Skalski was in action early in the fray, claiming two Dornier Do17 bombers shot down on 2 September. Next day he brought down an army co-operation Henschel Hs126 and shared in the destruction of a second, while on 4 September he claimed a Ju87 Stuka. Listed as Polish top-scorer with 4¼ victories, a study of claims made after the war led to the upgrading to confirmed of two other claims he had made for probable victories, his total for 1939 thus becoming 6¼.

Amongst the other Polish pilots, at least 17 more claimed two or more victories, including 2/Lt Wlodzimierz Gedymin (3½), the first pilot of the war to claim two victories in one combat, and 2/Lt Hieronim Durwal who claimed four victories. Many of these pilots later flew with the Polish units in Britain and added further to their successes. Both Mieczyslaw Mümler, leader of the Army Poznan Dyon, and the Pursuit Brigade's Aleksander Gabszewicz became noted leaders, while the Deblin Group's Henryk Szczesny took his score to over 10.

Amongst the Germans, top-scorer of the successful I(Z)/LG1 was Lt Werner Methfessel with four victories; subsequently he gained four more. In I/ZG76 two pilots each made three claims, one of them Wolfgang Falcke, later one of the founders of the Luftwaffe nightfighter force. Other pilots in this Gruppe who gained their first victories over Poland were Helmut Lent, later the first pilot to claim 100 victories at night. Gordon Gollob, who became the first fighter pilot ever to claim 150 victories (a total which he reached in the Soviet Union in August

LT STANISLAW SKALSKI OF 142 SQUADRON

1942), and another future nightfighter, Helmut Woltersdorf; the latter claimed two of his eight day victories over Poland, later adding 16 more at night.

Amongst other units, I(J)/LG2, the only Bf109E unit to see much action over Poland, saw first victories for future notables Erwin Clausen (132 victories) and Fritz Geisshardt (102). The defensive Gruppen flew sorties over the area, gaining a limited number of victories. Amongst those making their first claims here were I/JG21's Gustav Rödel (98 victories) and I/JG76's Hans Philipp (206 victories).

Thus the offensive work was left more to the Zerstörergruppen.

One such unit was I Gruppen of Zerstörergeschwader 2 (I/ZG 2), commanded by Hauptmann Hannes Gentzen. Gentzen first claimed on 4 September, when he shot down a PZL P.11 over its own airfield; on return from this sortie, he shot down one of the Bomber Brigade's P.37 Los bombers, while later in the day he claimed a further P.11. Subsequently, his unit slaughtered a formation of P.23 Karas light bombers, four of these being claimed by Gentzen to make him top-scorer in Poland with seven victories.

accomplished by Army Poznan's few fighters over Warsaw. On 16 September the Brigade's 54 available aircraft were re-organized into the Warsaw and Kracow Dyons and a reconnaissance unit of eight P.7s, but to no avail.

Other elements were in little better shape. By evening on 6 September the Bomber Brigade had lost 16 Los and 22 Karas bombers in 119 sorties, while the army units had lost a further 34 Karas. Amongst the reconnaissance units 37 of 77 available Lublin R XIIIs had been lost — 60 per cent of them to fire from their own troops on the ground! The Germans had at last gained their air supremacy, but by default. It was the threat to the Polish airfields occasioned by the advance of the land forces which had destroyed the cohesion of the air force, rather than attrition in the air — although the latter factor had been serious. Now the Luftwaffe came into its own.

Warsaw in danger
On 7 September, XVI Corps of 10th Army had broken through the defenses at Piotrkow, and by the next day, was within 125 kilometres of Warsaw. Indeed, on the afternoon of that day, Hs123s of II(Schlacht)/LG2 were attacking targets on the periphery of the city. No Polish reinforcements could be brought up due to the chaos on the railways caused by Luftwaffe attack. Meanwhile, however, on the same day air reconnaissance had discovered strong concentrations of Polish troops to the right of the 10th Army's advance, north-east of Lysa Gora and south of Radom.

This force, which was forming up in forests around Ilza, offered a threat to the flank of the drive on Warsaw. Having been appraised of the situation, General von Reichenau sought to turn it to German advantage with a major encircling move. XIV Corps swung right, past Radom to the Vistula at Deblin to cut off any retreat to the north. IV Corps followed more slowly to close the bottom of the pocket, while XV Corps moved forward on the far right to complete the encirclement. Early next morning the battle began, Luftwaffe Flak batteries playing an important part in support of the ground forces, while the Stukas were thrown in in force. For five days the trapped Poles were hammered by artillery and from the air, the survivors finally surrendering on 13 September.

Meanwhile, 10th Army's XVI Corps pressed on towards the capital, 4th Panzer Division reaching the outskirts during 9 September to be met by strong Polish resistance. The Luftwaffe was at once ordered to provide support and 140 Ju87s from StG77 and III/StG51 attacked, but without avail; 4th Panzer Division was forced to pull back due to lack of reserves. Indeed, the left flank of 10th Army was now dangerously exposed, as 8th Army had failed to keep up. This weakness had become apparent to the Poles, who sought to exploit it by a concentrated attack on the exposed flank. Twelve divisions were rushed to the Kutno region, some by a long forced-march, and on the night of 9–10 September, this force attacked southwards over the Bzura river, piercing the flank of the advanced elements of 8th Army. Realizing that a major threat to the whole advance had arisen, the German command turned 8th Army back to deal with this, while 10th Army's spearheads were pulled back from the Warsaw area.

Finally, on 11 September, came the call from Army Group South for maximum air support in the Kutno region. Luftflotte 4 now also had Fliegerdivision I from Luftflotte 1 attached to it, and all efforts were turned on the forces threatening 8th Army. As a first strike, Ju87s destroyed the bridges over the Bzura across which the Poles were advancing, cutting off their forward troops from the main body which effectively called a halt to their attack.

Throughout the next two days, the dreaded Stukas howled downwards again and again, while the Hs123 bi-planes of the ground attack II(Schlacht)/LG2 swept low over the area adding to the noise and confusion. The long columns held up by the destruction of the bridges were reduced to chaos by these close attacks, while the medium bombers of KG1, 4 and 26 added their weight to the assault from higher altitudes. Armor was destroyed, horses bolted and cohesion was lost.

After two days of attacks, the Polish advance had ground to a halt, while the northernmost German army — the 4th — had crossed the Vistula further north and moved south-east to cut the Poznan Army off as it attempted to withdraw. During the night of 12–13 September, the spear-heads were withdrawn back across the Bzura, but it was too late; the Poznan Army was now surrounded. The attacks continued from the air, the escorting fighters (particularly the Bf110s) now also coming down to low level to strafe. The effort was maintained at high intensity on 16 and 17 September, following which Polish resistance collapsed, some 170 000 troops surrendering during the next two days. Clearly, the Luftwaffe had played a decisive part in this major victory.

But what of the Polish air force during this time? As already noted, the fighters had been withdrawn and re-organized on 7 September, but to no good effect. Poznan Army's gallant III/3 Dyon had fought on under its commander, Major Mieczyslaw Mümler. Against the odds its few remaining P.11s faced, the unit could do little to change the ultimate conclusion but every day from 7–16 September, the unit added further victories to its tally, and when the collapse of the Army Poznan required a with-drawal, it had become the top-scoring Polish unit of the campaign with 31 victories.

The bombers, meantime, had attempted to maintain the fight. Bomber Brigade Los and Karas aircraft were out on 7 September, attacking targets on both the northern and central fronts. Such attacks continued for two more days, although four Karas were to be lost the next day, but on 10 September this Brigade too was reorganized. X/1 and XV/1 Dyons were ordered to collect 20 new Los bombers from store but only nine proved to be available, and they prepared for further operations with a combined strength of 30 aircraft. VI/6 Dyon was reformed with all the remaining aircraft of the Brigade's II/2 Dyons (21 and 22 Squadrons) and of the Army Air Force's 32 (Lodz) and 42 (Pomorze) Squadrons; as with the fighters, Army Poznan was permitted to retain its 34 Squadron.

Poles reorganize in vain

At the same time as the air force was reorganizing, so too were the ground forces which were now grouped into three commands — Northern, Central and Southern Fronts. Each front was allotted a single Karas squadron. Central Front got ex-Kracow 24 Squadron, Southern Front got ex-Karpaty 31 Squadron, brought up to strength by the remaining aircraft of the Bomber Brigade's 55 Squadron, and Northern Front received 41 Squadron, reinforced from the remnants of 51 Squadron.

So reorganized, the Bomber Brigade made its last major effort on 12 September, but the several raids mounted cost a further three Karas and one Los. Two days later 11 sorties

TOP: JUNKERS JU87B STUKA DIVE-BOMBER OF THE LUFTWAFFE.

ABOVE: PZL P.IIC FIGHTERS OF THE ARMY POZNAN'S DYON III/3.

were made, during which five Karas of 64 Squadron were attacked by seven Bf109s and were able to claim two shot down. That evening, however, VI Dyon was bombed at its Hutniki base, and five Karas were hit and written off. Next morning the attack was repeated and the unit ceased to exist — all 17 Karas were gone. Since 9 September the air force's problem had been compounded by an acute fuel shortage, and because of this operations were ended after the bombers' last efforts on 16 September. On this date, the Los Dyons were out twice, attacking armor near Hrubieszow and Wlodowa — their last sorties of the war. A few more sorties were flown by the fighters. At Deblin an impromptu unit had been formed by the instructors there, and flying the prototype PZL P-24 fighter with this unit, Lt Henryk Szczesny shot down two German aircraft on 14 and 15

POLISH AIR FORCE CLAIMS

UNIT	NO
Pursuit Brigade	
	45 (12 He111; 10 Ju87; 6 Bf110; 3 Do17; 3 Ju86; 1 Hs126; 10 unidentified)
Bomber Brigade	
Los Dyons	4 (3 Bf109; 1 He111)
Karas Dyons	2 (2 Bf109)
Army Support Air Force	
Dyon III/5 (Modlin)	4
Dyon III/4 (Pomorze)	21
Dyon III/3 (Poznan)	31
Dyon III/6 (Lodz)	13
Dyon III/2 (Kracow)	10
Independent Deblin Group	2
Total	132
Ground Defenses	89
Overall total	221

LUFTWAFFE CLAIMS

Detailed breakdown of German claims in Poland is not available.
I(Z)/LG1 was reputedly top-scorer with 30 aerial victories.
I/ZG2 was credited with 28 in the air and 50 destroyed on the ground.
I/ZG76 made 31 claims, but only 19 of these appear to have been confirmed.
Victories in smaller quantities were also credited to I/JG21, I/JG76 and I(J)/LG2.

POLISH AIR FORCE LOSSES

	ENEMY ACTION	OTHER CAUSES	TOTAL
Tactical Air Force			
Pursuit Brigade			
P-7, P-11a, P-11c			54
Bomber Brigade			
P-23 Karas	35	21	56
P-37 Los	14	12	26
Liaison			
R XIII			7
Transport			
Fokker FVII/3m			2
Total			145
Army Support Air Force			
Fighters P-7, P-11a, P-11c	40	20	60
Bomber/Reconnaissance P-23 Karas	21	35	56
Army Co-operation R XIII, RWD 14, LWS 3	54	20	74
Total			190
Total			335

LUFTWAFFE LOSSES

Reconnaissance Aircraft	63
Bf109	67
Bf110	12
Medium Bombers (He111, Do17)	78
Dive-Bombers (Ju87)	31
Transports (Ju52/3m)	12
Marine and Miscellaneous	22
Total	285

279 more aircraft of all types were damaged to over 10% and removed from unit strength for repair.

September. During the next two days, III/6 Dyon, now operating as part of the Pursuit Brigade, managed to get into the air, also claiming two further victories — the second of these by 2/Lt Tadeusz Koc being the last of the campaign.

Despite the knowledge that 100 Fairey Battle bombers and 11 Hawker Hurricane fighters were on the way to Rumania from England for the Poles, it was obvious that even if these arrived there was little hope that the fuel or organization to operate them would remain. Then on 17 September came the final blow; from the east, by prior agreement with the Germans, Soviet troops crossed the border to occupy territory lost by the Soviet Union to the Poles in 1919. There was no more the air force could do, and the Commander-in-Chief, General Rayski, ordered evacuation to Rumania.

Over the next 48 hours, 50 P.11s and P.7 fighters, 19 Los bombers, 11 Karas, 18 Lublin R XIII and RWD 14 Czapla army co-operation aircraft, 150 training aircraft (including 40-50 early-model Los and Karas aircraft), and 60 civil aircraft crossed the frontier, while 40 more trainers and light aircraft flew into Latvia. With the battle in the air all but won, the Luftwaffe had begun withdrawing many units to the West from 12 September onwards, leaving in the east only those elements essential to continue the level of support.

Meanwhile, however, Operation *Seaside* — the major bombing attack on Warsaw — was reinstated, and on 13 September, 183 bombers struck at the city, attempting to concentrate at this stage on defenses, public utilities, etc. Such precision is seldom possible by normal bombing methods however, and soon the city was on fire.

The German armies were now closing up to Warsaw and nearby Modlin as resistance of the Army Poznan ebbed, but the arrival in Eastern Poland of the Russians on 17

September, brought pressure from Hitler for an early end to hostilities. Warsaw, where the bulk of the remaining Polish forces were now entrenched and determined to fight to the last, was seen as the key, and an all-out air attack was ordered. Leaflets were dropped on the city during five of the next seven days, calling for surrender, but there was no response from the 100 000 troops in the city. Consequently, at 0800 hours on 25 September, something over 400 bombers, including eight Gruppen of Ju87s, attacked Warsaw three or four times each. Because so many of the medium bomber units had been withdrawn to the West, 30 transport Junkers Ju52/3ms were thrown into the fray to drop incendiaries, which were literally shovelled out of the aircraft's loading doors. By nightfall, 500 tons of high explosive and 72 tons of incendiaries had rained down on the city. There could only be one response in the circumstances; next day the defenders offered surrender, the Germans moving into the city on 27 September.

Meanwhile, the Stukas had turned their attack on Modlin, delivering a further 318 tons of bombs onto this fortress during 26 and 27 September; surrender followed here too the next day. The campaign was now all but over, but troops led by General Kleeberg continued to resist, engaging the Germans in battle on 1 October. These too ceased to resist on 5 October when their supplies of ammunition were exhausted. In little more than one month, a martial nation of proven courage had been totally destroyed by a new form of mechanical warfare. A form of aerial support to ground forces of a scope and effectiveness hitherto barely imagined had come of age.

C H A P T E R   T W O

THE BATTLE OF BRITAIN

JUNE – NOVEMBER 1940

Overleaf

As Dornier Do17Z bombers of Kampfgeschwader head over Kent to
attack London on 15 September, 1940, they are intercepted by Supermarine Spitfire Is from Fighter
Command's No 11 Group.

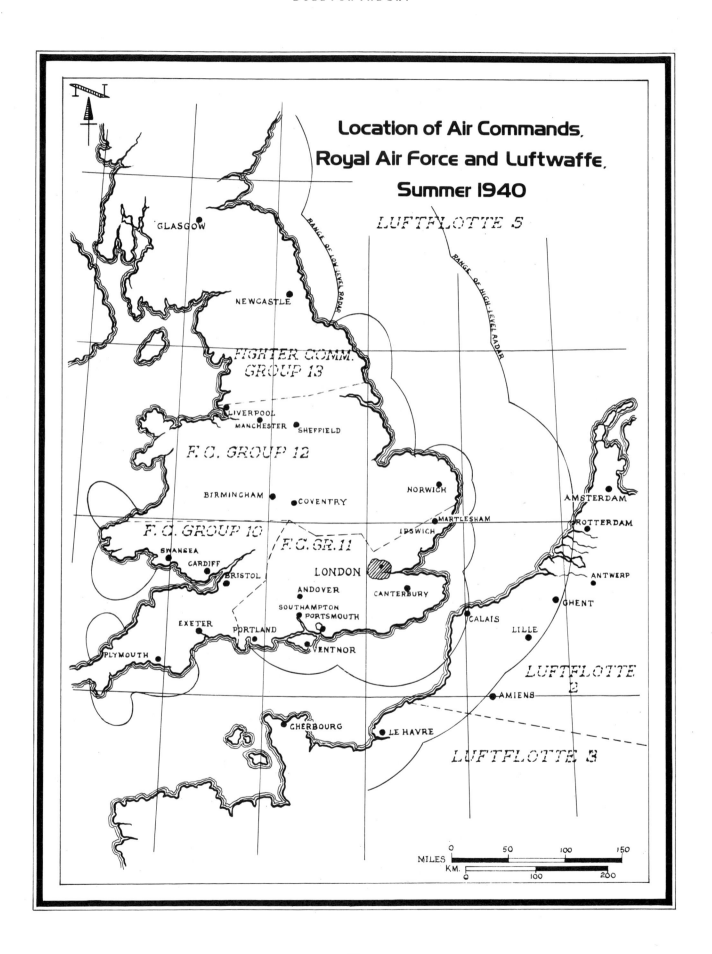

Of all the aerial battles which took place during World War II, few, if any, captured the imagination of the public and historians alike, or gained the fame of the Battle of Britain. Yet few were less decisive in their immediate results, although the long-term repercussions were tremendous.

With the fall of France in June 1940 Britain was left alone against one of the mightiest and most efficient war machines ever. In three short months the small British army had lost the best of its equipment and been reduced to little more than cadre strength. The Royal Air Force had suffered grievous losses of fighter and day bomber aircraft, only the as-yet hardly tested night bomber arm remaining relatively unscathed.

The traditional shield of England from the expansionists of Europe — the proud Royal Navy — had been forced to accept that, without air cover, it was extreme folly of the most dangerous kind to operate within range of Germany's land-based air force. For a badly-prepared island people, without powerful allies and with only the uncertain friendship of that slumbering giant, the United States, to fall back upon, it was a grim prospect.

But Britain possessed a number of advantages which stood her in good stead — not least her geographical position. To launch an invasion, the German Wehrmacht would first have to cross the English Channel with its unreliable weather and fierce currents — a major undertaking for a nautical power, much less a continental one, and one for which there were few recent precedents to call upon for experience. The Royal Navy, bloodied but unbowed, was still a force greatly to be reckoned with, while experience in Spain, Poland and France had convinced the Germans that no such undertaking could be considered without the maintenance of full air superiority as an absolute pre-requisite. And therein lay the rub, for the Royal Air Force had developed the most advanced air defense system that burgeoning science and the previous experience of combating German raiders during 1916–18 allowed.

This system was built not only around the finest and most modern fighter aircraft, well-trained pilots and well-developed maintenance and re-supply organization, but also a chain of radar stations — then known as radio location — which had rapidly been developed around the south-eastern and southern coastline of the country during the final years immediately preceding the outbreak of war. The information received from these early radars, which were known as the 'Chain Home' system, was fed to Group Headquarters where incoming raids were plotted on a central mapboard.

Direct radio and telephone transmission to major fighter airfields, known as sector stations allowed interceptions to be centrally controlled, while each sector had its own smaller operations room for the more intimate control of its allocated squadrons. Each sector station also had available and under its control two or three satellite airfields, at which some of its squadrons could be based as a dispersal against air attack and airfield overcrowding. The ten months of the 'Phoney War' and the Battle of France had allowed systems to be developed and honed to a fine edge of readiness against the regular reconnaissance flights and attacks on coastal shipping in which the Luftwaffe had indulged.

If the British fighter force had one major disadvantage compared with its Luftwaffe opponents at the start of 1940,

it was lack of operational experience. However, the hectic events over France, Belgium and Norway — and particularly the bitter fighting above the beaches of Dunkirk — had gone far to correct this particular deficiency, although sadly not far enough to save the lives of many desperately-needed but 'green' pilots when the days of reckoning arrived.

Despite the efforts of Fighter Command's chief, Sir Hugh Dowding, several squadrons of Hawker Hurricanes had been sent to France during the debacle, where they had been consumed, not so much by the fighting in the air as by the chaos on the ground. A frighteningly high number had been destroyed, many of them burnt on the ground to prevent them falling into enemy hands often as a result of relatively minor repair requirements. Even the carefully-husbanded and less numerous Spitfires had been thrown in over Dunkirk, where they had on several occasions been successful in gaining local air superiority.

However, the Luftwaffe too had suffered heavy losses during the fighting in France. Its units had moved fast across Europe, and time was now needed to rest, re-equip and consolidate before further major operations could be considered. This provided a breathing space for the RAF to rebuild its shattered squadrons — not only the fighters, but the day bombers of Bomber Command's No 2 Group, which had suffered far more heavily than the fighters, and which would be required to play an important part in the face of any invasion attempt.

RAF regroups and retrains

Aircraft production was not a problem. The United Kingdom went onto a full war footing in every aspect of the nation's life long before Germany did, and production of aircraft was soon catching up with, and indeed passing that achieved by German industry. This was in no small part owing to the dynamic efforts of Lord Beaverbrook, who had been appointed Minister of Aircraft Production by the new British Prime Minister, Winston Churchill, and to the system of 'shadow' factories that had been set up all over the country during the last years of uneasy peace.

It took much longer to select and train fighter pilots, and train them to a level at which they could hope to survive and play their part. During the 1930s the RAF had expanded rapidly, and many enthusiastic volunteers had been trained in their holidays and weekends as members of the Volunteer Reserve, while those who had joined the prestigious Auxiliary Air Force had reached a standard of proficiency comparable with the regulars. All had been called up in August 1939 and would play their part. But they were not enough; so every avenue had to be considered and tried.

Volunteers to fly fighters were called for from the bomber and army co-operation units, pilots who had survived the rigours of the Battle of France at the controls of a Fairey Battle or Bristol Blenheim undertaking a rapid conversion course before going to swell the ranks of a Hurricane or Spitfire squadron. Escapees from the occupied nations of Europe offered another ripe harvest, Poles, Czechs, Frenchmen and Belgians particularly coming forward in numbers. Many were already experienced and combat-hardened veterans — all needed rapid courses in English and in RAF procedures before joining British units, or being formed into national squadrons of their own. All these dedicated men gave particularly good service. Finally, the Admiralty was asked to loan a quantity of trained fighter pilots from the Fleet Air Arm, and the small but select band of individuals from this tiny air force eventually played a part out of all proportion to their numbers.

Throughout the second half of June 1940, as the French collapsed, the bombers of No 2 Group, usually well-escorted by Hurricanes and Spitfires, flew across the Channel day after day to hammer away at the advancing German columns, and to attack the airfields along the coast of France to which the Luftwaffe was now moving. Meanwhile, German reconnaissance aircraft strayed along the British eastern coastlines, and occasionally flew inland, while during the night of 18–19 June the first serious air raid on England was launched.

It was a fine moonlit summer's night, however, and as the Heinkel He111s droned in over East Anglia, the Blenheim IFs of the nightfighter squadrons were joined by Spitfires from several units; five of the raiders were shot down and two more claimed as probables, but it was a fore-taste of things to come. At the end of June the escorted raids by the RAF ceased, although for a few more days formations of fighters flew reconnaissances over the French coast. But the emphasis was changing, for from the start of July the Luftwaffe began steadily going over to the offensive and probing westwards across the sea.

There was little sense of urgency on the German side, where many considered that, with the fall of France, an accommodation with the British would soon be reached. Eventually, Adolf Hitler somewhat unenthusiastically ordered the preparation of plans for an invasion of Southern England codenamed Operation *Seelöwe* (Sea Lion). The essential preliminary was an air assault to gain that vital element of supremacy demanded by the admirals of the German Navy. This time would also allow the collection of barges from the waterways of Western Europe, and the build-up of supplies at ports of embarkation. Reich-

Marschal Hermann Göring, Commander-in-Chief of the Luftwaffe and First War fighter ace was enthusiastically optimistic that here was the ideal opportunity for his beloved air force to bring the British nation to its knees — or at least to the negotiating table — by air power alone.

The British under threat

For this task three Luftflotten (Air Fleets) were allocated. Luftflotte 2, the largest, was based in Belgium and Northern France, facing England from the east. Luftflotte 3 took station in Normandy and Brittany, to assault the south coast, while the much smaller Luftflotte 5 was already established in Norway and Denmark since the conquest of those countries during the spring. From here its units could threaten Scotland and the North of England.

On 30 June Göring issued orders for the first phase of the assault which was to gain and maintain air superiority over the Channel, and deny the coastal waterways to the cargo shipping that was constantly plying these sea routes with coal and other cargoes from north to south. This task was entrusted to Bruno Lörzer's II Fliegerkorps and VIII Fliegerkorps which was commanded by Wolfram von Richthofen, cousin of the famous 'Red Baron' of World War I, and like Lörzer, himself an ace of that war. Oberst Johannes Fink, Kommodore of KG2 was appointed 'Kanalkampfführer' to co-ordinate and organize operations. These would be undertaken mainly by the Dornier Do17Z bombers of KG2 and KG3, and by the Stukas of VIII Fliegerkorps; various fighter units would provide escort, the units most frequently to operate being from JG27 and 51, and the Zerstörer units, ZG26 and 76.

By this time the British intelligence organization, aided by information gathered from 'Ultra', the top-secret decoding device which had broken the German code, and by the radio-listening 'Y' Service, had a fair idea of the strength and dispositions of the Luftwaffe, which had been consistently overestimated earlier in the war. The Luftwaffe was ready for its new task — but only just. In fact it was in a far weaker state than might have been the case. Losses in action during May and June had totalled over 1100 aircraft, with a further 145 damaged. The intense nature of the operations undertaken had resulted in a further 216 being destroyed in accidents and due to mechanical failures. This total had included the loss of 235 Bf109Es, 106 Bf110s, 113 Ju87Bs and no less than 492 medium bombers, equivalent to about half the immediately available strength with which the Luftwaffe was to open the main phase of the Battle! But the Germans had the huge asset of experience. Large numbers of their aircrew had already seen action in Spain during the Civil War there; a number had been involved in the fighting over Poland, whilst nearly all had been active over France and the Low Countries, or Norway, during the past two months. Several Stuka and bomber pilots had already been awarded the coveted Ritterkreuz (Knight's Cross) for their service, as had two of the fighter pilots. Both the latter were veterans of Spain: Wilhelm Balthasar, Kommandeur of II Gruppe in Jagdgeschwader 2, had added 23 victories to the seven he had claimed in Spain to emerge as top-scorer of the 1940 *Blitzkrieg*, while Werner Mölders, German top-scorer in Spain with 14 victories there, had added 25 more since the start of the war.

Instigator of many of the excellent tactics employed by the German fighters, Mölders would be promoted as Kommodore of Jagdgeschwader 51 before July was out, taking over from an old World War I 'warhorse' Theo

A GROUP OF TYPICAL FIGHTER PILOTS OF RAF FIGHTER COMMAND (BOTH SERGEANTS AND OFFICER PILOTS), PLAY SHOVE-HA'PENNY BETWEEN SORTIES.

CLASSIC LUFTWAFFE FIGHTER OF THE BATTLE—THE MESSERSCHMITT BF109E. THIS IS AN AIRCRAFT OF I/JG2, SEEN ON A FRENCH AIRFIELD; IN THE FOREGROUND IS THE STANDARD OF THE JAGDVERBÄNDE (FIGHTER FORCE).

Osterkamp. The latter was then promoted 'Jafü 2' (Jagd-fliegerführer 2), in command of all the fighter units of Luftflotte 2.

Fighter Command faced the German threat at the start of July with its squadrons controlled by three groups. In the south No 11 Group controlled 17 squadrons of Hurricanes, eight of Spitfires and four of Blenheim IFs. No 12 Group in the Midlands and East Anglia had three squadrons of Hurricanes, five of Spitfires, one of Defiants and two of Blenheims. The whole of the North of England, Scotland, Northern Ireland and the Orkney and Shetland Islands came within the aegis of No 13 Group, which had nine squadrons of Hurricanes, six of Spitfires, one of Defiants and one of Blenheims. Five of these units were not fully operational yet, either new units working up, or still recuperating after service in France.

Further new units were being formed at this stage, but strength at the start of the month amounted to some 870 fighters, of which 645 were immediately serviceable. It should not be forgotten, however, that Fighter Command

was backed by more than 20 squadrons of Coastal Command around the coastal airfields of the country, four of which were equipped with Blenheim fighters, and ten with bomber or torpedo-bomber aircraft, together with a further dozen day-bomber squadrons of No 2 Group, and by a handful of Fleet Air Arm fighters and torpedo-bomber biplanes, all of which would play their part in forthcoming operations, as indeed would Bomber Command's not inconsiderable night-bombing force.

The Luftwaffe offensive begins

On 1 July the first attacks began; Ju87Bs of III/StG51 bombarded a convoy near Plymouth, escaping fighter interception from the sparse forces available in the south-west. Near Dover, Do17Zs of KG77, shortly to withdraw to Germany to re-equip with Ju88As, appeared off the coast in some numbers, three being lost here to fighter attacks and anti-aircraft gunfire. Three more of this Geschwader's aircraft were lost over other parts of south-east England. Three reconnaissance aircraft and an air-sea rescue floatplane were also lost in action during the day to make it a fairly expensive opening foray for the Luftwaffe.

A heavier attack was made by III/StG51 on 4 July when 33 of the Gruppe's Ju87Bs attacked Portland naval base at Weymouth, Dorset, sinking the auxiliary anti-aircraft vessel HMS *Foyle Bank*, and seriously damaging a tanker. The

Foyle Bank at 5582 tons was the largest vessel in dock, and indeed was the largest sunk throughout the Battle. Aboard the vessel Acting Seaman Jack Mantle continued to man his 'pom-pom' gun throughout the attack, although mortally wounded, later being awarded a posthumous Victoria Cross. The Stukas suffered only a single loss to gunfire, escaping fighter interception entirely. The attack showed up starkly the extent to which No 11 Group's defenses were stretched thin in the south-west of the country. However, Fighter Command did little better further east when well-escorted Do17Zs attacked a convoy off Dover. Hurricanes of 79 Squadron attempted a late interception, but were headed-off by the escort from II/JG51 which shot down Sgt Henry Cartwright, DFM, a Battle of France veteran credited with five victories.

First encounters

On 7 July came the first real clash between the opposing fighters. A British convoy was passing along the south coast in a west to east direction, and several interceptions of reconnaissance aircraft were made over or near it during the late morning. Towards evening, as it approached the Dover Straits, Bf109s were sent out on 'Freie Jagd' (free chase) missions to clear the skies of British fighters before a raid was launched on the ships. Spitfires from 54 Squadron rose to intercept one such incursion, gave chase to a lone He111 and were at once attacked by Messerschmitts which shot down two, and damaged a third British fighter.

When Do17Zs of KG2 arrived to attack just before dark, 64 and 65 Squadrons were scrambled, but a Bf109 sweep by JG51 caught the latter unit and sent down three of its aircraft, all the pilots being killed. The surviving pilots claimed three of the Messerschmitts in return, two of them by F/Sgt W H Franklin, DFM, who had recently claimed over five victories above Dunkirk, and who followed his first victim almost to France, but no Luftwaffe losses were recorded while II and III/JG51 claimed ten Spitfires.

Two days later the vaunted Bf110s appeared over England for the first time, III/ZG26 escorting a force of Ju88s and He111s, together with a Gruppe of Bf109s to bomb a convoy in the Thames estuary. Hurricanes of 151 Squadron attempted to intercept, but were unable to fight their way through to the bombers. The escorting fighters shot down one and damaged a second. More Hurricanes from 43 Squadron came to the assistance of 151, but that flown by the Commanding Officer, Sqn Ldr George Lott was hit and he baled out, blinded in one eye by splintered glass. Between them, the Hurricane pilots shot down three of ZG26's Bf110s in return and damaged a fourth.

That same evening Portland was again dive-bombed by 27 Stukas from StG77. This time, however, Spitfires from 609 Squadron which had recently arrived at the newly-completed airfield at Warmwell intercepted the bombers; that flown by the Kommandeur of I Gruppe, Hpt Freiherr von Dalgwick zu Lichenfels, who had recently been awarded the Knight's Cross, being shot down by Plt Off David Crook, one of 609's budding aces. A Bf110 from the escort provided by V(Z)/LG1 was also lost, but the crew were rescued from the sea.

During the day the RAF attempted to strike back. Twelve Blenheim IVs, from 21 and 57 Squadrons in Scotland, flew across the North Sea to bomb one of Luftflotte 5's airfields at Stavanger in Norway. While their bombs destroyed three Do215 reconnaissance aircraft of the Aufklarüngs gruppe ObdL, the bombers were set upon by

BRITISH

Supermarine Spitfire I
The classic British fighter of the Battle of Britain, world-renowned, and synonymous with the Battle and the British will to win which it inspired. Considered to be one of the most aesthetically beautiful aircraft ever built, the Spitfire was a low-wing monoplane of semi-monocoque construction, with an elliptical wing of slender section. Powered by a 1030 hp Rolls Royce Merlin II or III engine, the Spitfire achieved a top speed of 365 mph at 19 000 ft, a ceiling of 34 000 ft and a range of 375 miles. A very manoeuvreable aircraft, it was capable of turning more tightly than a Bf109E, but was outclimbed and outdived by the German fighter. When the Messerschmitt rolled sharply over into a dive the Spitfire was unable to follow as the carburettor-fed Merlin stopped firing momentarily due to gravity-inspired fuel starvation whereas the fuel injected DB601A of the Messerschmitt continued to operate undisturbed. Armament of the Spitfire I was eight 0.303 in Browning machine guns arranged along the length of the wing leading edge. While these gave a high density of fire, the small bullets lacked the weight to inflict really effective damage on aircraft which featured armor protection in other than relatively favorable situations.

Hawker Hurricane I of 242 Squadron, No 12 Group, Fighter Command, flown by Sqn Ldr D R S Bader

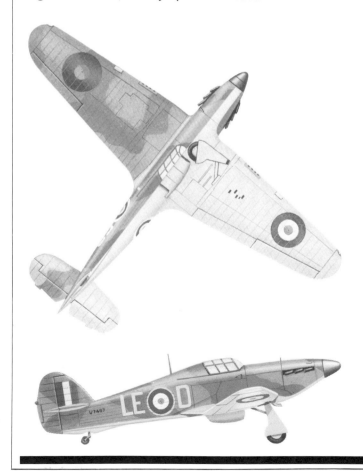

Heinkel He111H of II/Kampfgeschwader 53

Hawker Hurricane I
Powered by the same Merlin engine as the Spitfire, the Hurricane was a rather larger aircraft of slightly older and more traditional design, which featured a fabric-covered rear fuselage. Armament also comprised eight 0.303 in Brownings, but these were arranged in two tight groups of four in each wing. A tough, manoeuvrable aircraft, capable of taking considerable punishment, the Hurricane was more stable than the Spitfire and as a result was a better gun platform, but the overall performance was lower. Top speed was 324 mph at 16 250 ft and service ceiling was 34 200 ft. Climb rate, however, was virtually identical to that of the Spitfire, but range was only 425 miles. Generally, given the somewhat lower performance of the Hurricane, it enjoyed similar attributes to the Spitfire and suffered from the same disadvantages; it was, however, available in substantially larger numbers in 1940, and production tempo was considerably higher during the Battle.

Boulton-Paul Defiant I
The third single-engined low-wing monoplane fighter of the RAF in service in 1940 was also powered by a 1030 hp Merlin. The Defiant differed, however, in having no fixed forward firing armament, but featured instead a power-operated revolving gun turret in the fuselage immediately behind the pilot, in which a gunner manned a battery of four 0.303 in Brownings. Designed specifically as a bomber destroyer, which could fly alongside enemy aircraft, pouring a sustained fire into their unprotected flanks, the Defiant soon proved no match for hostile fighters due to the reduced performance occasioned by its greater weight. With a maximum speed of 303 mph at 16 500 ft, the aircraft had a service ceiling of 30 350 ft. When forced out of the day battle it became a moderately effective interim nightfighter.

Bristol Blenheim I and IV
Designed as a high speed day bomber, the Blenheim was a clean, relatively small twin-engined mid-wing monoplane. Possessed of a marked performance advantage when first introduced to service, it was already outclassed by contemporary fighter aircraft by 1940 and as a light bomber could operate safely by day only in conditions of cloud cover, or when heavily escorted. The earlier Mk I 'short-nosed' aircraft had already been superseded in the bomber squadrons when war began, but the substantial numbers available were fitted with a special pack under the fuselage containing four forward-firing 0.303 in Brownings, and these aircraft were then issued to a considerable number of fighter squadrons as interim equipment. By summer 1940 they were employed only as nightfighters.
    A few Blenheim IFs, together with numbers of Mk IV bombers similarly converted to the F-fighter role, were employed

by several Coastal Command units as long-range coastal patrol fighters. The bomber version of the Mk IV equipped all the squadrons of Bomber Command's No 2 Group in summer 1940 as well as two Coastal Command anti-shipping units. These aircraft played a major part in the Battle, attacking Luftwaffe airfields by day and night. Apart from the gun packs of the fighter versions, basic armament comprised a single fixed Browning machine gun in one wing and a 0.303 in Vickers 'K' gun in a power-operated dorsal turret for the Mk I, the turret guns being replaced by one or two Brownings in the Mk IV. Comparative performance was as follows:

	Mk I F	Mk IV
Engines	Two 840 hp Bristol	Two 920 hp Bristol
—	Mercury VIII radials	Mercury XV radials
Max speed	260 mph at 12 000 ft	266 mph at 11 800 ft
Ceiling	27 280 ft	22 000 ft
Range	1125 miles	1460 miles
Bombload	1000 lb	1320 lb

GERMAN

The Luftwaffe employed basically the same Messerschmitt Bf109E and Bf110C and D fighter aircraft, Junkers Ju87B dive bomber, and Heinkel He111H and P, and Dornier Do17 medium bombers that had been employed in Poland. All now carried a greater degree of armor protection for the crews and self-sealing fuel tanks, while the twin-engined bombers had received an increase in the defensive armament, the three 7.9 mm MG15 machine guns frequently being increased by the addition of between one and five flexibly-mounted guns. There was one major new addition, however:

Junkers Ju88A-1
A twin-engined low-wing monoplane, the Ju88 doubled as both a level and dive bomber. It also saw service during the Battle as a reconnaissance aircraft in its Ju88D version. One of the best and most versatile aircraft of the war, the Ju88 was also to see service as a Zerstörer and effective nightfighter. The 1940 bomber version was powered by two Junkers Jumo 211B-1 in-line engines with annular radiators which gave the visual appearance of being radials. These engines of 1210 hp each gave a top speed of 280 mph at 18 050 ft and a service ceiling of 32 150 ft — as good as a fighter! Range was 620 miles and offensive bombload was up to 3960 lb. Defense armament comprised the usual three 7.9 mm MG15s, increased subsequently to five such weapons.

Bf110s of I/ZG76 and Bf109s of II/JG77 which cut the formation to pieces. Each Gruppe claimed half a dozen Blenheims shot down, actual losses amounting to seven shot down and five damaged, one of which force-landed. Next day six of 107 Squadron's Blenheims attempted to attack Amiens airfield in Luftflotte 2's area, but once again disaster struck, five of them being shot down by Jafü 2 Bf109Es from III/JG3, which claimed seven.

Meanwhile during 10 July the Luftwaffe had launched a sufficiently major attack for the RAF to consider this to be the opening day of the Battle. Under cover of ZG26 Bf110s and JG3 Bf109Es, 26 Do17Zs from KG2 swept in to attack a large convoy in the Thames estuary. Three squadrons of Hurricanes and one of Spitfires were vectored to make an attack which was opened by 111 Squadron undertaking a squadron-strength head-on pass. A rare tactic at this stage of the war, it was later widely employed by the Luftwaffe against US bomber formations over Germany. One of the Hurricanes collided head-on with a I/KG2 Dornier, the ball of twisted wreckage falling to earth as the fighting continued above. A second Do17 was claimed collectively by 111 Squadron and two by 32 Squadron pilots, while four more were claimed to have been damaged by the Spitfires of 74 Squadron. Meanwhile 56 Squadron engaged the Bf109s of the escort, claiming three of these shot down, while two more were claimed damaged by the Spitfires.

Against the Bf109s 74 Squadron claimed two shot down and five damaged, Flg Off Henry Ferris of 111 Squadron claiming a third, although his Hurricane was badly damaged; three Spitfires were also damaged. Actual German losses appear to have totalled six; apart from the Dornier which had collided with Flg Off T P K Higgs, one more was shot down and a third so badly damaged that it force-landed and was written off. One of III/ZG26's Bf110s was also shot down and a second slightly damaged, while I/JG3 lost a single Bf109E. It seems that JG51 also became involved in this action, one Messerschmitt from II Gruppe being shot down over the Thames estuary, while one each from I and III Gruppen were damaged by Spitfires at this time.

Claims and losses
The results of this first large combat have been analyzed in some depth as they set the pattern for the coming weeks and months. Fighter Command claims were approximately double the number of known Luftwaffe combat casualties, and this was to be almost par for the course. On some occasions the discrepancy was smaller, on others larger. Only on those days of poor weather, when German aircraft appeared only singly were claims to be nearer to an accurate 'one-for-one' basis. Generally, however, the larger the numbers of aircraft and units engaged the larger would the discrepancy become. In July and August, however, analysis shows that two claims for one loss was the 'norm'.

Luftwaffe claims tended generally to be rather more accurate — especially those of the Bf109 pilots — but on this day, they were more than usually optimistic, pilots of JG51 claiming 13 fighters shot down, while III/ZG26 and various bomber gunners added claims for six more.

As the attack on the Thames estuary was underway 68 Ju88s from Luftflotte 3 flew in unopposed over the West Country to undertake damaging raids on Swansea and Falmouth in which they were totally unopposed. This again hammered home the inadequacy of existing defensive arrangements, and on 13 July No 10 Group was established with headquarters at Box in Wiltshire, headed by A V M Sir Christopher Brand — himself a notable World War I fighter pilot. A C M Dowding transferred a number of squadrons to the south-west from some of the northern bases in No 13 Group's area on the same date — the West Country would not be caught so unprepared again.

Several raids on convoys followed during the next few days, one of these on 11 July proving notable because for the first time Bf110s provided the escort for a formation of Ju87s heading once more for Portland. Three Hurricane flights were scrambled, that from 601 'City of London' Squadron arriving first and sailing into the bombers, claiming one shot down, five probables and one damaged. They then became engaged with the escorting Bf110s of III/ZG76, being joined by aircraft from 87 and 238 Squadrons; between them, the Hurricane pilots claimed five Bf110s shot down and three probables without loss. This was one of the days when RAF claims were rather more accurate — four Bf110s being lost by the Luftwaffe, together with one Ju87B from each of the Gruppen taking part (III/StG2 and IV(St)/LGI), while a third was damaged. Not so for the Germans, III/ZG76 claiming two Hurricanes and four Spitfires.

Fierce battles over England

The situation was very different on 13 July. Over Dunkirk, Defiants of 264 Squadron had enjoyed some apparently outstanding success during May, but this squadron was now resting. The second Defiant unit, 141 Squadron, was now operating from Hawkinge, and shortly after midday nine of this unit's aircraft began a patrol over the Channel. Suddenly the formation was attacked by ten Bf109Es of III/JG51, several of which approached from the Defiant's head-on blind spot. In seconds four Defiants had gone down into the sea, only a single pilot escaping with his life. As the remainder fought for survival one more was set on fire and subsequently blew up, while two others were badly hit, one of these crashing as it landed. Although three of the seven gunners baled out only one was found.

As the Defiants fought for life, Hurricanes of 111 Squadron came to their rescue, preventing total annihilation. The pilots of these Hurricanes claimed three Bf109s shot down, while the surviving Defiant crews reported that four more had been brought down by the turret gunners; in fact JG51 only lost one aircraft in this engagement and in turn claimed 11 Defiants and a Hurricane.

Mid-afternoon 32 Squadron also became engaged in a fierce battle with Bf109s, claiming five for one loss, while towards evening 43 Squadron was also engaged, claiming three for the loss of two Hurricanes and one damaged. One of those shot down was Flt Lt John Simpson DFC, at the time one of the unit's leading pilots. Already credited with seven victories, Simpson claimed two more in this fight,

although he was wounded and was out of action until November as a result. At least five other squadrons were engaged in fights on this date, claims for the day totalling over 20, yet Luftwaffe losses amounted only to five. Their own claims were for 21 fighters against nine actually lost and three damaged.

This day (13 July) was the worst day of the month for the RAF — and one of only two days on which their losses were heavier than the Luftwaffe. Every day of the month the Germans reappeared to attack convoys or occasional coastal targets. Whilst the fighting was hard, it was not yet really damaging, and Fighter Command was given much opportunity to learn some hard lessons. One was the need for an effective air-sea rescue service: the other was for the provision of individual dinghies for pilots shot down over the sea. The Germans already had these, and their chances of rescue from the choppy waters of the Channel by the He59 floatplanes of the Seenotstaffeln were far better than those of their British counterparts. In the event the RAF supply side was not found wanting — dinghies rapidly appeared, while an efficient system of high speed rescue launches was soon set up.

Meanwhile on 16 July Adolf Hitler had issued to his Chiefs of Staff the War Directive for the preparation of an invasion of England. On 19 July in the Reichstag he delivered his 'last appeal to reason' to the British to reach an accommodation. Now only 'blood, sweat and tears' awaited the defenders. While the daily shipping attacks were already taking on a pattern, there were various changes and highnotes. On 21 July V(Z)/LG1 first employed its Bf110s as fighter-bombers, carrying bombs underwing and leading the RAF to believe that a special bomber adaptation of the 110 (which it christened the 'Jaguar') had been introduced. This was not its only misapprehension during the battle. Clever German propaganda had led the British to believe that the Heinkel He113 fighter was in service. This was in fact a spurious designation for the He100D, only a small pre-production batch of which had been built — but throughout the fighting pilots frequently reported meeting, and shooting down 'He113s'.

The Dornier Do17Z bomber, with the revised angular and more bulbous cockpit area, was constantly misidentified as the 'Do215', a small production reconnaissance version of the Do17Z with the radial engines replaced by liquid-cooled powerplants. Misidentification of another kind occurred on 24 July, a day on which opposing fighters clashed violently. During the morning III/JG26 escorted 18 Do17s over the Medway area, where they were engaged first by Spitfires of 54 Squadron, and then others of 65 Squadron. The Messerschmitts were held in combat until low on fuel, when they had to dive away to make good their escape, leading the British pilots to believe that they had shot down many more than was the case. 54 Squadron claimed six and seven probables, and 65 added one more; actually JG26 lost three, and was able to shoot down two of 54 Squadron's aircraft in return: one of these crash-landed, but the other went down, taking with it Plt Off 'Johnny' Allen DFC, a fresh-faced young ace with more than eight victories.

German sweeps continue

More Spitfires of 610 Squadron had been despatched to patrol over the Dover area where it was hoped they might be able to cut off the retreat of the Germans on their return from the Medway. Instead they were well-positioned to

ROYAL AIR FORCE ORDER OF BATTLE (DAY UNITS), 8 AUGUST 1940

SECTOR STATION	BASE	SQUADRON	AIRCRAFT
FIGHTER COMMAND AIR CHIEF MARSHAL SIR HUGH DOWDING STANMORE, MIDDX			
11 Group Air Vice-Marshal Keith Park Uxbridge, Middx			
Debden, Essex	Debden,	17 Squadron	Hurricane
	Martlesham, Suffolk	85 Squadron	Hurricane
North Weald, Essex	Rochford, Essex	56 Squadron	Hurricane
	North Weald	151 Squadron	Hurricane
	Martlesham, Suffolk	25 Squadron	Blenheim IF
Hornchurch, Essex	Hornchurch	41 Squadron	Spitfire
	Hornchurch	54 Squadron	Spitfire
	Hornchurch	65 Squadron	Spitfire
	Hornchurch	74 Squadron	Spitfire
Biggin Hill, Kent	Biggin Hill	32 Squadron	Hurricane
	Biggin Hill	610 Squadron	Spitfire
	Gravesend, Kent	501 Squadron	Hurricane
	Manston, Kent	600 Squadron	Blenheim IF
Kenley, Surrey	Kenley	615 Squadron	Hurricane
	Kenley	64 Squadron	Spitfire
	Croydon, Surrey	111 Squadron	Hurricane
Northolt, Middx	Northolt	1 Squadron	Hurricane
	Northolt	257 Squadron	Hurricane
Tangmere, Hampshire	Tangmere	43 Squadron	Hurricane
	Westhampnett, Sussex	145 Squadron	Hurricane
	Tangmere	601 Squadron	Hurricane
10 Group Air Vice-Marshal Sir Christopher Brand Box, Wiltshire			
Pembrey, South Wales	Pembrey	92 Squadron	Spitfire
Filton, Somerset	Exeter, Devon	87 Squadron	Hurricane
	Exeter, Devon	213 Squadron	Hurricane
St Eval, Cornwall	St Eval	234 Squadron	Spitfire
	Roborough, Devon	247 Squadron	Gladiator
		(one flight)	
Middle Wallop, Hampshire	Middle Wallop	238 Squadron	Hurricane
	Middle Wallop	609 Squadron	Spitfire
	Middle Wallop	604 Squadron	Blenheim IF
	Warmwell, Dorset	152 Squadron	Spitfire
12 Group Air Vice-Marshal Trafford Leigh-Mallory Watnall, Nottingham			
Church Fenton, Yorkshire	Church Fenton	73 Squadron	Hurricane
	Church Fenton	249 Squadron	Hurricane
	Leconfield, Yorks	616 Squadron	Spitfire
Kirton-in-Lindsay	Kirton-in-Lindsay	222 Squadron	Spitfire
	Kirton-in-Lindsay	264 Squadron	Defiant
	Ringway	264 Squadron, 'A' Flight	Defiant
Digby, Lincolnshire	Digby	46 Squadron	Hurricane
	Digby	611 Squadron	Spitfire
	Digby	29 Squadron	Blenheim IF
Coltishall, Norfolk	Coltishall	242 Squadron	Hurricane
	Coltishall	66 Squadron	Spitfire
Wittering, Northamptonshire	Wittering	229 Squadron	Hurricane
	Wittering	266 Squadron	Spitfire
	Colly Weston, Northants	23 Squadron	Blenheim IF
Duxford, Cambridgeshire	Duxford	19 Squadron	Spitfire
13 Group Air Vice-Marshal Richard Saul Newcastle-Upon-Tyne			
Wick, Caithness, N Scotland	Wick	3 Squadron	Hurricane
	Castletown, N Scotland	504 Squadron	Hurricane
	Suburgh, Shetlands	232 Squadron	Hurricane
		(one flight)	
Dyce, Scotland	Dyce	603 Squadron, 'A' Flight	Spitfire
	Montrose, Scotland	603 Squadron, 'B' Flight	Spitfire
Turnhouse, Scotland	Drem, Scotland	605 Squadron	Hurricane
	Turnhouse	232 Squadron	Hurricane
	Turnhouse	253 Squadron	Hurricane
	Prestwick, Scotland	141 Squadron	Defiant
Usworth, Durham	Acklington, Northumberland	79 Squadron	Hurricane
	Usworth	607 Squadron	Hurricane
	Acklinton	72 Squadron	Spitfire

SECTOR STATION	BASE	SQUADRON	AIRCRAFT
Catterick, Yorkshire	Catterick	219 Squadron	Blenheim IF
Aldergrove, N Ireland	Aldergrove	245 Squadron	Hurricane

BOMBER COMMAND   AIR MARSHAL SIR CHARLES PORTAL   HIGH WYCOMBE, BUCKS

2 Group Air Vice-Marshal J M Robb Huntingdon			
West Raynham, Norfolk		18 Squadron	Blenheim IV
		101 Squadron	Blenheim IV
Horsham, St Faith, Norfolk		114 Squadron	Blenheim IV
		139 Squadron	Blenheim IV
Walton, Norfolk		105 Squadron	Blenheim IV
Bodney, Norfolk		82 Squadron	Blenheim IV
Wyton, Huntingdonshire		15 Squadron	Blenheim IV
Oakington, Cambridgeshire		218 Squadron	Blenheim IV
Wattisham, Suffolk		107 Squadron	Blenheim IV
		110 Squadron	Blenheim IV
Lossiemouth, Scotland		21 Squadron	Blenheim IV
		57 Squadron	Blenheim IV

COASTAL COMMAND   AIR CHIEF MARSHAL SIR FREDERICK BOWHILL   NORTHWOOD, MIDDX

15 Group Liverpool			
Oban, West Scotland		210 Squadron	Sunderland I
Aldergrove, N Ireland		233 Squadron	Hudson I
		502 Squadron	Anson I
18 Group Rosyth, East Scotland			
Thornaby, Yorkshire		220 Squadron	Hudson I
		608 Squadron	Anson I, Botha I
Leuchars, East Scotland		224 Squadron	Hudson I
Wick, North Scotland		42 Squadron	Beaufort I
		269 Squadron	Hudson I
Stranraer, North Scotland		240 Squadron	Short Stranraer
Sullum Voe, Shetlands		201 Squadron	Sunderland I
		204 Squadron	Sunderland I
Sumburgh, Shetlands		248 Squadron	Blenheim IVF
		254 Squadron	Blenheim IF, IVF
16 Group Chatham, Kent			
Thorney Island, Hampshire		59 Squadron	Blenheim IV
Detling, Kent		53 Squadron	Blenheim IV
Detling, Kent		500 Squadron	Anson I
Bircham Newton, Norfolk		206 Squadron	Hudson I
		235 Squadron	Blenheim IVF
North Coates, Lincolnshire		22 Squadron	Beaufort I
19 Group Plymouth, Devon			
St Eval, Cornwall		217 Squadron	Beaufort I
		236 Squadron	Blenheim IF, IVF
Pembroke Dock, South Wales		209 Squadron	Saro Lerwick I
The following fighter units became operational during the Battle after 8 August 1940:			
		1 Squadron, Royal Canadian Air Force	Hurricane
		302 (Polish) Squadron	Hurricane
		303 (Polish) Squadron	Hurricane
		310 (Czech) Squadron	Hurricane
		312 (Czech) Squadron (From 2 October)	Hurricane
		306 (Polish) Squadron (From 8 November)	Hurricane
		308 (Polish) Squadron (From 24 November)	Hurricane
		421 Flight	Spitfire
		422 Flight	Hurricane
		Fighter Interception Unit	Blenheim IF/Beaufighter
		Air Fighting Development Unit	Various

TYPICAL LUFTWAFFE ORDER OF BATTLE AS AT 13 AUGUST 1940

LUFTFLOTTE 2 BRUSSELS, BELGIUM
GENERALFELDMARSCHALL ALBERT KESSELRING

I Fliegerkorps Beauvais, France Generaloberst Ulrich Grauert

UNIT	BASE	COMMANDER	AIRCRAFT
Kampfgeschwader 1	Rosiers-en-Santerre	Oberstlt Exss	
Stab	Rosiers-en-Santerre		Heinkel He111
I Gruppe	Montdiddier		Heinkel He111
II Gruppe	Montdiddier		Heinkel He111
III Gruppe	Rosiers-en-Santerre		Dornier Do17Z
Kampfgeschwader 76	Corneilles-en-Vexin	Oberstlt Stefan Frohlich	
Stab	Corneilles-en-Vexin		DornierDo17Z
I Gruppe	Beauvais		Dornier Do17Z
II Gruppe	Creil		Junkers Ju88A
III Gruppe	Croneilles-en-Vexin		Dornier Do17Z
5(F)/122			Heinkel He111/Junkers Ju88D
4(F)/123			He111/Ju88D/Bf110

II Fliegerkorps Ghent, Belgium General Bruno Lurzer

UNIT	BASE	COMMANDER	AIRCRAFT
Kampfgeschwader 2	Arras	Oberst Johannes Fink	
Stab	Arras		Dornier Do17Z
I Gruppe	Epinoy		Dornier Do17Z
II Gruppe	Arras		Dornier Do17Z
III Gruppe	Cambrai		Dornier Do17Z
Kampfgeschwader 3	Le Culot	Oberst Wolfgang von Charniers Glisczinski	
Stab	Le Culot		Dornier Do17Z
I Gruppe	Le Culot		Dornier Do17Z
II Gruppe	Antwerp/Duerne		Dornier Do17Z
III Gruppe	St Trond		Dornier Do17Z
Kampfgeschwader 53	Lille-Nord	Oberst Stahl	
Stab	Lille-Nord		Heinkel He111
I Gruppe	Lille-Nord		Heinkel He111
II Gruppe	Lille-Nord		Heinkel He111
III Gruppe	Lille-Nord		Heinkel He111
Stukageschwader 1			
II Gruppe	Pas de Calais		Junkers Ju87B
Lehrgeschwader 1			
IV (St) Gruppe	Tramecourt		Junkers Ju87B
Erprobungs gruppe 210			
1,2 Staffeln	Calais-Marck		Messerschmitt Bf110
3 Staffel	Calais-Marck		Messerschmitt Bf109E
Lehrgeschwader 2			
II(Sch) Gruppe	St Omer		Messerschmitt Bf109E

IX Fliegerkorps Sovesterburg, Holland Generalmajor Joachim Coeler

UNIT	BASE	COMMANDER	AIRCRAFT
Kampfgeschwader 4	Sovesterburg	Oberstlt Hans-Joachim Rath	
Stab	Soesterburg		Heinkel He111
I Gruppe	Soesterburg		Heinkel He111
II Gruppe	Eindhoven		Heinkel He111
III Gruppe	Amsterdam "Schipol"		Junkers Ju88A
Kampfgruppe 100	Vannes, Brittany		Heinkel He111
Kampfgeschwader 40			
Stab	Brest, Brittany		Focke-Wulf FW200
I Gruppe	Brest, Brittany		Focke-Wulf FW200
Kampfgruppe 126	Coastal Detachments		Heinkel He111
Kustenfliegergruppe 106	Coastal Detachments		Heinkel He115/Dornier Do18
3(F)/122			Ju88D/He111

Jagdfliegerfuhrer 2 Wissant, France Generalmajor Theodor Osterkamp

UNIT	BASE	COMMANDER	AIRCRAFT
Jagdgeschwader 3	Samer	Oberstlt Carl Vick	
Stab	Samer		Messerschmitt Bf109E
I Gruppe	Colombert		Messerschmitt Bf109E
II Gruppe	Samer		Messerschmitt Bf109E
III Gruppe	Desvres		Messerschmitt Bf109E
Jagdgeschwader 26	Audembert	Maj Gotthard Handrick	
Stab	Audembert		Messerschmitt Bf109E
I Gruppe	Audembert		Messerschmitt Bf109E
II Gruppe	Marquise		Messerschmitt Bf109E
III Gruppe	Cuffiers		Messerschmitt Bf109E
Jagdgeschwader 51	Wissant	Maj Werner Mölders	
Stab	Wissant		Messerschmitt Bf109E
I Gruppe	Wissant		Messerschmitt Bf109E
II Gruppe	Wissant		Messerschmitt Bf109E
III Gruppe	St Omer		Messerschmitt Bf109E
Jagdgeschwader 52	Coquelles	Maj von Merhart	
Stab	Coquelles		Messerschmitt Bf109E
I Gruppe	Coquelles		Messerschmitt Bf109E
II Gruppe	Peuplingne		Messerschmitt Bf109E
Jagdgeschwader 54	Campagne	Maj Martin Mettig	
Stab	Campagne		Messerschmitt Bf109E
I Gruppe	Guines		Messerschmitt Bf109E
II Gruppe	Hermalinghen		Messerschmitt Bf109E
III Gruppe	Guines		Messerschmitt Bf109E
Lehrgeschwader 2			
I(J) Gruppe	Calais-Marck		Messerschmitt Bf109E
Zerstörergeschwader 26	Lille	Oberstlt Joachim Huth	
Stab	Lille		Messerschmitt Bf110
I Gruppe	Yvrench		Messerschmitt Bf110
II Gruppe	Crecy		Messerschmitt Bf110
III Gruppe	Barley		Messerschmitt Bf110
Zerstörergeschwader 76	Laval	Maj Walter Grabmann	
Stab	Laval		Messerschmitt Bf110
II Gruppe	Abbeville		Messerschmitt Bf110
III Gruppe	Laval		Messerschmitt Bf110

LUFTFLOTTE 3 PARIS, FRANCE
GENERALFELDMARSCHALL HUGO SPERRLE

IV Fliegerkorps Compeigne, France Gen. Kurt Pflugbeil

UNIT	BASE	COMMANDER	AIRCRAFT
Lehrgeschwader 1	Orleans/Bricy	Oberst Alfred Bulowush	
Stab	Orleans/Bricy		Junkers Ju88A
I Gruppe	Orleans/Bricy		Junkers Ju88A
II Gruppe	Orleans/Bricy		Junkers Ju88A
III Gruppe	Chateaudun		Junkers Ju88A
Kampfgeschwader 27	Tours	Oberst Behrendt	
Stab	Tours		Heinkel He111
I Gruppe	Tours		Heinkel He111
II Gruppe	Dinard		Heinkel He111
III Gruppe	Rennes		Heinkel He111
Stukageschwader 3			
Stab			Do17/He111
Kampfgruppe 806,	Nantes		Junkers Ju88A
3(F)/31			Bf110/Do17/Hs126A

UNIT	BASE	COMMANDER	AIRCRAFT
V Fliegerkorps, Villacoublay		Generalleutnant Robert Ritter Von Greim	
Kampfgeschwader 51	Orly	Oberst Dr Fisser	
Stab	Orly		Junkers Ju88A
I Gruppe	Melun		Junkers Ju88A
II Gruppe	Orly		Junkers Ju88A
III Gruppe	Etampes		Junkers Ju88A
Kampfgeschwader 54	Evreux	Oberstlt Höhne	
Stab	Evreux		Junkers Ju88A
I Gruppe	Evreux		Junkers Ju88A
II Gruppe	St Andre-de-L'Eure		Junkers Ju88A
Kampfgeschwader 55	Villacoublay	Oberst Alois Stöckl	
Stab	Villacoublay		Heinkel He111
I Gruppe	Dreux		Heinkel He111
II Gruppe	Chartres		Heinkel He111
III Gruppe	Villacoublay		Heinkel He111
VIII Fliegerkorps Deauville		Generalmajor Wolfram Freiherr von Richthofen	
Stukageschwader 1	Angers	Maj Hagen	
Stab	Angers		Dornier Do17
I Gruppe	Angers		Junkers Ju87B
III Gruppe	Angers		Junkers Ju87B
Stukageschwader 2	St Malo	Maj Oscar Dinort	
Stab	St Malo		Dornier Do17
I Gruppe	St Malo		Junkes Ju87B
II Gruppe	Lannion		Junkes Ju87B
Stukageschwader 77	Caen	Maj Chemens Graf von Schönborn	
Stab	Caen		Dornier Do17
I Gruppe	Caen		Junkers Ju87B
II Gruppe	Caen		Junkers Ju87B
III Gruppe	Caen		Junkers Ju87B
Lehrgeschwader 1			
V(Z) Gruppe	Caen		Messerschmitt Bf110
Lehrgeschwader 2			
II(F) Gruppe	Boblingen, Germany		Dornier Do17F
2(F)/11	Le Bourget		Bf110/Do17
2(F)/123			Junkers Ju88D
Jagdfliegerfuhrer 3 Cherbourg Oberst Werner Junck			
Jagdgeschwader 2	Evreux	Oberstlt Harry von Bülow	
Stab	Evreux		Messerschmitt Bf109E
I Gruppe	Beaumont-le-Roger		Messerschmitt Bf109E
II Gruppe	Beaumont-le-Roger		Messerschmitt Bf109E
III Gruppe	Le Havre		Messerschmitt Bf109E
Jagdgeschwader 27	Cherbourg-West	Maj Max Ibel	
Stab	Cherbourg – West		Messerschmitt Bf109E
I Gruppe	Plumetot		Messerschmitt Bf109E
II Gruppe	Crepon		Messerschmitt Bf109E
III Gruppe	Carquebut		Messerschmitt Bf109E
Jagdgeschwader 53	Cherbourg	Maj Hans-Jürgen Craman-Taubadel	
Stab	Cherbourg		Messerschmitt Bf109E
I Gruppe	Rennes		Messerschmitt Bf109E
II Gruppe	Dinan		Messerschmitt Bf109E
III Gruppe	Sempy and Brest		Messerschmitt Bf109E

UNIT	BASE	COMMANDER	AIRCRAFT
Zerstörergeschwader 2	Toussee-la-Noble	Oberstlt Friedrich Vollbracht	
Stab	Toussee-le-Noble		Messerschmitt Bf110
I Gruppe	Amiens		Messerschmitt Bf110
II Gruppe	Guyancourt		Messerschmitt Bf110

LUFTFLOTTE 5 STAVANGER, NORWAY GENERALOBERST HANS-JURGEN STUMPFT

UNIT	BASE	COMMANDER	AIRCRAFT
X Fliegerkorps		Generaleutnant Hans Geisler	
Kampfgeschwader 26	Stavanger	Oberstlt Robert Fuchs	
Stab	Stavanger		Heinkel He111
I Gruppe	Stavanger		Heinkel He111
II Gruppe	Stavanger		Heinkel He111
Kampfgeschwader 30	Aalborg, Denmark	Oberstlt Loebel	
Stab	Aalborg		Junkers Ju88A
I Gruppe	Aalborg		Junkers Ju88A
III Gruppe	Aalborg		Junkers Ju88A
Zerstörergeschwader 76			
I Gruppe	Stavanger		Messerschmitt Bf110
Jagdgeschwader 77			
II Gruppe	Stavanger and Trondheim		Messerschmitt Bf109E
Küstenfliegergruppe 506	Stavanger and Trondheim		Heinkel He115C
1(F)120	Stavanger		He111/Ju88D
1(F)121	Stavanger		He111/Ju88D
AufklObDL	Stavanger		Dornier Do215
Aufklgr22	Stavanger		Dornier Do17P
(Det)	Vlissingen, Germany		Messerschmitt Bf110

NB Certain other units also took part in operations during the Battle, and there were various redesignations during the fighting which are set out below:

KüF1Gr196: Coastal reconnaissance unit with Arado Ar196 floatplanes

KüFlGr406: Based on the French and Dutch coasts in detachments with Dornier Do8 flyingboats

KüFlGr906: Based at Ijmuden and Schellingwoude on the Dutch coast with Heinkel He115B floatplanes

Aufklaringsgruppe 14: Based at Caen, Cherbourg and Plumetot with Bf110s and Do17P reconnaissance aircraft

KAMPFGESCHWADER 77: Stab I, II and III Gruppen took part in early operations in July 1940, equipped with Do17Z. The Geschwader was then withdrawn to equip with Ju88As, returning to operations from Caen, Neufchatel and Amiens airfields in early September.

KÜSTENFLIEGERGRUPPE 606: This coastal reconnaissance-bomber unit was equipped with Do17Zs, and was based in the Brest area. During September it was employed as an additional bomber unit when night attacks began.

KAMPFGRUPPE 806: This unit began the Battle as a Küstenfliegergruppe, but was reclassified as a conventional bomber Gruppe in August.

STUKAGESCHWADER 51: This Geschwader in fact only comprised III Gruppe which was involved in the first actions at the start of July. On 6 July it became II/StG1. Similarly on this date I(St)/TrGr186 became III/StG1. Also on 6 July I/StG76 became III/StG77.

STUKAGESCHWADER 3: I Gruppe was formed during summer 1940 from elements of I/StG76.

ZERSTÖRERGESCHWADER 2: II Gruppe was added at the start of the Battle by the redesignation of I/ZG52.

JAGDGESCHWADER 77: I Gruppe, which was left on Home Defense, became IV/JG51 in late 1940. III Gruppe was formed in midsummer, also for Home Defense, by the renumbering of II(J)/TrGr186.

'bounce' an incoming sweep by III/JG52, claiming three of the Messerschmitts definitely shot down and three more unconfirmed: three did in fact fail to return, including that flown by Oblt Ehrlich, the 8 Staffel Commander.

Another 610 Squadron pilot shot down an aircraft which he believed to be a Vought V.156F dive-bomber — an aircraft believed to have been taken over from the French Aeronavale by the Luftwaffe; it was indeed very similar, but it was a Blackburn Skua fighter/dive-bomber of the Fleet Air Arm on Channel patrol. Another leading RAF fighter pilot was lost on this date when Plt Off Jack Hamar DFC, a six-victory member of 151 Squadron, was killed in a take-off crash; not all losses were to enemy action.

Another fighter versus fighter engagement of some note occurred on 28 July when 74 Squadron was ordered off to cover Hurricanes intercepting bombers over the coast. The Spitfire unit, led by an indomitable flight commander, the South African 'Sailor' Malan, engaged elements of I and II/JG51, which were covering the bombers, led by their famous Geschwader Kommodore, Werner Mölders. In the fighting which followed, Mölders' Messerschmitt was hit and very badly damaged, the great man himself receiving slight wounds; he was obliged to crash-land on return. One of I/JG51's rising 'Experten', Oblt Richard Leppla, claimed to have shot down the Spitfire responsible. JG51 came off somewhat the worst in this engagement however; apart from Mölders, Hpt Eichele of I Gruppe was shot down and killed, as was a pilot of II Gruppe, while one more Bf109E from each Gruppe was damaged and both had to force-land on return. 74 Squadron claimed four and five damaged, one of the confirmed successes by Malan, but lost two Spitfires, one pilot managing to bale out, although wounded; Mölders, Leppla and one other pilot each claimed Spitfires shot down.

Next day 48 Ju87Bs from IV(St)/LG1 and II/StG1, covered by over 80 Bf109Es from JG51, raided Dover.

Spitfires of 41 Squadron and Hurricanes of 501 Squadron intercepted, the Hurricanes getting to the Stukas and claiming three shot down, two probables and four damaged, together with a Bf109. Soon, 41 Squadron became heavily engaged with the escort, claiming four Bf109s and a single Ju87, but losing one Spitfire shot down, while four more were damaged and all crashed on landing, although none of the pilots were hurt. During the later stages of the fight, 56 Squadron also ran into the escort, losing one Hurricane and pilot, but claiming one Messerschmitt shot down. Claims against the dive-bombers proved accurate, two from each Gruppe being lost and a fifth damaged, but not a single escorting Messerschmitt failed to return, or even suffered damage. I and II/JG51 claimed 11 British fighters.

Convoy attacks

Later in the day a new German unit, Erprobungsgruppe 210, which had been formed as a fighter-bomber test unit with two Staffeln of bomb-carrying Bf110s and one of Bf109Es, undertook its initial operation by raiding a coastal convoy east of Harwich, escorted by more Bf110s from ZG26. The new unit claimed hits on two ships, and although intercepted by Hurricanes of 151 Squadron, returned with only one aircraft damaged, the gunner being wounded — this was claimed probably destroyed by the Flg Off K H Blair as 151's only success of the combat. The escorting Bf110 pilots claimed four Hurricanes shot down without loss; two were actually hit and force-landed.

THE MOST NUMEROUS BRITISH FIGHTER AVAILABLE IN 1940 WAS THE HAWKER HURRICANE I. THIS PHOTO OF AN AIRCRAFT OF 71 'EAGLE' SQUADRON WAS TAKEN EARLY IN 1941, BUT ILLUSTRATES WELL THE TYPICAL MARKINGS OF SUCH AN AIRCRAFT DURING THE BATTLE.

THE BEST GERMAN BOMBER OF 1940 WAS THE JUNKERS JU88A, WHICH WAS IN SERVICE IN SMALLER NUMBERS THAN THE HE111 AND DO17Z. THIS EXAMPLE HAS BEEN BROUGHT DOWN ON BRITISH SOIL IN A RELATIVELY UNDAMAGED STATE.

The close of July did not bring to an end the convoy battles, although operations during early August were at a somewhat reduced level. On 8 August, however, reconnaissance indicated to the Germans the presence of a big convoy — CW9, codenamed 'Peewit', comprising some 20 cargo vessels with naval escort, which was attempting to sail from the Medway, through the Straits and round to Swanage. At once Luftflotte 3 was ordered to launch a maximum effort against it, and so great was the strength of attack and the numbers employed that many historians have taken this as the opening day of the Luftwaffe's main attack on England. But it was not so — essentially it was a continuation of the July battles.

Early in the morning elements of Luftflotte 3 were already out after a convoy which had sailed west from Weymouth. As Ju87s of II/StG1 and Bf109s of I/JG27 appeared, they were attacked by Hurricanes of 145 Squadron, two Ju87s and three Bf109s being shot down for the loss of two Hurricanes. Later in the morning Jafü 2 despatched a strong fighter sweep over the Folkestone, Dover, Margate area which became engaged with Spitfires from 41, 64 and 65 Squadrons.

In the typical confusion of such an engagement 64 Squadron claimed two Bf109s shot down, together with a probable and two damaged for the loss of one Spitfire, while two pilots of 41 Squadron claimed seven between them — four credited to Flt Lt J T Webster and three to Plt Off R W Wallens. However, 65 Squadron made no claims and lost two aircraft and their pilots. II and III/JG51 and III/JG26 claimed nine Spitfires between them, shot down four barrage balloons, and also claimed an aircraft identified as a Hampden, which is in fact believed to have been a Blenheim fighter of 600 Squadron, shot down as it took off from Marston airfield by Oblt 'Mickey' Sprick of III/JG26. Sprick's unit suffered the only casualty, one Bf109E being shot down.

Now the first strike on convoy 'Peewit' was on the way, however, with 57 Ju87s from StG2, 3 and 77 covered by 20 Bf110s of V(Z)/LG1 and Bf109Es of JG27 approaching the south coast under full surveillance by the Isle of Wight radar stations. Even before the attack on the shipping had started, Hurricanes were engaging the dive-bombers and their escorts in a battle which continued throughout the bombing. Three Ju87s of I/StG3 were shot down and three more from this unit and StG2 were damaged; V(Z)/LG1 lost one of its Bf110s, with three more badly damaged and two damaged to a lesser extent. The JG27 escorts lost three Bf109s. Amongst the interceptors, 609 Squadron claimed two Ju87s and three Bf110s, 238 Squadron two Bf110s, two Bf109s and five probables, while 145 Squadron was also heavily involved, claiming a number of Ju87s and Bf110s. The Luftwaffe pilots claimed 15 British fighters and nine barrage balloons shot down, but on this occasion RAF losses were very much lower. However, the bombing was effective and four merchant ships were sunk, with seven other vessels damaged.

Three hours later the attackers were back in force for a final attack on the ships which had now reached Weymouth Bay. Eighty-two Ju87s escorted by 68 Bf109s and Bf110s again hit the ships hard, but 43, 145 and 152 Squadrons were on the spot to intercept, shooting down three of II/StG77's Stukas and damaging four others, two so badly that they were write-offs. Escorting fighters claimed 14 British fighters and three No 2 Group Blenheims which passed their formation, but suffered heavily for their efforts, losing four Bf109Es from II/JG27 including the Gruppenkommandeur, Maj Werner Andres, who became a prisoner. The 'Peewit' convoy finally limped into Swanage harbor with only four ships undamaged; seven had been sunk and six more had been badly damaged, many making for the nearest port for refuge; four of the escort vessels had also been hit.

Claims generally for the day were rather optimistic. Over 'Peewit' JG27 claimed 15 victories, II/JG53 claimed seven and V(Z)/LG1 another six; for the day Luftwaffe claims included 45 Spitfires and Hurricanes, whereas combat losses of these fighters amounted only to 17. Fighter Command claimed 55 against 26 actual losses — 145 Squadron was top of the league with 23 victories in three separate engagements, which included 13 Ju87s, seven Bf109s, and three Bf110s. The unit suffered five losses, but amongst the other pilots Flt Lt Adrian Boyd had claimed five, Sqn Ldr John Peal, Flt Lt Roy Dutton and Plt Off Weir three each, while four other pilots had claimed two apiece.

The beginning of the Luftwaffe's main assault, 'Adler Tag' (Eagle Day), should have started on 10 August but bad weather forced a cancellation for three days.

The big raids begin

Meanwhile, however, 11 August saw the biggest raid yet during the morning. The day began with a number of 'Freie Jagd' sweeps by the Bf109s, several of which were intercepted, and then an attack was made on Dover by the EGr 210 'Jabos'. A force of 165 aircraft then approached Portland, comprised of 54 Ju88s from I and II/KG54, 20 He111s of KG27, 61 Bf110s of I and II/ZG2, and 30 Bf109s from III/JG2. Five squadrons (87, 145, 152, 213 and 238) were scrambled to intercept, while aircraft of 601 and 609 Squadrons which were already in the air, were vectored to the area. The latter hit the ZG2 formation and five Bf110s went down including that flown by the Gruppenkommandeur of I Gruppe, Maj Ott.

Most of the fighters became involved with the escorts as the Ju88s dive-bombed and the Heinkels attacked from higher up. JG27 arrived to provide withdrawal support as the German formations turned for home, and when the fighting ceased a total of 18 Luftwaffe aircraft had gone down, including six Bf109s and five Ju88s, but 16 Hurricanes had been lost, 13 pilots being killed and two wounded — a very high proportion. Two squadrons (145 and 238) were hard hit, each suffering four losses; one Spitfire from 152 Squadron also failed to return. It had been an

expensive raid in terms of unit commanders for the Germans however; apart from Ott, Majors Schlichting and Leonardi, Kommandeurn respectively of II/KG27 and II/KG54, were also lost.

Later in the day another big raid developed over convoy 'Booty' off the east coast near to Harwich, as EGr 210 swept in to attack, followed by Do17s of KG2 and Bf110s of ZG26, and then more Do17s and some Ju87s and Bf109s. Again five squadrons (this time 17, 54, 74, 85 and 111) engaged them. Four Bf110s and two Bf109s were shot down and a number of other aircraft damaged, but eight more British fighters were lost, including five from 111 Squadron. This raised losses for the day to 31 to set against German losses of 35 — although claims had totalled 76.

The next day (12 August) brought yet more raids. Starting again with the usual 'Freie Jagd' sorties to draw off the British fighters, EGr 210 then attacked a number of coastal radars, those at Dover, Pevensey and Rye being put temporarily out of action. This was followed by a raid on Hawkinge forward airfield by Ju88s of II/KG76, and then by dive-bomber attacks on two convoys. The big raid of the day was launched on Portsmouth by KG51 Ju88s escorted by 120 ZG2 and 76 Bf110s, and 25 JG53 Bf109s. Fifty-eight fighters were scrambled from the south-western airfields, but the defenses had been taken by surprise and the raid which hit the dockyard and town proved very effective. Fifteen of the Ju88s peeled off to attack the Ventnor radar on the Isle of Wight, but were met by Spitfires of 152 and 609 Squadrons. Consequently, KG51 was badly mauled, losing ten of its aircraft, and the Kommodore, Oberst Dr Fisser. The day ended with an attack on Manston, Kent's most easterly airfield, by Do17s of KG2. During a day which had brought 70 more claims for Fighter Command, 22 defending fighters had been lost. The balance looked good — but actual German losses had only been 29.

During the period of the convoy attacks, 18 small merchant steamers had been sunk, while the Royal Navy had lost nine armed trawlers, two yachts, a tanker and a mooring vessel to air attack, as well as the ill-fated AA auxilliary. Throughout this period efforts by both No 2 Group and Control Command to attack the Luftwaffe airfields and the possible invasion ports by day had not ceased. By the end of July German fighter claims for the month included 59 Blenheims, 13 of them on 9 July, seven one day later and nine on 18 July, while seven Lockheed Hudsons had also been claimed. During this period No 2 Group alone had lost 31 Blenheims in action, three more being so badly damaged as to be written off.

The main assault

At last on 13 August, 1940, 'Adler Tag' arrived — but got off to an immediate bad start as the first raid had to be recalled. The fighters received the message, but 74 Do17 bombers of KG2 did not, and continued unescorted to bomb Eastchurch airfield. As they turned for home they were fiercely attacked and lost five of their number. In the afternoon Ju87s appeared in force to attack coastal radars and various airfields, but while Hpt von Brauschitsch led 40 Stukas from IV(St)/LG1 in a damaging attack on the non-Fighter Command field at Detling, an attempt to bomb Middle Wallop by II/StG2 led by Maj Walter Ennerccerus, was intercepted by Spitfires of 609 Squadron with disastrous results — six of the nine bombers in one formation were shot down. Forty Ju88s from KG54 and 80 from LG1 then approached the south coast, feinting

THIS Bf109E OF JAGDGESCHWADER 2 IS THE PERSONAL AIRCRAFT OF MAJ HELMUT WICK, KOMMODORE OF THE UNIT AND TOP-SCORING FIGHTER PILOT OF THE BATTLE. NOTE THE VICTORY 'BARS' ON THE RUDDER.

towards Portland, but attacking Southampton. Fighters intercepted, shooting down four KG54 bombers and three from LG1, while eight more suffered damage; four escorting Bf110s of V(Z)/LG1 were also shot down, and an equal number damaged.

The day had cost the Luftwaffe 43 aircraft — by far the highest losses yet (against RAF claims of 79), while the defender's losses had been held at a relatively low 14 — eight of these from 56 and 238 Squadrons, which suffered equally. The greatest successes had been over the south coast where 609 Squadron had claimed 13 victories, 238 and 601 Squadrons adding 11 each. However, the RAF had fared worse elsewhere.

No 2 Group despatched 12 Blenheims of 82 Squadron to attack KG30's airfields at Aalborg in Denmark. Eleven were shot down by Flak and Bf109s of II/JG77, four of them by Uffz Menge. It was the worst day of another expensive month which eventually cost the Group 28 Blenheims shot down and eight damaged beyond repair.

Raids continued on 14 August, but the next day ushered in the most violent and costly of the whole Battle — and it was to be 'Black Thursday' for the Luftwaffe. Eighty-seven Ju87s from IV(St)/LG1 and II/StG1 attacked Hawkinge and Lympne airfields, while Bf110s strafed Manston again. Twenty-five EGr 210 'Jabos' raided Martlesham airfield in Suffolk, intercepting Hurricanes being 'bounced' by escorting Bf109s. The Luftwaffe now believed that their attacks of the previous few days had drawn all Fighter Command's reserves from the north, and consequently Luftflotte 5 was now brought into the fighting. During the morning 63 He111s from KG26, escorted by 21 Bf110Ds of I/ZG76, headed across the North Sea for Newcastle.

The RAF defenses were still very much alive, however. Spitfires of 41 and 72 Squadrons with Hurricanes of 79 and 605 Squadrons intercepted and claimed 30 victories while in fact they shot down seven Heinkels and seven Messerschmitts — still an impressive feat — including that of the Kommandeur of I/ZG76, Hpt Restmeyer. As the Germans headed back in scattered bunches, one more bomber was downed by a Coastal Command Blenheim fighter.

Further south the fighting continued unabated. EGr 210 returned to attack Kenley airfield, but the 15 Bf110s and eight Bf109s missed their target and attacked Croydon by mistake. Caught by Hurricanes of 32 and 111 Squadron, the unit lost six Bf110s and a Bf109, including the whole Stabsschwarn, with the Kommandeur, Hpt Walter Rubendchorffer. Meanwhile, Biggin Hill was raided by Do17s, while bombers from KG1 and 2 attacked Hawkinge and radar stations on the Kent coast. A dozen Ju88s from I/LG1 attacked Middle Wallop and 15 more from II Gruppe made for Worthy Down. Little damage was done and eight were lost to fighters, five from a single Staffel.

Eighty-eight Do17s from KG3 achieved more success when they approached north Kent under heavy escort from JG51, 52 and 54. Eastchurch airfield and the Short Brothers aircraft factory at Rochester were hit, with production of the new four-engined Stirling bomber being disrupted at the latter target. Losses to the defenders here were low as the escorts were efficient and the JG26 'Freie Jagd' had taken the 'sting' out of the defenses. The Geschwader claimed 22 victories, 18 of them by III Gruppe — three of these credited to the Kommandeur, Adolf Galland.

Towards the end of the afternoon Luftflotte 5 tried again. Fifty unescorted Ju88s from KG30 in Denmark attacked Driffield airfield in North Yorkshire, where about 12 Bomber Command Whitleys were destroyed on the ground. However, 73 and 616 Squadrons intercepted effectively, claiming 18 bombers shot down; only seven were lost, but this was more than enough — Luftflotte 5 did not attack again during the Battle. Indeed, before August was out KG26 and 30 moved south into Luftflotte 2's area to join the main assault.

The cost to the Luftwaffe on 15 August was 72 aircraft — its highest losses on any day during the Battle. The Bf110s had suffered particularly heavily with 12 of II and III/ZG76, and six of EGr 210 to add to those lost by Luftflotte 5's I/ZG76. Fighter Command had claimed 152 victories for 32 combat losses, so the day appeared an outstanding success. There was no let up however, and the Luftwaffe came back in force on 16 August to attack airfields and radar stations in Kent, Hampshire and Sussex. In these raids 46 further losses were inflicted by the defenders, who claimed 81 victories for a loss of 23 of their own. One formation of Do17s from KG2 attempting to attack Hornchurch was turned back, but a second attacked, losing three aircraft, with one of which Flt Lt Henry Ferris, one of 111 Squadron's leading pilots collided.

Counting the cost

The worst losses of the day for the RAF were suffered by 266 Squadron which lost five Spitfires to the marauding Bf109s. It was at Tangmere that the Germans suffered their worst defeat however, for when StG2 attacked this airfield nine of its Ju87s were shot down and three more damaged by 43 Squadron. However, the Germans managed to destroy five Blenheim fighters of the Fighter Interception Unit and a Hurricane on the ground. Amongst Fighter Command personnel lost was one of 213 Squadron's aces, French-Canadian Flg Off J E P Laricheliere. It was on this date that the Command gained its only Victoria Cross of the war. Flt Lt J B Nicholson of 249 Squadron was shot down by a Bf109 but stayed in his blazing cockpit long enough to claim a Bf110 shot down before baling out; already suffering from burns, he was then shot at and wounded by Home Guards as he floated down on his parachute!

This scale of losses did bring a respite from the German attacks on 17 August with only reconnaissance aircraft appearing, but on 18 August the Luftwaffe was back in force, intent on taking out the main sector fighter airfields. Do17s and Ju88s, of KG76 bombed Biggin Hill and Kenley causing much damage; at Kenley six of 615 Squadron's Hurricanes were destroyed on the ground, together with four others and a Blenheim. Yet more of the Geschwader's Dorniers attacked Croydon, but these were intercepted, two being shot down at once and two later going down in the Channel. In all the unit lost six Do17s and two Ju88s with three more aircraft damaged during these raids. In one aircraft the pilot was killed but the flight engineer, Oberfeldwebel Illg, took over the controls and flew back to France to make a successful crash-landing. He was awarded a Knight's Cross for this effort, but within a week was a prisoner after having been shot down on a subsequent sortie.

The day was marked particularly by the losses suffered by the Stukas of StG77. Attacking Poling radar station, Ford and Thorney Island airfields on the Hampshire coast, the unit was engaged by 43, 152, 601 and 602 Squadrons which claimed 34 Ju87s shot down — 14 of them by 602 alone; 43 Squadron's Jim Hallowes was credited with three Stukas for the second time in three days. Actual losses were

LEADING FIGHTER ACES OF THE BATTLE OF BRITAIN

As a battle for air supremacy, the Battle of Britain produced many high-scoring fighter pilots on both sides – pilots who played a part in the fighting out of all proportion to their numbers. The Luftwaffe paid more attention to personal scores, and expended more effort than did the RAF in checking their validity as far as was possible. Their policy of retaining successful units and pilots at the front as long as possible assisted many German pilots to build up big scores.

The Luftwaffe

As mentioned, several of the leading pilots had seen service in Spain and amassed good scores there, while a number had also done well in France. At the end of June, therefore, Mölders had claimed 25 victories since the beginning of the war, Balthasar 23, Wick 14 and

OBLT HANS 'ASSI' HAHN, III/JG2.

Galland 13. Balthasar increased his score to about 31, but on 4 September he was badly wounded and saw no further action for several months. Galland reached his 20th victory on 15 August, closely followed by two of Mölders pilots, Walter Oesau of III Gruppe and Horst Tietzen of II Gruppe, but the latter was shot down and killed on 18 September at a time when he was leading the top-scoring Staffel (5/JG51) of the top-scoring Gruppe in the top-scoring Geschwader.

By the end of August Helmut Wick too had reached 20, while during September seven more Jagdflieger reached this magic figure. Early September proved to be a more costly period, however. The day after Balthasar had been lost to III/JG3, Oblt Franz von Werra, adjutant of II/JG3, was shot down and became a prisoner.

A day later on 6 September, Hpt Joachim Schlichting, Kommandeur of III/JG27 was also shot down and became a captive. On 9 September one of III/JG53's leading pilots, Oblt Schultz-Blanck, was shot down and killed with his total approaching double figures. The month saw new records reached, however, Mölders recording his 40th victory on the 21 September and Galland his four days later; Wick also reached 40 on 6 October, having claimed five victories in a day on the previous date.

A further five pilots reached 20 before the end of November 1940, but the three leaders were by then still far ahead of anyone else. Mölders became the first to reach 50 on 22 October, closely followed by Galland. Wick, now Kommodore of JG2, was pursuing them closely, again claiming five in a day on 6 November.

At last on 28 November he shot down two in the morning to pass Mölders, raising his score to 55. On a later sortie that day he led his Stabschwarme down onto Spitfires of 609 Squadron, shooting down his 56th and last victim. He was at once shot down himself by Flt Lt John Dundas DFC and Bar for the latter's 13th victory; moments later Dundas went down to his own death, shot down by Wick's wingman, Rudi Pflanz, another budding 'Experte'. Mölders ended the Battle with his 55th victory on 1 December, while Galland finished the year as the new No 1, with 58. Behind them were Hpt Walter Oesau whose score was close to 40, Hpt Hans-Karl Mayer, who had reached 38 before being shot down and killed by the British ace Desmond McMullen on 17 October, and Hpt Herman-Friedrich Joppien with 31.

JG51 had been by far the most successful of the fighter units during the year. Amongst the leading pilots, other than Mölders, Tietzen (II Gr), Oesau (III Gr) and Joppien (I Gr) were Priller, who served with II Gruppe before leading I/JG26, and Lignitz who was with III Gruppe prior to taking command of III/JG54; Heinz Bär, highest-scoring NCO pilot with 13 victories also served with the Geschwader. The greatest single gathering of 'stars' was in Galland's old III/JG26, which boasted Müncheberg (23 victories), Schöpfel (22), who took command when Galland became Geschwader

MAJ ADOLF GALLAND, JG26.

Kommodore, Sprick (20) and Ebeling (18), who became a prisoner of war on 5 November. Leading pilots of the Geschwader's other Gruppen were Pingel (15 + victories) in I Gruppe, and Adolph (15 + victories, ex-III/JG27) in II Gruppe.

Amongst the other Geschwadern Wick's JG2 had Machold (28) and Krahl in I Gr Schnell in II Gr and 'Assi' Hahn in III Gr. In JG3 were Lutzow in I Gr, von Werra in II Gr and Berram in III Gr, while von Maltzahn's JG53 had included Mayer in I Gr, Bretnutz in II Gr and two notables in III Gr, (Oblt Hans von Hahn, who departed to command I/JG3 during August (10 +) and Lt Erich Schmidt (18)).

JG54 had its 'stars' as well — Philipp and Hrabak in II Gr and Oblt Hans-Ekkehard Bob (18) in III Gruppe. I(J)/LG2 was still led by Oblt Ihlefeld, whose score by the end of the year stood at 25. Probably the least successful of the Jagdgeschwadern had been JG27 and JG52. In the former the three most successful pilots had been Oblt Gerhard Homuth in I Gr (15), Oblt Günther Rödel in II Gr (14) and Oblt Erbo Graf von Kageneck in III Gr (13). JG52 alone failed to produce an 'Experte' of note during 1940 — an odd situation, as it was to end the war as the highest scoring Geschwader of the Luftwaffe.

The Zerstörergruppen, of which so much had been hoped, had achieved much less success. The doyen of these pilots was Oblt Hans-Joachim Jabs of II/ZG76, who had claimed eight over France and added a further 12 during August and September 1940. In the same unit were Erich Groth, the Kommandeur and Heinz Knacke, each credited with 12 victories, and Walter Borchers credited with a similar total. The unit's III Gruppe was led by Rolf Kaldrack who had 11 victories, while the Kommodore, Maj Walter Grabmann, claimed six. I Gruppe's presence with Luftflotte 5 in Norway prevented its pilots operating over England more than once during the Battle, although several had scored well during the earlier fighting over Norway, and during defensive operations there.

ZG26 lost two of its leading pilots during the Battle, Lt Walter Manhard of III Gr becoming a prisoner on 3 September after nine victories, while from the same unit ten victory 'Experte' Fw Walter Scherer was shot down and badly

MAJ WERNER MÖLDERS, JG51.

HPT GÜNTHER LÜTZOW, I/JG3.

THE INTERNATIONAL RAF

1 FLT LT J A A GIBSON (NEW ZEALANDER), 501 SQUADRON. 2 WG CDR F V BEAMISH (IRISH), 151 SQUADRON. 3 SGT J FRANTISEK (CZECH), 303 SQUADRON. 4 FL OFF W L McKNIGHT (CANADIAN) WITH (RIGHT) SQN LDR D R S BADER (ENGLISH), 242 SQUADRON. 5 FROM LEFT TO RIGHT, FLG OFF Z HENNEBERG (POLISH), FLT LT J A KENT (CANADIAN), AND PLT OFF M FERIC (ALSO POLISH) FROM 303 SQUADRON. 6 FLG OFF A G LEWIS (SOUTH AFRICAN), 249 SQUADRON. 7 SQN LDR R R S TUCK (ENGLISH), 257 SQUADRON. 8 FLT LT P C HUGHES (AUSTRALIAN), 234 SQUADRON. 9 PLT OFF H M STEPHEN (SCOTS) AND (RIGHT) FLG OFF J C MUNGO-PARK (ENGLISH), 74 SQUADRON.

injured on 25 September, also becoming a prisoner of war.

Other III Gruppe pilots who were credited with more than the odd victory included Johann Schalk, the Kommandeur, Sophus Baagoe, Helmut Haugk and Richard Heller. I Gruppe's Wilhelm Mackrocki had nine victories and Wilhelm Spies about ten, while II Gruppe's 'Experte' was Theodor Rossiwall. The ill-fated ZG2 produced no notables, nor did V(Z)/LG1, but in Erprobungsgruppe 210 Lt Edward Tratt was able to claim 12 victories by the end of 1940 — well on his way to his final position as the Luftwaffe's top-scoring Zerstörerflieger.

The Royal Air Force
Like the Luftwaffe, the RAF had a number of pilots available in July 1940 who had already claimed some victories over France and the Channel. Many of these added further to their successes during the Battle, ending the year as Fighter Command's top scorers. They were not necessarily the most successful during the period of the Battle itself,

however. While natives of the United Kingdom Allard, Lacey, Crossley, Lock and McKellar ended the year with at least 20 individual victories each, the leading lights of the summer battles were much more representative of the growing Commonwealth, and indeed international, flavor.

While Eric Lock of 41 Squadron had gained the lead by the end of November with 18, he was only just ahead of Josef Frantisek, a Czech member of 303 Polish Squadron, who claimed 17. 'Ginger' Lacey and Archie McKellar, two more of the British top scorers, were credited with 15 each during the Battle, as was the little-known Brian Carbury, a New Zealander in 603 Squadron. Another New Zealander, Colin Gray, was credited with 14, a score equalled by Australian Pat Hughes and the Pole, Witold Urbanowicz. At least 16 more pilots had totals of individual victories in double figures.

While many pilots built up their scores in a steady manner throughout the fighting there were some whose actions were more

mercurial. Between 12–25 August Mike Crossley claimed 12 victories and one shared, including two Ju88s, a Do17 and a share in another on 15 August, a Bf109, Bf110 and Ju88 one day later and a Bf109 and Ju88 on 18 August, also claiming a Bf110 probable on this latter date.

With 234 Squadron Pat Hughes claimed 13 and one shared between 14 August and 5 September, including three Bf110s on 4 September. The next day he collided with his last victim, a Do17, and crashed with it to his death. On 24 August Sgt Ronnie Hamlyn of 610 Squadron flew three times, claiming a total of five victories — a Ju88 and four Bf109s, this feat being equalled during the day by a Polish pilot with 501 Squadron, Sgt Antoni Glowacki, who claimed three Bf109s and two Ju88s. On the last day of the month Brian Carbury matched them when he was credited with five Bf109s.

Eric Lock claimed two Bf109s and two He111s, but a new record was set on 27 September by South African Albert Lewis of 249

Squadron. Lewis had already been credited with five in a day over France in May with 85 Squadron. Now he flew four sorties, claiming four Bf109s, two Bf110s and a probable and a Ju88 to raise his score to 18; the very next day he was shot down and badly burned.

One more outstanding exploit of this nature remained. On 7 October Archie McKellar, who had been credited with three and a probable on 15 September, claimed five Bf109s, four of them in a period of ten minutes. While obviously the majority of leading RAF fighter pilots flew Hurricanes or Spitfires, a few operated the unsuccessful Defiants. The most notable Defiant crew comprised Flight Sergeants Edward Thorn (pilot) and Frederick Barker (gunner). This pair had claimed seven and one shared during May 1940, adding five more during the Battle of Britain, including the Bf109 which was responsible for shooting their Defiant down during one combat on 26 August. Unlike most Defiant crews, they survived the Battle.

quite bad enough, with 18 lost or written off and four more damaged; amongst those lost was Hpt Maisel, the I Gruppenkommandeur.

Such losses were unsupportable, and the Stukageschwadern were pulled out of the Battle. Göring blamed the Jagdflieger, demanding that in future they should give much closer escort to the bombers, at the expense of their 'Freie Jagd' activities. This would give advantage to the defenders, for it forced the Bf109 pilots into a basically defensive role, also reducing their time over England as more fuel was expended maintaining formation with the bombers.

There were other losses however, for while escorting bombers over Southern England the Gruppen of ZG26 were badly savaged by several squadrons of Spitfires and Hurricanes, losing 14 with five more damaged; it seemed that the Zerstörern would themselves require fighter escort in the future. Eighteen Bf109Es, including six each from JG3 and 27, and seven He111s from several units brought German losses for 18 August to a hefty 65, second only to 15 August. RAF claims had reached 130, but its losses were at the highest level they were ever to reach — 36 in the air and seven on the ground. 32 Squadron lost six aircraft and 501 Squadron seven — four of them in a few seconds to Oblt Gerhard Schöpfel of III/JG26 as they climbed up over Kent. 111 and 615 Squadrons each lost four, the former unit losing another of its aces — Flt Lt S D P Connors — while Flt Lt R H A Lee of 85 Squadron, another Fighter Command notable, failed to return.

It was not only the RAF that suffered in this way, for on 18 August II/JG51 lost one of its great 'Experten', Hpt Horst Tietzen, while III/JG26 lost Lt Gerhard Müller-Duhe (5 victories), and Oblt Helmut Tiedmann (6 victories) of I/JG3 became a prisoner. Activity continued at a less intensive level during the next five days, but resumed on 24 August with heavy attacks on Hornchurch and North Weald sector stations, and Portsmouth and on several other airfields.

The Portsmouth attack, by 50 LG1 Ju88s escaped interception, but over North Weald KG53 lost five of its He111s, and over Hornchurch three Ju88s of KG76 were shot down by the Defiants of 264 Squadron. The latter were themselves hit by the escorts, losing four of the ill-fated turret fighters. Twenty-nine losses were suffered by the Germans, but while Fighter Command had claimed 70 to actually destroy a similar total on 12 August, on this occasion only 53 claims were submitted. Twenty-six fighters were lost in return, 32 Squadron worst hit with five losses.

Raiding by night

By now, the Luftwaffe had begun a series of widespread night raids, and during the night of 25–26 August RAF Bomber Command retaliated with an attack on Berlin, which incensed the German leaders. Relatively limited activity over England on 25 August was followed by another round of sustained attacks on the main sector airfields the next day. Forty He111s and 12 Do17s attacked first, bombing the area around Dover. Forty more Dorniers from KG2 and 3 then headed for Hornchurch and Debden sector stations, but were intercepted and turned back with the loss of six bombers — a major failure. Forty-eight He111s of KG55 then raided Portsmouth, but this was to be the last daylight attack by Luftflotte 3 bombers for some three weeks.

Their major duty now became attacking fighter production factories in the Midlands by night, while Luftflotte 2 maintained the day offensive in the south. This allowed most of the Jafü 3 fighters to be moved into the Jafü 2 area to increase by a considerable amount the number of Bf109s available for escort. The change in role for Luftflotte 3 had an immediate impact on the level of nocturnal activities, and during the night of 28–29 August between 130 and 150 He111s and Ju88s from KG27, 55, KGr806 and KGr100 raided Liverpool.

Fighter Command casualties were continuing to run at fairly high levels compared to the numbers of Luftwaffe machines actually shot down, given the disparity in strength between the two forces. Fifty-seven claims on 25 August had brought 20 actual successes, although 35 more fell the next day against 59 claims. Losses amounted to 47 on these two days, 30 of them on 26 August when 616 Squadron lost six Spitfires in a single combat. The next three days remained quieter, although on 29 August 150 Bf110s and 500 Bf109s appeared in one of the biggest sweeps undertaken. Despite the numbers involved, no heavy fighting resulted, each side suffering the loss of only nine fighters during the day.

Luftwaffe pressure increases

The Battle entered its critical phase for Fighter Command on 30 August when no less than 30 Gruppen of bombers appeared over Kent in a two-hour period. While RAF fighters attacked 40 He111s and 30 Do17s and their escorts all the way into the target — albeit without inflicting substantial losses — Ju88s got through unopposed and made a most successful attack on Biggin Hill which caused much material damage and loss of life. Thirty more He111s from KG1 attacked north of the Thames, but were harder hit, losing five. Twenty-two of the defending fighters went down including no less than eight from 222 Squadron — although only one pilot was killed. Against these losses, 58 victories were claimed, (only 23 German aircraft were lost).

Whole Geschwadern of fighters now appeared to escort single Gruppen of bombers, and the fighting on 31 August proved to be some of the most expensive of the whole Battle for Fighter Command. Raids were made on five sector airfields, six radar stations and several other targets during the day. Five of 30 KG3 Do17s were shot down while attacking Hornchurch, but eight more from II/KG76 made another successful low level attack on Biggin Hill, which was now barely able to operate. The escorts were all over the defenders, shooting down 32 of them for the loss of only 11 Bf109s. JG26 alone submitted 18 claims, three of them by III Gruppe's Oblt Ebeling. Another three of 54 Squadron's Spitfires were destroyed by bombs as they were taking off from Hornchurch, but once again all the pilots survived. However, these depredations failed to stop the defenders making 77 claims which cost the Luftwaffe an actual 38 aircraft, including seven Bf110s, four of them from V(Z)/LG1 in the Croydon area.

Early September saw the attacks redoubled, with no letup for the defenders on the hard-pressed No 11 Group airfields. Do17s again bombed Biggin Hill on 1 September, while 18 He111s from I/KG1 bombed Tilbury docks under a massive escort of three Geschwadern of fighters. Next day successful attacks were made on seven airfields, and Fighter Command knew it was in real trouble. A subtle change in events was noticeable at this point, for while it had tended to be the inexperienced units newly-entering action in the south which had been hardest hit in previous recent battles,

THIS HE111 BOMBER DID NOT MAKE IT HOME, CRASH-LANDING IN THE SEA AS IT ATTEMPTED TO MAKE FOR ITS BASE. THE CHANNEL PROVED TOO MUCH FOR MANY DAMAGED LUFTWAFFE AIRCRAFT.

now suddenly it was the longer-serving experienced squadrons which began to be cut to pieces.

On 2 September the 28 German aircraft lost (30 claimed) included six Bf110s from ZG2, but the RAF's 24 losses included Sgt W L Dymond DFM (11 victories) of 111 Squadron and 43 Squadron's Plt Off Tony Woods-Scawen DFC (7 victories) both of whom were killed. Only the day before the experienced 85 Squadron had lost five Hurricanes, one of the pilots killed having been Woods-Scawen's twin brother, Patrick (12 victories).

The Vickers aircraft factory at Brooklands was the main target on 4 September, when in heavy fighting RAF pilots claimed 54 victories. Only 22 actually went down, but included amongst this total were no less than 16 Bf110s, which were fast becoming a liability to the Luftwaffe rather than an asset. III/ZG26 lost nine — six in one attack by Hurricanes of 253 Squadron — while V(Z)/LG1 lost four more and EGr 210 lost their new Kommandeur, Hpt Boltenstern. Fighter Command lost 22 on this date, including five from 66 Squadron. Next day 68 Dorniers and Heinkels from KG2, 3, 26 and 53 bombed oil tanks at Thameshaven, while Biggin Hill was attacked yet again by other bombers. This time it was 41 Squadron which suffered heavily, five Spitfires being shot down, those killed including Flt Lt J T Webster (14 victories); 73 Squadron lost four Hurricanes, while in 501 Squadron one of the first Polish airmen to see action with the RAF, Stanislaw Skalski, ace of the Polish campaign was shot down and wounded for the second time in the month.

Fighter Command was by now at its lowest ebb. Pilot supply was a major problem, and several of the main southern sector stations on which the defense rested had been bombed almost to extinction. The coastal radar had also been heavily damaged, and it was only with difficulty that the defensive system was being maintained, although good progress was being made in moving the sector control rooms into makeshift secondary locations.

Desperate days for the RAF

The fighters continued to do their best, and during 6 September several large attacks on the south-east were successfully broken up. However, German bomber losses were falling off after reaching 107 since 24 August. Nevertheless, losses suffered on 6 September were the highest in the month thus far and included the Gruppenkommandeur of III/JG27 and two Bf109Es from II(Sch)/LG2 which had recently arrived at Calais-Marck airfield to commence operations with its new fighter-bombers. These losses raised the total suffered during the first six days of September to 125 — 235 had been claimed — but the RAF had lost 119 in the same period. After its losses on 1 September 85 Squadron had been withdrawn to rest; on 6 September it was 601 Squadron which was hard hit, its four losses including Flg Off Carl Davis DFC (11 victories) and Flg Off Willie Rhodes-Moorhouse DFC (9 victories), son of the World War I VC. Losses of men like this showed just how tired many of No 11 Group's units had become — so 601 Squadron too, was rested.

New units were now beginning to take their place in the line. The fiery Poles of 302 and 303 Squadrons had entered action at the end of August, the latter unit with particular success, 26 victories being claimed during the squadron's first week in the line. But on 6 September this unit too had fallen foul of the Jagdflieger, losing five Hurricanes

ONE OF THE MANY ILL-FATED BfIIOC ZERSTÖRERN LOST
DURING THE BATTLE. THIS WAS OF 2 STAFFEL, FROM I/ZG26,
BROUGHT DOWN ON 11 SEPTEMBER 1940.

including that flown by the Polish commanding officer, who was killed, and the RAF joint commanding officer, who was wounded.

Relief for the hard-pressed RAF was at hand, however, but from the least expected source — the Reichmarschall of the Luftwaffe himself! Goaded by Hitler following the bombing of Berlin by the RAF, driven by his own ambition, and advised by the wishful thinking of his Intelligence Staff and some of his commanders that Fighter Command was all but finished and that either all RAF reserves must by now have been consumed, or alternatively that further attacks on the airfields could only lead to a withdrawal to those north of London, beyond the range of the Jagdflieger, he ordered the main weight of attack turned onto London — just as the defenders were on maximum alert for an invasion.

London becomes the target

This had worked at Warsaw and Rotterdam, but London was a different proposition. Vastly larger, it soaked up the weight of attack which the Luftwaffe could apply like a vast sponge. Obviously a dreadful experience for the civil populace, it at least took the weight off the fighter squadrons, allowing them to recuperate, and to concentrate their efforts on the enemy in the air. Coming just at a time when Dowding's policy of rotation was in some danger, it allowed more of those units which had been bearing the brunt of the fighting to be moved north for much needed rest and the training of reinforcement pilots. In their place came the more newly-formed units — including the first of the Polish and Czech squadrons — ready for the fray.

It was afternoon on 7 September before the first attack came in on London — and so vast was the formation that only London could be the target. A total of 348 bombers from KG1, 2, 3, 26 and 76, escorted by 617 fighters — nearly 1000 aircraft — headed for the East London docks, which were brutally bombed. 19 and 41 Squadrons (Spitfires), 111 and 249 Squadrons (Hurricanes) intercepted first, but the inexperienced pilots of 249 were hard hit by the escorts, losing six aircraft, although only one pilot was killed. More squadrons joined the running battle, including elements of the Duxford Wing from No 12 Group. Seventy-one victories were claimed by 17 squadrons, but actual losses amounted to 34, 12 of them bombers and seven Bf110s. Most units claimed between one and five victories, but Duxford's 242 Squadron claimed ten, and the Poles of 303 Squadron 14. RAF losses were almost the same as those they had actually inflicted — 35. With dusk 318 Heinkels and Dorniers returned to stoke the fires started during the day; London's ordeal had begun.

The attack was resumed with several more late afternoon raids on 9 September. The biggest was by 26 He111s of II/KG1 escorted by 20 Bf110s of III/ZG76 and 60 Bf109s of JG3 which attempted to raid the Royal Aircraft Establishment at Farnborough. Attacked all the way in, the formation was met by 70 British fighters over Croydon and began to break up. At this stage it was joined by 40 Ju88s of KG30, under attack by Hurricanes of 253 and 303 Squadrons; one Heinkel, five Ju88s, four Bf110s and three Bf109s were lost. Further north the Duxford Wing attacked a formation of Do17s, claiming 19 shot down, but no losses of these bombers were recorded at all! This contributed considerably to the RAF's overclaiming a total of 51 against actual Luftwaffe losses of 23. The RAF itself lost 22, six of them from 607 Squadron, which was not able to record any claims in return.

Again after a day's respite the raiders were back on 11 September, and again it was afternoon before they arrived. A heavy raid towards London by KG26 lost most of its escort when the Bf109s ran short of fuel; and the Bf110s drew off to await the bombers' return from the target, and to escort them home. Sixty fighters — mainly Hurricanes — from 17, 56, 73, 222, 249 and 303 Squadrons attacked, claiming 29 victories — 17 of them by the Poles; actual losses suffered totalled seven He111s with ten more damaged. Some other British squadrons attempted to attack from too low an altitude, and suffered heavy losses to the escort. A raid on Portsmouth and Southampton was also interrupted, costing KG1 five more Heinkels, but during the day 16 squadrons suffered a total of 36 losses.

This seemed a fair balance for the 89 victories claimed by pilots of 23 different units — but overclaiming had again been heavy, and only 22 aircraft had actually been lost by the Luftwaffe, although a considerable number of others were damaged. During the day six Coastal Command Blenheim fighters of 235 Squadron escorted a dozen Fleet Air Arm Fairey Albacore biplane bombers to attack Calais. The escort was attacked by JG26 and lost two of their number, while claiming two of the Messerschmitts shot down in return. In all, 15 bombers were lost over the Channel ports with evening — mainly to Flak — to make 11 September a bad day for the RAF.

Luftwaffe reverses

After desultory clashes on 14 September, the climax was reached the next day, a day which dealt a bitter blow to the Luftwaffe. It started well enough for them when 18 Bf110s of EGr 210, making their first major attack for over ten days, attacked the Woolaston Spitfire factory at Southampton without loss. Then, the first major attack of the day on London was launched by 100 Do17s of KG3, but flying into a strong head wind and approaching slowly, they were picked up early by the radar, their escort being forced to turn back due to lack of fuel long before the target was reached. Four squadrons attacked first, and then all five squadrons of the strengthened Duxford Wing arrived. The Dorniers jettisoned their bombs and turned back, less six of their number. Fighter Command claims were massive — particularly those of the Duxford units.

The second wave to approach comprised 150 Heinkels and Dorniers from KG2, 53 and 76, which were intercepted all the way to their target, releasing their bombs over South and East London. Fourteen Do17s, eight of them from KG76, and ten He111s, six from KG53 and others from elements of KG1, 4 and 26, were lost as 170 No 11 Group fighters attacked over Kent, followed by the Duxford Wing, six more No 11 Group units and two from No 10 Group. JG26 and 54 did what they could, but RAF losses were moderate. Subsequently, 27 He111s of III/KG55 attacked Portland, but two squadrons intercepted, shooting down one of the bombers.

By the end of the day the Kampflieger had suffered a major defeat. Thirty-five bombers had been lost and so many others damaged that a quarter of the force available was out of action. Fighter Command had lost 28 fighters, but claimed a great victory, the 185 claims submitted by 28 squadrons exceeding even 15 August. There had been heavy overclaiming again however, particularly by the Duxford units, where 19 Squadron alone had claimed 13 victories and 242 Squadron 12, with 303 Squadron's Poles adding 14 more claims as No 11 Group top-scorer. No other units had

claimed more than nine.

In the final analysis Luftwaffe losses were not as heavy as either 15 or 18 August, amounting to 55 aircraft, but the proportion of bombers was particularly heavy and damaging. From now on most of the Heinkels and Dorniers were turned over to night operations, the day offensive maintained only by the much smaller number of Ju88s, and by the bomb-carrying fighters of EGr 210 and the Zerstörergeschwadern. More importantly, with the debacle of 15 September having proved that Fighter Command was still very far from being destroyed, Hitler ordered the postponement of Operation Seelöhe indefinitely since it seemed unlikely that full air superiority would now be available before the onset of worse weather.

German efforts redoubled

The first resumption of the German attack by day occurred on 18 September, when III/KG77, recently returned to operations after conversion to Ju88s, made an afternoon attack on London, under heavy escort. No less than 14 squadrons scrambled over 100 fighters to meet this raid and the bombers suffered heavily, losing nine of their number, including Maj Maxim Kleis, the Gruppen-kommandeur, and five aircraft from 8 Staffel alone. Once again figures were distorted by the over-optimism of the Duxford Wing units, which claimed 30, but appear only to have accounted for four. Several fighter sweeps had been engaged earlier in the day, total British claims reaching 53 for a loss of 11 with actual Luftwaffe combat losses 17.

During the next week most activity by day revolved around high-altitude fighter incursion and fighter-bomber (Jabo) activity, although the weight of the offensive at night increased and intensified. Not until later in the month did the bombers return, and when they did, it was the West Country that was the priority target. On 25 September 58 He111s from KG55 attacked the Bristol Aircraft factory at Filton, while some Ju88s of LG1 attacked Portland as a diversion. The main raid was successful, eight new aircraft being destroyed on the ground and considerable damage inflicted. Three squadrons (238, 152 and 609) intercepted the bombers on their way out, claiming 18 victories between them. In fact they shot down five of the bombers and two Bf110s of III/ZG26 which were making a sweep in support.

KG55 were back next day, again escorted by ZG26, and this time to attack the Woolaston Spitfire factory at Southampton, which was badly damaged. The defenders were late getting off, and while several squadrons attacked, only one of the 59 Heinkels was lost — although 303 Squadron included nine of these bombers amongst its 13 claims! Two Bf110s were also lost, but total German aircraft combat casualties for the day amounted to five against Fighter Command claims of 31 for the loss of nine.

The heaviest fighting since 15 September came on 27 September — and for the Luftwaffe losses of virtually the same proportions — although British claims were on this occasion rather more modest, and in line with the July-August factors. It was largely the day of the Jabo, for early on Bf110s from V(Z)/LG1 and II/ZG76 swept in over the south carrying 500kg bombs, under an 'umbrella' of Bf109s, while in the west more of these aircraft from EGr 210 attacked, covered by others of ZG26. Both formations were intercepted and 17 Bf110s shot down, including seven from the LG1 formation, six from ZG26 and three of EGr 210, the unit's latest Kommandeur, Hpt Martin Lutz included.

BATTLE OF BRITAIN: VARIOUS STATISTICS

Note: every source seems to differ in figures given for the Battle, and the losses of each side particularly seem to be collated with reference to different criteria. The author has in some cases added his own assessments of losses, which include aircraft shot down, crash-landed or force-landed in a seriously damaged state or written off due to the degree of damage.
In comparing Fighter Command totals of claims for aircraft shot down, the author has again provided figures from his own research which lead him to believe that the totals previously published include unconfirmed and 'probable' claims.

Numbers of aircraft available to Luftwaffe units, 10 August 1940

	On Strength	Serviceable
Long Range Reconnaissance	100	71
Fighters (Bf109Es)	934	805
Destroyers (Bf110s)	289	224
Bombers	1481	998
Dive-Bombers	327	261
Ground Attack	39	31
Coastal	93	80

Average daily availability of Fighter Command aircraft

	On Strength	Serviceable
July	871–1052	644–658
August	1061–1181	708–764
September	1161–1048	746–715
October	1048–1064	734–747
November	1064	721

Average production of British fighter aircraft during the Battle

Hurricanes	55–65 per week
Spitfires	30–40 per week
Defiants	10 per week
Beaufighters	5 per week

British aircraft losses, 1 July – 31 October 1940

	Destroyed	Damaged
Bombers	367	116
Fighters	1140	710
Other Types	96	50

Alternative figures of fighter aircraft losses, 1 July – 2 November 1940

	Destroyed	Damaged
Hurricanes	619	137
Spitfires	373	101
Defiants	24	11
Blenheim IF	44	14

Aircraft of Fighter Command attacked on the ground, 15 August – 25 September 1940

	Destroyed	Damaged
Hurricanes	16	11
Spitfires	7	10
Blenheim IF	7	5
TOTAL	30	26

(of these, 42 were the result of attacks in the week ending 21 August)

Fighter Command pilot casualties, July – October 1940

	Killed, Missing or Prisoner	Wounded or Injured
July	74	49
August	148	156
September	159	152
October	100	65
TOTAL	481	422

RAF Fighter Command claims, July – November 1940

Period	Claims	Author's Figures	Actual Losses	Author's Figures	Damaged
10 Jul – 7 August	188	217	192	148	77
8 August – 23 August	755	711	403	363	127
24 August – 6 Sept	643	577	378	336	115
7 Sept – 30 Sept	846	757	435	336	162
1 Oct – 31 Oct	260	203	325	195	163
1 Nov – 30 Nov		196*		146*	
Total	2692		1733		644

*Includes claims for 20 Italian aircraft and 9 actual losses

Luftwaffe losses to enemy action, July – November 1940 (Destroyed: Damaged)

	July	August	Sept	Oct	Nov	Total
Long-Range Reconnaissance	18:2	13:1	16:3	8:1	7:n/a	62:7
Single-Engined Fighter	34:6	177:24	187:17	104:24	51:n/a	553:71
Twin-Engined Fighter	19:4	114:32	81:17	10:1	6:n/a	230:54
Bomber	76:12	183:48	165:58	64:24	78:n/a	566:142
Dive Bomber	12:8	47:14	—	—	14:n/a	73:22
Coastal	11:0	19:2	8:2	7:0	8:n/a	53:4
Total	170:32	533:121	457:97	193:50	164:n/a	1537:300

Heaviest combat losses (30 or more aircraft lost)

LUFTWAFFE		FIGHTER COMMAND*	
15 August	72	18 August	36
18 August	65	11 Sept	36
15 September	55	31 August	35
27 September	53	7 September	35
16 August	46	15 August	32
13 August	43	11 August	31
30 September	41	26 August	30
31 August	38	27 September	30
11 August	35	*Including Coastal Command Fighters	
26 August	35		
7 September	34		
6 September	33		

Meanwhile, a further attempt to attack Filton by 30 He111s and escorting Bf110s was foiled by Hurricanes, the defenses in the west having again been strengthened, and this force was obliged to jettison its bombs and turn away.

Fifty-five Ju88s of I and II/KG77 then set off to bomb London, but reached their rendezvous late and missed their escort. The RAF took full advantage of this error, putting up 120 intercepting fighters which shot down 12 of the bombers. Jafü 2 Bf109s reacted to desperate calls for help and arrived to inflict heavy casualties on the Fighter Command formations, but too late to save the bombers.

No less than 28 squadrons had been engaged, and had claimed 120 victories, the fourth and last time on which British claims exceeded 100 in a day during the Battle. Top-scorer was again 303 Squadron with 14 claims, while 504 Squadron claimed six Bf110s and 17 Squadron five. Over 20 Bf109s were shot down in the heavy fighter versus fighter battle which occurred, 19 Squadron alone claiming seven of these aircraft, but Fighter Command's losses amounted to

Confirmed victories claimed by RAF fighter squadrons, July – November 1940

S–Spitfire, H–Hurricane, D–Defiant, B–Blenheim, G–Gladiator.
NB (c) Coastal Command Squadron, (n) Night Fighter Squadron

Squadron	Score	Type	Squadron	Score	Type
303 Squadron	126½	H	615 Squadron	36½	H
602 Squadron	102	S	65 Squadron	34½	S
603 Squadron	98	S	253 Squadron	33	H
92 Squadron	94²/₅	S	1 Squadron	32	H
501 Squadron	93	H	616 Squadron	31	S
41 Squadron	92²/₅	S	151 Squadron	30	H
609 Squadron	90⅓	S	1 (Canadian) Sqn	28½	H
74 Squadron	86	S	257 Squadron	28	H
213 Squadron	81	H	46 Squadron	27½	H
249 Squadron	75	H	79 Squadron	27	H
601 Squadron	73½	H	302 Squadron	26½	H
234 Squadron	73	S	504 Squadron	21	H
32 Squadron	71	H	607 Squadron	21	H
610 Squadron	71	S	229 Squadron	20½	H
43 Squadron	70	H	73 Squadron	19½	H
238 Squadron	69½	H	264 Squadron	16	D
242 Squadron	68½	H	611 Squadron	15	S
19 Squadron	68	S	235 Squadron(c)	13	B
17 Squadron	67½	H	266 Squadron	10	S
72 Squadron	61½	S	141 Squadron	6	D
54 Squadron	60	S	25 Squadron(n)	4	B
56 Squadron	59½	H	236 Squadron(c)	3	B
85 Squadron	59	H	29 Squadron(n)	2	B
152 Squadron	59	S	219 Squadron (n)	2	D
605 Squadron	56½	H	3 Squadron	1	H
87 Squadron	54	H	232 Squadron	1	H
145 Squadron	54	H	254 Squadron(c)	1	B
66 Squadron	50	S	312 Squadron	1	H
222 Squadron	49²/₅	S	600 Squadron(n)	1	B
111 Squadron	47½	H	604 Squadron(n)	1	B
64 Squadron	43	S	23 Squadron(n)	0	B
310 Squadron	40	H	245 Squadron(n)	0	H
			247 Squadron	0	G
			248 Squadron(c)	0	B
			263 Squadron	0	G

30 aircraft on this date — the highest since 11 September.

The last occasion on which bombers played a major part by day occurred on 30 September, which began with an attempt by 200 aircraft to attack London, with three Ju88s shot down. Later KG30 tried to get through but failed, two more bombers going down. KG55 made a fourth and final assault in the west, this time with Yeovil as the target. As on 27 September the bombers were turned back, and four of the Heinkels were lost. There was heavy fighting between the opposing fighters, total Luftwaffe casualties amounting to 41 on this date — Fighter Command submitted 44 claims for the loss of 23 Spitfires and Hurricanes, 16 squadrons being engaged.

September had proved to the Germans that until Fighter Command could be defeated, the daylight offensive had become just too expensive in terms of attrition to the bomber force, and all further activity by the Kampfflieger during the autumn was by night. RAF Bomber Command was already similarly convinced as during September No 2 Group had been obliged to undertake more of its activity by night in what was its busiest month of the year. The result had been a substantial fall-off in casualties compared with recent months, 19 Blenheims failing to return during September, and six more being written-off due to damage.

Following the heavy fighting of late September, October was ushered in on a much quieter note. Now, as the long summer days shortened and more of the German bomber units became committed to the increasing scale of night bombardment now being inflicted on the population of the industrial towns of England, day operations began to develop to a new pattern. Daily formations of Bf109s swept high over the southern counties on their 'Freie Jagd' sorties, sometimes accompanied by small numbers of bomb-carrying fighters which then dived to low level to release their explosive cargoes on targets of opportunity — airfields, radar sites, rail or road targets etc. Other fighter-bombers swept in at low level for surprise 'hit-and-run' attacks, while occasionally the raiders were accompanied by a small formation of Ju88s.

Fighter Command holds the line
Still the Luftwaffe hoped to draw into combat and thereby weaken the defending fighters, pending any resumption of the main offensive in the following spring. Such tactics could scarcely be of more than nuisance value, but they had the effect of keeping the RAF constantly 'on the hop', and of whittling away at Fighter Command strength. This was now beginning to climb back up towards early August levels, as production made good the losses, and new units — particularly those of the Free European personnel — approached operational readiness. Early versions of the improved Spitfire and Hurricane Mark IIs were also now starting to appear, and while many of the front line units were tired, Fighter Command was in increasingly good heart.

There was an upsurge of activity on 5 October when several attacks were intercepted; claims totalled 23, but reality brought actual victories over two EGr 210 Bf110s, a II(Sch)/LG2 Bf109, and six fighter Bf109s, with several more of each damaged; a Spitfire and six Hurricanes were lost to the German fighters in return, four more Spitfires being damaged.

The most active day of the month occurred on 7 October when 25 Ju88s of II/KG51 attacked the Westland factory at Yeovil, escorted by 50 Bf110s from II and III/ZG26. The formation was hard hit by Hurricanes and Spitfires from No 10 Group airfields, two Ju88s and seven Bf110s being shot down. The arrival of withdrawal support Bf109s saved the formation from even heavier losses, and inflicted casualties of two Spitfires and a Hurricane on the British force, a further Hurricane falling to fire from the bombers' gunners. Elsewhere over south-east and southern England interception of 'Freie Jagd' and 'Jabo' (fighter-bomber) activity cost the Luftwaffe four fighter-bomber and eight fighter Bf109Es. Six more RAF fighters — mainly Hurricanes from 501 and 605 Squadrons — were lost, while two 607 Squadron aircraft collided and crashed. On this date 29 claims brought 21 actual German losses, shot down or crash-landed due to damage.

Aerial fighting was thereafter of a desultory nature for the rest of the month, enlivened on only four or five days. On 15 October RAF losses actually exceeded those of the Luftwaffe — this had also happened on 6 October. During several dogfight engagements 46 Squadron was badly 'bounced' and lost four Hurricanes, while 92 Squadron lost three Spitfires: other losses amounted to a further eight British fighters. In return JG2 and JG27 each lost three Bf109Es, and JG3 an additional pair. Two days later a formation from Jagdgeschwade 53 was mauled by Spitfires of 41, 222 and 603 Squadrons, losing three aircraft. One of these was flown by one of the leading Jagdflieger

'Experten', Hpt Hans-Karl Meyer, of I Gruppe (Kommandeur) and victor of 38 combats, while a second was piloted by one of his Staffelkapitän, Oblt Walter Rupp of 3 Staffel, who was also killed: it is believed that Mayer fell to one of the leading RAF fighters, Desmond McMullen of 222 Squadron.

Another day of whirling, contrail-marked fighter combats came on 25 October during which seven RAF fighters were shot down by the Messerschmitts and two more collided while engaged with them. The German fighters came off worst on this occasion, 11 Bf109s from five different units failing to return. Fighter Command enjoyed a somewhat larger success four days later when a 'Jabo' attack by II(Sch)/LG2 escorted by JG51 was well 'bounced' over Kent; three of the fighter-bombers went down, including that flown by 5 Staffel commander Oblt Bern von Schink, while JG51 lost five more — all without loss to the RAF. During various sweeps four more Bf109s were shot down for the loss of three RAF aircraft, and a fifth was brought down over the Isle of Wight by AA fire.

The most successful Luftwaffe operation was an attack on North Weald airfield by the bomb-carrying Bf109s of 3/EGr 210, which arrived just as the Hurricanes of 249 and 257 Squadron were taking off. Two of the latter units' aircraft were destroyed by the bombs, but Flt Cdr R A 'Butch' Barton, a Canadian flight commander in 249 Squadron, gave chase as the Messerschmitts turned for home, and shot down Oblt Otto Hintze, the Staffelkapitän, who became a prisoner after baling out. Elsewhere, Ju88s of I/LG1 got through to make an unintercepted attack on Portsmouth, while Ramsgate was bombed by Italian Fiat BR20 bombers, escorted by Fiat CR42 biplane fighters.

This was the first daylight appearance of aircraft from a Regia Aeronautica task force which had recently arrived in Belgium at the insistence of Benito Mussolini to add their

EQUIPMENT OF THE NIGHT FIGHTER SQUADRONS OF FIGHTER COMMAND IN SUMMER 1940 WAS THE BRISTOL BLENHEIM IF— SOMETIMES MISTAKEN BY HURRICANE AND SPITFIRE PILOTS FOR JU88s!

relatively modest weight to the offensive against the common enemy — though rather late in the day. Their first operation had been a night attack on Harwich on 25–26 October: more was seen of them during November.

It was, however, by night that the main battle was now being fought. On all but two nights during October bombers had appeared over England, and some of the raids had been devastatingly heavy and effective. On the night of 14–15 October, 69 Do17s had attacked Coventry, while 200 He111s and Ju88s bombed London: another similarly heavy raid hit the capital again next night. While the Battle of Britain was fast phasing out by day, it was gathering strength in the hours of darkness where what was to become known as the 'Blitz' was getting into its stride.

Combating the 'Blitz'

Here the British defenses were in a much more parlous state. A few early Airborne Interception radar sets were being installed in some of the inadequate Blenheim IFs, and a few — a very few — of the powerful new Bristol Beaufighters were joining the squadrons. However, at this stage most of the defense rested on the guns and on day fighters — Hurricanes and Defiants — co-operating with the searchlights and hoping to have the good fortune to spot raiders visually. Indeed, towards the end of 1940, several day-fighter squadrons converted to the night-fighting role to meet the new threat. Initially, however, the advantage was all with the Germans. The new radio direction-finding aids — 'Knikkebein' and 'X-Gerat' — were employed by the specialist He111s of Kampfgruppe 100, which acted as 'pathfinders' for the main force.

Raids increased in intensity during November. Seventy-seven He111s of KG26 bombed London during the night of 13–14 November, while 63 more from KG55 had Birmingham as their target. Next night 12 KGr 100 'Pathfinders' led 437 aircraft from KG1, 3, 26, 27, 55, LG1 and KFlGr 606 to Coventry where the city was all but destroyed by 394 tons of high explosive, 56 tons of incendiaries and 127 parachute mines. A new, deadly word was coined — to

'Coventrate'. Five nights later it was the turn of Birmingham as KGr 100 led 369 aircraft of KG26, 54, 55 and KFlGr 606 to this target. By the end of the month 1150 twin-engined bombers were available for night raids, and an average of 200 per night were appearing over England. This weight of attack continued for the next two months, during which 13 900 tons of bombs were dropped. There was little that the British could do at this stage, but losses to the enemy were minimal in percentage terms for the efforts expended.

TOP-SCORING RAF FIGHTER PILOTS BY LATE 1940 (ONLY THOSE TAKING PART IN THE BATTLE OF BRITAIN INCLUDED)

NAME	SCORE	DURING JUNE-NOVEMBER PERIOD	NATIONALITY	SQUADRON
Flt Lt G Allard	23 & 2 shared	9 & 2 shared	British	85
Plt Off J H Lacey	23	14 & 1 shared	British	50 1
Sqn Ldr M N Crossley	20 & 2 shared	13 & 2 shared	British	32
Flt Lt A A McKellar	20 & 2 shared	15 & 1 shared	British	605 KIA 1 11 40
Plt Off E S Lock	20 & 1 shared	18 & 1 shared	British	41 WIA 17 11 40
Flt Lt W D David	19 & 2 shared	6 & 1 shared	British	87, 213
Flg Off A G Lewis	18	9	S African	85, 249 WIA 28 9 40
Sqn Ldr A G Malan	17 & 5 shared	8 & 1 shared	S African	74
Sqn Ldr R R S Tuck	17 & 4 shared	10 & 1 shared	British	92, 257
Sqn Ldr R G Dutton	17 & 3 shared	7 & 3 shared	British	145
Plt Off H J L Hallowes	17 & 2 shared	9 & 1 shared	British	43
Sgt J Frantisek	17	17	Czech	303 KIFA 8 10 40
Plt Off A C Deere	16 & 2 shared	4	N. Zealander	54
Plt Off C F Gray	16 & 2 shared	14 & 2 shared	N. Zealander	54
Flg Off W L McKnight	16 & 2 shared	6 & 2 shared	Canadian	242
Flg Off B J G Carbury	15 & 2 shared	15 & 2 shared	N. Zealander	603
Plt Off R F T Doe	15	15	British	234, 238
Plt Off H M Stephen	14 & 9 shared	11 & 3 shared	British	74
Sqn Ldr A H Boyd	14 & 3 shared	8 & 3 shared	British	145
Flt Lt P C Hughes	14 & 3 shared	14 & 3 shared	Australian	234 KIA 7 9 40
Sqn Ldr J Ellis	14 & 2 shared	11 & 1 shared	British	610
Flt Lt J T Webster	14 & 2 shared	7 & 1 shared	British	41 KIA 5 9 40
F/Sgt G C Unwin	14 & 2 shared	11 & 2 shared	British	19
Sgt R T Llewellyn	14 & 1 shared	11 & 1 shared	British	213
Flt Lt J I Kilmartin	14 & 1 shared	1	Irish	1, 43
Sqn Ldr W Urbanowicz	14	14	Polish	303
Flg Off Count M B Czernin	13 & 5 shared	8 & 5 shared	British	17
F/Sgt W H Franklin	13 & 3 shared	8	British	65 KIA 12 12 40
Plt Off J C Freeborn	13 & 2 shared	10 & 2 shared	British	74
Flt Lt J C Dundas	13 & 1 shared	8	British	609 KIA 28 11 40
Flg Off H M. Ferris	12 & 3 shared	3 & 3 shared	British	111 KIA 16 8 40
Flg Off D A P McMullen	12 & 3 shared	11 & 3 shared	British	54, 222
Flg Off P P Woods-Scawen	12 & 3 shared	6 & 2 shared	British	85 KIA 1 9 40
Flt Lt S D P Connors	12 & 1 shared	5 & 1 shared	British	111 KIA 18 8 40
Sqn Ldr D R S Bader	12	11	British	242
Flt Lt R F Boyd	11 & 2 shared	11 & 2 shared	British	602
Plt Off T F Neil	11 & 2 shared	11 & 2 shared	British	249
Sgt A V Clowes	11 & 1 shared	5 & 1 shared	British	1
Flg Off C R Davis	11 & 1 shared	11 & 1 shared	S African	601 KIA 6 9 40
Sgt W L Dymond	11 & 1 shared	11 & 1 shared	British	111 KIA 2 9 40
Sqn Ldr A R D MacDonnell	11 & 1 shared	11 & 1 shared	British	64
Plt Off C F Currant	10 & 5 shared	10 & 5 shared	British	605
Flg Off J C Mungo-Park	10 & 4 shared	10 & 1 shared	British	74
Flg Off J W Villa	10 & 4 shared	10 & 4 shared	British	72, 92
Flt Lt W G Clouston	10 & 3 shared	4 & 1 shared	N. Zealander	19
Flt Lt J A A Gibson	10 & 1 shared	9	N. Zealander	501
F/Sgt F W Higginson	10 & 1 shared	7 & 1 shared	British	56
Plt Off H C Upton	10 & 1 shared	10 & 1 shared	Canadian	43, 607, 145
Flt Lt J W C Simpson	10	3	British	43
DEFIANT TEAM				
F/Sgt E R Thorn (pilot)	12 & 1 shared	5	British	264
F/Sgt F J Barker (gunner)	12 & 1 shared	5	British	264

Meanwhile, November saw a renewal of activity by day, so far as the weather allowed, for coastal convoys had once again resumed their progress along the eastern and southern coastlines of England. Fighting with Messerschmitts on 1 November brought ten claims (four actual losses), but cost the lives of two leading fighter pilots, 605 Squadron's Flt Lt Archie McKellar and 74 Squadron's Flt Lt W H Nelson (6 victories). Skirmishing continued on most days, with losses on both sides, 145 Squadron which had now returned to action being hard hit on 7 November with losses of four Hurricanes shot down and one crash-landed.

Next day Ju87 dive-bombers were challenged in force for the first time since August, when aircraft of StG77, I/StG3 and IV(St)/LG1 attacked two Royal Navy destroyers east of Clacton. Fourteen Hurricanes of 17 Squadron led by Wg Cdr Farquhar hit the dive-bombers hard, 15 being claimed together with several probables. In the Luftwaffe loss lists two were recorded, one each by I/StG3 and IV(St)/LG1, but it is known that StG77 also lost six — reputedly four to fighters and two to the guns of HMS *Winchester*.

Three days later on 11 November 17 and 603 Squadrons

AWARDS OF RITTERKREUZ TO LUFTWAFFE MEMBERS DURING THE BATTLE OF BRITAIN

DATE	NAME	UNIT	VICTORIES AT DATE
JAGDFLIEGER			
1 Aug	Maj Adolf Galland	III/JG26	17
20 Aug	Hpt Walter Oesau	III/JG51	20+
	Hpt Horst Tietzen	II/JG51 (KIA 18 Aug)	20+
22 Aug	Oberstlt Harry von Bülow – Bothkamp	JG2	6+
	Oberst Max Ibel	JG27	
	Gen Maj Theo Osterkamp	JG51, Jafu	6++
27 Aug	Oblt Helmut Wick	I/JG2	20
3 Sept	Hpt Hans-Karl Mayer	I/JG53 (KIA 17 Oct)	20+
5 Sept	Werner Machold	I/JG2	21
11 Sept	Hpt Gerhard Schöpfel	III/JG26	20
13 Sept	Oblt Herbert Ihlefeld	I(J)/LG2	21+
14 Sept	Oblt Joachim Müncheberg	III/JG26	20
	Hpt Rolf Pingel	I/JG26	15+
16 Sept	Oblt Hermann-Friedrich Joppien	I/JG51	21
18 Sept	Hpt Günther Lutzow	I/JG3	15+
	Maj Wolfgang Schellmann	JG2	10+
21 Sept*	Maj Werner Mölders	JG51	40+
24 Sept	Oblt Hans Hahn	III/JG2	20
	Hpt Wolfgang Lippert	I/JG53,II/JG27	12+
25 Sept*	Maj Adolf Galland	JG26	40
1 Oct	Lt Gustav Sprick	III/JG26	20
6 Oct*	Maj Helmut Wick	JG2	42
19 Oct	Oblt Josef Priller	II/JG51	20
21 Oct	Hpt Dietrich Hrabak	II/JG54	16
22 Oct	Oblt Hans Philipp	II/JG54	20
	Hpt Heinz Bretnutz	II/JG53	20
28 Oct	Hpt Otto Bertram	III/JG2	13
5 Nov	Oblt Heinz Ebeling	III/JG26 (POW 5 Nov)	18
	Oblt Arnold Lignitz	III/JG51	
		III/JG54	19
9 Nov	Lt Siegfried Schnell	II/JG2	20
13 Nov	Hpt Walter Adolph	III/JG27, II/JG26	15+
	Hpt Karl-Heinz Krahl	I/JG2	15
14 Dec	Hpt Joachim Schlichting	III/JG27 (POW 6 Sept)	3+
	Oblt Franz von Werra	II/JG3 (POW 5 Sept)	8 and 5 on ground
30 Dec	Maj Günther Freiherr von Maltzahn	JG53	13
ZERSTÖRERFLIEGER			
5 Sept	Obstlt Johann Schalk	III/ZG26	
11 Sept	Obstlt Joachim-Friedrich Huth	ZG26	
14 Sept	Obstlt Walter Grabmann	ZG76	6
1 Oct	Obstlt Hans-Joachim Jabs	II/ZG76	
	Maj Wolfgang Falck	I/ZG1.NJG1	
	Hpt Erich Groth	II/ZG76	12
6 Oct	Hpt Wilhelm Makrocki	I/ZG26	9
13 Oct	Obstlt Friedrich Vollbracht	ZG2	2

again engaged Ju87s (this time heavily escorted) over the Thames estuary. Four Bf109s and three Ju87s were claimed, again with several probables in addition. On this occasion III/StG1 lost two Stukas, while JG51 and 53 lost five Bf109s between them, including that flown by Oblt Georg Claus (17 victories) who had for long been Mölders' wingman. Two hours later the Italians appeared in some strength, ten BR20 bombers escorted by 40 CR42s approaching Harwich. Hurricanes from 46 and 257 Squadrons attacked from opposite sides, but at the same time. Nine BR20s were claimed shot down, together with

four CR42s, and three probables. Actual casualties were more mundane: three BR20s lost and three damaged, one of these crash-landing on return, while three CR42s also went down. Squadrons 41 and 249 appeared on the scene late, claiming one 'Ju86' believed to have been a mis-identified BR20, and an He59 air-sea rescue seaplane shot down, plus a couple of CR42s damaged.

On 14 November Spitfires from 66 and 74 Squadrons again intercepted Ju87s, this time over the Dover area. Sixteen Stukas were claimed, 14 of them by the 'Tigers' (74 Squadron), while each unit also claimed an escorting Bf109.

DATE	NAME	UNIT	VICTORIES AT DATE
2 Nov	Hpt Rolf Kaldrack	III/ZG76	11
	Hpt Heinz Nacke	II/ZG76	12
SCHNELLKAMPFFLIEGER			
19 Aug	Hpt Walter Rubensdorffer	ErpGr210 (KIA 15 Aug)	
1 Oct	Hpt Martin Lutz	ErpGr210 (KIA 27 Sept)	
	Oblt Wilhelm-Richard Rössiger	ErpGr210 (KIA 27 Sept)	
24 Nov	Hpt Otto Hintze	ErpGr210 (POW 29 Oct)	
STUKAFLIEGER			
(Nine awards were made on 21 July 1940, but related to earlier operations over France and Poland)			
19 Aug	Hpt Anton Keil	III/StG51	
		II/StG1	
18 Sept	Oblt Johannes Brandenburg	I/StG2	
14 Dec	Hpt Waldemar Plewig	II/StG77 (POW 8 Aug 40)	
KAMPFFLIEGER			
16 Aug	Fw Otto Eichloff	II/KG30	
27 Aug	Maj Dipl Ing Dietrich Freiherr von Massenbach	II/KG4	
5 Sept	Hpt Otto Höhne	KG4	
	Oblt Heinrich Paepcke	II/KG30	
18 Sept	Maj Heinz Cramer	II/LG1	
30 Sept	Oblt Bernhard Jope	I/KG40	
1 Oct	Obfw Wilhelm-Friedrich Illg	III/KG76 (Flight Engineer)(POW)	
	Obstlt Benno Kosch	II/KG1	
3 Oct	Obst Wolfgang von Chamier-Gliczinski	KG3	
13 Oct	Hpt Erich Bloedorn	III/KG4	
	Oblt Hajo Herrmann	II/KG30	
14 Oct	Maj Friedrich Kless	II/KG55	
	Oblt Dietrick Peltz	Stab/KG77	
21 Oct	Maj Joachim Hahn	KüFlGr606	
	Maj Edgar Petersen	I/KG40	
	Maj Walter Storp	II/KG76	
24 Oct	Hpt Hans-Joachim Helbig	II/LG1	
2 Nov	Obst Karl Angerstein	KG1	
24 Nov	Hpt Robert Kowalewski	II/KG26	
	Oblt Gerhard Richter	III/LG1	
	Oblt Siegmund-Ulrich Freiherr von Gravenreuth	I/KG30	
25 Nov	Oblt Hermann Kühl	I/KG4	
3 Dec	Hpt Wilhelm Dürbeck	III/LG1	
30 Jan. 41*	Maj G Martin Harlinghausen	X Fliegerkorps	

+ indicates earlier victories in Spain (not included in these scores)
++ 32 victories in World War 2
* indicates award of the Eichenlaube (Oak leaves) to the Ritterkreuz

ONE OF TWO Bf109Es SHOT DOWN ON 23 NOVEMBER, 1940 IS RECOVERED BY BRITISH SERVICEMEN WITH THE AID OF SOME TRADITIONAL HORSEPOWER.

Only two Ju87s were recorded as lost by III/StG1, but again there may have been other unrecorded losses; JG51 lost one Messerschmitt — and a second a few minutes later to the joint fire of Hurricanes from 46 and 249 Squadrons. Next day Spitfires of 41 and 602 Squadron engaged a flock of Bf109s, claiming eight — in fact two were lost by II/JG54. An hour later 17 and 257 Squadron intercepted Bf110 'Jabos' of EGr 210 and escorting Bf109s of JG26. Three Bf110s were accounted for by 17 Squadron while 257 brought down one Bf109 — they claimed two. Maj Galland shot down 17's leading ace, Flg Off Manfred Czernin, who baled out, and then claimed two of 257's Hurricanes as his 54th and 55th victories; one actually fell and the other was damaged.

The month continued with desultory combats on a daily basis against fighter sweeps, 'Jabos' and reconnaissance aircraft, odd victories being claimed. On 23 November the Italians returned, the CR42s making a fighter sweep. Spitfires of 603 Squadron intercepted them off Dover and claimed seven shot down, with four more probables or damaged. Three were hard hit and crash-landed, with two of the pilots being killed. About ten more were damaged, three of their pilots being wounded, but all got back to their airfield in Belgium.

The battle ends

The final engagement of note occurred on 27 November when Spitfires of 41, 66 and 74 Squadrons engaged Bf109s of I/JG51, claiming ten shot down. The German unit was hard hit, and lost six aircraft on this occasion. The month had been a profitable one for the RAF, for while 196 claims had been made (146 actual losses, a number of them to AA fire at night), Fighter Command had lost only 31 Hurricanes and Spitfires, with 19 more damaged.

Was the Battle of Britain the victory it was believed to be? The British say yes, the Germans no. Certainly the Luftwaffe had been prevented from gaining aerial superiority over Southern England — partly by Göring's decision to switch the attack to London, but also in no small part by the RAF's own efforts. Without this superiority the invasion of England had to be postponed and it had become too costly to continue daylight bomber operations. However, the night attack was maintained with the bomber force undiminished, continuing throughout the winter and spring of 1941. While the British night defenses became more effective, it was the withdrawal of units elsewhere in April and May 1941 which brought the 'Blitz' to a close. The German fighters were still making sweeps and 'Jabo' attacks on England throughout the spring, and while Fighter Command was then also undertaking some offensive operations in the other direction, it was at a cost.

The Luftwaffe awaited a resumption of the offensive in Spring 1941, strengthened and with its new Bf109F fighters coming into service — albeit against a strengthened Fighter Command. If they had returned, might they not have learned the lessons of September 1940 and concentrated on the fighter airfields and radar sites until a conclusion was reached? Was the Luftwaffe defeated? We speak here of an air force which in early 1941 swept through the Balkans in a month, drove the Royal Navy from the Mediterranean and supported Rommel in North Africa. The air force which, in June 1941, despite the necessity to maintain a viable presence in Western Europe and in Africa, struck eastwards and in a few weeks virtually destroyed the massively numerically-strong Soviet Air Force. Hardly the actions of a beaten force. The Luftwaffe had suffered grievous losses in the summer of 1940, and had suffered a setback, but was it not Hitler's decision that the United Kingdom was all but finished and was hardly worth the trouble invading, which truly brought the Battle of Britain to its conclusion?

CHAPTER THREE

INVASION OF THE PHILIPPINES

DECEMBER 1941

Overleaf

Mitsubishi A6M2 Zero fighters of the Tainan Kokutai of the Imperial
Japanese Navy, sweep in low to strafe Clark Field, Luzon, in the Philippines at midday on 8 December,
1941. They catch parked Boeing B-17D Fortress bombers of the 19th Bomb Group and
Curtiss P-40B fighters of the 20th Pursuit Squadron on the ground as the latter attempt to take-off
to intercept.

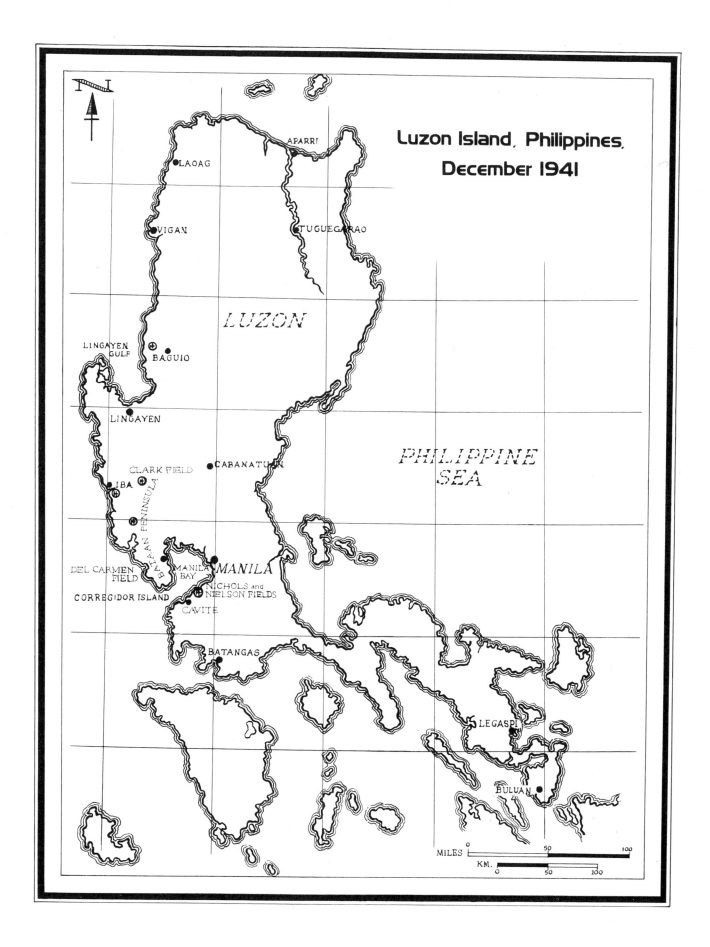

N

Luzon Island, Philippines,
December 1941

APARRI

LAOAG

VIGAN

TUGUEGARAO

LUZON

LINGAYEN
GULF

BAGUIO

LINGAYEN

*PHILIPPINE
SEA*

CLARK FIELD

CABANATUAN

IBA

BATAAN PENINSULA

DEL CARMEN
FIELD

MANILA
BAY

MANILA

NICHOLS and
NELSON FIELDS

CORREGIDOR ISLAND

CAVITE

BATANGAS

LEGASPI

BULUAN

MILES 0   50   100

KM. 0   50   100

As 1941 approached its end, the prospects of war with Japan had become very real for the United States of America, for that neutral and isolationist power had — for the best of reason — pushed militarist, expansionist Japan to the very brink. For some four years past the Japanese had been committed to a war of territorial expansion in China, to deter them from which the US had imposed various embargos on the supply of vital raw materials. Japan was denied iron and oil, but also rubber, cut off by the British in collaboration with the US government. Subsequently, Japan's assets in the US were frozen, and finally even her import of scrap metal was halted.

Desperately short of domestic natural resources, the Japanese were placed in an impossible situation. They either had to undertake a humiliating climb-down, with all the loss of face so unacceptable to any nation, much less a proud Oriental power, or they had to seize the rich oil and rubber-producing territories of Malaya and the East Indies. The latter course would bring them into unavoidable armed conflict with both Britain and the US.

Britain was embroiled in a war far away in Europe which was stretching her to the limits of her capacity and resources, while the other threat to Japanese security, her old enemy Soviet Russia, was similarly involved. True the US was still neutral, but her industries were busy providing equipment to keep the British and Russians supplied, while her own forces were still at little more than normal peace-time establishment levels.

Japan on the other hand was already on a war footing, her army, navy and air forces superbly equipped, combat experienced and ready for action. Support and co-operation might well be expected from Germany and Italy, with whom the Japanese were now joint signatories of the Axis Pact, and who appeared to be winning their war in the West. Might not a sudden, audacious blow of great magnitude so shatter the British and Americans as to bring them to the negotiating table? The time seemed right.

Target Philippines

To achieve this, however, it would be necessary not only to invade Malaya and the East Indies, but also the US-occupied Philippine Islands which were situated nearby, and from which offensive operations against the Japanese in their newly-conquered territories could otherwise be mounted. Any war in the east would essentially be a naval one, however, and the bulk of the US naval strength was located far away in mid-Pacific at bases in the Hawaiian Islands, as was much of the air power. A massive pre-emptive strike here would also be an essential pre-requisite for any successful venture. Consequently, the preliminaries were put in hand, the Imperial Navy planning a great strike by its powerful aircraft carrier fleet on the Hawaiian bases, whilst strong air and ground forces were assembled in Indo-China and Formosa ready to move south. The newly-formed Southern Army under General Count Hisaichi Terauchi was to undertake operations against the Philippines, Malaya, Burma and the East Indies.

While the American, British, Dutch and Australian commands with interests in the threatened areas each had their own armies, navies and air forces, and plans had been discussed for these to operate in conjunction with each other in the case of hostilities, in the event the sheer force of the initial Japanese assault tended fully to overwhelm each national contingent in the defense of its own territory. With

only limited degrees of overall command and little commonality of equipment, there was much less co-ordinated action than had been planned or hoped for. So while it must be remembered that other Japanese units — air, land and naval — were similarly involved close by, those engaged in the Philippines were able to carry on their own campaign, little affected by what was going on elsewhere.

Consequently, amongst the elements being readied for the great adventure, the Japanese allocated for initial involvement only in the Philippines, the 14th Army under Lt Gen Masaharu Homma, the Imperial Army Air Force's Southern Army Direct Command, located on the island of Formosa, and the Imperial Naval Air Force's land-based 21st and 23rd Air Flotillas, also based on Formosa. These would be supported as necessary by elements of the Imperial Fleet. The 14th Army comprised ten divisions and three mixed brigades, while the strength of the two air forces was as follows:-

	Fighters	Medium Bombers	Light Bombers	Reconn-aissance	Totals
Army	72	18	54	11	155
Navy	114	117	—	12	243
	186	135	54	23	398

Additionally, the Navy had available a detachment of 24 flyingboats for a total operational strength of 422 aircraft.

The Philippines had been seized from Spain by the US at the turn of the century during the Spanish-American War, but were now approaching planned independence. There had been considerable resistance to the prospect of continued US military bases in the islands following independence, as a result of which for some time little had been done to increase or modernize the garrison, since it was considered that US forces would withdraw as soon as the Filipinos could take over their own defense.

The threat of war with Japan had halted this trend, and in October 1940 48 out of 60 Seversky P-35A fighters which had been ordered by the Swedish government, were reallocated, being sent to the Philippines instead. These were followed in 1941 by Douglas B-18A bombers and Curtiss P-40B fighters to replace the resident Martin B-10s and Boeing P-26As, most of these latter obsolescent types being passed on to the embryo Philippine Air Force. When General Douglas MacArthur arrived in May 1941 to take over command of the Filipino-American forces, he pressed for a greater commitment — particularly of air power — so that a more aggressive defensive policy might be adopted. As a result more fighters were sent, together with quantities of the four-engined Boeing B-17 — the famous Flying Fortress.

The strength of 265 aircraft (inclusive of reserves) which was available to the US Far Eastern Air Force in December 1941 was approximately equal to that of the Royal Air Force in Malaya and Singapore, and the Dutch Air Force in the East Indies. Because of the preponderance of modern P-40s and B-17s, it was, however, the most powerful and effective air force available to the Allies in the area, and was the one part of the arsenal facing the Japanese capable of posing a real threat to them. Immediately available aircraft with operational units included 102 fighters, 36 heavy bombers and 30 flyingboats.

On the ground, the army could muster a total of 120 000

US FAR EASTERN AIR FORCE 8 DECEMBER 1941

V INTERCEPTOR COMMAND

UNIT	BASE	AIRCRAFT
24th Pursuit Group	Clark Field	
3rd Pursuit Squadron	Iba	18 Curtiss P-40E
17th Pursuit Squadron	Nichols Field	18 Curtiss P-40E
20th Pursuit Squadron	Clark Field	18 Curtiss P-40B
35th Pursuit Group detachment (attached 24th Pursuit Group)		
21st Pursuit Squadron	Del Carmen	18 Curtiss P-40E
34th Pursuit Squadron	Nichols Field	18 Seversky P-35A

V BOMBER COMMAND

UNIT	BASE	AIRCRAFT
19th Bombardment Group	Clark Field	
28th Bomb Squadron	Clark Field	9 Boeing B-17
30th Bomb Squadron	Clark Field	9 Boeing B-17
93rd Bomb Squadron	Del Monte	9 Boeing B-17
14th Bomb Squadron	Del Monte	9 Boeing B-17

NB All B-17s were of the early C and D models. The 28th Squadron had been in the Philippines for 15 years; the 14th Squadron had just arrived from Oahu, Hawaii.

Philippine Air Force		
6th Pursuit Squadron	Batangos	12 Boeing P-26A
US Navy Air Force		
Patwing 10	Subic Bay	30 Consolidated PBY Catalina

With reserves, the US/Filipino air forces had available on 8 December 1941, 35 B-17C and D heavy bombers, 18 Douglas B-18A and 12 Martin B-10B medium bombers, 105 P-40s, 48 P-35As and 16 P-26As, together with numbers of North American A-27s, various observation aircraft and trainers. At Nichols Field was the US 2nd observation Squadron which would play no part in operations. The Headquarters of the 27th Bombardment Group was at Neilson Field, but as yet no aircraft had arrived for it. Two B-10Bs had been handed to the PAF's 10th Bombardment Squadron, but all other B-10Bs and B-18As were on the strength of the B-17 and fighter squadrons as transport and liaison aircraft. The A-27s, attack versions of the well-known A-6 Texan (Harvard) trainer, had been ordered by the Thai Air Force, but seized by the US Government; they were supplied to the fighter units for use as trainers. Two other PAF Squadrons existed, the 5th Photo and 9th Observation and Attack Squadrons, but only the latter had any aircraft – two Douglas O-46s. The various other observation aircraft in Luzon included elderly Thomas Morse O-19s, the much more modern Curtiss O-52s and some Grumman OA-9 amphibians.

JAPANESE AIR FORCE UNITS OPERATING OVER THE PHILIPPINES 8 DECEMBER 1941

IMPERIAL NAVY AIR FORCE

UNIT	BASE	AIRCRAFT
21st Air Flotilla		
Kanoya Kokutai	Taichung	27 Mitsubishi G4M1
1st Kokutai	Tainan	36 Mitsubishi G3M2
Toko Kokutai (detachment)	Polan	24 Kawanishi H6K
23rd Air Flotilla		
Takeo Kokutai	Kangshan	54 Mitsubishi G4M1
Tainan Kokutai	Tainan	45 Mitsubishi A6M2
		12 Mitsubishi A5M4
		6 Mitsubishi C5M
3rd Kokutai	Kangshan	45 Mitsubishi A6M2
		12 Mitsubishi A5M4
		6 Mitsubishi C5M

IMPERIAL ARMY AIR FORCE

5th Air Division

UNIT	BASE	AIRCRAFT
4th Flying Battalion		
8th Sentai	Chiatung	27 Kawasaki Ki48
		9 Mitsubishi Ki15
		2 Mitsubishi Ki46
14th Sentai		18 Mitsubishi Ki21
16th Sentai	Chiatung	27 Mitsubishi Ki36
50th Sentai	Hengchan	36 Nakajima Ki27
24th Sentai	Chaochou	36 Nakajima Ki27
10th Independent Hikotai		
52nd Independent Chutai	Pingtung	13 Mitsubishi Ki15
74th Independent Chutai	Pingtung	10 Tachikawa Ki36
76th Independent Chutai	Pingtung	9 Mitsubishi Ki15
		2 Mitsubishi Ki46
11th Transport Chutai		Various

men in ten divisions — a most impressive force on paper. Numbers were illusory, however, for only 20 000 of these men were regular soldiers, the rest reservists of the Citizen National Army. The greater part of the latter were untrained and had little equipment — not even steel helmets and proper boots in most cases. Many were illiterate, or did not speak the same language as their officers. The only effective formations were the Philippine Division, which included the only all-American regiment on the islands, the 31st Infantry Division, and the Filipino/American Philippine Scouts. Just before the outbreak of hostilities MacArthur had managed to squeeze further reinforcement in the shape of 108 M-3 Stuart light tanks, which were formed into the Provisional Tank Group, and the 200th Coast Artillery Regiment with 12 3-inch guns and 25 self-propelled 75 mm anti-aircraft guns.

The Philippine-based US Asiatic Fleet, commanded by Admiral T C Hart, had no capital ships at all — battleships or carriers. It possessed three cruisers, only one of which carried 8-inch guns, 13 destroyers (two of which were undergoing refit), two seaplane tenders, six gunboats and 29 submarines. It was hardly a force capable of challenging anything the Japanese might put to sea, and could only offer a real threat if combined with the British and Dutch navies.

The Japanese plan called for simultaneous actions, including the great strike on the bases in Hawaii, particularly the Pearl Harbor naval base; an invasion of Southern Thailand, coupled with strikes on airfields in Northern Malaya; and a strike on the US airbases in Southern Luzon in the Philippines. At two of the three points of impact all went according to plan. The audacious Pearl Harbor strike exceeded the most optimistic expectations for it, while little effective opposition was met on the Kra Isthmus, linking Malaya and Thailand. But in the Philippines little happened — initially!

A faltering start

The reason coincidentally was similar to the situation facing the Luftwaffe on 1 September 1939, for with the dawn a thick blanket of fog had rolled in from the sea over the Formosan airfields on which the aircraft of the Imperial Naval Air Force waited ready to take off for their targets around Manila. The Japanese waited in trepidation; now surely the dreaded Flying Fortresses would appear overhead and destroy their aircraft on the ground! They might well have done so, for news of the Japanese attacks reached

Manila early on 8 December, providing the US command with the luxury of five full hours' warning before anything serious transpired. Indeed, a pre-emptive strike on Formosa was considered, but was decided against, a purely defensive posture being adopted. Not for the first time a dictatorship had underestimated the confusion and indecision which tends to overwhelm democracies thrust suddenly into war.

Certainly the Americans had full notice that there had been no error in the reports, for at dawn a small force of aircraft comprising 13 Nakajima B5N bombers and nine escorting Mitsubishi A5M fighters were led from the light aircraft carrier *Ryujo* by Lt Takahide Aioi to attack the naval base at Davao on the southern coast of Mindanao, the most southerly large island of the Philippines group. Here the bombers attacked the seaplane tender USS *Preston* without effect, while the fighters strafed and destroyed two naval PBY Catalina flyingboats of PatWing 10. Anti-aircraft fire hit three of the attackers, one bomber coming down in the sea where the crew were swiftly rescued by a Japanese destroyer. A second strike three hours later by five aircraft achieved little and cost one of the fighters.

Meanwhile on Formosa the fog had not had the same affect on some of the Army Air Force airfields, and two formations of the Army's shorter-range aircraft had got into the air, 25 Kawasaki Ki48 light bombers attacking Tuguegarao airfield in northern Luzon at 0700 hours, while 18 Mitsubishi Ki21 medium bombers hit the town of Baguio in the middle of the island at the same time. Neither of these formations met any opposition, but the raids did galvanize the US authorities into some action. As the raids were reported, two fighter squadrons were ordered off to patrol to the north of Manila in case of any attempt to attack the capital, while all flyable B-17s at Clark Field were ordered off for their own safety, 15 of the 19 bombers getting into the air. The 16 at Del Monte were considered to be safely dispersed.

Had the Imperial Japanese Naval Air Force (IJNAF) aircraft on Formosa got off on time, these moves by the Americans might well have coincided with their arrival, but

as it was nothing appeared, and by 1100 hours all the B-17s had landed again. One of them was then despatched to patrol towards Formosa, another heading off to the north of Luzon. Meanwhile fighter patrols had been organized, the P-40Es from the 3rd, 17th and 21st Squadrons cruising over Iba and Clark airfields, and the fortress island of Corregidor in Manila Bay, until fuel ran low. Seven SCR 270 radar sets had been delivered to Luzon recently, but only one, which had been set up at Iba, was so far operational, the crews keeping a close watch on their 'scopes. The patrolling fighters had all begun landing by 1230 hours, and the 20th Squadron was just about to send up its P-40Bs to cover Clark Field while they were refuelled, when the Japanese arrived. The sheer ill-fortune of the Americans could hardly have been greater had the Japanese been able to plan their arrival to coincide with the moment of greatest weakness. The results were catastrophic.

The sun had finally burned away the fog over Formosa by mid morning, and the relieved Japanese, hardly able to believe their luck, had swiftly launched two strong strikes on the Manila area. The capital and its adjacent air and naval bases were beyond the range at which escorted bombers could be operated by the Army, hence the allocation of this target area to the Navy. First off were 26 of the older Mitsubishi G3Ms of the 1st Kokutai, 27 newer Mitsubishi G4Ms of the Takao Kokutai, and 36 escorting Mitsubishi A6M fighters of the Tainan Kokutai — the famous Zeros, soon to become the very symbol of Japanese qualitative superiority over the Allies.

This combined force made for Clark and Del Carmen airfields, immediately followed by 54 more G4Ms from the Takao and Kanoya Kokutais and 53 A6Ms of the 3rd

Kokutai (strengthened with elements of the Tainan Ku), which were to attack Iba. A total of six aircraft were forced to turn back for one reason or another, but the remaining 190 droned on towards their targets.

It was at Iba that the first bombs fell, crashing down without prior warning at 1235 hours (unreported by the Iba radar), just as one flight of 3rd Squadron P-40Es were landing from their patrol. The explosions wrecked the leading fighter just as it touched down, but some of the escorting Zeros were already after the others, shooting down four of them as they attempted to land. Two more of the 3rd's P-40s which had not yet gone into the landing pattern, attempted to engage the Japanese fighters without success, and one was hit, being forced to crashland.

The second flight, comprising six more P-40Es, gave up any hope of getting down at Iba, and flew instead to Clark Field, where the other Japanese formation had opened its attack at 1240 hours, just as the 20th Squadron was scrambling four of its P-40Bs to intercept. The initial cascade of bombs destroyed five more P-40Bs as they were waiting to get onto the runway, while Tainan Ku Zeros which then swept down to strafe, as had those of 3rd Ku at Iba, wrote 'finis' to yet another five. The quartette of American fighters which had got into the air engaged the Zeros, three of which were claimed shot down, two by Lt Randall B Keator, which included the first US fighter victory in the Philippines.

The Japanese exact a heavy toll

The Tainan Ku fighters over Clark were now joined by those of the 3rd Ku which had run out of targets at Iba. There were plenty of aircraft around at this main airfield for them to attack, which they did in the most damaging manner. When the six 3rd Squadron P-40Es from Iba also arrived here it was to find the area alive with Zeros, and whilst they attacked with vigour, Lt Grant Mahoney claiming one shot down, the American flight lost three of their own aircraft. The 17th and 21st Squadrons returned to their airfields without seeing anything, and low on fuel, although a section of Tainan Ku A6Ms strafed the 21st's base at Del Carmen in their absence. One section of the 21st did run into some of the Japanese fighters, two of which were claimed by Lt Jack Donaldson, while 34th Squadron P-35As also skirmished with them, Lt Ben Brown claiming one shot down, with Japanese claims including one P-35, although none were actually lost. During their successful attacks on the US airfields, the two Zero units had claimed 15 fighters shot down and seven more probably so — USAAF losses were actually nine — while 47 more were claimed destroyed on the ground, 33 of them in flames. Seven Zeros were lost, five of them Tainan Ku aircraft, and an eighth pilot was wounded; none of the bombers failed to return.

The cost had indeed been devastating; apart from the nine P-40s shot down, ten more had been destroyed on the ground, and so too had 12 of 14 serviceable B-17s at Clark. In addition, two more unserviceable bombers were written off — these were taxied out of their burning hangar in an effort to save them, only to bring them right into the fighters' fire. Only the absence of the two on reconnaissance prevented the whole force at this field being destroyed. In addition to these grievous losses, some 25–30 miscellaneous aircraft had also been destroyed including B-10s, B-18As, A-27s, O-52s, O-49s, O-46s, O-19s, OA9s, a Sikorsky amphibian, and a pair of Beechcraft light aircraft.

MAIN AIRCRAFT TYPES EMPLOYED DURING THE PHILIPPINES CAMPAIGN

AMERICAN

Curtiss P-40B Tomahawk and P-40E Kittyhawk
Main fighter equipment of the USAAF at the outbreak of war was the Curtiss P-40. A conventional low-wing monoplane with an in-line engine, the earlier P40B version was powered by a 1150 hp Allison V-1710-33. Armament comprised two 0.50 in Browning machine guns mounted above the engine and synchronised to fire through the propeller disc, and four wing-mounted 0.30 in Brownings. The P-40E differed in having the oil cooler and engine radiator brought further forward under the nose in a more prominent fairing, and a revised armament comprising six wing-mounted 0.50 in Brownings. A fairly heavy aircraft, the P-40 lacked any supercharging to its Allison engine, which was rated for low altitude, and consequently performance fell off rapidly at high altitude. Although fairly manoeuvreable, it could not compare in this sphere with the light, nimble Japanese fighters. However when US pilots avoided dogfights and used the aircraft's attributes of fast diving speed, heavy firepower and tough construction to make rapid dive attacks on their opponents, zooming straight back up to higher levels for safety, they could achieve good results. Performance of the P-40B included a maximum speed of 352 mph at 14000 ft, a range of 730 miles and a service ceiling of 32400 ft; the P-40E was somewhat faster, reaching 362 mph at 15000 ft, but with a reduced range of 650 miles and a service ceiling of 29000 ft.

Republic (Seversky) P-35A
The P-35 was the first modern cantilever monoplane fighter to enter service with the USAAC, in 1937. It was a rather portly low-wing monoplane with an attractive semi-elliptical wing planform. The undercarriage did not retract fully into the wings, but folded back into streamlined fairings. The A version was an up-gunned export model with a more powerful 1050 hp Pratt

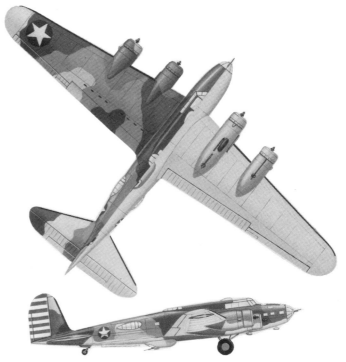

Boeing B-17D Fortress of the 19th Bombardment Group (Heavy)

and Whitney R-1830-AS radial engine, 120 of which were built for Sweden. The second 60 were requisitioned by the US Government in October 1940 and 48 were sent to the Philippines. The P-35A carried one 0.50 in and one 0.30 In Browning machine guns mounted above the engine in the nose, and two more 0.50 in guns in fairings under the wings. Maximum speed was 310 mph at 14 300 ft, range was up to 950 miles, and service ceiling 31 400 ft. The aircraft was totally out-classed by the Japanese A6M.

Boeing P-26A
A classic American fighter of the early thirties, the P-26A was totally obsolete by 1941. A low wing wire-braced monoplane with an open cockpit and a fixed, heavily-spatted undercarriage, this attractive but outdated little aircraft had been 'passed down' to the Filipinos – it saw service nowhere else during the war. Powered by a 600 hp Pratt and Whitney R-1340-27 Wasp radial, its best speed was 234 mph at 7500 ft; service ceiling was 27 400 ft and range 570 miles. It was armed with either two 0.30 in Browning machine guns, or one 0.30 in and one 0.50 in gun, both carried in the nose.

Boeing B-17D Fortress
A large, four-engined low wing monoplane bomber powered by four 1200 hp Wright R-1820-65 Cyclone radial engines, the B-17D was the best bomber in service in the Pacific area in 1941. With a service ceiling of 37 000 ft and a range with 4000 lb of bombs of 2000 miles, the aircraft was difficult to intercept. At optimum height of 25 000 ft its top speed was 323 mph. Although the B-17D was not fitted with any power-operated gun turrets, it was quite heavily armed with pairs of hand-held 0.50 in Browning machine guns in dorsal and ventral hatch positions, and another of these guns in each of two side hatch positions; a single 0.30 in gun was fitted in the nose cone for use by the bombardier.

Consolidated PBY-5 Catalina
A sturdy, ubiquitous patrol flyingboat, the PBY featured a parasol wing mounted on a pylon above the fuselage, to which it was braced with pairs of struts. Powered by two 1200 hp Pratt and Whitney R-1830-82 radial engines, the aircraft had a range of 1945 miles, a service ceiling of 21 600 ft and a top speed of 200 mph at 5700 ft. It was armed with one 0.30 in bow gun, one more for underside defense in a tunnel, and a 0.50 in gun in each of two large perspex 'blisters' on the sides of the fuselage. Offensive load could include either four 325 lb depth charges, 4000 lb of bombs or two torpedoes.

JAPANESE

Mitsubishi A6M2 Zero-Sen
The famous Zero fighter was a low-wing monoplane of clean but orthodox design. Very light and supremely manoeuvreable, it also possessed a very long range, particularly when fitted with an under-fuselage long-range tank. Powered by a 925 hp Nakajima Sakae 12 radial engine, it had a maximum speed of 336 mph at 19 685 ft and a service ceiling of 33 790 ft. It was armed with two 7.7 mm Type 97 machine guns in the nose and two 20 mm Type 99 cannon in the wings.

Nakajima Ki27
The main Japanese Army fighter in 1941, the Ki27 — known to the Allies by the codename 'Kate' — was a small, light, low-wing monoplane with very low wing loading which made it extremely manoeuvreable. Fitted with a fixed, neatly spatted undercarriage, and powered by a 710 hp Nakajima Ha1B radial engine, it reached 286 mph at 16 400 ft. It was armed only with two nose-mounted 7.7 mm Type 89 machine guns.

Mitsubishi G3M2
The oldest Japanese bomber in service in 1941, the G3M was a mid-wing monoplane with twin fins and rudders, powered by two 1075 hp Kinsei 45 engines. These gave a top speed of 232 mph at 13 715 ft and a service ceiling of 29 950 ft. The bomber had a range of 2722 miles and carried 1764 lb of bombs or

Mitsubishi A6M2 Zero-Sen of the 3rd Kokutai, IJNAF

torpedoes. It was armed with pairs of 7.7 mm Type 92 machine guns in each of two perspex blisters on the fuselage sides, and a 20 mm Type 99 cannon in a dorsal blister.

Mitsubishi G4M1
Built as a replacement for the G3M 'Nell', the G4M 'Betty' was a somewhat portly medium bomber monoplane with a low-mid wing. As befitted a Naval aircraft, it had a very long range of 3750 miles. Powered by two 1530 hp Mitsubishi MK4A Kasei 11 radials, it had a top speed of 266 mph at 13 780 ft and carried an offensive load of 1764 lb bombs or torpedoes. Defensive armament was four 7.7 mm Type 92 machine guns situated in nose, dorsal and two side blisters, plus a 20 mm Type 99 cannon in the tail.

Mitsubishi Ki21-IIa
The Army's main medium bomber in 1941, the Ki21-IIa (codename 'Sally') was a clean, low-mid wing monoplane powered by two 1500 hp Mitsubishi Ha101 engines. Performance was higher than Navy medium bombers, top speed being 302 mph at 15 485 ft and service ceiling 32 810 ft. Range however was 1680 miles, and bomb load 1653 lb normal, or 2205 lb maximum. Armament comprised five 7.7 mm machine guns, one in a remote-controlled barbette in the far tail, the others in nose, dorsal and ventral positions.

Kawasaki Ki48
A twin-engined light bomber, the Ki48 ('Lily') was powered by two 1000 hp Ha25 engines providing a maximum speed of 300 mph at 11 480 ft, and a ceiling of 31 000 ft. Range was 1750 miles, bombload 1100 lb, and armament four 7.7 mm machine guns in nose, dorsal and ventral positions.

Reconnaissance Aircraft
Both Army and Navy employed a number of basically similar two-seat reconnaissance/light bomber types. All were clean monoplanes powered by radial engines, all featured fixed, spatted undercarriages and light armaments. These included the Navy's Mitsubishi C5M and the Army's Mitsubishi Ki15 and Ki30.

At Iba the sole operational radar station had also been destroyed. It seems that further fighters were destroyed on the ground at Iba and Del Carmen, for total losses listed for the day increase the total of P-40s to over 50, and include three P-35As. The Japanese were back after dark, bombing Nicholls Field, where at least two B-18As were destroyed, and also attacking Fort McKinley. Nicholls was now evacuated as being too exposed for defense; the 34th Squadron moved to join the 21st at Del Carmen.

Next day bad weather over Formosa grounded the

Japanese and brought a welcome respite. Although Clark Field was barely useable, the beginnings of a striking force was reborn from the ashes. The two B-17s which had been away on reconnaissance were back and were serviceable. Close inspection showed that three of the wrecked bombers were repairable — and there were still 15 more remaining at Del Monte, plus a further damaged machine. However, the air raid warning system was in tatters and effective resistance to further attacks was not going to be easy. To compound the defenders' problems, during the day two 21st Squadron P-40s collided while taking off, one of them crashing into a B-17. Soon afterwards two more 17th Squadron P-40s crashed during a scramble, five of the best aircraft having been lost without the Japanese firing a shot! Nevertheless, at last a strike on Formosa was planned, and at dusk seven B-17s moved up to Clark from Del Monte and eight to San Marcellino, ready for a morning attack on 10 December.

Plans were soon changed next morning, however, when Lt Grant Mahoney undertook a reconnaissance up the west coast in his P-40 and spotted a Japanese landing force at Vigan. This comprised six transport vessels with an escort of

LEFT: CURTISS P-40C OF THE USAAF IN 1941. THIS AIRCRAFT IS SIMILAR TO THOSE EMPLOYED BY THE 20TH SQUADRON OF THE 24TH PURSUIT GROUP AT CLARK FIELD.

BELOW: TYPICAL OF THE BOMBERS HEADING FOR THE USAAF'S AIRFIELDS IN THE MANILA AREA ON 8 DECEMBER, 1941 WERE THESE MITSUBISHI G4MIS. LATER GIVEN THE ALLIED CODENAME 'BETTY', THESE LONG-RANGING AIRCRAFT WERE THE MOST MODERN BOMBERS AVAILABLE TO THE JAPANESE AT THE START OF THE WAR.

three cruisers and seven destroyers, landing 2000 men of the Kanno Detachment. Unknown to the Americans at this time, a similar convoy was unloading another 2000 men of the Tanaka Detachment at Aparri on the opposite coast. These landing parties were after airfields and, while those at the landing areas were swiftly taken, the troops split up into parties and had soon secured those at Tuguegarao and Laoag also. Another field on the small island of Batan, to the north of Luzon, had also been seized without opposition on 8 December. Nakajima Ki27 fighters of the IJAAF's 24th Sentai had already moved to this island and were available to cover these new landings.

At once on receipt of Mahoney's report five B-17s were despatched to bomb the shipping at Vigan, followed by P-40Es of the 17th Squadron, carrying bombs, and then by 16 P-35As. Half this latter force turned back due to trouble with the worn engines of these rather elderly fighters, and the pilot of another baled out when his engine actually failed. The Fortresses rained large quantities of 100 lb bombs on the ships without undue success, but the P-40s managed to cause some damage to the cruiser *Naka*, although two of the fighters were lost — ostensibly because of yet more engine problems, but possibly to Japanese fighters, the Ki27 pilots claiming one US fighter shot down during the morning. When the remaining seven 34th Squadron P-35As arrived, they strafed until a mine sweeper blew up — but the explosion destroyed one of the fighters as it passed over, Lt Samuel Marrett being killed.

Meanwhile the IJNAF on Formosa was preparing to rejoin the fray. Firstly, 17 A6Ms led by a C5M reconnaissance aircraft were despatched by the Tainan Ku to take over defense of the Vigan landing fleet from the Army

Ki27s. Behind them came 27 G3M bombers from the 1st Ku, heading for Cavite Navy Yard, followed by 27 G4Ms which were to attack Nicholls Field, and 27 more making for Del Carmen, both the latter formations drawn from the Takao Ku. The whole bomber force was escorted by 22 more Tainan Ku A6Ms, 34 more of these from the 3rd Ku being led by three C5Ms, to sweep over the Manila area. This time Army bombers joined the main attack, Ki21s of the 14th Sentai receiving Iba as their target.

The heavy fighting continues
Del Carmen was the first of the targets to be reached, but the Takao Ku bombers found it covered by cloud and headed instead for Manila. Despite the deflection of the bombing force, the Tainan Ku Zeros went in under the clouds and caught the recently-landed P-35As on the ground, destroying 12 of the fighters outright and damaging six more; the 34th Squadron had virtually ceased to exist. With news of the attack on Del Carmen, all P-40s at Clark Field had been ordered to scramble. 17th Squadron aircraft reached the area and attacked the Zeros, Lieutenants George Kiser and William Sheppard claiming two apiece, while the Japanese pilots claimed three of the Curtiss fighters in return. The 17th did indeed lose three, while the Tainan Ku lost one, with three more damaged.

Even as this fighting was at its height bombs from the G3Ms and G4Ms began tumbling towards their targets. Cavite Navy Yard was devastated, while Nicholls Field and Manila City were also hard hit. As the city came under attack, all P-40s were ordered to head there, arriving to find not the bombers, but more Zeros of the 3rd Ku, the opposing fighters tearing into each other. Pilots of the 20th

ABOVE LEFT: FIRST OF THE JAPANESE AIRCRAFT TO OPERATE
FROM PHILIPPINES SOIL WERE THE NAKAJIMA KI27 FIGHTERS
OF THE ARMY AIR FORCE'S 50TH SENTAI, WHICH FLEW IN TO
APARRI ON 11 DECEMBER. ONE OF THIS UNIT'S AIRCRAFT IS SEEN
HAVING ITS ENGINE STARTED BY A HUCKS STARTER.
ABOVE: A6M2 ZERO FIGHTER OF THE TAINAN KOKUTAI
DURING THE LONG FLIGHT BETWEEN FORMOSA AND THE
MANILA AREA. LT WAKOO'S V-117 CARRIES A LONG-RANGE
FUEL TANK BENEATH THE FUSELAGE.

Squadron claimed five or six of the A6Ms shot down, Lieutenants Joseph Moore and Carl Gies each claiming two, but against the weight of opposition, 11 P-40s were lost.

The 3rd Ku lost only one of its fighters initially, but 16 more were hit and four of these were obliged to make force-landings as they made the return flight to Formosa. Finding no US fighters over Manila on arrival, the Zero pilots had gone down to strafe first, but must have attacked many of the wrecks left on 8 December, for their claims totalled 34 destroyed on the ground, including six B-17s, none of which were lost on 10 December; most of those destroyed were trainers, liaison aircraft or obsolete types, actual losses being well below the claimed level. The Zeros had then climbed up to meet the attacking P-40s and in the dogfight which followed had over-claimed or double-claimed quite extensively, believing that they had shot down 27 and three probables. Enthusiasm was getting the better of their judgement for when they also encountered some patrolling PBY Catalina flyingboats of PatWing 10 during their mission, three of these were claimed to be shot down while only two were actually lost.

The Americans were attempting to strike back in the meantime. Three other PBYs had bombed Japanese shipping, claiming a hit on a battleship — in fact they had near-missed the cruiser *Ashigawa*. Six B-17s from the 14th Squadron had also gone out after ships, the Aparri force being their main target. Little damage was done, but after one B-17C flown by Lt Colin Kelly Jnr had bombed one vessel without success (although later he was to be credited, incorrectly, with having sunk the battleship *Haruna*) it was intercepted by some of the Tainan Ku Zeros which had been patrolling over Vigan. Repeatedly the Zeros attacked without apparent effect, but at last it began to burn as it neared Clark Field. Kelly ordered his crew to bale out, which they did while he held the aircraft steady, but it blew up before he could follow them. The first US air hero of the war, he was awarded a posthumous DSO, while an address in his honor was read by the President personally over the radio.

This was the first time the Japanese had encountered one of the Fortresses in the air but already the bomber was something of a legend in its own time for its supposed invincibility. Even though the C and D model B-17s used initially in the Philippines were less heavily-armed than the later and much more numerous Es, Fs, and Gs, it was still a formidable opponent, difficult to catch with its high speed and altitude.

An hour or so later more B-17s attacked, this time being intercepted by Army Ki27s from the 50th Sentai which managed to inflict severe damage on one of the bombers despite their light armament. The forces remaining available to the US command for aerial operations were now critically weakened; by the end of the day no more than 22

TWO LEADING PILOTS OF THE PHILIPPINES CAMPAIGN – DECEMBER 1941

One pilot who stood out amongst those of the US air forces in the Philippines was Lt Boyd D 'Buzz' Wagner. During two raids on the airfields captured by the Japanese army in Northern Luzon, Wagner had been credited with shooting down five Nakajima Ki27 fighters and destroying at least as many more on the ground. Awarded a DSC, he was evacuated before the fall of Bataan and later served in New Guinea as a staff officer with 5th Air Force Fighter Command as Director of Fighters at Port Moresby.

He occasionally flew on operations, and on 30 April, 1942 led a flight of Bell P-39 Airacobras of the 35th Fighter Group over Lae, New Guinea, claiming three Zeros shot down to become 5th Air Force top ace, a position he held for several months. After returning to the US in 1943, he crashed at Elgin Air Force Base during a routine flight in a P-40 and was tragically killed outright.

Saburo Sakai

Saburo Sakai was an NCO pilot with the Tainan Kokutai on Formosa in December 1941, having seen action over China during 1938-41. He took part in the first strike over the Philippines on 8 December 1941, sharing the first victory here against the US — one of the intercepting P-40s over Clark Field. Two days later he was involved in the combat with Colin Kelly's B-17 and subsequently gained numerous victories during raids on the Dutch East Indies, claiming his 13th on 28 February 1942. He later operated from Lae, northern New Guinea, gaining many victories against US and Australian aircraft here — particularly P-40s and P-39s.

When the US landings on Guadalcanal began on 8 August 1942 he was top Navy fighter pilot with 58 victories, although many of these were shared or probables. Over Guadalcanal, he was credited with four more victories, but was badly wounded and lost an eye. He subsequently became an instructor and test pilot, but returned to combat over Iwo Jima in June 1944 with the Yokosuka Kokutai. On the last day of the war he and another pilot jointly shot down a B-29 bomber, making his total stated score 64.

Commissioned an Ensign in March 1945, he was one of only three Navy pilots to have his achievements recognized while still alive.

LT BOYD D 'BUZZ' WAGNER, 24TH PURSUIT GROUP.

P-40s, eight P-35As, 18 B-17s, and 24 PBYs remained serviceable, although mechanics were working round the clock to add to this number. Fortunately for the US forces, 11 December proved to be another day of bad weather which brought a lull in the assault again, although three more B-17s and a P-40 were lost in accidents. Arrangements could now be made for the personnel of the 3rd Pursuit Squadron to be shipped out, as they no longer had any aircraft available, while the 17th and 20th Squadrons were amalgamated. Meanwhile, the 21st left Del Carmen for the strip at Hermosa.

Japanese positions are secured

The Japanese too were on the move. The landings in the north had met no real resistance, since the US command correctly assessed them to be preliminaries to something larger. As a result the newly-captured airfields could be confirmed as secure, and during 11 December the Ki27s of the 50th Sentai flew in to Aparri. Next day a further landing was made at Legaspi in the very far south of Luzon, and this too was virtually unopposed. Once again possession of a strategically-placed airfield was the main Japanese purpose, but following their successful landing here, the Kimura Detachment advanced north up the Bicol Peninsula to the narrow neck of land at Atimonen, where it links with the main land mass of Luzon. Here, however, they were repulsed with heavy losses — in the only successful engagement of the campaign for the Filipino forces.

While their initial landings at Legaspi were under way on 12 December, IJNAF units again took off from Formosa for a third heavy strike against the Luzon air bases. Thirty-six G3Ms of the 1st Ku split into two formations to attack Clark and Iba, while 27 Kanoya Ku G4Ms also raided the former airfield, and 52 more of these bombers from the Takeo Ku raided the Philippine Air Force's fighter base at Batangas. Escort was this time provided by 3rd Ku A6Ms, while the Tainan Ku fighters flew an independent sweep to Subic Bay, seeking the Navy PBYs at anchor. They found what they were looking for, sweeping in low to leave four of the Catalinas in flames, with two or three more damaged.

Meanwhile, the main force had come in beneath cloud to attack Iba and Clark Field, but the reduced altitude necessary brought them within range of the AA defenses, 12 G3M bombers of the 1st Ku being hit. Five P-26As of the Philippine 6th Pursuit Squadron had been scrambled on this occasion, Capt Jesus Villamor leading these to attack a formation of 27 bombers, one of which he was credited with shooting down. This may have been one of the 1st Ku G3Ms, which force-landed near Clark Field. 3rd Ku A6M fighters attacked the little force of elderly interceptors, one flown by Lt Antonio Mondigo being shot down at once, the pilot baling out, while two more were badly shot up. As the Japanese followed the Filipinos back to Batangas, a sixth

P-26A, which had been sent off on a reconnaissance, arriving back low on fuel was also shot down.

Fighting was so fierce that several sections of Zeros attacked the P-26As at once, each believing that they were responsible for despatching the defenders, so that eight claims were submitted. At Batangas it was thought that the 6th Squadron had accounted for one Zero as well as its single victory over the bombers — the latter being the first such claimed since the raids had begun.

With the fight over and the Japanese bombers safely dispersed, one Chutai from the 3rd Ku then flew over to repeat the earlier strafe on Subic Bay, claiming a further six PBYs in flames. Several of these were obviously aircraft already hit by the Tainan Ku pilots, for *total* PatWing 10 losses during the two attacks amounted to seven PBYs destroyed. The PAF also reported that one formation of Japanese aircraft had struck their airfield at Maniques, where the 7th Advanced Training School Squadron, 10th Bombardment Squadron (equipped only with two B-10s) and 8th Air Base Unit were situated; 11 of the 17 aircraft at this airfield were destroyed.

The US offers little resistance

The main point of interest to the Japanese concerning the raids of 12 December was the very limited opposition encountered — only five old Filipino fighters; and now the assault would be stepped up. With fighter support now available in Northern Luzon, the IJAAF joined the assault on the Manila area airfields. On 13 December, eight 24th Sentai Ki27 fighters strafed Del Carmen airfield while nine more from the 50th Sentai attacked Clark Field. The 24th Sentai then attacked the same target, followed by six Ki21 bombers of the 14th Sentai, while a force of 17 of the lighter Ki48s from the 8th Sentai flew from Formosa to bomb Baguio, and 50th Sentai fighters shot-up Cabantuan for their second target of the day. The Navy units then followed up with a further round of bombing and strafing attacks on Del Carmen, Nicholls and Iba Fields, Olongapo and Camp Morphie.

Eleven G4Ms of the Kanoya Ku were hit by AA over Nicholls, but little other opposition was met. A few P-40s appeared and were engaged by the Zeros, each of the fighter units suffering one loss, while one US fighter was claimed shot down, and four more were claimed on the ground at Del Carmen. The Japanese Army aircraft then returned to attack again.

However, the US were able to offer some resistance in the shape of Lt Boyd Wagner of the 17th Squadron. He was flying up to Aparri in a P-40E on a reconnaissance when he was intercepted by two Ki27s, both of which he shot down. He then strafed the airfield, claiming between five and seven more destroyed on the ground. At this point he was attacked by three more Ki27s, but managed to down two more of these before escaping. This one attack would seem to have accounted for a good proportion of the 18 Ki27s lost in the Philippines by the IJAAF during the first eight days of the war.

However, the next day the Japanese Army Air Force maintained the assault on Luzon, while the Navy began moving a small air contingent to the newly-captured airfield at Legaspi in Southern Luzon. Six Takeo Ku G4Ms, and nine Tainan Ku A6Ms, plus a couple of reconnaissance C5Ms, moved in here. No sooner had they arrived than three B-17s approached to bomb the vessels offshore, since it had been reported that an aircraft carrier was present.

This was not the case — it was a seaplane tender, the *Chitose*, which was supporting the landings. One Mitsubishi F1M float biplane from this vessel and two A6Ms intercepted as the trio of bombers attacked singly.

The first bomber was shot down, the second escaped interception and the third was badly damaged: it flew back to Del Monte, but arrived in darkness, and trying to find the airfield could only succeed in crash-landing at Cagayen. The crew claimed three attacking fighters shot down — whereas none had actually been lost. A more effective attack on the Japanese at Legaspi was made that evening, however, by a lone P-40, which inflicted damage on two A6Ms and five of the G4Ms.

Continued Army and Navy air attacks on the airfields on 15 December were designed more to keep them neutralized than to inflict further damage, for there was now little remaining to attack. The series of major assaults which had virtually destroyed US air power in the Philippines had cost the IJNAF just ten bombers (four G4Ms and six G3Ms) and 23 A6M fighters to all causes: four bomber crews and 13 fighter pilots had been killed.

The Americans were now carefully husbanding the aircraft remaining to them but on 16 December three P-40s, each carrying six 20lb bombs, flew north to attack Vigan airfield. Here Lt Russell M Church Jnr's aircraft was hit by AA and set on fire, but he completed his attack before crashing in flames. A single Ki27 took off to intercept, but was shot down by Boyd Wagner for his fifth victory — the first ace of the war for the US forces, he was awarded a DSC.

Strafing and bombing attacks by Japanese aircraft continued daily, while on 19 December the airfield at Del Monte was at last discovered by four A6Ms from Legaspi. Reporting four B-17s and seven twin-engined bombers here, the Japanese pilots claimed two of the former and three of the latter in flames, and the rest destroyed. In fact no B-17s were hit, though three B-18As were destroyed. This attack did, however, precipitate the withdrawal of the surviving B-17s to Australia, which had already been ordered, and 13 left that evening. On the same day PatWing 10 left Subic Bay for Borneo with its last ten PBYs. Only a remaining handful of fighters were left. Japanese air forces had done their job well.

Japanese pressure increases

Next day more Japanese forces landed at Davao in Southern Mindanao, where a base for attacks on Borneo was desired. Eight Kawanishi H6K flyingboats bombed Del Monte to prevent any interference while A6Ms strafed other airfields in Southern Luzon. General Homma was now close to launching his main invasion, and on 21 December a force of Navy floatplanes arrived at Vigan to support it. This included 12 F1M biplanes, an E-13A and three Kawasaki E-7K cruiser floatplanes. Over the next few days these aircraft joined in the general assault on the Luzon airfields and other targets.

Raids in general were stepped up again and A6Ms strafed Batangas, claiming five fighters destroyed here — probably the residue of the Filipino P-26As. Then, on 22 December a force of 76 transport vessels covered by seven cruisers and 20 destroyers sailed into Lingayen Gulf on the western side of Central Luzon and began landing 80 000 troops. US fighters were immediately sent off to bomb and strafe, but caused little damage, one P-40 being claimed shot down by patrolling Ki27s. B-17s then struggled

THIS RARE PHOTO DEPICTS ONE OF THE USAAF'S SEVERSKY P-35A FIGHTERS OF THE 34TH PURSUIT SQUADRON CAPTURED ALMOST INTACT BY THE JAPANESE ON A PHILIPPINE AIRFIELD.

through from Australia to bomb, but gained no hits. The Filipino-American forces could do little more than make a fighting retreat as the Japanese advanced south through the central plain towards Manila.

Two days later another force of 24 transports, a cruiser and six destroyers sailed into Lamon Bay, to the east of Manila, to begin a further set of landings by the 16th Division. The remaining US fighters, all now concentrated into the 17th Squadron, moved to Pilar airstrip on the Bataan Peninsula on the opposite side of Manila Bay to the capital, and from here 12 P-40s and six P-35As were despatched against these new landings. Patrolling F1M float biplanes shot down two of the P-35As, and little damage was done to the Japanese forces.

American evacuation begins

So good had been the progress of the Lingayen invasion that the floatplane detachment at Vigan was withdrawn on Christmas Day. Nevertheless, on 26 December a strong force of G3Ms and G4Ms from Formosa bombed shipping in Manila Bay, claiming three merchant ships sunk and other vessels damaged. On 27 December Manila was declared an open city to protect it from further bombing since it could clearly not be defended, and the remaining elements of the defense forces began withdrawing into the defensible Bataan Peninsula where they would make their last stand. With them went 20 P-40s and two P-35As. Even as the evacuation began Navy bombers again attacked Manila Bay, this time claiming nine merchant vessels sunk and six damaged. Army fighters claimed two P-40s shot down over Lingayen.

The last major involvement of the IJNAF in the fighting occurred on 29 December when the fortified island of Corregidor, off the southern tip of the Bataan Peninsula (at the mouth of Manila Bay) was attacked in a rare combined Army/Navy effort. Eighteen 14th Sentai Ki21s, 22 8th Sentai Ki48s, 18 16th Sentai Ki30s, 41 Takao Ku G4Ms and 36 1st Ku G3Ms unloaded a considerable tonnage of high explosive onto the very small island under a protective 'umbrella' of Ki27s from the 24th and 50th Sentais; opposition was minimal and there were no Japanese casualties.

Thereafter the air battle was virtually over. The Navy bombers turned their attention elsewhere as the Army prepared to reduce the defenders of Bataan in a mainly ground operation. In this they were supported by a reducing force of IJAAF units, while the last of the US fighters continued to operate from time to time, generally in a reconnaissance role, but with an occasional fighter-bomber attack when a special target presented itself.

On 31 December 17 American fighter pilots were evacuated as their services were no longer needed, while on 2 January, 1942 the Japanese 14th Army occupied Manila and the Cavite Navy Yard. The defenders of the Bataan Peninsula held on until final surrender on 9 April and Corregidor finally capitulated on 6 May when all hope was gone. By this time, however, US/Australian forces had gone onto the offensive in New Guinea, while but a few days later the whole course of the Pacific War was changed by the unexpected and stunning US victory at the aircraft carrier Battle of Midway. But that was the future. At the end of 1941, the Philippines invasion stood out as the most shattering and complete defeat US armies were ever to suffer, and as one of the swiftest and most total defeats of one modern air force by another to occur during the entire Second World War.

CHAPTER FOUR

THE LONG STRUGGLE FOR MALTA

1940-1942

Overleaf

Supermarine Spitfire V fighters of 126 Squadron, RAF, taxi towards the
runway as yet another dive-bomber attack erupts on Luqa airfield, Malta, in summer 1942. A damaged
Spitfire returns to make an emergency landing.

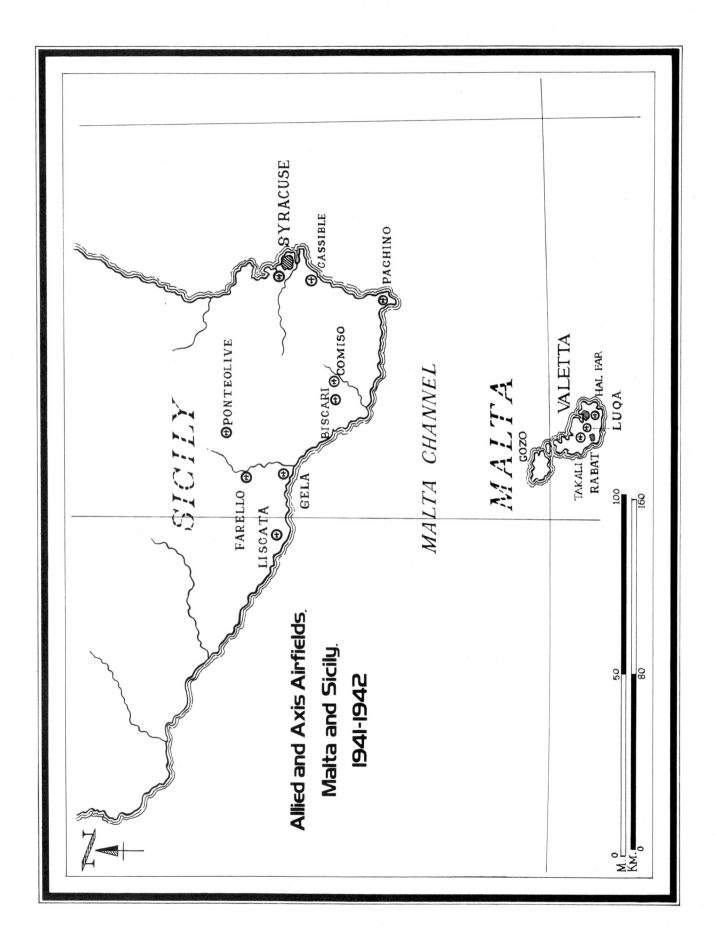

SICILY

SYRACUSE

CASSIBLE

PACHINO

PONTEOLIVE

COMISO

BISCARI

FARELLO

LISCATA

GELA

MALTA CHANNEL

MALTA

VALETTA

HAL FAR

GOZO

LUQA

TAKALI

RABAT

Allied and Axis Airfields.
Malta and Sicily.
1941-1942

N

M. 0   50   100
KM. 0   80   160

The little island of Malta lies strategically in the middle of the Mediterranean Sea. Situated approximately 60 miles to the south of Sicily, it is well-placed to dominate the sea routes between North Africa and Southern Europe. Sitting astride the narrow central 'waist' of the sea, it is also positioned to deny east–west passage to vessels travelling between the Suez Canal and the straits of Gibraltar.

Its promise as an offensive base from which to deny supplies and reinforcements to the Italian army in Libya was obvious to both Axis and Allied high commands. Consequently, Malta became a priority target for Italy's Regia Aeronautica, while even before the outbreak of hostilities, efforts had been put in hand by the British to provide some form of defense.

Initially, the defense comprised a handful of Royal Navy Sea Gladiator biplanes, taken over by the RAF and manned by a number of staff and flyingboat pilots. These undertook the initial interceptions of the first Italian raids. They were soon joined by a few Hurricanes and ferry pilots, diverted from last minute reinforcement flights to Egypt via France and Tunisia. The fall of France prevented any further such flights, but on 2 August 1940 the old aircraft carrier *Argus* flew off 12 Hurricanes of 418 Flight within range of Malta. These were flown by trained fighter pilots, some of whom already had experience of operations over Dunkirk, and together with the elements already on the island, these formed the nucleus of a new unit, 261 Squadron, which was then formed.

Preoccupied elsewhere, the Axis reduced the number of raids, expecting a British capitulation. This did not come. Indeed the British redoubled efforts to strengthen Malta. As soon as war had broken out a squadron of Royal Navy torpedo-bombers — Fairey Swordfish biplanes — had flown to the island from Southern France (830 Squadron). These had been joined in September by a few Martin Maryland reconnaissance-bombers which formed 431 Flight for long-range reconnaissance duties. Next month came 148 Squadron with Vickers Wellington night bombers, while big, four-engined Short Sunderland flyingboats from Egypt used the island's floatplane facilities at Kalafrana Bay as an operating and refueling base. Efforts to reinforce the fighters proved less successful when *Argus* flew off another dozen Hurricanes on 17 November. This time the ship launched its cargo too far west of the island and only four arrived, the rest ditching in the sea when their fuel ran out; several of the pilots were lost.

Despite this setback, two convoys loaded with supplies reached the island unscathed during this period, 60 000 tons of fuel, ammunition, spares and food being unloaded. By the close of 1940 the defending fighters had claimed 45 Italian aircraft destroyed, for relatively minimal losses. The Regia Aeronautica admitted the loss of 23 bombers and 12 fighters to the British defenses, a further 187 bombers and seven fighters having suffered damage, mainly to AA shell splinters.

By now, the Wellingtons were regularly attacking targets in southern Italy, Sicily, Albania and in the Tripolitanian province of Libya, while Swordfish attacked supply shipping on its way from Italy to Libya. The reconnaissance Marylands were very active in seeking the supply convoys and also played a part in the attack by Swordfish from the British carrier HMS *Illustrious* on the Italian Battle Fleet in Taranto harbor during November which resulted in two battleships being sunk. Indeed, at the end of the year 431 Flight, strengthened by the arrival of several more aircraft, was expanded into 69 Squadron.

However, because of Italian setbacks, Mussolini now asked Hitler for aid and he acquiesced, but a prerequisite was to neutralize British naval power in the Mediterranean to secure the sea supply lines. So, late in December 1940 the first elements of the Luftwaffe's X Fliegerkorps, a formation experienced in anti-shipping operations, began arriving in Sicily from Norway and France.

By early January 1941 Fliegerkorps X had available two Gruppen of Ju87B dive-bombers, one Gruppe of He111 medium bombers, one Gruppe of Bf110C heavy fighters, and a reconnaissance Staffel of Ju88 aircraft. The Luftwaffe first struck on 10 January when Major Walter Enneccerus led the Stukas of II/StG2 in a damaging attack on the carrier *Illustrious* as she passed close to Malta, the attack subsequently being repeated by I/StG2. Heavily-damaged, the carrier limped into Malta's Grand Harbour for urgent temporary repairs, while the remains of her fighter unit, the Fairey Fulmar-equipped 806 Squadron, flew in to the island's airfields. Next day II/StG2 went out again after the rest of the Mediterranean Fleet, which was retiring to Alexandria, and sank the cruiser *Southampton*.

Germany turns its attention to Malta

Thereafter, the focus of attack was turned on Malta, and particularly on *Illustrious* in the dockyard. Further reinforcement followed, two Gruppen of Ju88A bombers reaching Sicily early in January, followed by a third in mid-February. Daily through late January big formations of German bombers appeared overhead, escorted by Bf110s, and by Italian Fiat CR42 and Macchi C 200 fighters. While the Hurricanes put up a hard fight and took a heavy toll of the raiders, the sheer numbers involved, coupled with attacks on the airfields, soon began to take their toll. Nonetheless, the carrier escaped further damage whilst repairs were made, and on 23 January it was able to set sail for the United States, where more complete repairs could be undertaken in conditions of complete safety.

Thereafter the attacks reduced somewhat, particularly when several Staffeln of Ju87 and Bf110s were diverted to Libya to support the fledgling Afrika Korps there. A single reinforcement of six Hurricanes had been flown to Malta from North Africa at the end of January, together with about double that number of pilots, but this did not even make good recent losses. However, 261 Squadron was about to enter its most difficult period, for on 9 February 7/JG26 arrived in Sicily, led by one of the Luftwaffe's top 'Experten' of the Battle of Britain, Oberleutnant Joachim Müncheberg, who had 23 victories to his credit already. Müncheberg made his first claim for a Hurricane shot down over Malta three days later and thereafter this single Staffel, with never more than nine Messerschmitt Bf109E fighters available, was to rule the skies.

Fliegerkorps X renewed its attacks on Malta on 1 March and a series of hard and costly interception battles followed. Nearly all the Wellingtons were destroyed on the ground, Royal Navy warships and the Sunderland flyingboats were prevented from using the island, and Malta's offensive capacity reduced almost to nil. Early in March five more Hurricanes were flown across from Africa, followed later in the month by a detachment of seven from 274 Squadron, but most of these quickly fell victim to the marauding Bf109Es.

At last at the start of April came another delivery of

MAIN ROYAL AIR FORCE UNITS OPERATING OVER MALTA

UNIT	AIRCRAFT	DATE
FIRST PERIOD, JUNE 1940 – FEBRUARY 1942		
Fighter Units		
261 Squadron	Hurricane I	Aug 40 – May 41
806 Squadron (Det)	Fulmar I	Jan 41 – Mar 41
185 Squadron	Hurricane I, IIA,B,C	May 41 – Feb 42
249 Squadron	Hurricane I,IIA,B	May 41 – Feb 42
46 Squadron		
(renumbered 126)	Hurricane II,B,C	Jun 41 – Feb 42
MNFU (1435 Flight)	Hurricane II,B,C	Dec 41 – Feb 42
800 Squadron (Det)	Fulmar I	May 41 – Nov 41
242 Squadron (part)	Hurricane II,B,C	Nov 41 – Feb 42
605 Squadron (part)	Hurricane II,B,C	Nov 41 – Feb 42
Strike Fighter Units detached to Malta		
252 Squadron (Det)	Beaufighter I	May 41
252/272 Squadron (Det)	Beaufighter I	Jul 41 – Aug 41
272 Squadron (Det)	Beaufighter I	Aug 41 — Sept 41
113 Squadron (Det)	Blenheim IVF	Sep 41
252 Squadron (Det)	Beaufighter I	Dec 41
Bomber Units Serving on Malta, 1940-42		
148, 37, 38, 221 (Special Flight),		
104, 40 Squadrons	Wellingtons	
21, 139, 82, 110, 105,		
107, 18 Squadrons	Blenheim IV	
830 Squadron, Fleet Air		
Arm	Swordfish	
828 Squadrons, Fleet		
Air Arm	Albacores	
NB Bomber Squadrons arranged in order of arrival on Malta		
Reconnaissance Units		
431 Flight		Sep 40 – Jan 41
Became 69 Squadron		Jan 41 – Feb 42

UNIT	AIRCRAFT	DATE
SECOND PERIOD, MARCH-NOVEMBER 1942		
Fighter Units		
249 Squadron	Spitfire V	Mar 42 – Nov 42
126 Squadron	Hurricane IIB,C;	
	Spitfire V	Mar 42 – Nov 42
185 Squadron	Hurricane IIB,C;	
	Spitfire V	Mar 42 – Nov 42
1435 Flight	Hurricane IIB,C;	
	Beaufighter I	Mar 42 – Aug 42
229 Squadron	Hurricane IIC	Mar 42 – May 42
601 Squadron	Spitfire V	Apr 42 – Jun 42
603 Squadron	Spitfire V	Apr 42 – Jul 42
229 Squadron		
(reformed)	Spitfire V	Aug 42 – Nov 42
1435 Squadron		
(reformed)	Spitfire V	Jul 42 – Nov 42
89 Squadron (Det)	Beaufighter I	Jun 42 – Nov 42
NB 242 and 605 Squadrons amalgamated into 185 Squadron in March 1942. 229 and 1435 Squadrons reformed mainly from 603 Squadron personnel		
Strike Fighter Units		
235 Squadron (Det)	Beaufighter I	Jun 42 – Aug 42
252 Squadron (Det)	Beaufighter I	Jul 42
248 Squadron	Beaufighter I	Jul 42 – Aug 42
252 Squadron (Det)	Beaufighter I	Aug 42
227 Squadron*	Beaufighter I	Aug 42 – Nov 42
*formed from the 235 Squadron Detachment		
Bomber Units		
37 Squadron	Wellington	Feb 42 – Mar 42
104 Squadron	Wellington	May 42 – Jun 42
38 Squadron (Det)	Wellington	Jun 42
217 Squadron (Det)	Beaufort	Jun 42
39 Squadron	Beaufort	Sep 42 – Oct 42
830 Squadron, FAA	Swordfish; Albacore	Mar 42 – Nov 42
Reconnaissance Units		
69 Squadron	Maryland; Baltimore;	
	Spitfire	Mar 42 – Nov 42

fighters by carrier, HMS *Ark Royal* flying off 12 new Hurricane IIAs, returning later in the month to deliver a further 23. 7/JG26 had been transferred briefly to southern Italy for operations over Yugoslavia on 6 April; when it returned to Sicily it was joined for a few days by the similarly-equipped III/JG27, which operated over Malta briefly before returning to Germany. While occasional raids continued to be made, particularly by night, the Luftwaffe effort was waning as units began withdrawing north prior to the assault on the Soviet Union, and by the end of May all had gone except 7/JG26 and a single reconnaissance Staffel.

British defenses are strengthened
The reduction in the German effort over Malta coincided with a British build-up there. During April a destroyer flotilla again moved to the island, while early May brought further deliveries of Hurricanes, together with the arrival of a squadron of Bristol Beaufighter twin-engined strike fighters. There were now some 50 Hurricanes on the island and on 12 May 1941, a second squadron — 185 — was formed at Hal Far. Mid May saw the arrival of 82 Squadron from the United Kingdom via Gibraltar. This was a light bomber squadron from Bomber Command's No 2 Group, equipped with Bristol Blenheim IVs. It was the first of several units which were to be despatched in rotation to the island for temporary attachment during which they would undertake low-level anti-shipping operations.

Some larger deliveries of Hurricanes were made during late May and early June from the carriers *Furious*, *Victorious* and *Ark Royal*, but many of these flew on to the Middle East after refueling, to join the forces supporting the army in Egypt. They were led to their destination by the Beaufighters of 252 Squadron, which ended their brief stay on the island. Of those that stayed, 249 Squadron arrived on 21 May, taking over from 261 Squadron. The remnants of this tired unit flew to Palestine where the squadron was disbanded. Early in June came 46 Squadron's air party; a ground echelon was formed for the unit on the island, and it was renumbered 126. Surplus Hurricanes were then formed into a special nightfighter flight which was subsequently to be numbered 1435.

With the departure of the Luftwaffe, more Italian units had returned to Sicily, including units of Savoia S.79 bombers which had been the main type employed during 1940, Cant Z.1007bis, and Fiat BR20s — the latter for use mainly by night. For fighter operations several Gruppi of Macchi C 200 monoplanes and a few CR42 biplanes arrived. Early in June 7/JG26 left for Africa, having claimed 41 victories over Malta — most of them Hurricanes; 19 of these had been credited to Müncheberg alone!

Italian tactics mainly involved the despatch of large formations of fighters, grouped around a small nucleus of perhaps three bombers, in an effort to bring the Hurricanes

MAIN LUFTWAFFE UNITS OPERATING OVER MALTA

UNIT	AIRCRAFT	UNIT	AIRCRAFT
FIRST PERIOD, JANUARY – JUNE 1941		**THIRD PERIOD, JULY – AUGUST 1942**	
Stukageschwader 2		**Jagdgeschwader 53**	
I, II Gruppen	Junkers Ju87B	Stab, II Gruppe	Messerschmitt Bf109F
Kampfgeschwader 26		**Jagdgeschwader 77**	
II Gruppe	Heinkel He111H	I Gruppe	Messerschmitt Bf109F
Lehrgeschwader 1		Küstenfliegergruppe 606	Junkers Ju88A (Became I/KG 77)
Stab, II, III Gruppen	Junkers Ju88A	Kampfgruppe 806	Junkers Ju88A (Became III/KG 54)
Kampfgeschwader 30		**Kampfgeschwader 77**	
III Gruppe	Junkers Ju88A (from February)	Stab, II, III Gruppen	Junkers Ju88A
Zerstörergeschwader 26		1(F)/121	Junkers Ju88D
III Gruppe	Messerschmitt Bf110	**FINAL PERIOD, OCTOBER 1942**	
Jagdgeschwader 26			
7 Staffel	Messerschmitt Bf109E (from February)	**Jagdgeschwader 27**	
Jagdgeschwader 27		I Gruppe	Messerschmitt Bf109F/G
III Gruppe	Messerschmitt Bf109E (May only)	**Jagdgeschwader 53**	
1(F)/121	Junkers Ju88D	Stab, I, II, III Gruppen	Messerschmitt Bf109F/G
SECOND PERIOD, DECEMBER 1941 – MAY 1942		**Jagdgeschwader 77**	
		I Gruppe	Messerschmitt Bf109F/G
Kampfgeschwader 54		**Kampfgeschwadre 54**	
I Gruppe	Junkers Ju88A	Stab, I, III Gruppen	Junkers Ju88A
Kampfgeschwader 77		**Kampfgeschwader 77**	
II, III Gruppen	Junkers Ju88A	Stab, I, II, III Gruppen	Junkers Ju88A
Küstenfliegergruppe 606	Junkers Ju88A	**Lehrgeschwader 1**	
Kampfgruppe 806	Junkers Ju88A	II Gruppe	Junkers Ju88A
Stukageschwader 3		**Kampfgeschwader 100 (part)**	Heinkel He111H
Stab, I, II, III Gruppen	Junkers Ju87B (later Ju87D)	**Stukageschwader 3**	
Jagdgeschwader 53		II Gruppe	Junkers Ju87D (did not operate)
Stab, I, II, III Gruppen	Messerschmitt Bf109F	1(F)/121	Junkers Ju88D
Jagdgeschwader 3		**Schlachtgeschwader 2**	
II Gruppe	Messerschmitt Bf109F	I Gruppe	Messerschmitt Bf109E/F (late October only)
Nachtjagdgeschwader 2			
I Gruppe	Junkers Ju88C		
Zerstörergeschwader 26 (part)			
III Gruppe	Messerschmitt Bf110		
1(F)/121	Junkers Ju88D		

up to fight. In this they were usually successful, and many dogfights were fought over the island. However, the RAF pilots usually managed to shoot down more than they lost, and little damage was done on the ground by the minimal attack forces.

Now the Blenheims ranged far and wide over the Mediterranean, attacking supply convoys with telling effect. Even more effective were the activities of the island's destroyer flotillas, which on several occasions were successful in wiping out complete convoys which had been spotted for them by the persistent Marylands of 69 Squadron. More Beaufighters, this time of 272 Squadron, and further Wellington squadrons soon also reached the island, which was now fast becoming a major offensive base under the direction of the aggressive air commander, Air Vice-Marshal Hugh Pugh Lloyd, who had been sent out from England to orchestrate just such a 'hornet's nest'.

'Stocking up' continues

The last supply ships to reach Malta had done so in January 1941, before the start of the German offensive on the island. With the departure of the Luftwaffe further vessels were now sent to the island, 65 000 tons of supplies being delivered during July and 85 000 tons in September — but these were to be the last for a long time. So secure now was Malta that during October the Hurricane squadrons were able to begin some offensive operations over Sicily, some of their aircraft carrying a 250 lb bomb beneath each wing.

During October 1941 the Regia Aeronautica introduced into service the first of their improved Macchi C 202 fighters, powered by licence-built German Daimler-Benz DB 601 engines. These new aircraft were superior to the Hurricanes and whenever encountered proved difficult and dangerous opponents. They were still few in number, however, and their initial impact was small. Malta continued to strike and to strike hard, although the anti-shipping operations of the low-flying Blenheims proved extremely costly and each of the rotating detachments to the island tended to end when the unit had lost all its aircraft, rather than when it flew out of Malta.

On 12 November *Ark Royal* and *Argus* returned, carrying the greater part of the air parties of two new squadrons, 242 and 605, which were flown to the island. As the carriers returned to bring the rest of these units and a third

LUFTWAFFE JAGDFLIEGER OF 7/JG26 TRIES LOCAL TRANSPORT IN SICILY, SPRING 1941. BEHIND HIM IS ONE OF THE UNIT'S BF 109E FIGHTERS WHICH RULED THE SKIES OVER MALTA AT THIS TIME.

MAIN REGIA AERONAUTICA UNITS OPERATING OVER MALTA

UNIT	AIRCRAFT
FIRST PERIOD, JUNE 1940 – FEBRUARY 1941	
2ª Squadra Aerea	
1ª Divisione Aerea CT	
1° Stormo CT (17°, 157° Gruppo)	Fiat CR32, CR42
6° Gruppo Autonomo	Macchi C 200
3ª Divisione Aerea BT	
11° Stormo BT (33°, 34° Gruppo)	Savoia S-79
34° Stormo BT (52°, 53° Gruppo)	Savoia S-79
41° Stormo BT (59°, 60° Gruppo)	Savoia S-79
11ª Divisione Aerea BT	
30° Stormo BT (87°, 90° Gruppo)	Savoia S-79
36° Stormo BT (108°, 109° Gruppo)	Savoia S-79
96° Gruppo Ba'T	Savoia S-85 (later Junkers Ju87B)
SECOND PERIOD, JUNE 1941 – DECEMBER 1941	
30° Stormo BT (87°, 90° Gruppo)	Savoia S-79 (left August)
10° Stormo BT (30°, 32° Gruppo)	Savoia S-79
43° Stormo BT (31°, 99° Gruppo)	Fiat BR20M
23° Gruppo Autonomo CT	Fiat CR42
7° Gruppo CT	Macchi C 200
101° Gruppo Ba'T	Junkers Ju87B
278ª Squadriglia AutAS	Savoia S-79sil
282ª Squadriglia AutAS	Savoia S-79sil
54° Stormo CT (10°, 16° Gruppo)	Macchi C 200
9° Stormo BT (29°, 33° Gruppo)	Cant Z.1007bis (from August)
4° Stormo CT (9°, 10° Gruppo)	Macchi C 202 (from September)
3° Stormo BT (55°, 116° Gruppo)	Fiat BR20M (from October)
THIRD PERIOD, 1942 (AT VARIOUS TIMES)	
4° Stormo CT (9°, 10° Gruppo)	Macchi C 202 (April-May only)
51° Stormo CT (20°, 155° Gruppo)	Macchi C 202 (from June)
54° Stormo CT (7°, 16° Gruppo)	Macchi C 200; C 202 (to July only)
153° Gruppo CT	Macchi C 200
2° Gruppo CT	Reggiane Re2001
22° Gruppo CT	Reggiane Re2001
7° Stormo BT (4°, 25° Gruppo)	Savoia S-84
9° Stormo BT (29°, 33° Gruppo)	Cant Z.1007bis
88° Gruppo BT	Fiat BR20M
116° Gruppo BT	Fiat BR20M
10° Stormo BT (30°, 32° Gruppo)	Savoia S-79
132° Gruppo AS	Savoia S-79sil
101° Gruppo Ba'T	Junkers Ju87B (July only)
102° Gruppo Ba'T	Junkers Ju87B

squadron, *Ark Royal* was torpedoed by a submarine and sank. No more Hurricanes would be brought in thereafter. Since August 1940, 12 separate carrier deliveries of Hurricanes had been undertaken, 361 fighters being ferried, of which 303 reached Malta; about 150 of them flew on to North Africa. Two more deliveries had been made, one of Swordfish to reinforce 830 Squadron, and one in October 1941 bringing in the Fairey Albacore torpedo-bombers of 828 Squadron; all these aircraft had arrived safely. Eighteen more Hurricanes had reached Malta from North Africa during this period.

The importance of Malta

During mid November the long-awaited offensive by the British 8th Army had begun in Libya, and after hard fighting the Italo-German forces under General Erwin Rommel had been driven right back into Tripolitania again. The Axis armies found themselves critically short of supplies of all types, particularly of petrol. Malta's depredations had borne fruit and had played a genuine and substantial part in the result. So, the Luftwaffe was once more ordered to Sicily to neutralize this stubborn island for a second time. Campaigning in Soviet Russia had now settled into stalemate with the onset of winter and consequently late in November Feldmarschal Albert Kesselring's Headquarters arrived in Sicily, followed over the next few weeks by the operational units of II Fliegerkorps, several of which had first returned to Germany to re-equip. He eventually had five Gruppen of Ju88A bombers — two of them specialized anti-shipping units; four Gruppen of the latest Messer-schmitt Bf109F fighters; four Gruppen of Ju87Bs, and the usual back-up reconnaissance, liaison, transport and rescue Staffeln.

On arrival, however, one fighter Gruppe, III/JG53, and one of Stukas, I/StG3, were at once rushed to Africa where the situation was critical; III/JG53 would return early in January 1942. Operations by the German units began in mid December, and by the turn of the year the RAF in Malta was in dire trouble again. Against the Bf109F the Hurricane was completely outclassed, while the fast and heavily-armored Ju88 was a very difficult opponent also. By the end of the month only nine confirmed and eight probable victories had been claimed against a loss of ten Hurricanes in combat, but a substantially larger number on the ground.

The close of 1941 saw the end of the Hurricane's heyday on Malta, although it was to remain the main defense for several more months. Since June 1940 the defending fighters had claimed 199 confirmed and 78 probable victories, to which the AA defenses had added about 50 more claims. The cost in combat had been at least 90 Hurricanes, three Fulmars and one Gladiator; ten more Hurricanes and two Fulmars had been lost in accidents and many more had been destroyed on the ground.

Amongst the other units operating from the island up to the end of 1941, eight Marylands and two other reconnaissance aircraft, three Beaufighters and one fighter-Blenheim, and a very large number of bombers had been lost in action, with considerable additional numbers destroyed on the ground by bombing. Actual Axis losses amounted to 135 bomber types — 80 of them German — and 56 fighters, plus a number of other reconnaissance, rescue and transport aircraft. 261 Squadron's Sgt F N Robertson had been credited with ten victories, and Flt Lt J A F Maclachlan of this unit had claimed 8, a total equalled by Wg Cdr A C Rabagliati of 126 Squadron.

1942 was to prove the toughest, hardest-fought and most critical phase of the long siege. The first two months of the year saw desultory Luftwaffe raids on the island which the defending Hurricanes were hard-pressed to intercept. The January figures tell the story: only one victory could be claimed plus five probables and 12 damaged for the loss of eight Hurricanes. February saw some small improvement, with nine claimed shot down against losses of 11 Hurricanes in combat.

The other side of the coin was even grimmer, however. Fliegerkorps II had been joined by two Staffeln of Bf110s from III/ZG26 in Libya and by nightfighter elements of I/NJG2 from Germany, this latter unit flying fighter versions of the Ju88. Scouring the seas around Malta these twin-engined fighters intercepted the bomber and reconnaissance aircraft of Malta's striking force, more than 20 of these being shot down during the first two months of the year. By the end of February the air element of the striking force was down almost to zero.

Efforts to reinforce the island continued through February and March. The Beaufighters of 252 Squadron flew in again, together with the Wellingtons of 37 Squadron and reinforcement fighter pilots who were carried to Malta in a Sunderland flyingboat. Then on 7 March the carrier *Eagle* flew off 15 Spitfire Vs to re-equip 249 Squadron; these were the first fighter versions of the famous Spitfire to serve anywhere outside the United Kingdom, and were a most welcome reinforcement. They were few in number, however, and were too late to prevent the demise of the air striking force. The last of the Blenheim squadrons to operate from the island had been disbanded just before their arrival, while on 9 March the last of the recently arrived Wellingtons were destroyed on the ground.

Immediately after the arrival of the Spitfires, Fliegerkorps II opened a new offensive, formations of escorted Ju88s and offensive patrols of Bf109s appearing throughout the day on numerous occasions. The Spitfires were never able to operate at strengths greater than six aircraft, and within a few days two, three or four were all that could be scrambled at any one time, though often in company with four or six Hurricanes which continued to do the best they could. A dozen fighters were lost by the defenses during such operations in March, while 29 more aircraft were destroyed on the ground, but claims rose steeply to 31 confirmed, 20 probables and 65 damaged.

On 20 March a small convoy was again fought through to the island to deliver 5000 tons of supplies, while next day nine more Spitfires were flown off *Eagle*, this time for 126 Squadron. They came just in time, for 249 Squadron was already down to its last serviceable Spitfire, and the new aircraft had to be shared with the pilots of this unit. An

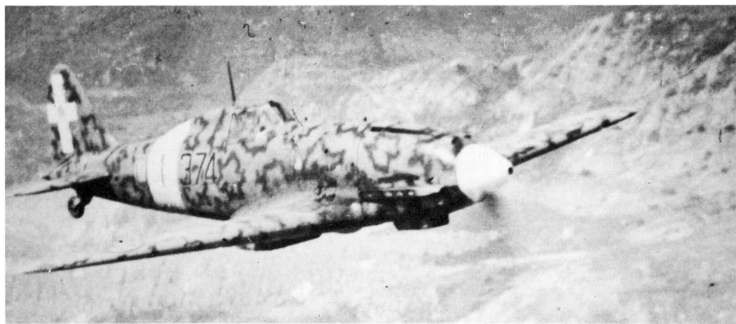

attempt to fight through a further convoy from the eastern end of the Mediterranean a few days later was foiled by the Luftwaffe, which inflicted heavy losses on the ships involved.

Crisis on the island

Malta was now beginning to get critically low on food, fuel and ammunition and a mere 5000 tons could not keep the defenses going for long. On 27 March, 11 Hurricane IIC fighters were flown in by pilots of 229 Squadron from North Africa, while two days later *Eagle* returned for a third time with seven more Spitfires; another eight Hurricanes would come from Africa late in April. From this area also came a few Beaufighter nightfighters to reinforce the few remaining Hurricanes of Malta's night-defense flight.

By now Fliegerkorps II was at full strength, its bomber force having been reinforced further by elements of LG1 from Crete, while improved Ju87D versions of the Stuka began reaching StG3 during late March. In April the attack continued at full intensity, the defenders operating as best they could. Indeed, April probably saw the defenses at their hardest pressed, and this became known as 'the cruellest month'; the island was now well on the way to becoming the most bombed place on earth. Yet still it continued to hold out; although bombed so heavily, their homes, towns and villages a mass of rubble and with morale frequently suffering, the population continued to give their support to the defenders. Malta's limestone rock, never far below the surface of its sparse vegetation, was easily worked, allowing deep air raid shelters and stores to be formed, and blast-proof aircraft pens built in profusion. Every night the day's bomb craters in the airfields would be filled in with the broken rock and rolled level with the few precious remaining steamrollers.

Help was on the way again, however. *Eagle* could carry only a small number of Spitfires at a time, while the newer *Victorious* could not fit them on its lifts to the hangars below deck because these had been designed to cope only with naval aircraft with folding wings. Consequently, Winston Churchill sought the aid of the Americans in solving the dilemma, the President, Franklin D Roosevelt agreeing to loan to the Royal Navy the carrier USS *Wasp* and her crew for a short period for such ferry duties. *Wasp* was ideal for the job and 47 Spitfires were loaded aboard her during April for delivery.

These were not the usual batches of replacement aircraft, but two full squadrons released from Fighter Command – 601 and 603, both well-known units of the Auxiliary Air Force. All but one of the fighters flew off safely on 20 April, but the Luftwaffe's reconnaissance aircraft had spotted their arrival, and no sooner were they on the ground than the Ju88s and Bf109s arrived to attack. The existing fighter defenses rose to the challenge, claiming seven and seven probables for the loss of three in combat, but by the end of the day 601 Squadron alone had lost two destroyed on the ground by bombs, while no less than 15 more had suffered damage.

Next day the Germans launched 325 bomber sorties over the Maltese airfields, where only 27 of the new Spitfires were serviceable and available to intercept. By the latter part of the month the defenders were lucky to be able to scramble six Spitfires to intercept an incoming raid, plus two more to cover them as they landed, when they were easy prey for marauding Messerschmitts which patrolled around

MAIN AIRCRAFT TYPES EMPLOYED OVER MALTA

BRITISH

Supermarine Spitfire VC (Trop) of 249 Squadron

Supermarine Spitfire V
Developed from the Mk I used in the Battle of Britain, the Mk V was powered by a Merlin 45 of 1470 hp, which provided an improved performance of 374 mph at 13 000 ft, a service ceiling of 37 000 ft and a range of 470 miles. Armament featured two 20 mm Hispano cannon in the wings and four 0.303 in Browning machine guns, two in each wing.

Hawker Hurricane I and II
The same Hurricane I as employed during the Battle of Britain, but fitted with a Vokes tropical air filter beneath the nose in many cases. Subsequently the eight-gun Mk IIA, 12-gun Mk IIB, and Mk IIC armed with four 20 mm Hispano cannon were all employed over the island.

Bristol Beaufighter
A large, heavy two-seat fighter, the Beaufighter was employed both as a long-range offensive aircraft by day, attacking Axis airfields and shipping, and as a nightfighter, in which role Airborne Interception radar was carried. Powered by two Bristol Hercules XI radial engines of 1590 hp each, the Beaufighter was a pugnacious-looking low-wing monoplane with a maximum speed of 323 mph, a range of 1500 miles and a service ceiling of 28 900 ft. It was heavily armed with four 20 mm Hispano cannon under the nose, which could be rearmed in flight by the observer, and six Browning machine guns, four in the right wing and two in the left. During 1942 many aircraft carried a single flexible 0.303 in Vickers 'K' machine gun in the rear dorsal observation 'blister' for use by the observer/navigator.

GERMAN

Basically the same Messerschmitt Bf109E and Bf110C and D fighters, Junkers Ju87B dive-bomber, Ju88A and Heinkel He111H bombers were employed as in the Battle of Britain.

Messerschmitt Bf109F and G
From late 1941 onwards the main fighter type employed over Malta by the Luftwaffe was the much-developed F model of the

Bf109. Powered by a 1300 hp Daimler-Benz DB 601E-1 in-line engine, the aircraft featured a revised, lighter but more effective armament of one 20 mm MG151 cannon, mounted on the engine center-line to fire through the propeller hub. The MG151 had a far higher muzzle velocity and resulting trajectory than the older MG FFs of the Bf109E, allowing for more accurate gunnery. Two 7.9 mm MG17 machine guns were mounted above the engine, firing through the propeller arc. Top speed was 390 mph at 22 000 ft, service ceiling 37 000 ft and range 440 miles.

Towards the end of the siege early examples of the 'Gustav' (the G model) began appearing. This differed mainly in having the DB601 engine replaced by a 1475 hp DB 605A-1, while after the initial batch, the fuselage-mounted MG17 guns were replaced by 13 mm MG131s. Although possessing a somewhat better service ceiling at 38 500 ft, and a marginally increased range, the greater weight of the aircraft resulted in there being no improvement in top speed.

Junkers Ju87D
In summer 1942 the first examples of the improved Ju87D began arriving in Sicily. This aerodynamically cleaned-up version of the Stuka featured a more powerful engine, the Junkers Jumo 211J-1 of 1400 hp. Forward-firing armament remained the same at two wing-mounted 7.9 mm MG 17s, but rear defense was increased to two flexible 7.9 mm MG81s. Bombload remained basically unchanged, but performance was substantially increased to 255 mph maximum speed at 13 500 ft; service ceiling dropped slightly to 23 950 ft, but range was increased to 510 miles.

ITALIAN

Fiat CR42 Falco
One of the last of the classic open-cockpit, fixed-undercarriage biplane fighters, the CR42 saw wide service on all fronts with the Regia Aeronautica and in experienced hands could be a formidable opponent for a Hurricane. Powered by an 850 hp Fiat A-74 RC 38 radial engine, it was armed with two 12.7 mm Breda-SAFAT machine guns in the fuselage. It reached a maximum speed of 266 mph at 13 120 ft, had a service ceiling of 33 30 ft, and a range of 488 miles.

Macchi C 200 Saetta
A rugged and manoeuvreable low-wing monoplane fighter, the MC 200 suffered from lack of power from its 870 hp Fiat A-74 radial engine, and lack of firepower from its two 12.7 mm Breda-SAFATs. Top speed was 312 mph at 14 750 ft, service ceiling 29 200 ft and range 354 miles. The MC 200 saw widespread action over Malta during 1941.

Macchi C-202 Folgore
Developed from the MC200, the MC202 was re-engined with a 1175 hp Alfa Romeo RA1000 Monsoni in-line engine — a licence-built version of the German DB601A. Manoeuvreable and tough, it had a maximum speed of 370 mph at 16 400 ft, a service ceiling of 37 730 ft and a range of 475 miles. This excellent performance was marred as in all Italian fighters prior to 1943 by its weak armament of two low-velocity 12.7 mm Breda-SAFAT guns in the nose, and its lack of reliable radio communication.

Reggiane Re2001 Falco II
Similarly powered and armed to the MC 202, the Re2001 was another manoeuvreable low-wing monoplane fighter, built in smaller numbers. Its performance was rather lower — maximum speed 337 mph at 16 400 ft, service ceiling 39 200 ft and range 466 miles. It was mainly employed as a fighter-bomber.

Savoia S-79 Saparviero
Because of the lack of suitably powerful engines, three of the four major bomber types employed by the Italians in the 1940–1942 period were powered by three, rather than the normal two engines. The oldest, but most numerous of these was the S-79, powered by 780 hp alfa Romeo 126 RC34 radial engines. A low-wing monoplane, the S-79 could carry up to 2750 lb of bombs up to 1180 miles. Top speed was 267 mph at

13 120 ft, and service ceiling was 21 320 ft. It was armed with three 12.7 mm Breda-SAFAT machine guns, one of them fixed to fire forward, and one 7.7 mm Lewis gun.

In 1942 the developed S-79-IIsII version was employed as a torpedo-bomber, powered by 1000 hp Piaggio P-XI RC 40 radials which marginally increased both top speed and service ceiling.

Savoia S-84
The cleaner and later-designed S-84 featured a twin fin and rudder instead of the single empennage of the S-79. Powered by three 1000 hp Piaggio P-XIs, it was used as a bomber and torpedo-carrier. Its performance was little different from that of the S-79, with top speed 266 mph, service ceiling 29 512 ft and range 1130 miles.

Cant Z.1007bis Alcione
Very similar in general design to the S-84, and Z-1007bis was also powered by a trio of P-XI engines and was produced in both twin- and single-tail versions — the former the more numerous. Constructed all of wood, the Z-1007bis was armed with two 12.7 mm and two 7.7 mm machine guns, and while normal bombload was 2600 lb, up to 4410 lb could be carried. With a top speed of 280 mph at 15 000 ft, this was the fastest of the Italian bombers. Service ceiling was 26 500 ft and range 1242 miles.

Fiat BR20M Cicogna
Employed only by night over Malta, the BR20M was the only twin-engined medium bomber employed by the Italians against the island. Of low-mid wing configuration with twin fins and rudders, the BR20M was of conventional design and powered by two 1000 hp Fiat A-80 RC 41 radial engines; it was armed with three 12.7 mm Breda-SAFAT guns in nose, ventral and dorsal positions. Bombload was 2200 lb, top speed 267 mph, service ceiling 22 140 ft and range 1242 miles.

Junkers Ju88A-4 of I/Kampfgeschwader 77

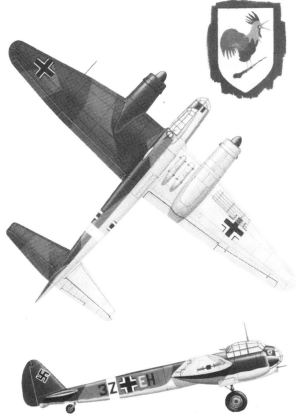

ACES OF THE BATTLE OF MALTA

Malta differed from other air battles in which the Luftwaffe was involved in that it produced no great 'Experten' with scores markedly in excess of the most successful of their opponents. Indeed the scores of the more successful on each side were remarkably similar, and the RAF in fact produced more high scorers than did the Germans.

True, the Luftwaffe units came and went, while the defenders were there all the time, but the RAF pilots all undertook operational tours and were then rested in a manner which was not adopted in the German units. It was just a tough theater, with the Germans opposed mainly by good quality fighter aircraft, manned by some of the most aggressive and skilled pilots in the RAF. There were simply not the opportunities available to them to build up big scores as they did in North Africa and Russia, and even on the West Front.

Spitfire aces

Amongst the first Spitfire pilots to reach Malta in March 1942, several became leading aces on the island, most going on to add further to their successes later in the war. The defense of Malta was very much a Commonwealth affair, and the leaders were from a wide variety of origin. In that first batch were New Zealander Ray Hesselyn, who claimed 12 victories over the island, Johnny Plagis, a Rhodesian of Greek parentage, who claimed 11 and Paul Brennan, a 10-victory Australian. Hesselyn later raised his score to 21½ before becoming a prisoner of war; Brennan died in an accident in 1943, and Plagis ended the war as a Wing Leader with 16 victories. Pete Nash was the first of the English Malta Spitfire aces, but was killed in action after claiming 9½ victories over the island.

FLG OFF G F 'SREWBALL' BEURLING, 249 SQUADRON.

More aces soon followed, including Tim Goldsmith (12½) and 'Slim' Yarra (12) from Australia, Claude Weaver III (11½), an American volunteer, Pat Schade, a Malayan-born Englishman (12½), and fellow-Englishman Ron West (9). Some of the greatest came in with the Spitfires carried by the USS Wasp, including Canadians Wally Mcleod (13), John McElroy (10), 'Billy the Kid' Williams (10), and the greatest of them all, George 'Screwball' Beurling. The most successful nightfighter in the island was another Canadian, 'Moose' Fumerton (9).

George Beurling lacked the educational qualifications to join the RCAF in 1940, so worked his way to Britain, and joined the RAF. He gained two early victories, but was in trouble for breaking away from formations to attack every aircraft in sight, and requested a posting to Malta. He arrived with the second Wasp delivery, and on 6 July shot down three Axis fighters. When he claimed three Macchi 202s on 11 July his score on the island had already risen to nine and he was awarded a DFM. On 27 July came his greatest day when he claimed two Macchis, two Bf109s and two more damaged; one of the Italian fighters was flown by the ace Niclot-Doglio. He claimed eight more during the October 'blitz' to bring his score on the island to 26⅓, but on 14 October he was shot down and wounded after three victories. This dedicated fighter pilot, now a Flying Officer with DSO, DFC, DFM and Bar, was consequently evacuated back to England.

A year later, however, he added three further victories with a Canadian squadron, but he was killed in 1948 in a crash while delivering an aircraft to Israel.

One other great pilot to emerge from Malta was Wing Commander Adrian Warburton, without doubt

FLT LT H W MCLEOD, 1435 SQUADRON.

the RAF's greatest reconnaissance pilot of the war. Warburton arrived as a semi-trained pilot with 431 Flight in late 1941. For the next year he flew many long-range reconnaissances in his Maryland over Italy and North Africa. Whenever possible he and his crew also attacked enemy aircraft, between them claiming seven shot down and three destroyed on the ground. After a rest, he returned to command the first Spitfire reconnaissance flight on the island throughout the rest of the siege. He subsequently commanded a photographic reconnaissance wing in 1943, but was lost while flying back from England to Italy over the Alps on 12 April, 1944.

Luftwaffe 'Experten'

Amongst the Luftwaffe fighters, the units to see the longest service over Malta were the Stab (Headquarters flight) and II Gruppe of JG53, which were present virtually without rest from December 1941 until November 1942. During this period the Geschwader Kommodore, Oberstleutnant Freiherr Günther von Maltzahn, claimed 13 victories, while his wingman

the airfields in the hope of catching their opponents at just such a disadvantage.

April was the month of supreme effort for the Luftwaffe, which made 9465 sorties over the island and its environs, nearly twice the number made in even the busiest of other months. The German airmen found Malta one of the most testing of all targets; their losses were not vast but were frequent. The AA fire over the island was notoriously vicious while the resolution and persistence of the defending fighters had gained their grudging respect. April also saw the loss of two of Fliegerkorps II's leading fighter pilots, the first on 10 April when 40-victory 'Experte' Lt Herman Neuhoff of III/JG53 was shot down to become a prisoner, and the second on 14 April when Hpt Karl-Heinz Krahl, 24-victory Kommandeur of II/JG3, was shot down and killed by AA fire during a low-level attack on Luqa airfield. The cost to the RAF had been high, too; by the end of April the 229 Squadron air party had been virtually wiped out and ceased to operate, while of ten new Wellingtons which

in the Stabsschwarm, Lt Franz Schiess, claimed 10. Von Maltzahn was one of the great Luftwaffe leaders of the war, having led his unit throughout the Battle of Britain and in the Soviet Union, eventually finishing the war in command of all fighters in Italy.

OBLT JOACHIM MÜNCHEBERG, 7/JG26.

The most successful pilot of the 1940-41 period was Joachim Müncheberg, who claimed 18 over Malta and one over Yugoslavia to add to 23 earlier victories during the Battles of France and Britain. Müncheberg later flew briefly in the Desert before returning to the West Front and then seeing some service in the Soviet Union.

In late 1942 he returned to North Africa to become Kommodore of Jagdgeschwader 77. Here in 1943 he was killed over Tunisia with his personal score at 135.

I Gruppe produced no great 'Experten' over Malta — its frequent sojourns to the Eastern front never kept it long enough in Sicily.

Despite its long detachments in North Africa, III Gruppe gained 62 victories over Malta, with Hpt Helmut Belser the unit's top scorer here (eight of his 36 successes were claimed over the island). It was the long-serving II Gruppe which produced probably the top-scoring Luftwaffe pilot over the island — Hpt Gerhard Michalski, who claimed 26, virtually identical to the score credited to Beurling, the RAF's Malta No 1. In this same unit Ofw Herbert Rollwage made 20 claims, but none of the unit's other pilots appear to have totalled double figures.

When I/JG77 arrived in July 1942 it included a number of successful and high-scoring pilots amongst its members, who proceeded to achieve success against the (increased number of) Spitfires at a much faster rate than had their comrades in JG53. By the end of October Oblt Siegfried Freytag had claimed about 25 victories, gaining for himself the sobriquet 'Die Stern von Malta' (the Star of Malta). Ofw Walter Brandt claimed approximately 14 during this same period, while Lt Günther Hannak claimed 12, Lt Heinz-Edgar Berres 11, and Oblt Fredrich Geisshardt nine.

Gerhard Michalski had served with II/JG53 since 1940, and by the time the unit moved to Sicily in December 1941 had 22 victories, 13 of them in the Soviet Union. By mid July he had claimed 23 over Malta, adding only three more by early November. He received the Knight's Cross during

September of that year; added 11 more over Tunisia, Sicily and Italy during 1943; he then claimed a further 14 on home defense duties up to the end of the war, by which time he was Kommodore of JG4.

Siegfried Freytag was a Staffelkapitän with 49 victories over Soviet aircraft, and newly decorated with the Knights' Cross when he arrived in Sicily with I/JG77 in July 1942. After his 25 swift victories over Malta, he added about 22 more over North Africa and three over Sicily before being wounded in action. He subsequently gained a final three on home defense after recovery, and ended the war flying Me262 jets with is score at 102 plus 12 destroyed on the ground.

Italian top-scorers

Amongst the many Italian pilots the top-scorer was Sergente Teresio Martinoli, who operated over the island during two separate periods with the 9° Gruppo of 4° Stormo CT. He claimed five victories during late 1941 when the MC202 was first introduced into action, made a further five claims during May 1942, and later added at least 12 more victories to his name over North Africa and in Italy by September 1943. He then joined the Co-Belligerent Air Force to fly alongside the Allies, and shot down one German aircraft over the Balkans before being killed in a flying accident at Naples in July 1944.

Also in 4° Stormo (10° Gruppo) was one of Italy's two top scorers of the war, Capitano Franco Lucchini, who claimed five of his 26

MAJ GÜNTHER VON MALTZAHN, JG53 WITH OBLT FRIEDRICH GEISSHARDT (LEFT) , I/JG77.

victories over the island during 1942, and shared in five other successes.

The other Macchi C202 unit to operate over the island, the 51° Stormo CT, produced at least three leading pilots. Most successful was the commander of the Stormo, Colonello Dulio Fanali, who claimed nine of his 14 victories here, while Maresciallo Ennio Tarantola, a former Ju87 pilot, claimed five and two shared flying with the Stormo's 20° Gruppo. Capitano Furio Nicolot-Doglio of the 155° Gruppo claimed six, but was shot down and killed on 27 July 1942 by 'Screwball' Beurling.

---

arrived on 26 March, only two survived to fly out on 6 April.

The defenders' resolve stiffens

The German efforts suffered a setback again on 9 May when *Wasp* returned, accompanied by *Eagle*, and 64 more Spitfires were flown off. This time Malta was ready; existing fighters patrolled overhead, while new pilots landing found themselves bundled out of their cockpits which were at once taken over by the local pilots. Simultaneously, fast-working maintenance crews refueled and armed the aircraft in record time. By the time the Luftwaffe arrived, most were already back in the air and waiting for them. Next day the

---

LONGEST-SERVING LUFTWAFFE FIGHTER UNIT IN SICILY WAS II/JG53. AN AIRCRAFT OF THIS GRUPPE'S STABSKETTE IS SHROUDED AGAINST THE SUN'S HEAT ON A SICILIAN AIRFIELD.

---

tanker *Welshman* reached Malta after a fast lone run. Once more the Luftwaffe appeared in force, joined by elements of the Regia Aeronautica which had begun returning to Sicily late in April. Twenty-three victories were claimed by the defenses for the loss of four Spitfires. Although actual losses were lower by a fair margin, it was still one of the biggest defeats inflicted by the Malta defenses so far.

Raids continued throughout the rest of May, but at a reduced rate, and with Italian aircraft playing a bigger part than for many months. There were now substantial numbers of fighter pilots available on the island — far more than there were aircraft. Units shared available Spitfires (few Hurricanes were now remaining), the pilots of one squadron operating the morning of one day and the afternoon of the next, while another took over in the intervening period. Thus, although frequently having to take to the shelters both by day and night, pilots were at least afforded reasonable periods of rest between operations. However, the month did see the loss of some of the island's noteables

**SPITFIRE V BEING REFUELLED AND REARMED BY RAF AND RN
PERSONNEL. IT STANDS IN A TYPICAL MALTA ANTI-BLAST PEN
CONSTRUCTED FROM SAND AND STONE-FILLED SURPLUS
PETROL CANS.**

in action. On 9 May Plt Off G R Tweedale DFM, one of the
last of the Hurricane aces, was shot down and killed after
claiming seven victories over the island, while on 17 May the
first of the Spitfire aces, Plt Off Peter Nash, was also lost.

The sheer numbers of Spitfires now available allowed
claims to reach a record 111 for the month — more than
twice the number claimed during April — although losses in
combat rose to 25 fighters. The momentum of Spitfire
deliveries was being maintained, although *Wasp* was no
longer available. *Eagle* and *Argus* brought in 17 more on 19
May, while in early June *Eagle* returned twice more, laden
to capacity to deliver a further 63! Ten more Wellingtons
also flew in to maintain some semblance of offensive
action, which was being kept flickeringly alive by the surviving Royal Navy torpedo bombers flying by night.

The need to support other fronts was now making itself
felt on the Luftwaffe, and by the end of May many of
Fliegerkorps II's units had departed, II/JG3 and I/JG53 to
the Eastern Front, III/JG53, II/StG3, III/ZG26 and
I/NJG2 to North Africa, II/LG2 and I/KG54 to Greece
and Crete. Only II/JG53, the two specialist anti-shipping
Ju88 units, KFlGr 606 and KGr 806, plus a reconnaissance
Staffel, remained in Sicily. This allowed more Italian units
to return, and the MC 202 fighters of 4° Stormo CT — soon
to move to Africa themselves again — were joined by
Savoia S.84s, Fiat BR20s, Cant Z.1007bis, and Ju87B
bombers, and by more MC 202s and new Reggiane Re2001
fighters.

All these moves took place against a background of
crisis for the British in Africa, where Rommel's Gazala

offensive, launched in late May, was destroying the 8th
Army's armored formations and threatening to drive the
British back across Cyrenaica into Egypt. Malta was now
desperately short of supplies, and while control of at least
part of the North African coast remained in British hands, a
major supply effort was mounted.

From Gibraltar a heavily-escorted convoy of six
merchant vessels set out for Malta under the codename
'Harpoon', whilst from Egyptian ports 11 more cargo
vessels and a covering naval force headed west for the
island, covered by patrols supplied by the Western Desert
Air Force; this convoy was codenamed 'Vigorous'.

The 'Harpoon' convoy came under violent attack from
Italian units based in Sardinia, whilst the 'Vigorous' vessels
had to run the gauntlet of Axis units on Crete, Rhodes and
other Aegean islands. The results were near-catastrophic:
after the loss of two vessels and damage to two others, the
'Vigorous' ships were forced to give up and turn back,
nearly all their anti-aircraft ammunition exhausted. With
the benefit of aircraft carrier support, the 'Harpoon' convoy was fought through, but not without the loss of four of
the cargo vessels. Beaufighters of 235 Squadron had flown
out from England to Malta to help escort the convoy at long
range, but despite their and the Navy's efforts, which
inflicted heavy losses on the Regia Aeronautica, only 25 000
tons actually reached the island. On 15 June the Spitfire
squadrons were heavily engaged as Axis units from Sicily
tried desperately to complete the destruction of the convoy.
Just sufficient supplies were received, however, to keep the
island's defenses functioning and for Malta to remain a
thorn in the Axis side.

However, with the 8th Army in full retreat, it was now
Western Desert Air Force that was desperate for Spitfires
and Malta that was well-provided, and at the end of June
601 Squadron flew out to Egypt with a dozen aircraft. In
return a detachment of Beaufighter nightfighters were despatched to the island by 89 Squadron to replace the now-
defunct 1435 Flight.

Germany prepares to invade

Axis plans for the final subjugation of Malta were now
prepared and required a renewed aerial offensive and at the
end of June Fliegerkorps II was once again reinforced.
Ju88s of II and III/KG77 and Bf109s of the 'crack' I/JG77
moved to Sicily from the Soviet front. The new offensive
began on 1 July, almost equal effort being maintained
throughout the month by the Luftwaffe and the Regia
Aeronautica. While the intensity of attack was markedly
lower than in April — only 4000 Italo-German sorties compared with over 10 000 — so greatly strengthened were the
defenses that in terms of claims and losses, it was the
heaviest month of the siege. Victories confirmed totalled
149, with 38 probables and 140 damaged being claimed by
the defending squadrons for the loss in combat of 36 Spitfires, but less than a third of that number of pilots — a toll
taken mainly by the experienced pilots of I/JG77.

Losses were more than made good, however, for *Eagle*

AXIS SORTIES FLOWN OVER THE MALTA AREA, 1942

	Jan	Feb	Mar	Apr	May	Jun	Jul	Aug	Sep	Oct	Totals
German	1741	2299	4881	9465	3136	1373	2006	1847	1384	3371	31 503
Italian	709	791	806	858	1597	1520	1903	1285	1155	1787	12 411
Combined	2450	3090	5687	10 323	4733	2893	3909	3132	2539	5158	43 914

completed two further trips during the month with another 62 Spitfires. 603 Squadron was disbanded, since the ground party had now reached Egypt, but could not move over to Malta. Instead, two new Spitfire squadrons were formed on the island, one carrying the temporarily defunct 229 Squadron number, the other taking on the number of 1435 Flight to become the only four figure fighter squadron in the RAF — 1435 Squadron. July also saw the arrival of that doyen of the defense of Great Britain in 1940, Air Vice-Marshal Sir Keith Park, who took over the command from AVM Lloyd.

Despite the continued presence of the Luftwaffe in Sicily, the assault waned towards the end of July, and August proved a much quieter month in general. Mid month witnessed the last effort to fight through a convoy while the siege lasted. Once again, Beaufighters were detached to Malta, both from England and Africa, and these launched a series of strikes on Italian airfields in Sardinia in an effort to hold down the Italian torpedo-bombers there. The convoy for Operation *Pedestal* was the largest yet — 14 merchant vessels with a massive naval escort including four aircraft carriers, one of which — *Furious* — was carrying 38 more Spitfires.

The ships were met by a tremendous Axis attack effort on 12 August, and again next day; as the cargo vessels and their close escort came within range of air cover from the island they were attacked by Italian motor torpedo boats with telling effect. Only five vessels, one the tanker *Ohio*, reached Grand Harbour, and all had been damaged — but 55 000 tons of vital supplies were extricated from them, and the island fought on. During the return to Gibraltar the faithful old *Eagle* was sunk by a U-Boat's torpedoes. However, *Furious* returned on 17 August, delivering yet another 32 Spitfires for the island.

The rest of August remained relatively quiet, but this time the Beaufighters stayed on the island to provide a renewed strike element. September was so quiet a month that on occasion and for the first time Spitfires were able to go over to the offensive, sweeps being flown over the airfields of southern Sicily during the month. 126 Squadron even had a number of its aircraft fitted to carry 250lb bombs, joining the few remaining Hurricanes on the island which were being operated in the fighter-bomber role by some naval pilots.

It was the calm before the storm, however. In Africa Rommel's forces had suffered a severe defeat at the start of September and his supply lines across the Mediterranean were still threatened from Malta — indeed the faithful reconnaissance crews of 69 Squadron had continued to seek out the Axis convoys throughout the siege. Consequently, around the end of September strengthening of Fliegerkorps II again began. KFlGr 606 had now been redesignated I/KG77 to bring this Geschwader to full strength, while Stab and I/KG54 had returned to Sicily, KGr 806 becoming III/KG54. II/LG1 also returned to the island to bring bomber strength up to six Gruppen of Ju88s. Elements of the He111-equipped KG100 also arrived from France to undertake night raids. The two Jagdgruppen, I/JG77 and II/JG53, were reinforced by I/JG53, back from the Eastern front, and I/JG27 from North Africa, this latter unit being accompanied by II/StG3. The Regia Aeronautica provided three Gruppi of Cant Z.1007bis bombers, three of MC 202 fighters, a single Gruppo of Re 2001s and one of Ju87s.

Facing this force when the new offensive began on the morning of 11 October were five full squadrons of Spitfire

TOP-SCORING FIGHTER PILOTS OF THE BATTLE FOR MALTA

LUFTWAFFE

NAME	SCORE OVER MALTA	UNIT	FINAL SCORE FOR WAR	FATE
Hpt Gerhard Michalski	26	II/JG53	73	K 22 2 46
Oblt Siegfried Freytag	25	I/JG77	102	
Ofw Herbert Rollwage	20	II/JG53	102	
Oblt Joachim Müncheberg	18	7/JG26	135	KIA 23 3 43
Ofw Walter Brandt	14	I/JG77	57	
Obstlt Günther von Maltzahn	13	Stab/JG53	68	Died 24 6 53
Lt Gunther Hannak	12	I/JG77	47	POW 5 5 43
Lt Heinz-Edgar Berres	11	I/JG77	53	KIA 25 7 43
Lt Franz Schiess	10	Stab/JG53	67	KIA 2 9 43
Oblt Friedrich Geisshardt	9	I/JG77	102	WIA 5 4 43 Died of wounds 6 4 43
Hpt Helmut Belser	8	III/JG53	36	KIFA 19 6 42

REGIA AERONAUTICA

Serg Teresio Martinoli	10	9°Gr,4°St	23	KIFA 25 7 44
Col Dulio Fanali	9	51°St	14	
Cap Furio Nicot-Doglio	6	155°Gr,51°St	6	KIA 27 7 42
Cap Franco Lucchini	5	10°Gr,4°St	26	KIA 5 7 43
Maj Ennio Tarantola	5	20°Gr,51°St	10	

ROYAL AIR FORCE

NAME AND NATIONALITY				
Flg Off G F Beurling Canadian	26⅓	249	31⅓	KIFA 20 5 48
Flt Lt W McLeod Canadian	13	603/1435	21	KIA 27 9 44
F/Sgt P A Schade British	12½	126	12½	KIFA 31 7 44
Flg Off A P Goldsmith Australian	12¼	126	16¼	Died 25 3 61
Flg Off R B Hesseln New Zealander	12	249	21½	POW Oct 43
Flg Off J W Yarra Australian	12	185	12	KIA 10 12 42
Flg Off C Weaver III American	11½	185	13½	KIA 28 1 44
Flt Lt J Plagis Rhodesian	11	249/185	16	
Wg Cdr A C Rabagliati British	10¼	46/126	17¼	KIA 6 7 43
Flg Off V P Brennan Australian	10	249	10	KIFA 13 6 43
Flt Lt J F McElroy Canadian	10	249	16¼*	
Flg Off J W Williams Canadian	10	249	10	KIFA Oct 42
Sgt F N Robertson British	10	261	12	KIFA 1943
Flg Off P A Nash British	9½	249	12½	KIA 17 5 42
Flt Off R C Fumerton Canadian	9	89	14	
Flt Lt R West British	9	249/185	9	

*Includes two claimed with the Israeli Air Force, 1948.

BRISTOL BEAUFIGHTER I STRIKE-FIGHTER OPERATING FROM MALTA DURING SUMMER 1942. THESE AIRCRAFT FLEW FAR AND WIDE TO STRAFE AXIS AIRFIELDS AND SHIPPING IN SICILY, SARDINIA AND NORTH AFRICA.

Vs, led by experienced leaders and with a high proportion of experienced pilots. From the initial attacks the defenders were in a position to intercept every raid in strength. Again and again the formations of Ju88s, protected by swarms of Messerschmitts and Macchis, attempted to fight their way through to their targets. And again and again they were thwarted.

The battle is won

In seven days the RAF pilots claimed no less than 44 of the bombers shot down, plus 20 more probables and another 70 believed to have been hit sufficiently to damage them. There was the usual element of double-claiming here, but the actuality was bad enough — at least 30 Ju88s were lost and 13 more damaged seriously, some of them to write-off levels. Fighter losses were also far from light with at least a dozen Bf109s and MC 202s being shot down and another ten or so badly damaged. Although the cost to the defenders was high, with 27 Spitfires being shot down during the seven days, and more than 20 more crash-landing or suffering heavy damage, losses of pilots were substantially lighter.

On 18 October Kesselring called a halt. No further bomber raids were attempted by day, even with the heaviest of escorts. The Ju87s which the Germans and Italians had been holding in readiness had not even been risked, so strong was the opposition. It was a major victory for the Spitfires — and a hard-fought one. For several more days fighter sweeps continued to be made over the island, and the Bf109 fighter-bombers of I/Schlachtgeschwader 2 were rushed across from Africa to join the Italian Re 2001s in heavily-escorted attacks on the airfields. Meanwhile, the Ju88s and Ju87s joined the He111s and Z.1007bis in their nocturnal sorties over the island, but lost several more of their number before the end of the month to 89 Squadron's Beaufighters.

The Spitfires continued to give battle to the fighters and fighter-bombers on a reducing scale until the end of the month, and into early November, but on 29 October *Furious* returned for the last time with a final load of 31 Spitfires to bring the squadrons and reserves back up to

strength. This 13th delivery since March 1942 brought to 385 the number of Spitfires ferried to Malta. Twelve of these had returned with the carriers due to unserviceability and 34 had been lost to a variety of causes after flying off, but 367 had reached the island to become the heroes of the defensive force.

Meanwhile, on 26 October, I/JG27 had returned to North Africa where Montgomery's great offensive at El Alamein had begun. Early in November news of the great victory won began to reach Malta, but of greater immediate impact to the island were the events which occurred a few days later on 8 November when Anglo-American forces landed in French Morocco and Algeria, and advanced into Tunisia. At once Kesselring's air forces were redirected onto this new threat.

At a stroke the long Battle of Malta was over. There would be more air raids, but not of a serious nature, and within six months the island would have become a major base for the first Allied landings on European territory. Before November was out a supply convoy was sailed through to the island without loss, and Malta was ready to go over to the offensive. The defenders had won their battle, but as so often the campaign had been decided by events elsewhere. However, in the greater sense of things, Malta had played a major part in the defeat of the Axis armies in North Africa.

CLAIMS OF LUFTWAFFE FIGHTER UNITS OVER MALTA

Unit	Number
7/JG26	42
III/JG27	5
Stab/JG53	35
I/JG53	29
II/JG53	159
III/JG53	62
II/JG3	8
I/JG77	99 approx
I/JG27	7
Total	446 approx

CLAIMS BY MALTA DEFENSES, JUNE 1940 – OCTOBER 1942

	Confirmed	Probable	Damaged
German aircraft	574	231	622
Italian aircraft	286	85	191
Totals	860	316	813

ADMITTED AXIS AIRCRAFT LOSSES OVER MALTA

		1940	1941	1942 (to 8 Nov)
German	Bombers		80	172
	Fighters		6	99
Italian	Bombers	23	32	58
	Fighters	12	38	47
Totals		35	156	376 = 567

NB The 132 victims claimed in October and the single success added in the first week of November, brought claims by the defenses to 614 confirmed and 240 probables since the start of 1942; the AA gunners had claimed about 130 more. Against these claims the Germans and Italians had lost at least 376 fighters and bombers during 1942, to bring their losses over Malta since June 1940 to well over 575 aircraft of all types. In the same period the German fighter units had claimed about 446 victories, and the Italians many others.

CHAPTER FIVE

THE BATTLE FOR GUADALCANAL

AUGUST – NOVEMBER 1942

Overleaf

Us Marine Grumman F4F-4 Wildcat fighters intercept Mitsubishi G4M1 medium bombers of the Imperial Japanese Navy over Guadalcanal, as these attempt to attack Henderson Field during October, 1942.

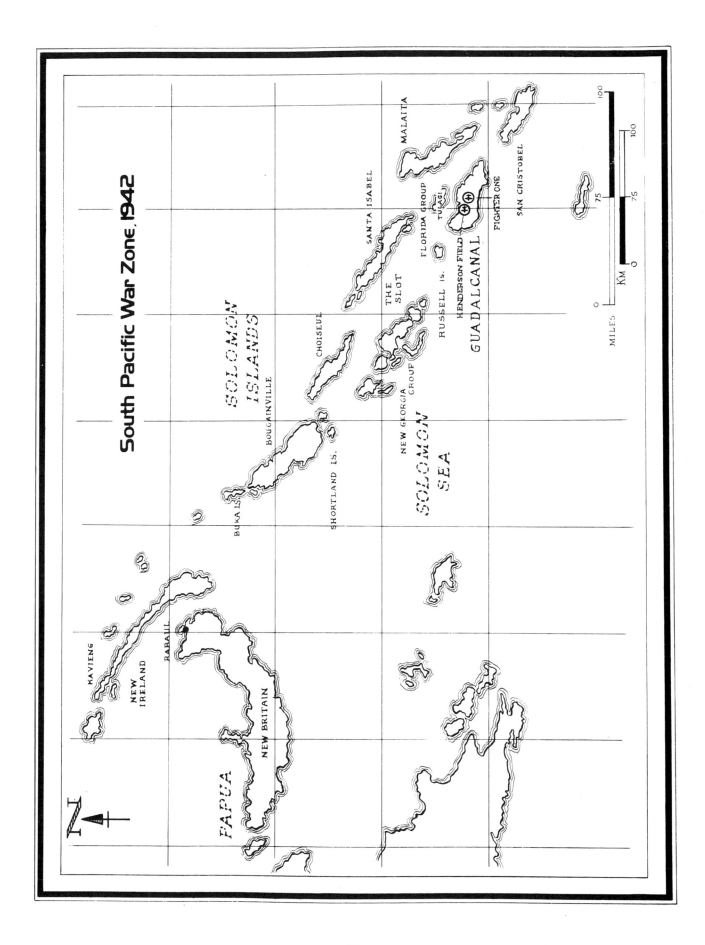

South Pacific War Zone, 1942

Droning slowly southwards over the blue sea, studded on each side by the islands of the Solomons chain, the 17 Mitsubishi A6M2 Zero-Sen fighters made steady progress. Below them Mitsubishi G4M1 twin-engined bombers formed three great arrowhead formations of nine aircraft each. Flying at the furthest extent of their range the Japanese fighter pilots required every ounce of the skill they had acquired over the past two years. Careful judgement was essential to coax the maximum from every drop of fuel by flying at optimum height, throttle setting and propeller pitch. They were heading for a rendezvous with a new opponent. It was late in the morning of August 7, 1942 and their destination was Guadalcanal.

During their initial lightning advance through the East Indies and South-West Pacific, the Japanese forces had reached New Guinea and the Northern Solomons by March 1942, but since then had been involved in a long, slogging fight with the US and Australian defenders around Port Moresby on the south coast of New Guinea. A major base area for fleet, air and ground forces had been set up by the Imperial Japanese Navy around Rabaul in New Britain, at the head of the Solomons chain, from where units, supplies and support could be fed into the New Guinea war zone. Steadily, small Japanese forces had trickled down the Solomons, posing a growing threat to the supply route between the US and Australia.

Australia was now the key. It constituted the one great base area from which the Allies could seek to halt the Japanese onrush and plan their own future counter-offensive. During the middle months of 1942, elements of the USAAF and the US Marine Corps' own air arm had been moved into the New Hebrides, to the south of the Solomons, to protect the US–Australia shipping route. It was at this stage that reconnaissance from the New Hebrides flown by B-17 Fortresses of the 11th Bomber Group, with photographers from the Marines' VMO-251 reconnaissance unit aboard, first spotted construction works for a new airfield on the South Solomons island of Guadalcanal. The threat that this activity posed could not be ignored. A US invasion of the island was immediately drafted, and so began one of the fiercest and most critical battles of World War II. Success or failure for the US in this conflict would depend to a critical degree upon air power.

Operation *Watchtower*

Up to this point the part played in the Pacific War by the US Marines had been small, though heroic. Their air units had defended little Wake Island at the outbreak of war, and taken the initial brunt of the Japanese onslaught at the Midway battle in June 1942. Only a single Marine fighter squadron had so far reached the New Hebrides, but Marine Air Group 23 (MAG 23) was at Ewa in the Hawaiian Islands, where its two fighter and two dive-bomber squadrons were being re-equipped and undergoing intensive training. The Marines were also selected as the invading ground force on Guadalcanal. General Archie Vandergrift's 1st Marine Division boarded the 23 transports of Rear Admiral Richard Kelly Turner's Task Force 62, ready to undertake Operation *Watchtower*, the first American offensive of the war.

The initial landings would be supported by carrier-borne air power, and the three aircraft carriers forming Task Force 61 under Vice Admiral Frank 'Jack' Fletcher were available for this task. The carriers *Saratoga* and *Enterprise*

had been operating in the Pacific since the start of the war and were now joined by *Wasp*, which had been delivering Spitfires to Malta. The American aviators felt they had the measure of their Japanese counterparts after their recent victories, but were still wary of the nimble and deadly Zero fighter. Although the Japanese carrier force had recently suffered serious losses, the remaining carrier air groups were well-trained, experienced and aggressive.

They would not immediately be met, for it was the Navy's formidable land-based elements which would carry the initial brunt of the action. On New Britain were the 24th and 25th Air Flotillas, which included under their command the 3rd and Tainan Kokutais with A6M2 Zero fighters, five of the six available Kokutais of Mitsubishi G4M medium bombers, the Yokohama Kokutai, equipped with H6K flyingboats and a variety of floatplanes, and a number of ancillary units. Most of these units were operating over New Guinea and northern Australia, but a detachment from the Yokohama Ku, including both Kawanishi H6K flyingboats and Nakajima-built floatplane versions of the Zero fighter — the A6M2-N — had been based at Tulagi, a small island off Guadalcanal, since late June to bring an element of air defense and reconnaissance capability to the Southern Solomons pending the availability of the airfield there. These aircraft had already been in action against US aircraft from the New Hebrides, culminating on 4 August when seven of the floatplanes intercepted three 11th Bomb Group B-17Es and NAP 1/C Shigeto Kobayashi rammed (or collided with) one of the big bombers, both aircraft crashing with the loss of everyone aboard.

The land-based Japanese fighters had yet to encounter US Marine or Navy aircraft. They were, however, the most experienced in the Imperial Navy, and had cut a swathe through the Dutch and USAAF aircraft that had opposed them in the Philippines and East Indies. Again in New Guinea they had been inflicting dreadful losses on the US and Australian defenders, and had to date suffered only minimal casualties themselves. They included almost all the top-scoring Japanese Navy pilots of the war so far, and were confident to the point of arrogance, sure both of their own skill and the superiority of their aircraft.

At dawn on 7 August, 1942, the US Marines stormed ashore — 19 546 of them — on Guadalcanal and Tulagi, while at sea the three aircraft carriers, the battleship *North Carolina*, 11 cruisers, 31 destroyers, five minesweepers and five oilers provided support and protection. Grumman F4F-4 Wildcats and Douglas SBD-3 Dauntlesses from *Wasp* swept over Tulagi harbor claiming the destruction of 21 moored waterborne aircraft; seven H6Ks and nine A6M2-Ns were actually lost, the Yokohama Ku Detachment ceasing to exist as the Marines poured across the little island, wiping out the small forces opposing them. On Guadalcanal itself, faced only by 600 soldiers and 1400 laborers, rather than the 5000 troops they were expecting, the Marines soon took the airfield, and the defenders forced into the jungle. Before the day was out Tulagi, Gavutu and Tanambogo Islands were in US hands, and 1500 defenders were dead. Marine casualties stood at 108 dead and 140 wounded.

First strike

When news of the US action reached Rabaul, the only immediate response the Japanese could make was to launch an air strike. Rear Admiral Sadayoshi Yamada's Air Flotilla 25th had been reinforced the day before by 15 A6M2

fighters and 16 Aichi D3A dive-bombers of the 2nd
Kokutai, while the A6Ms of the Tainan Ku and the G4Ms
bombers of the 4th Ku were in the process of being readied
for another raid over New Guinea. This mission was
immediately cancelled and orders were swiftly issued for an
attack on the shipping at Guadalcanal. A preliminary look
at the map alerted the pilots to the fact that this would be a
maximum range operation — it was fully 600 miles to the
target area.

Taking off at 0950 hours, the flight lasted some three
and a half hours, during which only one of the original 18
A6Ms was forced to turn back. The Tainan fighter pilots
were eager to meet their US counterparts for the first time.
In the event, they discovered that the carrier air groups
waiting for them were the toughest opponents they had ever
engaged.

By now F4Fs of Fighting Squadron VF-5 from *Saratoga*
and VF-6 from *Enterprise* were in the air, as were SBDs
from all three carriers. Eight VF-5 fighters reached the
bombers first, but were overwhelmed by the escorting Zeros
as the G4Ms made a bombing run which missed completely.
Lt James Southerland and Ens Joseph Daly each claimed
two of the bombers before being shot down in turn them-

BEFORE AND AFTER: THESE TWO GROUP PHOTOS OF THE
IJNAF'S TAINAN KOKUTAI INDICATE THE ATTRITION OF THE
GUADALCANAL CAMPAIGN. LEADING FIGHTER PILOTS
PRESENT IN THE PHOTO (ABOVE) TAKEN ON 4 AUGUST 1942,
INCLUDE: FRONT ROW, 4TH RT KAZUSHI UTO; SECOND ROW,
FAR LT SAHEI YAMASHITA; 2ND LT TAKATSUKA TORAICHI; 4TH
LT JUNICHI SASAI; 2ND RT TAKEYOSHI OHNO; THIRD ROW, 7TH
LT SABURO SAKAI; 8TH LT HIROYOSHI NISHIZAWA: 10TH LT
YOSHIO OHKI; 6TH RT TOSHIO OHTA.
(ABOVE RIGHT), TAKEN IN NOVEMBER 1942, SAKAI, OHTA,
TORAICHI, SASAI AND UTO ARE NO LONGER PRESENT. FRONT
ROW, 2ND LT TAKEO OKUMURA; 3RD LT OHKI; 3RD RT
NISHIZAWA; 4TH RT YAMASHITA; 5TH RT OHNO; SECOND ROW,
FAR LT OKANO; 3RD LT YOSHIICHI NAKAYA; 5TH LT MITSUO
HORI; 7TH RT KOZABURO YASUI. ALL NAMED WERE
CONSIDERED TO BE ACES.

selves as were three more of the US fighters, two others
being badly damaged. Daly and Southerland both lived to
tell the tale. Southerland's aircraft had already been badly

hit by fire from the bombers when he was given the coup de grace by one of the leading Japanese aces of the time, NAP 1/C Saburo Sakai.

As the Japanese bombers turned for home, ten more F4Fs, this time from VF-6, came after them, several of these fighters managing one attack before the Zeros could reach them. Three more G4Ms were claimed shot down, plus several 'probables', while Radio Electrician Thomas W Rhodes shot down a Zero. The cost was again high. Four F4Fs were shot down and one of the pilots was killed.

Meanwhile, Saburo Sakai's section of four had been attacked by an intrepidly flown lone Dauntless of Scouting Squadron VS-71. Turning on this, Sakai quickly shot it down, killing the gunner, although the pilot — Lt Dudley H Adams — survived. Sakai then spotted eight more SBDs of VS-5 and VB-6 which he took to be more F4Fs, diving on these from behind with one wingman. The gunners opened fire, and while Sakai hit one of the bombers, he was hit in return and badly wounded, splinters in both eyes nearly blinding him.

Counting the cost

The Tainan pilots returned to Rabaul triumphantly. In the whirling dogfights over the US Fleet they believed that they had shot down 38 F4Fs and probably 15 more, together with seven SBDs. NAP 1/C Hiroyoshi Nishizawa — later to become the top-scoring Japanese fighter pilot of the war claimed six F4Fs alone. Three other pilots made five claims apiece and four more claimed four.

Three pilots were missing, however. Two of these were the illustrious Sakai, whose score after this mission stood at 61, and NAP 1/C Motosuna Yoshida, a 12-victory ace. Long after the others had returned, Sakai's Zero appeared. Blind, blacking out, and in desperate pain, he had somehow managed to keep his Zero in the air and on course for the 560-mile flight back to Rabaul. Truly one of the epic flights of the war! The 4th Ku had lost three of its G4Ms over the target and two more had ditched on the way home due to damage; US claims totalled five of these bombers by the fighters and two by ships' anti-aircraft fire, but only two Zeros had been claimed (one of these was Sakai's aircraft, which was credited to the SBD gunners of VS-5).

The day was not over, however. Within two hours, nine D3A dive-bombers from the newly arrived 2nd Ku appeared overhead and attacked the shipping, damaging the destroyer *Mugford*. In reply, VF-5 and -6 Wildcats rose to the attack. At the end of a fierce action, 16 claims were made by the US fighters and two by anti-aircraft fire (considerably more than the numbers involved, it must be noted). Credit for three of these went to Lt (jg) Carlton Starkes of VF-5, two (and another shared) to Ens Mark Bright, and two each to three other pilots. In fact five were shot down over the target and the other four ditched later on the return flight to Rabaul, which was beyond the aircraft's range. It had been virtually a suicide mission.

Next day the Japanese returned. This time, 23 G4Ms carried torpedoes to attack the fleet. Three VF-6 F4Fs intercepted and claimed four bombers shot down, together with one of the 15 escorting Zeros. Of this tally, one of each was claimed by Machinist Donald Runyon (who had incidentally been credited with two of the D3As on the previous afternoon). The low-flying torpedo-droppers were prime targets for the ships' guns, which opened fire and destroyed 14. One G4M crashed into the deck of the transport *George F Elliott*, which had to be sunk when fires aboard became uncontrollable. The destroyer *Jarvis* was also damaged.

Controlling the lifeline

Now the Japanese were ready to make a seaborne riposte. After dark a force of five cruisers, two light cruisers and a single destroyer attacked the US vessels near Savo Island off the north-western tip of Guadalcanal, sinking the cruisers *Astoria*, *Quincy*, *Vincennes* and *HMAS Canberra*, while *Chicago* and one destroyer were damaged. In return they escaped with damage to only two of their own cruisers. Following this humiliating defeat, the US ships quickly began to withdraw, even though the unloading of supplies was unfinished. At dawn on 9 August, 16 G4Ms and 15 A6Ms returned to harrass the retreating vessels, sinking the damaged destroyer but losing three bombers to anti-aircraft fire.

Now the Japanese began to send vessels down the stretch of water which came to be known as 'The Slot', through the center of the two north–south chains of islands. The ships were bringing reinforcements to the troops holding out on Guadalcanal. Over the next three months the success or failure of this reinforcement and supply effort was the key to the campaign. By night the Japanese, trained for such operations, were for a time supreme. But by day, control of The Slot passed increasingly to Guadalcanal-based US air power. The initial Japanese effort was costly, however, for on 10 August the cruiser *Kako* was torpedoed and sunk by an American submarine.

Ashore the Marines were finding Guadalcanal no tropical paradise. It was a humid, jungle-clad and mosquito-infested nightmare. Unrelenting rainfall soon turned the black earth into a morass of mud where the troops and airmen, short of food, ammunition and supplies of all kinds, under almost constant sniper and artillery fire from the nearby Japanese, eked out a semi-subterranean existence in tents, dugouts and foxholes. The vital significance of Guadalcanal lay in its airfield, and Marine engineers were struggling to complete the works begun by the Japanese. The first resistance to this — other than by the garrison survivors — came on 11 August when half a dozen Zeros carried out a strafing attack. Eight G4Ms dropped the first bombs a week later on what was soon to be named Henderson Field, after a Marine dive-bomber pilot who had died at Midway. To most of the new occupants Guadalcanal would soon be known by its radio codename — 'Cactus'.

LAND-BASED UNITS OF THE IMPERIAL JAPANESE NAVAL AIR FORCE OPERATING OVER THE SOLOMONS, 7 AUGUST – 15 NOVEMBER 1942

UNIT	DESIGNATION ON BEING RENUMBERED	ARRIVAL/ DEPARTURE
FIGHTERS (Mitsubishi A6M2)		
Tainan Kokutai	251st Ku	7 Aug – late Oct
2nd Kokutai*	382nd Ku	7 Aug – 23 Aug
6th Kokutai	204th Ku	21 Aug –
3rd Kokutai	202nd Ku	1 Sept –
2nd Kokutai	582nd Ku	12 Sept –
253rd Kokutai	253rd Ku	Late Sept –
252nd Kokutai	252nd Ku	9 Nov –
(*2nd Kokutai included also an element of D3A dive-bombers)		
BOMBERS (Mitsubishi G4M1)		
1st Kokutai	752nd Ku	7 Aug –
4th Kokutai	702nd Ku	7 Aug –
Chitose Kokutai	703rd Ku	7 Aug –
Kiarazu Kokutai	disbanded	7 Aug –
Misawa Kokutai	705th Ku	7 Aug –
Mihoro Kokutai	701st Ku	
Kanoya Kokutai	751st Ku	
FLYINGBOATS/FLOATPLANES (Kawanishi H6K, Nakajima A6M2-N, Mitsubishi F1M etc)		
Yokohama Kokutai	801st Ku	7 Aug –
Kamikawa Maru Air Group		23 Aug –
14th Kokutai	802nd Ku	24 Aug –
Toko Kokutai	851st Ku	26 Aug –
CARRIER AIR GROUPS TEMPORARILY LAND-BASED (Mitsubishi A6M2 & 3, Aichi D3A, Nakajima B5N)		
Shokaku Air Group		29 Aug – 3 Sept
Hiyo Air Group		18 Oct –

The first aircraft to land on Henderson's runway of interlocked metal plates was a PBY-5A Catalina amphibious flyingboat which came in on 12 August; eight days later the first squadrons were flown into the island from the escort carrier *Long Island*. These, part of MAG (Marine Air Group) 23, were VMF-223 whose 19 F4F-4s were led by Maj John L Smith, and VMSB-232, with 12 SBD-3s led by a veteran Marine pilot, Lt Col Richard Mangrum. VMF-223's most inexperienced pilots had been exchanged at Efate on the way for eight of VMF-212's longer-serving men. The squadron also included three pilots who had seen service at Midway, most notably Capt Marion Carl.

Their arrival on 20 August was greeted by the opening that night of the first major land battle. Fanatical troops of the Ichiki Detachment, 900-strong and recently landed on the island, attempted to storm across the Tenaru River and were cut to pieces. Next day the 25th Air Flotilla struck again, 26 bombers and 13 Zeros appearing overhead. Four F4Fs intercepted six Zeros, but after firing at one of the Japanese fighters, Major Smith had to crash-land his damaged Wildcat. Reinforcements were on the way for both sides. Eighteen A6Ms of the 6th Kokutai arrived at Rabaul on 21 August after carrier-borne service at Midway, followed by floatplanes from the tender *Kamikawa Maru*.

US AVIATION UNITS BASED ON GUADALCANAL, 20 AUGUST – 15 NOVEMBER 1942

UNIT AND SERVICE	COMMANDER ON ARRIVAL	AIRCRAFT	ARRIVAL/ DEPARTURE
VMF-223. USMC	Maj John L Smith	F4F-4	20 Aug – 16 Oct
VMSB-232. USMC	Lt Col Richard C Mangrum	SBD-3	20 Aug – 12 Oct
67th Fighter Squadron USAAF	Capt Dale D Brannon	P-400, P-39D	22 Aug –
'Flight 300' (Part VS-5, VB-6) USN	Lt Turner Caldwell	SBD-3	24 Aug – 27 Sept
VMF-224. USMC	Maj Robert E Galer	F4F-4	30 Aug – 16 Oct
VMSB-231. USMC	Maj Leo H Smith	SBD-3	30 Aug – 2 Nov
VF-5, USN	Lt Cdr Leroy C Simpler	F4F-4	11 Sept – 12 Oct
VB-3. USN	Lt Cdr Louis J Kirn	SBD-3	12 Sept –
VT-8. USN	Lt Harold H Larsen	TBF-1	12 Sept –
VS-71 (Part) USN	Lt Cdr John Eldridge	SBD-3	28 Sept –
VF-71 (Part) USN		F4F-4	Late Sept – Oct
VMSB-141. USMC	Maj Gordon A Bell	SBD-3	6 Oct – 19 Nov
VMF-121. USMC	Maj Leonard K Davis	F4F-4	9 Oct –
VB-6. USN	Lt Cdr Ray Davis	SBD-3	14 Oct –
VMF-212. USMC	Lt Cdr Harold W Bauer	F4F-4	16 Oct – 22 Nov
VMSB-132. USMC	Maj Joseph Sailer Jnr	SBD-3	29 Oct –
VMF-112 USMC	Maj Paul J Fontana	F4F-4	2 Nov –
VMSB-142. USMC	Maj Robert H Richard	SBD-3	12 Nov –
VMSB-131. USMC	Lt Col Paul Moret	TBF-1	12 Nov –
339th Fighter Squadron (det), USAAF	Maj Dale D Brannon	P-38E	12 Nov –
39th Fighter Squadron (det), USAAF	Capt Robert Fauret	P-38E	13 Nov – 22 Nov
70th Bomb Squadron USAAF		B-26B	14 Nov –
Air Group 10 – USN			
VF-10		F4F-4)	
VS-10, VB-10		SBD-3)	14 Nov –
VT-10		TBF-1)	

BELL P-400 AIRACOBRA FIGHTERS OF THE 67TH FIGHTER SQUADRON. TAKEN OVER FROM BRITISH ORDERS, THESE WERE THE FIRST USAAF AIRCRAFT TO SEE SERVICE ON GUADALCANAL.

More H6K flyingboats from the 14th Kokutai reached Rabaul soon afterwards. At Henderson, 22 August saw the arrival of five P-400s (export versions of the Bell P-39 Airacobra fighter) of the 67th Fighter Squadron, USAAF, led by Captain Dale D Brannon.

Race to reinforce
Japanese efforts to reinforce the island were now redoubled, and these led to the first of two major carrier actions. A transport and four destroyers converted to the transport role were spotted approaching Guadalcanal from the north. They were carrying 1500 troops and were supported by two fleet carriers, a light carrier, a seaplane tender, two battleships, four cruisers, two light cruisers and 21 destroyers. The light carrier *Ryujo* was being employed as 'bait' to draw off any US carrier involvement, allowing the fleet carrier air groups an undisturbed opportunity to destroy the American capital ships. To face this threat, Admiral Fletcher headed back into the Solomons with two carriers, a battleship, three cruisers, one light cruiser and ten destroyers. This smaller force could, however, look to the land-based aviation on Guadalcanal for support.

During the afternoon of 23 August, 31 SBDs and six Grumman TBF Avenger torpedo-bombers from *Saratoga* took off to attack the transports. Failing to find them, they landed at Henderson Field and stayed there overnight, before returning to their parent vessel while scouts from *Enterprise* searched for the Japanese ships. Japanese reconnaissance aircraft were also out.

At midday, two Japanese H6Ks were shot down by VF-5 fighters. Early in the afternoon *Ryujo* launched 15 A6Ms and six Nakajima B5N bombers to attack Henderson Field, augmented by 20 G4Ms which had flown down from Rabaul. Fourteen F4Fs of VMF-223 and some 67th Squadron P-400s were scrambled, and — in their first major engagement over the island — the defenders claimed 21 victories. A Zero was credited to Capt Brannon and Lt Deltis H Fincher as the first USAAF victory in the South Pacific area. The Marines claimed seven more fighters; 11 of the single-engined B5Ns (again more than were actually taking part!) and two G4Ms, for the loss of four of their number. Actual losses of B5Ns and A6Ms were three and one respectively, but Lt Kenjiro Notomi's escorting Zero pilots were just as optimistic, claiming that they had seen 15 Wildcats shot down over Guadalcanal. Among the Marine

pilots, Marion Carl was credited with four victories, which with his earlier success over Midway made him the first Marine ace of the war. 2/Lt Zenneth Pond claimed three, and four other pilots received credit for two victories each.

The carrier battle starts

Ryujo had been spotted twice by PBY Catalinas, and was found again early in the afternoon by SBDs from *Enterprise* which then spotted the big carriers *Shokaku* and *Zuikaku*. The two scout bombers courageously dived and bombed *Shokaku*, causing slight damage. One was then shot down by Zeros as it attempted to attack a cruiser. On receipt of the initial sighting, *Saratoga* had launched 29 SBDs and seven TBFs led by Cdr Don Felt, the Air Group Commander. These attacked *Ryujo* at 1620 hours, achieving four bomb hits and one torpedo hit and they left her sinking. Defending fighters claimed 11 attackers, but the US force suffered no loss at all; most of the Japanese A6Ms were obliged to ditch in the sea. The stricken *Ryujo* was then attacked by seven 11th Bomb Group B-17s, which resulted only in a near-miss.

A Japanese floatplane had meanwhile spotted the US carriers. It had time to alert the Japanese fleet carriers before it was shot down in flames by a vigilant VF-6 F4F. Acting quickly on the information, the carriers launched a considerable attack-force, consisting of 54 D3A dive-bombers, 12 B5N torpedo-bombers and 19 A6Ms in two waves, an hour apart. Anticipating this attack, the US carriers put 53 F4Fs into the air in readiness, accompanied by SBD scouts. There was just time for the carriers to send up a further strike of SBDs and TBFs before the first wave of attackers arrived.

The first wave of ten Zeros and 27 D3As which homed in on the US Fleet met a host of Wildcats and SBDs which almost overwhelmed them. About 15 Japanese dive-bombers slipped through this net, striking and damaging *Enterprise*. Three hits put her out of action. The price of this one casualty was, however, high to the Japanese. Six of the ten Zeros went down as well as 18 D3As. High as these figures were, US claims in the aftermath of the battle were higher, totalling 51 — which was substantially more than the strength of the entire Japanese formation. VF-5 claimed 17 for the loss of four F4Fs and three pilots, while VF-6 claimed 27 for two losses. The SBDs claimed a further seven and even a VT-3 Avenger crew claimed one D3A and a probable. Indeed 32 of the total claims related to the dive-bombers, of which three and a probable were credited to Lt Hayden Jensen of VF-5. Lt Carlton Starkes was credited with three confirmed, as was VF-6's Machinist Donald Runyon. Gunner Charles Brewer of the same unit also claimed three, and no less than seven other pilots claimed two each. The returning A6M pilots of the *Shokaku* and *Zuikaku* claimed ten victories between them.

Amongst the bombers that left the US carriers just before the attack, two SBDs found the tender *Chitose* and damaged her with two hits. With their carrier out of action,

PLAYING AN IMPORTANT PART THROUGHOUT THE CAMPAIGN, BOTH FROM LAND BASES AND FROM THE US CARRIERS, WERE THE TOUGH, RELIABLE DOUGLAS SBD-3 DAUNTLESS DIVE-BOMBERS OF THE USN AND USMC. THESE BOMB-LADEN NAVY AIRCRAFT ARE JUST ABOUT TO TAKE OFF FROM THEIR CARRIER.

JOE FOSS — HERO OF GUADALCANAL

Joe Foss was far from being the typical carefree young fighter ace of popular mythology. Born in April 1915 of farming stock, his parentage was Norwegian and Scots-Irish. Following the death of his father while he was still a boy, Foss worked his way through college, and then trained as a civilian pilot during 1937.

He joined the US Marine Corps early in 1940, and a year later, on qualification, was made an instructor.

When war broke out he was at first refused active duty as a fighter pilot on the grounds that at 27 he was already too old. Undeterred, he kept trying and eventually obtained a posting to Fighting Squadron VMF-121 in California as Executive Officer with the rank of Captain, in August 1942. In September he married, but a month later found himself with the squadron flying into Henderson Field, Guadalcanal, to see active service.

During the unit's first rather unsuccessful engagement on 13 October he claimed the first victory for the squadron over a Zero fighter, although his own aircraft was badly shot-up. This did not affect his performance, and with the example before him of the island's leading aces, John Smith and Marion Carl, he was back in action next day, claiming another Zero. His first multiple claim came on 18 October when victories over two Zeros and a 'twin-tailed bomber' made him an ace. In a fierce dogfight on 23 October he claimed four Zeros, while two separate fights on 25 October added five more to raise his total by the end of October to 16 in 12 days. Already he was second only to Smith.

It was some days before he met Japanese aircraft again, but on 7 November his unit intercepted a formation of floatplanes over a convoy well to the north of Guadalcanal. Of the nine that were claimed, one Zero floatplane fighter and two F1M float biplanes were credited to Foss to equal Smith's total of 19. Five days later another interception of

JOE FOSS' 'FLYING CIRCUS'—A FLIGHT OF MARINE FIGHTING SQUADRON VMF-121 WITH A GRUMMAN F4F-4 WILDCAT FIGHTER ON GUADALCANAL; FOSS HIMSELF STANDS ON THE WHEEL OF THE AIRCRAFT.

a raid on Henderson was undertaken by VMF-121, Foss claiming two G4M bombers and a Zero to become the first American of World War II to reach 20 victories. Three days later on 15 November — the day on which Guadalcanal's security was at last made certain — he sent down another float biplane to bring his total to 23.

Now suffering severely from malaria, he was evacuated on 19 November for rest and recuperation, returning to Guadalcanal in January 1943. On 15 January over New Georgia he claimed

three more Zeros to bring his score to 26 — the first to equal the total of the great American ace of World War I, Eddie Rickenbacker. Eleven days later he was ordered home, but on the way suffered a recurrence of malaria that almost cost him his life. On reaching the US he was awarded the Congressional Medal of Honor and feted as a national hero.

During his time on the island, Foss had led his flight of eight to 72 confirmed victories, and five of his pilots also became aces, the most successful being Lt Bill Marontate with 13. They divided themselves into two four-man divisions — the 'Farm Boys' and the 'City Slickers'.

Foss later succeeded in civil life as well, entering politics and becoming Governor of South Dakota. Joining the USAF Reserve, he reached the rank of Brigadier General. At the time of writing he had become Commissioner of the American Football League at Dallas, Texas.

11 of the *Enterprise* SBDs were led by Lt Turner Caldwell to Henderson. They were destined to stay there as 'Flight 300' until September 27. The second wave of Japanese aircraft had meanwhile missed the carriers, and were eventually obliged to turn back. Several ran out of fuel and were forced to ditch.

A dozen SBDs from Henderson Field found the transport force led by the cruiser *Jintsu* on the morning of 25 August. VMSB-232's Lt Lawrence Baldinus put his bomb just forward of the warship's bridge, badly damaging her, while Ens Charles Fink (one of the *Enterprise* pilots) hit the transport *Kinryu Maru* amidships. Blazing from stem to stern, she had to be sunk by the destroyer *Mutsuki*, which stopped to pick up survivors. At this point eight B-17s of the 11th Bomb Group scored three hits on the destroyer while it was vulnerable, sinking it. VMSB-232 crews also claimed to have shot down two floatplanes which were escorting the ships. The Battle of the Eastern Solomons was over.

Next day the 25th Air Flotilla resumed battle. A strong force of G4Ms and escorting Zeros took off to attack Henderson. VMF-223 took up the challenge, claiming seven bombers and five fighters, three of the former being credited to Capt Loren Everton. Japanese losses were stated as only three bombers. This was misleading: Lt Junichi Sasai, one of the Tainan Ku's 'stars' with 27 victories, fell on this date to the F4Fs — possibly to Marion Carl, who claimed two Zeros. US losses included one F4F lost while on the ground, several aircraft damaged and 2000 gallons of precious aviation gasoline destroyed.

The island therefore welcomed the arrival of nine more Army P-400s on 27 August, just in time to meet a renewed threat. Four destroyers from Truk — the great Japanese Fleet base in the Caroline Islands — tried to run another 3500 troops down The Slot next day. Spotted by patrolling SBDs, they were attacked by 11 of the dive-bombers at evening; these for a single loss sank the *Asagiri*, which blew up, set the *Yugiri* on fire and brought *Sirakumo* to a halt. The survivors came ashore next day.

Fighting over the island

Shokaku's airgroup, which had landed at a new airstrip on Buka Island, began a series of operations on 29 August over Guadalcanal. In three days these were to cost them eight Zeros and six pilots. The first Japanese attack took place at noon, the attack force comprising 18 bombers and 22 fighters. Ten F4Fs and 14 P-400s scrambled to intercept the attackers, but the latter failed to reach the raiders' altitude. The Marines, however, did make contact, and in the fighting that ensued claimed five bombers and six Zeros for no losses of their own.

Shokaku sent out 18 A6M3s the next day on a sweep which caught four American P-400s on patrol over the transport *Burrows* aground on Tulagi. US reinforcements rose to the rescue in the shape of seven more P-400s and eight F4Fs. These attacked the Zeros, 16 of which were claimed for the loss of four P-400s and two pilots; actual losses amounted to seven A6Ms — a severe enough blow to the Japanese nonetheless. Two were credited to Capt Brannon of the 67th Squadron, but the rest were claimed by the Marines, Maj Smith personally claiming four and Capt Carl three. When 18 bombers and 22 Zeros came over later in the afternoon they escaped interception.

It was now clear that the P-400 was not suitable for the interception task, and the Army pilots were allocated the ground-support role instead, for the Airacobra was an excellent 'strafer'; defense of the island was left wholly in the hands of the Marines. In this however, they were joined during the day by the 19 newly-arrived F4Fs of Maj Bob Galer's VMF-224 which flew in with the 12 SBDs of VMSB-231 to bring MAG 23 to full strength.

US forces were, however, worsted in the next confrontation on 31 August. When 17 of VMF-224's new Wildcats were scrambled to intercept an incoming raid, three were lost with nothing to show for their efforts. Worse was to come. West of Santa Cruz Islands, the patrolling *Saratoga* was hit by a submarine torpedo and damaged, being forced to withdraw. With *Enterprise* under repair, only *Wasp* and *Hornet* — newly-arrived — were now available. It was fortunate for the Americans that the Japanese Fleet failed to venture into Solomons waters during September. Action centered instead over Henderson Field, where Japan's Rabaul-based units made nine more major raids during the month.

The first raid occurred on 2 September, when F4Fs from both squadrons intercepted 18 G4Ms and 22 A6Ms, claiming three bombers and four fighters without loss. Bob Galer, whose squadron recorded four of the successes on this occasion, was credited with a bomber and a fighter. During the day six Wildcats and two Airacobras strafed 15 landing boats which were bringing in part of a force of 5200 troops led by Maj Gen Kawaguchi. A single F4F was lost when it was hit by their return fire, crashing into the sea.

The September raids begin

A new fighter airfield was opened 2000 yards to the east of Henderson, on 9 September and was christened 'Fighter One'. Its opening was a memorable one. Twenty-six escorted G4Ms were that day intercepted by elements of both squadrons, which shot down five bombers and three Zeros for the loss of four Wildcats. One of these was flown by Capt Carl who baled out after claiming two bombers, and landed in the water. At this time Carl was top-scorer in the area with 12 victories over the island. He managed to get ashore and make contact with local natives who guided him back to Henderson. When he made it back to base, John Smith had claimed a further five victories to overtake him — much to his chagrin. It was a lead which he never recovered. VMF-223 had lost one of its other aces during this period however, 2/Lt Zenneth Pond, who was the pilot of the only F4F to be lost on 10 September when four more G4Ms were lost by the Japanese from a raiding force of 27 (the Marines claimed five).

Despite the efforts of the defenders, the Japanese had landed 6000 troops on Guadalcanal by 11 September. A raid on the airfields on that date destroyed a P-400 and wounded Capt Brannon and two other Army pilots on the ground; all three had to be evacuated. However, during the day — which saw six more bombers and a Zero go down for the loss of a single F4F — the 24 F4Fs of *Saratoga's* fighter squadron, VF-5, arrived on the island

OVERLEAF: MITSUBISHI G4MI BOMBERS OF THE MISAWA KOKUTAI PASS OVER RABAUL'S SIMPSON HARBOUR AS THEY HEAD OFF FOR ANOTHER ATTACK ON GUADALCANAL ON 28 SEPTEMBER, 1942. THE ATTRITION OF THE FIGHTING HERE SERIOUSLY WEAKENED THE IJNAF'S BOMBER ARM, WHICH PLAYED LITTLE FURTHER PART IN THE PACIFIC WAR'S MAJOR ACTIONS AFTER THIS PERIOD.

GRUMMAN F4F-4 WILDCAT FIGHTER TAKES OFF FROM 'CACTUS' FOR AN INTERCEPTION MISSION.

for land-based duty during the carrier's absence for repairs.

During their first operation from the island, 21 Navy Wildcats joined 11 Marine aircraft to intercept 42 G4Ms and their escort. Twelve bombers and three Zeros were claimed for the loss of one VF-5 aircraft (and damage to another). The 2nd Kokutai, making one of its first sorties over the island with 15 A6Ms, claimed 11 victories! All squadrons were up again two days later to meet a 20 Zero sweep. Three Zeros were claimed for the loss of two Wildcats. An escorted raid by 28 G4Ms followed which resulted in further claims for six bombers and two fighters at a cost of four F4Fs. It was a very bad day for the Japanese fighters, no less than three of their aces being killed, including Lt Takatsuka (16 victories) and NAP 2/C Uto (19 victories) of the Tainan Ku.

On the same day 17 more reinforcement F4Fs arrived, flown in from the two fleet carriers by Navy pilots, who then returned to their vessels. They were followed in the afternoon by more of *Saratoga*'s airgroup — the 12 SBDs of VS-3 led by Lt Cdr Louis Kirn and six TBF Avengers of VT-8 led by Lt Harold 'Swede' Larsen. Rabaul was also reinforced when the 26th Air Flotilla flew in, bringing 72 more bombers, 60 A6Ms and eight reconnaissance aircraft.

Life on 'Cactus' Island

Losses and casualties at the hands of the Japanese enemy were only part of the problem on Guadalcanal. A pair of SBDs were lost on 6 September when they flew into a weather front on their way to attack shipping in Gizo Harbor. Two days later, Wildcats took off in rain and fog. Conditions deteriorated still further and they were recalled. On landing one crashed into a bulldozer and four others suffered accidents. If this were not enough, during the night of 12–13 September fierce shelling by the Japanese killed three SBD pilots. Among them was Larry Baldinus who had been responsible for damaging the cruiser *Jintsu* the previous month. The Marine airmen were a tough lot, however, and when Lt Richard Amerine of VMF-224 was shot down early in September, he made his way back to Henderson after baling out, killing four Japanese soldiers en route.

A new service which played an increasingly important part in making life bearable was opened during the night of 5 September when a Douglas R4D (Dakota) transport landed to deliver supplies of cigarettes and candy, and to carry out wounded. Squadron VMJ-253 had just reached Tacoblan in the New Hebrides as the first part of the all-transport MAG 25, and was inaugurating a service which would grow swiftly.

Earlier in the month the floatplanes from the *Kamikawa Maru* had been detached from Rabaul down to Shortland Island. Three A6M2-N Zero floatplane fighters undertook a reconnaissance to the Guadalcanal area on 14 September. Here they were intercepted by VF-5 Wildcats which shot down all of them (four were claimed). Soon after midday, 28 G4M bombers arrived for a normal raid, escorted by 11 A6Ms of the 2nd Ku, whose pilots claimed 10 victories. The intercepting Marine F4Fs of VMF-223 claimed one G4M and also a 'twin-tailed bomber' — possibly one of the earlier Mitsubishi G3Ms which were now being used in small numbers to conserve the dwindling supply of G4Ms remaining. The defending fighters suffered no loss. Later another scramble took place involving both Navy and Marine fighters. A *Kamikawa Maru* Zero floatplane piloted by Lt Ono claimed one F4F shot down over Henderson (actually *none* were lost). NAP 2/C Matsutara Ohmura was shot down by Lt (jg) Elisha Stover of VF-5. It seems that the float Zeros were escorting other floatplanes, for Stover and Ens John Weslowski then claimed three twin-float single-engined biplanes near Savo Island, while Maj John Dobbin and Lt George Hollowell of VMF-224 each claimed three single-float biplanes — probably Mitsubishi F1Ms.

This unusual success was marred on 15 September by the news that the carrier *Wasp* had been sunk by a Japanese submarine to the south-east of the Solomons. The well-handled attacker also inflicted damage on the battleship *North Carolina*. Now only *Hornet* remained intact. Strength of the 'Cactus' air forces had reached 63 aircraft by mid-month however — 29 F4Fs, 26 SBDs, five TBFs and three P-400s — and these were soon joined by six more Navy TBFs, and then later in the month by a further ten SBDs and TBFs. The R4D transports began flying in pilots of VMF-121 and VMSB-141 from MAG 14 to reinforce the existing units. With them came Lt Col Cooley, the MAG 14 commander, on 23 September, who took charge of all bombers on the island. The Japanese still had the edge on these forces with 100 fighters and 80 bombers available at Rabaul. To balance this disproportion, the Americans could rely on the B-17s of the 11th Bomb Group — now reinforced up to four squadrons — which were regularly active throughout the Solomons from their base further south. The remaining five pilots and 11 gunners of *Enterprise* Flight 300, which had been on the island since the carrier battle, left at last on 27 September. They were replaced next day by six new SBDs and crews from VS-71

MAJ JOHN L SMITH LED THE FIRST MARINE SQUADRON IN TO GUADALCANAL'S HENDERSON FIELD ON 20 AUGUST, 1942. HIS VMF-223 PILOTS EMERGED WITH THE HIGHEST TOTAL OF VICTORIES DURING THE BATTLE FOR THE ISLAND, BEING CREDITED WITH 110 JAPANESE AIRCRAFT SHOT DOWN; 19 OF THESE WERE ACCOUNTED FOR BY SMITH, WHO RECEIVED THE CONGRESSIONAL MEDAL OF HONOR.

(ex-*Wasp*) and four more Avengers for VT-8. The residue of *Wasp's* fighter squadron, VF-71, would also soon arrive.

Defending furiously

The Japanese renewed their air assault the same day when 18 G4Ms came down The Slot, escorted by no less than 38 Zeros. Sixteen Wildcats from VMF-223 and -224 were quickly launched to attack the bombers, while 18 VF-5 fighters engaged the escort. Six of each were claimed without loss, two thirds of them by the Marines, but the Japanese bombing was all-too-accurate and ten SBDs and TBFs were destroyed or badly damaged on the ground. All three squadrons were scrambled again next day when 27 bombers returned, covered by 42 Zeros. Half of these were from the 2nd Ku which Cdr Yamamoto had led down to the new strip on Buka Island. From here the distance to the target was substantially reduced.

This time the defenders really hit the bombers hard, and claims indicated a tremendous success — 23 were claimed. Bob Galer, CO of VMF-224 was credited with three, Smith and Carl of VMF-223 claiming one each to raise their personal scores to 17 and 15½ respectively; and one was credited to Lt Col Harold Bauer, CO of VMF-212, who had come up from Efate to fly with Galer's unit. Nine of the claims were made by VF-5, three of whose pilots claimed two apiece; two Zeros were also claimed. The reality was more modest, but still represented a considerable achievement — seven bombers and one Zero fighter were lost at no cost to the Americans.

The last raid of the month occurred on 29 September. A further fighter Kokutai, the 253rd, had now reached the Solomons, and was based at Kavieng in New Ireland. Nine of this unit's A6Ms joined 18 others to escort nine G4Ms to Henderson. The Americans scrambled 30 F4Fs. In the furious engagement which ensued, the Japanese lost only one Zero, but made eight claims. Four were credited to Petty Officers Kenichi Abe and Ohkura of the 253rd Ku for the unit's first successes in this theater.

October proved to be a month of hard fighting, with frequent engagements both over the island and over shipping in The Slot. The month began badly for the Americans when 36 Zeros sweeping over the area caught six of the 33 Wildcats which were scrambled, at a disadvantage as they struggled for height. VMF-223 lost two of its fighters in the first pass; by the time the fight was over losses had risen to six for only four claims. John Smith had emerged from cloud to engage three A6Ms, claiming one shot down before his aircraft was shot up by the others and he was obliged to crash-land at Fighter One. VMF-224's Bob Galer claimed two Zeros but his F4F was also hit and he baled out.

The balance was redressed next day when 27 more A6Ms swept over 'Cactus'. This time only seven Marine Wildcats took off, but these managed to inflict heavy losses, claiming nine shot down while the AA defenses claimed two more; actual Japanese losses on this occasion totalled nine A6Ms. Marion Carl claimed one of these and Ken Frazier two, although forced to bale out himself, but honors for the day went to Lt Col Bauer, the visiting VMF-212 CO, who led a division of VMF-223 Wildcats in this interception, personally claiming four Zeros shot down and a fifth as a probable. Amongst the victims was a 3rd Ku ace, Ens Sadao Yamaguchi; he and his Shotai had just claimed three Wildcats between them when he was hit and force-landed on Guadalcanal. He was rescued by Japanese troops and subsequently returned to his unit to fight again.

It was now the better part of a month since Henderson Field's bombers had enjoyed any success against the shipping plying up and down The Slot — the nightly visitations by troop and supply-carrying destroyers and cruisers were now referred to collectively as the 'Tokyo Express' by the Americans. The situation was remedied on 5 October when Lt Cdr Lou Kirn led nine of his VS-3 SBDs after a destroyer force which had been spotted in the waters near Guadalcanal. Kirn personally got a hit on *Minegumo*, which was damaged, while three other pilots inflicted damage on *Murasame*. Later in the day VMSB-141 SBDs attacked two light cruisers and four destroyers north of New Georgia, Lt W H Fuller claiming a direct hit on one of the larger vessels, although no Japanese record of this attack has been found.

Fighting over The Slot

The SBDs and TBFs operating up and down The Slot were also frequently engaged by Japanese floatplanes, and occasionally by Zero fighters, their gunners making several claims against these during the month. Japanese reinforcement of the Guadalcanal forces was not being stopped, however, and during the night of 8–9 October the seaplane tender *Nissin* arrived to deliver much-needed heavy equipment. 'Cactus' air power had again been strengthened, 11 Bell P-39D Airacobra fighters flown by pilots of the USAAF's 339th Squadron having arrived on 7 October to fly with the 67th Squadron and its P-400s. With *Wasp's* SBDs and *Saratoga's* SBDs and TBFs, 81 aircraft were now available, and many of these were out over The Slot on 9 October to attack the retiring vessels of the 'Tokyo Express'.

Floatplanes were encountered seeking to defend the vessels and two of these were claimed shot down by the new P-39s; one of the Japanese pilots claimed two Airacobras in return, while another claimed an SBD and a probable. Floatplanes were again met next day when VMF-223 flew its last sorties from Guadalcanal to escort SBDs and TBFs after shipping near New Georgia.

Fifteen A6M2-Ns and assorted biplane floatplanes attempted to 'bounce' the formation, but three of each type were claimed shot down by the Marines, including one by John Smith who thereby raised his score to 19. A seventh was claimed by a VMF-224 pilot as this unit's Wildcats were completing a strafing attack on six warships. Japanese witnesses reported seeing two of the A6M2-N pilots shoot down 'at least four' US aircraft before they fell themselves; one of these was NAP 2/C Nishiyawa, who had claimed the two P-39s on the previous day.

Meanwhile, on 5 October VMF-121 had flown off the escort carrier *Copahee* Maj Leonard K Davis leading his unit of 20 brand new F4F-4s to the island. On 11 October the Japanese were back in force for the first time in a week, 17 Zeros sweeping over the island, followed by a bombing force of 30 G4Ms, escorted by another 30 A6Ms. Thirty-one Marine and eight Navy Wildcats, three P-400s and nine P-39s took off to intercept, claiming nine of the bombers and four Zeros for the loss of one P-39. Either on this or a subsequent mission the 6th Ku reported losing five A6Ms during a patrol in foul weather on this date, one of those missing being flown by 9-victory ace Juzo Okamoto.

After dark the 'Express' was back, landing artillery, tanks and troops without hindrance. A covering force of three cruisers and two destroyers moved in to shell US positions, but was met by a US naval force comprising two

OPERATING FROM THE NEW HEBRIDES IN SUPPORT OF THE DEFENDERS OF GUADALCANAL THROUGHOUT THE 1942 FIGHTING, THE BOEING FORTRESS BOMBERS OF THE 11TH BOMB GROUP WERE IN FACT THE FIRST US AIRCRAFT TO APPEAR OVER THE ISLAND.

cruisers, two light cruisers and five destroyers. In the Battle of Cape Esperance which followed, the Americans drove off the Japanese at the cost of one destroyer, sinking one cruiser and one destroyer in doing so.

With the dawn, US aircraft were out again after the Japanese naval forces, 16 SBDs spotting three destroyers to the north of Russell Island, which they attacked, damaging the *Murakumo*. They were followed by six more SBDs from VS-3, VS-71 and VMSB-141 led by Lt Cdr Lou Kirn, six TBFs of VT-8, and 14 F4Fs. Three of the dive-bombers near-missed the damaged *Murakumo* while an Avenger put a torpedo into her; she sank that afternoon. The bombers were out again before darkness fell, obtaining hits on *Natsugumo* which caused the destroyer to blow up and sink at once.

During 12 October, VMF-223 became the first unit to finish its tour on Guadalcanal and leave the island for a rest. Since 20 August the squadron had claimed 110 victories — 47 of them over A6M Zero fighters, at a cost of ten pilots. They had produced eight aces, including two of the leaders, John Smith with 19 and Marion Carl with 16½; Smith subsequently became the island's first airman to be awarded the Congressional Medal of Honor. Next day the unit was followed off the island by the surviving crews of VMSB-232.

The punishment continues

The successful efforts of the SBDs and TBFs on 12 October brought speedy retribution next day. Twenty-four G4Ms and 15 A6Ms raided Henderson Field, and the 42 F4Fs and 13 Airacobras sent off after them were late in scrambling and could not prevent an accurate bombing attack. One G4M and one A6M were claimed for the loss of a Wildcat which was hit by fire from the bombers. Later in the day 18 more bombers appeared again with escort. The newly-arrived VMF-121 went up after them, but only one F4F made contact when Lt Joe Foss became separated and engaged a Zero, shooting it down before his own aircraft was hit and damaged by others.

During these raids Henderson Field received 13 bombs on the runway and lost 5000 gallons of fuel which was hit and burnt. But that was only the beginning! At dusk a 150mm artillery piece which had recently been landed by the Japanese and soon became known as 'Pistol Pete', began shelling the airfield. Then at 0400 hours the area erupted in explosions. The Imperial Japanese Navy (IJN) had despatched two battleships, *Haruna* and *Kongo*, to bombard the airfield, and in a short period these two armored giants hurled over 900 14-inch shells onto the American base. Before dawn G4Ms were back to shower the area with more bombs.

Dawn on 14 October found a sorry picture; while some aircraft had been destroyed, many others were damaged and rendered unserviceable. Of 41 F4Fs, 29 were flyable, but only seven of the 39 SBDs were immediately available, and no TBFs. The USAAF could field four P-400s and just two of six P-39s. Over 40 men had been killed including Maj Bell, CO of VMSB-141, a flight commander, an executive officer and two other pilots. Radio communications had been destroyed and nearly all available fuel had gone up in flames. When 25 G4Ms appeared overhead that morning nothing opposed them and they were able to bomb Henderson at their leisure.

The Americans recovered quickly, however, and when 15 more bombers returned with a Zero escort, 24 Wildcats from VF-5, VMF-121 and -224 met them, claiming 11 bombers and three fighters shot down for the loss of just one F4F. Scouts flew out over The Slot and these soon reported the approach of six Japanese transports escorted

ABOVE: AICHI D3A DIVE-BOMBERS APPEARED FREQUENTLY OVER THE SOLOMONS, SOME FLYING FROM AIRFIELDS IN NEW BRITAIN, WHILE OTHERS OPERATED FROM THE DECKS OF THE VARIOUS JAPANESE CARRIERS. HERE ONE OF THESE AIRCRAFT HEADS OUT OVER THE COAST IN THE RABAUL AREA GOING DOWN THE SLOT TOWARDS GUADALCANAL.

RIGHT: A BOMB-LADEN D3A TAKES OFF FROM A RABAUL AIRFIELD.

by destroyers, and a bombardment force of two cruisers and two destroyers. Four SBDs went out to attack early in the afternoon, followed by nine more, but their assaults were ineffective — and they certainly did not prevent Henderson Field being bombarded again that night.

On 15 October five of the transports were seen unloading troops and supplies off Tassafaronga with a covering patrol of fighters overhead. It was too late to stop their arrival, but it could still be made expensive. Three SBDs attempted to get off, but two ran into craters from the bombardment. Eventually a force did take off. It comprised a single PBY amphibian carrying two torpedoes, a dozen SBDs, four F4Fs, three P-39s and one P-400, the Army aircraft all carrying bombs. Over the ships five Zeros and a float biplane were claimed shot down for the loss of two P-39s, one F4F and three SBDs, but three of the transports were hit and left beached and on fire.

Eleven B-17s from Espiritu Santo then attacked and hit another, all four vessels being damaged beyond repair; the two survivors withdrew. 'Cactus' was building up again, for during the day six more SBDs flew in together with fuel-carrying R4Ds. Next morning Dauntlesses and Airacobras were out to strafe the newly-arrived Japanese troops on several occasions.

American comings and goings
The remaining MAG23 aircrews departed on 16 October, after Bob Galer had led VMF-224 on a last strafe of the beached transports. The fighter pilots were joined on the R4Ds by those of VF-5 and the dive-bomber crews of VMSB-231. The second Marine fighter unit to go had claimed 56½ victories for the loss of seven Wildcats, while the Navy pilots had lost eight pilots (five killed and three wounded) against claims for 45½ during their time on the island.

The departure of VMF-224 was followed immediately by the arrival of VMF-212. After his brief and fruitful visit to the island, 'Joe' Bauer had returned to Espiritu Santo to collect his unit, but as he led the 18 F4Fs on the approach to the island he saw nine D3A dive-bombers which were attacking the destroyer/transport McFarland, being unloaded at the time. The attackers had just hit a fuel barge when Bauer broke away from his formation and attacked, shooting down four of them; the AA defenses claimed a fifth.

Aichi dive-bombers were again over the island next day (17 October) when a group of 18 D3As and 18 A6Ms, drawn equally from the two aircraft carriers Hiyo and Junyo, approached to attack two US destroyers. They were intercepted by eight Wildcats of VMF-121, Maj Davis and his pilots submitting claims for six D3As and four A6Ms for the loss of one F4F; Davis and three other pilots each claimed two. Six of Junyo's nine D3As failed to return from this sortie, while amongst the Zeros Hiyo's Lt (jg) Kaname Harada (9 victories) was badly wounded. Following this action Hiyo suffered engine trouble and was forced to return to Japan for repairs, her air group being put ashore at Rabaul to continue action over Guadalcanal.

The day saw the departure of Lt Cdr Lou Kirn and the last seven crews of VS-3, but the SBDs remained active. During the afternoon Lt (jg) C H Master of VS-71 on a scouting sortie over Rekata Bay, saw an F1M float biplane taking off and at once shot it down. He was then attacked by four more F1Ms and an A6M2-N, and was himself shot down by the latter, flown by NAP 3/C Hisao Jito; he and his gunner got ashore safely.

No let up for the defenders
While the actions of 17 October saw the last attempts to run ships down The Slot for some days, it certainly did not indicate a quieter time for the Americans on Guadalcanal. Shelling by 'Pistol Pete' effectively closed down Henderson Field for the next five days while the defenders of the Lunga perimeter awaited a renewed assault by the reinforced Japanese ground forces. Luckily for the Americans, this did not come until 23 October and even then was ill-co-

ordinated and poorly executed. Prepared and ready for the attacks, the Marine and Army infantry in their trenches and foxholes were able to drive off all attempts with heavy losses to the attackers.

Air raids continued undiminished, and during the next six days there were attacks on every day — with continued heavy over-claiming by both sides. On 18 October 15 G4Ms and nine A6Ms attacked, 15 Marine Wildcats intercepting with, for the first time, two flown by VF-71 pilots. Claims were submitted for seven bombers and 15 Zeros, 19 of them by VF-121. Among the Japanese pilots, Wt Off Yoshio Hashiguchi and his two 3rd Ku wingmen claimed five F4Fs and two probables between them. Actual losses on this date only amounted to two G4Ms and four A6Ms for two F4Fs!

A Zero sweep on 19 October was followed by raids by escorted G4Ms on 20, 21 and 23 October. During these three attacks, eight G4Ms and 37 A6Ms were claimed shot down, 21 of the fighters being claimed on 23 October, 11 by VMF-121, nine by VMF-212, and one by a P-39. On 22 October D3A dive-bombers appeared over the island again, and five of these were claimed by VMF-121. The total cost of these five days amounted to five F4Fs shot down, but one of the two lost on the third day was flown by 7-victory ace Gunner 'Tex' Hamilton, who was killed. In this same combat the Tainan Ku lost another of their great aces, Wt Off Toshio Ohta failing to return after being seen to get his 34th victory.

Weather was bad at this time, heavy rain turning the air-fields into quagmires as artillery shelling and suicidal charges by 'Banzai' shouting Japanese assault troops reached their climax on 25 October — 'Dug-out Sunday' to the defenders of Lunga and Henderson Field. Early on this day six SBDs set off for the usual morning search of The Slot; they soon found trouble, spotting first three destroyers, and then five more with the light cruiser Yura heading south obviously intending to make a further bombardment. At once a strike of five SBDs was prepared and led off by Lt Cdr John Eldridge, the larger force of ships being found soon after midday. Eldridge personally put a 1000lb bomb through the cruiser's deck, and two other pilots near-missed her. Bomb-carrying P-39s then attacked, hitting the Yura again with a light bomb, while the Akizuki was damaged for the second time by near misses. By now Yura was burning, but her ordeal was not yet over as four B-17s appeared high overhead, claiming a further hit. As evening drew on she was sunk by torpedoes from her escorting destroyers, and the rest of the force withdrew followed by the limping Akizuki; there was no bombardment that night.

The island was still under air attack, however, several Zero sweeps coming over. During the morning of 25 October Marine Wildcat pilots claimed ten A6Ms shot down, while during an afternoon raid, five G4Ms and eight more Zeros were claimed; 14 of these successes were credited to VMF-121, while the handful of VF-71 pilots registered their sixth and last claim over Guadalcanal. Amongst the A6M pilots lost, two more Japanese aces were included — Petty Officers Yoshimura and Moriura.

Japanese assault coordinated
A greater threat to the security of the island now arose. While the Japanese Army and Navy seldom managed to co-ordinate their major efforts, late October 1942 saw an exception to the rule. In conjunction with the land offensive, a strong carrier task force was again assembled to

sweep into the area and destroy any remaining US sea power. Thus on 25 October Vice Admiral Nagumo's force approached the area from Truk. In the van was the Advance Force of two battleships, four heavy cruisers, one light cruiser, 14 destroyers and Rear Admiral K Kakuta's Carrier Division 2, including the fleet carrier *Junyo*. Following came Nagumo with Carrier Division 1 — *Shokaku*, *Zuikaku*, and the light carrier *Zuiho*, supported by two more battleships, four heavy cruisers, a light cruiser, 16 destroyers and four oilers.

Three US task forces under the overall command of Vice Admiral Halsey were standing by to the east of the Solomons in case of any such intrusion, but these had a strength only about half that of the Japanese force. *Enterprise* in Task Force 16 was supported by one battleship, one heavy and one anti-aircraft cruiser, and eight destroyers. In Task Force 17 *Hornet* was backed by two heavy and two anti-aircraft cruisers and six destroyers while Task Force 64 comprised one battleship, one heavy and one light cruiser, and one anti-aircraft cruiser, and six destroyers.

PBY flyingboats and B-17s searched throughout 25 October, and the Japanese vessels were spotted at noon. At once *Enterprise* launched 48 aircraft to search, many of them armed. Nothing had been found as dusk approached, but one F4F crashed into the sea and three SBDs and three TBFs ran out of fuel and ditched while waiting to land-on. Unbeknown to the Americans, the Japanese had in fact been preparing to withdraw again, since Henderson Field was still in US hands, and they only turned back on the Army's assurance that it would be captured during 25 October.

The Battle of Santa Cruz
Early on 26 October, 16 *Enterprise* SBDs were off again, but even as they began their searches numerous reports of sightings came from PBYs. Sixteen floatplanes and eight B5N bombers had been launched by the Japanese on a similar search, and these soon found the US fleet. Then began a confused series of engagements;

0650   Two SBDs found the Japanese carriers; they tried to attack, but were intercepted by eight A6Ms. Escaping into cloud, they claimed three of the Japanese fighters shot down.
0700   From Carrier Division 1 *Shokaku*, *Zuikaku* and *Zuiho* launched 21 A6Ms, 21 D3As and 20 B6Ns to attack the US Fleet. Nine more A6Ms, 19 D3As and 16 B6Ns were ready to follow. *Junyo* launched 12 A6Ms and 17 D3As.
0730   *Hornet* launched 15 SBDs led by Lt Cdr Gus Widhelm and six TBFs, escorted by seven VF-72 F4Fs, led by Lt Cdr Henry G Sanchez.
0800   *Enterprise* launched eight TBFs led by the Air Group Commander, Cdr Richard Gaines, three SBDs and eight F4Fs led by Lt Cdr James H Flatley and Lt John Leppla. About the same time two of the scouting SBDs flown by Lt S Birney Strong and Ens Charles Irvine, dived on *Zuiho* and gained two hits on the stern with their 500 lb bombs; this carrier was badly damaged and put out of the battle. They were chased by Zeros, the gunners claiming two shot down, but although one Dauntless was damaged, both escaped. Two other SBDs attacked the cruiser *Tone* and gained near misses. Another pair claimed two more intercepting A6Ms shot down for a total of

seven claimed during the search missions.
0815   *Hornet* launched nine more SBDs, nine TBFs and seven F4Fs, the formation led by Cdr Walt Rodee. The two carrier forces were about 200 miles apart, and the two strike forces passed close by each other.
0830   As the *Enterprise* group was still climbing the first Japanese strike passed. Six A6Ms from *Zuiho* broke off and attacked, shooting down three TBFs, including that flown by Cdr Gaines. Lt Leppla's division of F4Fs attempted to intercept, but he and two others were shot down; the fourth escaped badly shot-up. Leppla and his pilots were credited with three Zeros shot down, while Avenger crews of VT-10 claimed three more. Lt Cdr Flatley then attacked and shot down another. The *Zuiho* Zeros lost four of their number, but claimed 14 US aircraft shot down. One more TBF and one F4F turned back due to engine trouble.
0900   The Japanese sighted *Hornet* (*Enterprise* was hidden briefly in a rain squall). They had got to within 50 miles before being picked up on the US radar. Thirty-eight F4Fs were up to intercept but were still too low. *Enterprise*'s Fighter Direction Officer gave confused vectors, but *Hornet*'s then took over and directed two VF-72 divisions right into the approaching formation. They attacked just as the D3As entered their dive, claiming several; next they saw the B5Ns coming in low and attacked these. VF-10 then joined the fight, claiming more D3As and Zeros. However, *Hornet* was hit by three bombs and two torpedoes and by the *Shokaku* dive-bomber commander's D3A, which he dived into the ship after being hit by AA. The first Japanese strike had lost 25 of 58 aircraft.
0940   Close behind came the second strike of 20 *Zuikaku* D3As, 12 *Shokaku* B5Ns and 23 A6Ms from all three carriers. These and the *Junyo* aircraft attacked *Enterprise* and the battleship *South Dakota*. Many F4Fs were already out of ammunition, but two VF-72 divisions were able to claim nine D3As and two probables, while VF-10's Lt Stanley 'Swede' Vejtasa, who had already claimed two D3As during the attack on *Hornet*, added five B5Ns and a probable, while other pilots from his unit claimed four more and another seven probables. SBDs of VB-8 returning from attacking the Japanese carriers, claimed four D3As and a B5N, while one of the scouting SBDs of VS-10 on return from the original scouting mission claimed one more D3A. *Enterprise* was hit by two bombs, but was still able to operate; *Hornet* was taken in tow by a cruiser. The second Japanese strike lost 20 aircraft, plus another four which ditched on the way back; the *Junyo* force lost nine plus two ditched.

Results of the battle
During the fighting over the US carriers VF-72 had claimed seven D3As and nine probables, seven A6Ms and three probables, and five B5Ns — all the latter by Ens George L Wrenn — in the first wave; and nine more D3As and two probables, in the second. VF-10 claimed seven D3As and three probables, a Zero and nine B5Ns plus eight probables. The SBDs had added six more for total claims in defense of 51 and 25 probables. Eight VF-72 F4Fs and seven from VF-10 had been shot down, or had ditched out of fuel, while

US CARRIER AIR GROUPS OPERATING IN THE SOLOMONS

CARRIER	UNIT	AIRCRAFT
GUADALCANAL LANDINGS, 7–9 AUGUST		
USS *Saratoga* – Air Group 3	VF-5	34 F4F-4
	VS-3, VB-3	37 SBD-3
	VT-8	16 TBF-1
USS *Enterprise* – Air Group 6	VF-6	36 F4F-4
	VS-4, VB-6	36 SBD-3
	VT-3	15 TBF-1
USS *Wasp* – Air Group 7	VF-71	29 F4F-4
	VS-71, VS-72	30 SBD-3
	VT-7	13 TBF-1
BATTLE OF THE EASTERN SOLOMONS, 24–25 AUGUST		
USS *Saratoga* – Air Group 3	VF-5	36 F4F-4
	VS-3, VB-3	37 SBD-3
	VT-8	15 TBF-1
USS *Enterprise* – Air Group 6	VF-6	36 F4F-4
	VS-5, VS-6,	
	VB-6	37 SBD-3
	VT-3	15 TBF-1
BATTLE OF SANTA CRUZ ISLANDS, 26 OCTOBER		
USS *Hornet* – Air Group 8	VF-72	36 F4F-4
	VS-8, VB-8	36 SBD-3
	VT-6	16 TBF-1
USS *Enterprise* – Air Group 10	VF-10	34 F4F-4
	VS-10, VB-10	36 SBD-3
	VT-10	13 TBF-1

JAPANESE CARRIER AIR GROUPS OPERATING IN THE SOLOMONS

CARRIER	AIRCRAFT
BATTLE OF THE EASTERN SOLOMONS, 24–25 AUGUST	
Ryujo	16 A6M
	21 B5N
Shokaku	26 A6M
	14 D3A
	18 B5N
Zuikaku	27 A6M
	27 D3A
	18 B5N
BATTLE OF GUADALCANAL, 17 OCTOBER	
Junyo	24 A6M
	21 D3A
	10 B5N
Hiyo	A6M
	B5N
BATTLE OF SANTA CRUZ ISLANDS, 26 OCTOBER	
Junyo	24 A6M
	21 D3A
	10 B5N
Shokaku	13 A6M
	20 D3A
	23 B5N
Zuikaku	27 A6M
	27 D3A
	18 B5N
Zuiho	18 A6M
	5 B5N

seven more VF-10 machines had been damaged.

The escort of the first strike from *Zuikaku* claimed 14 victories, seven and two probables by Lt (jg) Yashio Ohishi's section of four, while *Junyo*'s 12 Zero pilots claimed a further nine and five probables, but lost their ace Suzuki. In the second wave Wt Off Katsuma Shigemi's four *Zuikaku* aircraft claimed nine more, while *Zuiho*'s 14 fighters claimed four for two losses during this mission; sections of *Shokaku* fighters took part in both strikes, claiming five victories, so that total claims over the US carriers by the Japanese fighters came to 41 and five probables, plus the Air Group 10 aircraft claimed by *Zuiho*'s fighter en route.

Meanwhile, at 0930 hours the first *Hornet* strike force had found *Shokaku* and *Zuikaku*. The TBFs were too low and failed to make contact. However, the 15 SBDs and their escort headed for the carriers, although intercepted by defending A6Ms which shot down two SBDs and two F4Fs, damaging a third Wildcat and wounding its pilot; this ditched later. Two more Dauntlesses were damaged including Widhelm's, whose engine finally failed. He broke away, Lt James E Vose taking over the lead. As Widhelm glided down he was attacked again, but ditched safely; he and his gunner were picked up by a PBY two days later. The remaining Dauntlesses fought their way through, claiming 'at least 15 Zeros' shot down, and then dived on *Shokaku*, gaining between three and six damaging hits which put her out of action.

Enterprise's three SBDs attacked the battleship *Kirishima*, obtaining two relatively ineffectual hits, while the four TBFs launched torpedoes at a cruiser, but missed. A single A6M attacked as they turned for home, but was claimed shot down by gunners. The final strike attacked the cruiser *Chikuma*, claiming four hits and actually gaining three; the warship was badly damaged. All remaining strike aircraft made it back to the US carriers.

During the attack on the Japanese vessels, by both the scouting SBDs and the strike forces, *Shokaku* and *Zuikaku* had launched 51 A6Ms, these claiming 12 and three probables. Five *Zuikaku* fighters were lost, while *Shokaku*'s ace, NAP 1/C Shigetaka Ohmori (13 victories) was reported killed when he rammed an SBD to prevent it bombing his carrier.

As *Enterprise* limped away, overloaded with aircraft, she flew off 13 SBDs to the New Hebrides to make more room aboard. Nine SBDs had been destroyed aboard the carrier during the attacks on her to bring total US air losses to 74, only about 20–25 of which had been due to Japanese fighters, which had claimed 66 and seven probables.

The battle was not yet over, however, for at 1515 hours seven B5Ns and eight A6Ms from *Shokaku* and *Junyo* attacked *Hornet* again; the tow was cut and the carrier was hard hit, and was ordered abandoned. Four aircraft were shot down during this attack and three more ditched. Finally at 1200 hours six more A6Ms and four D3As from *Junyo* attacked unhindered, gaining a bomb hit on the deck. It was the end, and *Hornet* was set afire by US destroyers — eventually by gunfire, after 16 torpedoes had failed to do the job! Still she would not sink, but soon after midnight two Japanese destroyers fired four more torpedoes into her, and at last she went down.

The Battle of Santa Cruz had been a tactical victory for the Japanese, and the IJN could have taken control of the seas round Guadalcanal. Aircraft losses had been too high, however, about 90 aircraft lost to all causes, and although 84 remained serviceable aboard *Zuikaku* and *Junyo*, the fleet withdrew to Truk. During the day apart from the 49 victories and 27 probables claimed by the F4Fs, and 29 claimed by the SBD and TBF crews, 32 claims had been made by the anti-aircraft gunners aboard *South Dakota*, 26 of which received confirmation.

The results of the Santa Cruz battle had an important bearing on the future course of the Guadalcanal fighting, but still did not end it. Bad weather and events elsewhere kept the skies over the island quiet until 30 October, during the afternoon of which VMF-121 claimed four bombers shot down, their description indicating that they were

probably B5Ns. Earlier in the morning VMF-212 had escorted SBDs to Rekata Bay, where four A6M2-Ns and a number of F1M floatplanes were seen, three of the former and two of the latter being claimed shot down. One A6M2-N is known to have been lost and one badly damaged, NAP 3/C H Jito of the 14th Ku claiming two victories in return.

The 'Tokyo Express' was back on 1 November, landing 1500 men; indeed, during the first ten days of the month 65 destroyer-loads of troops and two cruiser-loads were delivered to Guadalcanal, but most were quickly trapped into pockets and reduced by the US ground forces.

Reinforcements badly needed

By now, everyone on the island was exhausted, and early in November the VS-71 and VB-6 contingents left, while

MAIN AIRCRAFT TYPES EMPLOYED DURING THE BATTLE FOR GUADALCANAL

AMERICAN

Grumman F4F-4 Wildcat
Main US Navy and Marine Corps fighter aircraft of the early war years. A tough, manoeuvreable radial-engined mid-wing monoplane, powered by a 1200 hp Pratt and Whitney R-1830 –86 Twin Wasp engine, the Wildcat was armed with six 0.50 in Browning machine guns in the wings and could carry two 100 lb bombs. Top speed was 318 mph at 19 400 ft, service ceiling 34 900 ft, and normal range 770 miles. The Wildcat was stronger and more heavily armed than the Japanese Zero, and dived faster; in all other aspects it was outclassed.

Bell P-400/P-39D Airacobra
The Airacobra was an unorthodox low-wing monoplane fighter with a tricycle undercarriage, and with a 1140 hp Allison V-1710-35 in-line engine in the fuselage behind the pilot, driving the propeller by an extension shaft. The aircraft was armed with a 37 mm cannon firing through the hollow prepeller shaft (replaced by a 20 mm weapon in the P-400 versions), plus two 0.50 in Brownings in the nose firing through the propeller disc, and four 0.30 in guns in the wings. Although fast, with a maximum speed of 360 mph at 15 000 ft, the aircraft's performance fell off rapidly at higher altitude, and it proved disappointing as an interceptor or dog-fighter. However it was excellent as a ground strafer and ship attack aircraft. Service ceiling was 32 100 ft, and normal range 600 miles.

Douglas SBD-3 Dauntless
The classic US Navy and Marine dive and scout bomber, the single-engined Dauntless was a low-wing monoplane two-seater, powered by a 1000 hp Wright R-1820-52 engine. Armed with two nose-mounted 0.50 in Browning guns for the pilot, and a pair of flexible 0.30 in Brownings for the gunner for rear defence, the aircraft could carry a 1000 lb bomb, or a 500 lb and two 250 lb weapons. It had a top speed of 250 mph at 16 000 ft, a service ceiling of 27 100 ft and a range of 1345 miles as a bomber, extended to 1580 miles in its scouting role. Early in the war it frequently doubled as a fighter in defense of the US carriers.

Grumman TBF-1 Avenger
First introduced at Midway, the Avenger saw its first full-scale employment during the Guadalcanal actions. A large mid-wing monoplane torpedo-bomber, it was powered by a single Wright R-2600-8 engine of 1700 hp, giving it a top speed of 271 mph at 12 000 ft, a service ceiling of 22 400 ft, and a range of 1215 miles, increased to 1450 miles as a scout. A crew of three was

Grumman F4F-4 Wildcat of the US Marine Corps

carried, the pilot with a single fixed, forward-firing 0.30 in Browning in the nose, the gunner with a 0.50 in Browning in a power-operated rear turret, and another 0.30 in Browning that could be fired through a hatch in the underside of the fuselage by the bombardier. The aircraft could carry a bombload of 2000 lb or a torpedo in an internal bomb-bay.

VMSB-132 arrived, led by Maj Joseph Sailer. On 2 November, reports were received of a large destroyer force landing troops by night and Lt Cdr John Eldridge led off three SBDs to attack in the dark. Eldridge had headed 11 strikes in the previous five weeks and was one of the most experienced dive-bomber men to serve on the island. What precisely happened remains uncertain, but Eldridge and a Marine pilot both crashed on Santa Isabel Island, the third SBD disappearing completely.

At this time General Louis Woods arrived to take over the 'Cactus' command from General Roy Geiger, and on 7 November he despatched a late afternoon strike by seven SBDs, three TBFs, eight bomb-carrying P-39s and 23 F4Fs after the 'Express', which was bringing in a further 1300 men, covered by A6M2-N and F1M floatplanes. As the formation approached, five floatplanes made to attack the

Marine F4Fs, but the P-39 pilots jettisoned their bombs and intercepted, claiming two of each type shot down. The Marines of VMF-121 then turned on the remainder, claiming six A6M2-Ns and three F1Ms without loss; three were credited to 2/Lt Bill Marontate, and two to Capt Joe Foss, bringing his score to 19, equal to John Smith's record. One more A6M2-N was claimed by a VT-8 TBF crew.

A total of six A6M2-Ns had actually been present, from the 802nd Ku, as the 14th Ku had been renumbered at the start of the month. Led by Lt Hidero Goto, the formation lost five in the first pass, then the sixth. Meantime, the SBDs had attacked and badly damaged two destroyers, *Takanami* and *Naganami*, which were forced to turn back.

Reinforcements continued to arrive for both sides, six more VMSB-132 SBDs flying into Guadalcanal on 7 November, while the A6Ms of the 252nd Ku reached

---

JAPANESE

The Mitsubishi A6M-2 Zero fighter and Mitsubishi G4M-1 medium bomber were basically the same aircraft as those employed during the Philippines invasion, and already described. The Nakajima A6M2-N was the basic Zero fighter mounted on a single main float with a pair of small outrigger floats for waterborne operations.

Aichi D3A
This low-wing monoplane with fixed, spatted undercarriage, was the main Japanese naval dive-bomber. Powered by a 990 hp Mitsubishi Kinsei 43 radial engine, the very manoeuvreable D3A could double as a fairly formidable fighter when necessary. Carrying a crew of two, the aircraft could carry a single 551 lb bomb beneath the fuselage and another of 132 lb beneath each wing. It was armed with two fixed forward-firing 7.7 mm machine guns and one flexible weapon of similar calibre for rear defense. Top speed was 240 mph at 9845 ft, service ceiling was 30 050 ft, and range 915 miles.

Nakajima B5N2
A single-engined low-wing monoplane torpedo-bomber and reconnaissance scout, the B5N was powered by a 1000 hp Nakajima Sakae 11 radial engine. Carrying a crew of three, it was armed with only a single flexibly-mounted 7.7 mm Type 92 machine gun for rear defense, but carried a 1764 lb torpedo or bomb load of similar weight. Maximum speed was 229 mph at 6560 ft, service ceiling 24 280 ft, and range 1404 miles.

Mitsubishi F1M2
A two-seat biplane floatplane, with a similar central float arrangement to that of the A6M2-N fighter, the F1M was a general-purpose reconnaissance aircraft, capable of doubling as a fighter, powered by a single 875 hp Mitsubishi MK2 Zuisei 13 radial engine. It was armed with two fixed 7.7 mm machine guns above the engine, and one similar flexible gun for rear defense; it could carry two 132 lb bombs. Top speed was 230 mph at 11 290 ft, service ceiling was 30 970 ft and range 360 miles.

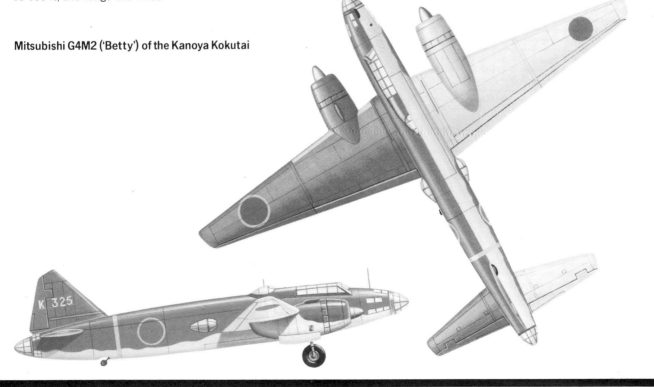

Mitsubishi G4M2 ('Betty') of the Kanoya Kokutai

CLAIMS OF US FIGHTER SQUADRONS, GUADALCANAL 7 AUGUST – 15 NOVEMBER 1942

SQUADRON	NUMBER
LAND-BASED	
VMF-223	110
VMF-121	108½
VMF-212	82
VMF-224	56½
VF-5*	45½
VMF-112	36
67th Fighter Squadron	18
VF-10*	8
VF-71	5½
VMO-251	4
CARRIER-BASED	
VF-6	43
VF-5*	33
VF-72	29
VF-10*	22

*Thus VF-5's total for the whole campaign, operating from both carriers and Guadalcanal, was 78½, and VF-10's was 30.
NB Victories credited to pilots while attached to other squadrons are included in the score of their own units.

US FIGHTER PILOTS CLAIMING FIVE OR MORE VICTORIES OVER THE GUADALCANAL AREA, 7 AUGUST – 15 NOVEMBER 1942

NAME	UNIT	NUMBER	FINAL SCORE
Capt Joseph J Foss*	VMF-121	23	26
Maj John L Smith*	VMF-223	19	19
Capt Marion E Carl	VMF-223	15½	18½
Maj Robert E Galer*	VMF-224	14	14
2/Lt Eugene A Trowbridge	VMF-223	13 (Poss 6)	13 (Poss 6)
2/Lt Kenneth De F Frazier	VMF-223	12½	13½
Lt Col Harold W Bauer*	VMF-212	10	10 KIA 14 Nov
Capt Loren D Everton	VMF-212	10	10
1/Lt Jack E Conger	VMF-212	10	10
2/Lt William F Marontate	VMF-121	10	13 KIA later
2/Lt Thomas H Mann Jnr	VMF-121	9	9
1/Lt George L Hollowell	VMF-224	8	8
2/Lt Charles M Kunz	VMF-224	8	8
Machinist Donald E Runyon	VF-6	8	11
Maj John F Dobbin	VMF-224	7½	7½
Lt Stanley W Vejtasa	VF-10	7¼	10¼
Machine Gunner Henry B Hamilton	VMF-212	7	7 KIA 21 Oct
Lt Hayden M Jensen	VF-5	7	7
2/Lt Joseph L Narr	VMF-121	7	7 KIA 11 Nov
Ens Francis R Register	VF-5,6	7	7
2/Lt Roger A Haberman	VMF-121	6½	6½
1/Lt Gregory K Loesch	VMF-121	6½	8½
2/Lt Lt Kenneth A Pond	VMF-223	6	6 KIA 10 Sept
Lt (jg) Carlton B Starkes	VF-5	6	6
1/Lt Robert F Stout	VMF-212	6	6
Maj Frederick R Payne	VMF-212, 213	5½	5½
Ens George L Wrenn	VF-72	5¼	5¼
Ens Mark K Bright	VF-5	5	9
Maj Leonard K Davis	VMF-121	5	5
2/Lt Cecil J Doyle	VMF-121	5	5 KIA 7 Nov
1/Lt Frank C Drury	VMF-212	5	6
Maj Paul J Fontana	VMF-112	5	5
2/Lt William B Freeman	VMF-121	5	6
2/Lt Charles Kendrick	VMF-223	5	5 KIA 2 Oct
A P I/C Lee P Mankin Jnr	VF-5, 6	5	5
2/Lt Hyde Phillips	VMF-223	5	5
2/Lt Orvin H Ramlo	VMF-223	5	5
Ens John M Wesolowski	VF-5	5	7

*Pilots awarded the Congressional Medal of Honor for actions over Guadalcanal

Rabaul two days later. On 11 November nine D3As and 12 A6Ms from the *Hiyo* airgroup flew down to attack transport shipping at Guadalcanal, followed by 25 G4Ms and 26 more A6Ms, including 11 from the 252nd Ku on their first mission over the island, to attack Henderson Field.

Marines of VMF-112, -121, -212 and newly-arrived elements of VMO-251 and some P-39s all attacked, claiming six Zeros and six D3As, four of them by VMF-121's 2/Lt Thomas H Mann. The cost was high, six F4Fs being lost; *Hiyo*'s fighter leader, Lt Cdr Tadashi Kanako, claimed three of these. Against the following bomber formation 17 more Wildcats and again some P-39s were scrambled, one Zero and seven G4Ms being claimed for the loss of one more F4F — the first victory in the area for the 252nd Ku. Two of the bombers were added to the fast-growing score of VMF-121's Bill Marontate.

Fighting intensifies

The situation at Guadalcanal was now approaching its climax, and the next four days saw some of the most violent and incessant fighting yet. The Japanese, in a final desperate attempt to recover control of the island, had assembled a fleet of 12 heavy transports with 13 500 troops aboard, plus heavy artillery and other equipment, and a covering naval force.

The Americans too were bringing in more forces both by air and sea. During 12 November the ten SBDs of VMSB-142 flew in led by Maj R H Richard, accompanied by eight TBFs of the first Marine torpedo-bomber squadron, VMSB-131. Around noon eight of the big, new twin-engined Lockheed P-38 Lightning fighters of the USAAF's 339th Squadron arrived, led by Maj Dale Brannon, who had previously brought in the first P-400s. Next day eight more of these potent fighters arrived, this time aircraft of the 39th Fighter Squadron on detachment from the US 5th Air Force in New Guinea.

It was against the transport shipping anchored off Lunga that the Japanese first reacted, 19 torpedo-carrying G4Ms and eight escorting A6Ms from the 252nd Ku sweeping in low to attack the 30 vessels. They flew into a maelstrom of intense anti-aircraft fire, coupled with interception by 15 F4Fs and eight P-39s. Seventeen of the bombers were claimed by the defending fighters and five by the AA crews — more than were taking part — while seven Zeros were also claimed, all for the loss of three Wildcats and one Airacobra. (The 252nd Ku pilots claimed eight US fighters shot down.) Twelve of the victories were credited to VMF-121, four of whose pilots claimed two G4Ms each, while ten went to VMF-112, and the balance to P-39s.

A powerful naval force was spotted on its way down The Slot, however, and another night of bombardment was anticipated by the defenders. It was not to be, however, for as the two battleships, one cruiser and 15 destroyers approached Guadalcanal, bent on pounding Henderson Field again, they were intercepted in the darkness by a smaller US force of five cruisers and eight destroyers.

This, the First Battle of Guadalcanal, has since been

LEADING JAPANESE FIGHTER PILOTS KILLED OR SERIOUSLY WOUNDED DURING THE BATTLE FOR GUADALCANAL

DATE	NAME	UNIT	SCORE AT TIME	FATE
7 Aug 42	Pty Off 1/C Saburo Sakai	Tainan Ku	61	Wounded
	Wt Off Mototsuna Yoshida	Tainan Ku	12	Killed
24 Aug 42	Pty Off I/C Yoshio Iwaki	Carrier Pilot	8	Killed
26 Aug 42	Lt Junichi Sasai	Tainan Ku	27	Killed
2 Sept 42	Pty Off 2/C Takaichi Kokubu	Tainan Ku	11	Killed
13 Sept 42	Lt Toraichi Takatsuka	Tainan Ku	16	Killed
	Pty Off 2/C Kazushi Uto	Tainan Ku	19	Killed
	Pty Off 3/C Susumu Matsuki	Unknown	9	Killed
14 Sept 42	Pty Off 1/C Koichi Magara	Unknown	8	Killed
11 Oct 42	Pty Off 1/C Juzo Okamoto	6th Ku	9	Killed
17 Oct 42	Lt(jg) Kaname Harada	'Hiyo'	9	Wounded
21 Oct 42	Wt Off Toshio Ohta	Tainan Ku	34	Killed
25 Oct 42	Pty Off 3/C Keisaku Yoshimura	Tainan Ku	12	Killed
	Pty Off 3/C Toyoo Moriura	Unknown	8	Killed
26 Oct 42	Pty Off 1/C Shigetaka Ohmori	'Shokaku'	13	Killed
	Wt Off Kiyanobu Suzuki	'Junyo'	9+	Killed
13 Nov 42	Lt Shigehisa Yamamoto	252nd Ku	?	Killed
14 Nov 42	Lt Cdr Tadashi Kaneko	'Hiyo'	8+	Killed

described as the 'fiercest naval battle ever fought'. Whether this epithet is truly deserved, it certainly proved a violent encounter. In 34 minutes the outgunned, but resolutely handled US cruisers pumped 85 shells into the battleship *Hiei*, and also sank two Japanese destroyers, preventing the planned bombardment and forcing the Japanese to break off and withdraw before the dawn brought air attack. The cost was sacrificially high; the cruisers *Atlanta* and *Juneau* were both sunk during the engagement, as were four destroyers, while the damaged cruiser *Portland* was finished off by a destroyer next day.

With dawn on Friday, 13 November, the SBDs and TBFs were out searching for survivors of the night's events. Five US and two Japanese ships were seen wrecked or burning, while the ultimate demise of the stricken *Portland* was also witnessed. But the big find was the unmistakable bulk of a battleship off Savo Island: it was the damaged *Hiei*, with a cruiser in attendance.

At once SBDs and TBFs were sent off in relays to attack; at 0615 hours the dive-bombers gained the first bomb hit, and soon afterwards a TBF managed a torpedo strike. Further help was at hand, for on news of the strength of the Japanese force, the hastily repaired *Enterprise*, backed by the fast, modern battleships *South Dakota* and *Washington*, had headed for the area. A dawn search after a suspected carrier found nothing, so a strike of nine Avengers was launched, escorted by six VF-10 F4Fs. This force found the slow-moving *Hiei* mid-morning and attacked, gaining a further torpedo strike. They then landed at Henderson Field to refuel and rearm before joining Marine aircraft for a further attack.

Meanwhile, the Marine fighters had been heavily engaged. Earlier in the morning strong forces of A6Ms had been despatched from Rabaul to cover the wounded battleship, but the Wildcat pilots had engaged these with great vigor, claiming nine shot down during the two hours up to 0830. Victories were credited to pilots from VMF-112, -121, -212, and VMO-251.

From the island Air Group 10's six TBFs and six F4Fs, now joined by eight Marine SBDs and two more Wildcats, attacked the battleship again, as she lay dead in the water. One further torpedo and three bomb hits inflicted further damage. Then 17 B-17s appeared overhead, dropping 56 bombs which were claimed to have gained one hit and one near miss. By early evening the battleship had suffered five direct bomb hits, three delivered by VMSB-132 SBDs, and ten torpedo strikes; after contributing two of these, the remaining crews of VT-8 left the island to rest. At 1800 hours *Hiei* was finally abandoned and scuttled; she sank later that evening — the first Japanese battleship to be lost in the war.

Japanese efforts redoubled

With darkness on 13 November the Japanese warships were back, however, and this time three cruisers and four destroyers were able to fire nearly 1000 not very well aimed rounds onto Henderson Field and the fighter strips. Two F4Fs and an SBD were destroyed, 17 more Wildcats and one P-38 suffering damage.

Dawn on 14 November still found the defenders with nearly 50 available aircraft, however, including 14 F4Fs, 16 SBDs and ten P-38s. Advised by Intelligence that the major Japanese convoy and its covering force were still on their way, *South Dakota* and *Washington* with four supporting destroyers had increased their speed towards Guadalcanal during the night. At dawn on 14 November *Enterprise* again launched scouts and CAP fighters to seek any opposition, as a Japanese carrier presence was still feared. Nothing transpired, but three of VT-10's TBFs still at Henderson Field joined three Marine TBFs, five SBDs and seven F4Fs on a search up The Slot.

Four cruisers and six destroyers were found 170 miles to the west, including the ships which had shelled during the night. While the SBDs gained two hits on the light cruiser *Maya*, the TBFs got four torpedoes into the heavy cruiser *Kinugasa*. *Enterprise* search aircraft also found the force, one pair of SBDs attacking a damaged cruiser which both hit with 500 lb bombs, then returning to land at Henderson. Another pair attacked other cruisers, claiming one direct hit, but the successful aircraft failed to return. Next on the scene were 17 *Enterprise* SBDs with 1000 lb bombs, and these made an unopposed attack, completing the sinking of *Kinugasa*, and damaging *Isuzu*, *Chokai*, *Maya* and a destroyer; all 17 of them reached Guadalcanal.

The tide turns

Meanwhile, two more scouting SBDs had found the transports further east, some 120 miles north of Guadalcanal;

the 11 ships were escorted by 12 destroyers and seven A6Ms. The two intrepid American pilots attacked at once, gaining a near miss and a hit on a transport. Again the successful SBD was lost, shot down by one of the A6Ms. News of the sighting had reached Guadalcanal, however, and at once a strike was prepared, 19 SBDs, seven VT-10 TBFs and a dozen escorting Wildcats going off.

Two transports were torpedoed and one bombed, two sinking and one turning back in a damaged condition. Six escorting Zeros were claimed shot down by VMF-112's Wildcats. Next out were 17 more SBDs which sank a further transport and claimed two intercepting A6Ms shot down. B-17s from Espiritu Santo also joined the attack, while the afternoon saw a further raid by 22 Marine and Navy dive-bombers, these gaining hits in three of the transports.

This time both A6Ms and floatplanes were encountered overhead, the Dauntless crews claiming one of each, while the escorting VMF-112 Wildcats were credited with six float biplanes and two Zeros. Another Zero was credited to Lt Col 'Joe' Bauer, Commanding Officer of VMF-212, who was flying a VMF-121 F4F in a section with Joe Foss and one other pilot. The trio had just strafed the ships when the Japanese fighters appeared, and Bauer was seen by Foss to shoot one down before his own aircraft was hit and he was forced to bale out. Although seen in his dinghy, dusk was approaching and he was never found. The 10-victory ace was the highest-scoring American fighter pilot lost during the battle; he was later awarded a posthumous Congressional Medal of Honor.

While this attack was underway eight more SBDs and 12 VF-10 Wildcats had arrived from Enterprise's deck, and the dive-bombers had claimed hits on six of the seven remaining transports, while the fighters strafed, and also claimed one Zero shot down. All 20 aircraft then flew to Guadalcanal.

The last major strike was made by 16 Navy and Marine SBDs, four TBFs, and then seven more SBDs. With the Japanese fighting fiercely for their very existence, this force met the strongest opposition in the air, VB-10 losing three SBDs with two more badly damaged by Zeros. One further transport was sunk, leaving only four, all of them damaged, together with about six of the escorting destroyers. The rest of the escort force had picked up large numbers of the troops and crews from the sunk vessels, and returned to Rabaul with them aboard.

During this day of major action, the Marine and Navy fighters had between them claimed a total of 19 victories, plus one 'snooping' flyingboat claimed by a section from the carrier, while the SBD and TBF crews had added nine more. At least three Japanese fighter units had been involved in the day's events, the 252nd Ku claiming 14 victories, but losing Lt M Suganami; while the Hiyo detachment lost their commander, Lt Cdr Tadashi Kaneko, as he was leading 11 fighters to cover the convoy. The 582nd Ku (the old 2nd Ku renumbered) also provided a patrol of eight Zeros; one of these was flown by ace Lt (jg) Kazuo Tsunoda, who claimed one victory, but was then shot down, force-landing in the sea. He was rescued by a passing destroyer.

One last Japanese effort
As night fell the four surviving transports and four escorting destroyers headed on towards Tassafaronga Point where the former beached themselves. In support of them, another striking force came near to bombard the island yet again. This time it comprised the battleship Kirishima, two

cruisers, two light cruisers, and nine destroyers. As it approached, it was met by the US fast battleships and their destroyer escort in the first direct capital ship engagement of the Pacific war.

Kirishima opened fire first, hitting South Dakota with 42 shells before the latter could sink the destroyer which was illuminating her and cause the volume of fire to slacken. The flash of Kirishima's guns had allowed Washington to pinpoint her, however, and moments later the Japanese battleship was wrecked by the impact of nine 16-inch and 40 5-inch shells; shattered, she had to be scuttled — the second battleship lost in three nights. Apart from the damage to South Dakota, the US force lost three of its four destroyers sunk, but it was nonetheless a major victory.

With dawn on 15 November 'Cactus' was ready to strike again — and stronger than ever. Thanks to the presence of all the aircraft of Air Group 10 apart from 14 F4Fs left on the Enterprise for her protection, Guadalcanal had 79 aircraft ready for action, including 24 F4Fs, 23 P-38s and P-39s, 16 SBDs, seven TBFs and nine of ten Martin B-26 Marauder twin-engined bombers, fitted to carry torpedoes; these aircraft of the USAAF's 70th Bomb Squadron had only just flown in on 14 November.

Early in the morning P-39 pilots spotted three transports beached at Tassafaronga and the fourth coming in. Over the next hour 13 SBDs and a single TBF obtained seven hits on three of the vessels, while five P-39s hit the fourth with 500 lb bombs. Three of the new B-26s then appeared to hit one of the ships with a 1000 pounder. Two F1M float biplanes which intervened were shot down by VMF-121 Wildcats, one by Capt Joe Foss for his 23rd victory. The transports were all wrecked, and as a result of the air attacks less than half of the 13 000 troops who had originally set out in 12 vessels eventually got ashore, and those without most of their weapons and equipment.

During the afternoon 11 A6Ms swept over the island, being engaged by 15 Wildcats from VF-10 which claimed six and four probables for one loss. 'Pistol Pete' then opened up on Henderson Field but was swiftly silenced by two well-directed 500 lb bombs from patrolling P-39s. By the day's end there were no more targets; Lunga and Henderson Field were secure.

It was the end for the Japanese — and they now at last accepted this fact. True, the fighting was not over by any means — it would be February 1943 before the last of their troops were evacuated — and the air raids would continue. But the effort to eject the Americans had come to an end — the cost entailed was too high. This realization marked the turning point of the war, and Guadalcanal provided the base from which an ever-more offensive campaign would be launched to clear the Solomons and neutralize the great southern base at Rabaul.

During the period from 7 August to 15 November, 1942 Guadalcanal-based aircraft (mainly SBDs) had sunk or wrecked 20 ships and damaged 14 more. Marine Wildcat pilots had claimed 407 victories, to which must be added 59 more by Guadalcanal-based Navy squadrons, and 18 by the Army's P-39s and P-400s, plus over 20 claimed by the bomber crews. Estimated actual Japanese losses to these units give a total of 260 aircraft. 'Cactus' had lost 101 aircraft, but of 126 Marine and 34 Navy fighter pilots who had served on the island only 38 had been killed or seriously wounded, and of these 17 fell during their first week on the island. Guadalcanal was indisputably a great American victory in every respect.

BREAKING THE MARETH LINE

MARCH 1943

Overleaf

The crew of this 88 mm anti-tank gun which has been holding up 8th
Army Sherman tanks, have been forced to take cover as bomb-carrying Curtiss Kittyhawks of Western
Desert Air Force sweep through the approaches to the Tebaga Gap during the Mareth
Battle on 26 March, 1943. A Hawker Hurricane IID 'tank-buster' aircraft shot down during
an earlier attack, has crash-landed close to the gun pit, which
has already suffered casualties.

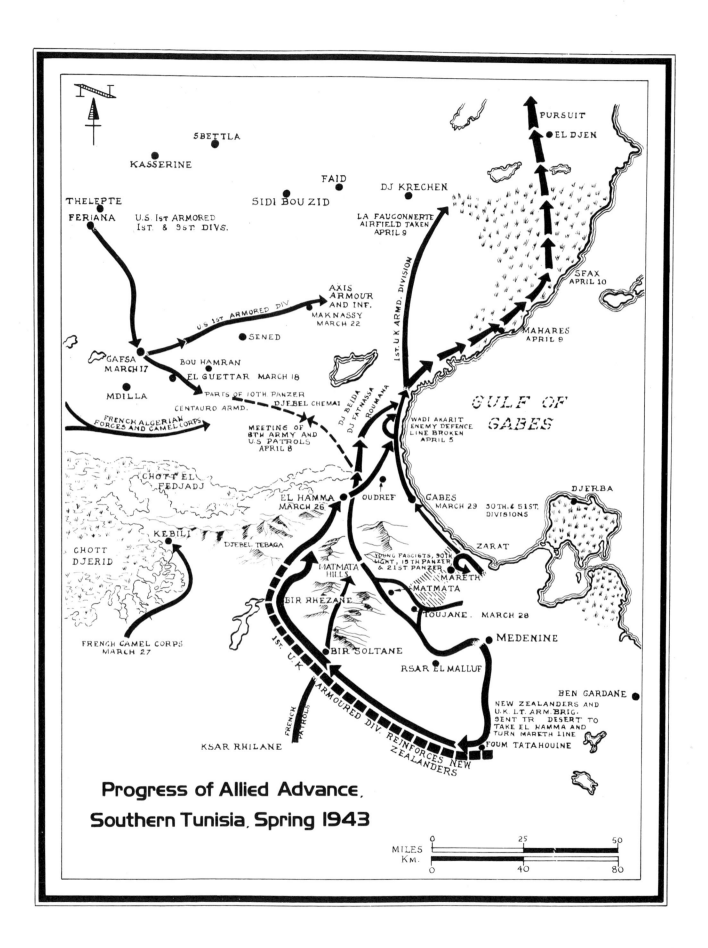

N

SBETTLA

KASSERINE

THELEPTE
FERIANA

FAID

DJ KRECHEN

SIDI BOU ZID

U.S. Ist ARMORED
Ist. & 9ST. DIVS.

LA FAUGONNERTE
AIRFIELD TAKEN
APRIL 9

PURSUIT
EL DJEN

AXIS
ARMOUR
AND INF.
MAKNASSY
MARCH 22

U S Ist ARMORED DIV

SENED

GAFSA
MARCH 17

BOU HAMRAN
EL GUETTAR MARCH 18

MDILLA

PARTS OF IOTH. PANZER
CENTAURO ARMD.   DJEBEL CHEMAI

FRENCH ALGERIAN
FORCES AND CAMEL CORPS

MEETING OF
8TH ARMY AND
U.S PATROLS
APRIL 8

CHOTT EL
FEDJADJ

KEBILI

CHOTT
DJERID

DJEBEL TEBAGA

EL HAMMA
MARCH 26

OUDREF

DJ BEIDA
DJ FATNASSA
ROUMANA

1st. U.K ARMD. DIVISION

SFAX
APRIL 10

MAHARES
APRIL 9

GULF OF
GABES

WADI AKARIT
ENEMY DEFENCE
LINE BROKEN
APRIL 5

GABES
MARCH 29   30TH.& 51ST.
DIVISIONS

DJERBA

ZARAT

YOUNG FASCISTS, 90TH
LIGHT, 15TH PANZER
& 21ST PANZER

MATMATA
HILLS

BIR RHEZANE

MATMATA

TOUJANE. MARCH 28

FRENCH CAMEL CORPS
MARCH 27

BIR SOLTANE

RSAR EL MALLUF

MEDENINE

BEN GARDANE

1ST. U.K. ARMOURED DIV. REINFORCES NEW ZEALANDERS

FRENCH PATROLS

NEW ZEALANDERS AND
U.K. LT. ARM. BRIG.
SENT TR   DESERT TO
TAKE EL HAMMA AND
TURN MARETH LINE

KSAR RHILANE

FOUM TATAHOUINE

Progress of Allied Advance,
Southern Tunisia, Spring 1943

MILES
KM.

0   25   50

0   40   80

Until the great Normandy invasion of June 1944, the Western Allies were denied a major battle ground with the bulk of the German armies in Europe. Here the land war was fought out in all its ferocity to the east, where the Wehrmacht and the Red Army were locked in mortal combat for four terrible years.

Driven from the mainland in 1940, the British and their various allies lacked the strength to fight their way back into France and the Low Countries for several years. During this period they could maintain military pressure on their enemies only from the air and sea, and on the periphery. In the air they struggled to overcome initial German superiority in order to mount a sustained offensive of sufficient weight materially to affect the German effort in the east.

At sea the British were fighting a life-and-death struggle to secure and safeguard the shipping routes so vital to maintain the war effort. Without the food, raw materials and flow of armaments from the factories of North America, the war would be lost in any event.

That left the periphery, where a mixture of circumstance and special interest caused the coastal areas of North Africa to become the focus of the British Army's main efforts throughout the mid-war years. The entry of Benito Mussolini's Fascist Italy into the war in June 1940, the fall of France and the Axis occupation of Greece turned the Mediterranean Sea into a sphere of Axis influence where before it had seemed secure. Vital oil supplies in Iraq and Iran were now under threat of German domination, while the route to India and the Far East via the Suez Canal was virtually denied to Britain.

Sustaining a precarious hold on the island of Malta to allow interruption of Axis supply lines to Africa, as has already been recounted, the British built upon their military presence in Egypt to launch an attack on the Italian colony of Libya. Success here brought German involvement to prevent the collapse of Hitler's southern ally, and soon the fighting developed into a major campaign which ebbed and flowed along the several hundred miles of barren coastline from the Egyptian frontier to Tripoli in Libya.

The RAF learns its lesson

While in Germany and the Soviet Union military aviation had developed largely as an adjunct to and support of the armies on the ground, this had not been the case with the Royal Air Force. During 1918 support of the ground forces had been developed to a fairly advanced level, but in the struggle to maintain the independence of the RAF between the wars, and to promote the primacy of pure airpower, the expertise had been lost. As a result World War II found the RAF behind the Luftwaffe in this respect and it was in North Africa that the tactical use of airpower had to be relearned and reapplied.

The battles of 1941 had been hard and costly, but by the end of that year the British were beginning to win the reinforcement battle and were steadily overtaking the Axis forces in Africa in numbers, if not in quality of equipment, both on the ground and in the air. Despite the outbreak of war in the Far East at the end of 1941, the following year saw a steady increase in the size and power of the British presence, although some stinging and humiliating defeats continued to be inflicted during the first half of 1942 — due in the main to superior generalship and the better equipment of the German element of the Axis North African forces.

Through the first 18 months of the war here the RAF had based its forces mainly upon twin-engined medium and light bombers, and upon fighters which escorted them, and fought for air superiority against their opposite numbers. However, during 1942 the RAF relied increasingly upon its fighters to take up the offensive role, carrying bombs to attack Axis lines of communications, supply depots, concentration areas and coastal shipping. This was an interdiction role, however, and still supported the efforts of the ground forces only in an indirect manner.

The RAF at this time remained short of experienced pilots, and apart from formation leaders, most units were crewed largely by young, raw pilots produced in growing numbers by the rapidly expanding Commonwealth Air Training Plan. Coupled with their own inexperience, the Hurricane, Tomahawk and Kittyhawk fighters which they flew were outclassed in several respects by the Messerschmitt Bf109F and Macchi C 202 fighters of the Luftwaffe and Regia Aeronautica by which they were opposed. As a result losses were high throughout the period, the very experienced German fighter pilots particularly taking a very high toll in return for relatively light losses, even when heavily outnumbered themselves.

Despite these disadvantages, steadily growing numbers, determinedly aggressive tactics, and gradually improving equipment allowed the RAF's Desert Air Force to gain the initiative to an increasing degree. At first the light bombers had suffered heavy losses, but by mid 1942 the dedication and sacrifice of their fighter escorts had rendered them almost invulnerable. The British fighters had also managed to get through to the Axis bombers, dive-bombers and fighter-bombers on numerous occasions, and to inflict steadily growing losses upon them. Eventually, despite their individual prowess, the Axis fighters were rarely able to fight their own bomb-carrying aircraft through unscathed. When the last fully successful Axis offensive was launched in mid 1942 at Gazala, the RAF fighter-bombers and light bombers played a major part in slowing down and disrupting the pursuit of the 8th Army as it retreated to its defensive positions at El Alamein.

Desert Air Force is strengthened

The arrival of General Bernard Montgomery as commander of the 8th Army at this stage coincided with a change in British fortunes, and in a number of developments within the Desert Air Force. A new anti-tank aircraft, the Hurricane IID had made its debut. A standard Hurricane fighter, modified to carry a pair of 40 mm anti-tank cannon beneath the wings, the aircraft was consequently slow, unmanoeuverable and rather vulnerable, but proved a most accurate and effective weapon against vehicles of all types, including tanks, in conditions of air superiority. The first Spitfires also reached Africa, and while barely a match for, rather than superior to, the main Axis fighters, their very presence began to improve the situation, although losses remained high.

At the same time elements of the US Army Air Force had begun to arrive to fly in Desert Air Force, although no US ground forces were to join 8th Army. Flying P-40F Warhawk fighters and North American B-25 Mitchell medium bombers, the American units offered no significant improvement in quality of equipment over the RAF units, but did bring to the battle vital numbers of experienced, peacetime-trained airmen.

This rejuvenated Allied airpower played a big role in

MESSERSCHMITT BF109G-2 FIGHTERS OF **I/JG77** IN FLIGHT OVER SOUTHERN TUNISIA EARLY IN 1943. THE NEAREST AIRCRAFT IS FLOWN BY THE GRUPPENADJUTANT, OBLT HEINZ-EDGAR BERRES, ONE OF THE UNIT'S LEADING 'EXPERTEN'.

breaking up Axis concentrations during the successful defensive Battle of Alam el Halfa at the start of September 1942, and was then extremely active throughout the great Alamein battle of late October/early November. Still, however, the role remained one of interdiction rather than direct battlefield support. However, the degree of co-operation and liaison between army and air force commanders at all levels was steadily improving as the contribution offered by airpower was increasingly seen and appreciated by men on the ground.

Just as the Alamein battle was won and the Axis began retreating westwards back across Libya, came news of Anglo-American landings in French North-West Africa to their rear. It seemed that the war in Africa was all-but over! The United States had been reluctant to become involved in the Mediterranean and Middle East, which they saw as peripheral and more concerned with British interests in Empire and spheres of influence after the war. Their desire was for an early invasion of Western France to confront the major forces of the German army on the mainland where their defeat was the only sure way of bringing the war to a swift end.

British experience at Dieppe in August 1942 and the reasoned argument of Winston Churchill and his Chiefs of Staff compelled the US to agree with reluctance that no such invasion could be launched with any chance of success before mid 1943 at the earliest. The British formula was to clear North Africa and then strike from the south into Italy, the Balkans or even Southern France — all immortalized by Churchill as the 'soft underbelly of Europe'. Consequently, the US now agreed to operations to speed the expulsion of the Axis from Africa, culminating on 8 November, 1942 in

the landings in French Morocco and Algeria, and the swift drive into Tunisia.

The gamble almost came off, as British and American forces moved with all speed eastwards to occupy Tunisia. They were foiled, however, by the swift reaction of the Axis in rushing forces from Sicily to Tunis and by the weather which slowed the Allied advance. Thus the end of 1942 found a strong Italo-German army holding northern and central Tunisia, while the Afrika Korps was retreating steadily westwards from Alamein towards Tripoli and the border with southern Tunisia. Facing the Axis in northern Tunisia was the British 1st Army supported by the RAF's 242 Group; to the immediate south was the US II Corps, with the XII Air Support Command of the US 12th Air Force, reinforced by the recently-liberated but still ill-equipped French army from Morocco and Algeria. Experienced units of the Luftwaffe flew in from Sicily, Western Europe and the Eastern Front, and were soon giving the Anglo-American air forces as bad a time as were their colleagues in Libya.

Meanwhile, 8th Army's pursuit of the Afrika Korps across Libya was steady if rather slow. The Axis fought rearguard actions, but offered no sustained resistance as ports like Tobruk, Derna and Benghazi fell once again into Allied hands. During January 1943 Tripoli, the Libyan capital, at last fell after a token defense and by early

DESERT AIR FORCE, MARETH AREA, MARCH 1943

UNIT	AIRCRAFT
244 WING	
92, 145, 601, 1 SAAF Squadrons	Spitfire V
73 Squadron (night intruder)	Hurricane IIC
417 Squadron (held for defense of Tripoli)	Spitfire V
239 WING	
112, 250, 260, 450, 3 RAAF Squadrons	Kittyhawk II & III
7 SAAF WING	
2 SAAF, 4 SAAF, 5 SAAF Squadrons	Kittyhawk I & II
57TH FIGHTER GROUP, USAAF	
64th, 65th, 66th, 319th Squadrons	P-40F Warhawk
79TH FIGHTER GROUP, USAAF	
85th, 86th, 87th, 316th Squadrons	P-40F Warhawk
232 WING	
55, 223 Squadrons	Baltimore III & IIIA
3 SAAF WING	
12, 24 SAAF Squadrons	Boston III
21 SAAF Squadron	Baltimore III & IIIA
12TH BOMBARDMENT GROUP (M), USAAF (part only)	
83rd, 434th Squadrons	B-25C Mitchell
MISCELLANEOUS UNITS	
6 Squadron (anti-tank)	Hurricane II D
40 SAAF Squadron (tactical reconnaissance)	Spitfire V
60 SAAF Squadron (photo-reconnaissance)	Mosquito II, Baltimore
1437 Strategic Reconnaissance Flight	Baltimore
2 Photographic Reconnaissance Unit	Spitfire, Hurricane
89 Squadron (nightfighter – defense Tripoli)	Beaufighter
37, 40, 70, 104 Squadrons	Wellington

AXIS AIR FORCES, MARETH AREA, MARCH 1943

UNIT	AIRCRAFT
LUFTWAFFE	
JAGDGESCHWADER 77	
Stab, I, II, III Gruppen	Bf109G
SCHLACHTGESCHWADER 2	
I Gruppe	Bf109E
STUKAGESCHWADER 3	
I, III Gruppen	Ju87D
RECONNAISSANCE STAFFELN	
4 (H)/12 (tactical reconnaissance)	Bf109F
1 (F)/121 (strategic reconnaissance)	Ju88D
2 (F)/123 (strategic reconnaissance)	Ju88D
REGIA AERONAUTICA	
3° Stormo CT	
18°, 23° Gruppo CT	MC 202
614ª Squadriglia (liaison)	Various

February nearly all Axis forces had withdrawn across the frontier into Tunisia, the Afrika Korps taking up positions in the old French fortifications of the Mareth Line.

Tightening the knot

Steadily the 8th Army closed up to the line, the first Allied units crossing into Tunisia on 22 February. Meanwhile, however, to secure his rear from any attempt by the Allied forces in Algeria to press east to the Tunisian coast and cut the Afrika Korps off from the Axis forces in the north, the German commander, Erwin Rommel, swung a part of his forces northwards to attack the US II Corps at Kasserine. Gambling that the 8th Army would not be ready to attack at Mareth for some weeks, he left only a screen here while his desert veterans administered a fearful drubbing to the inexperienced Americans — this was only prevented from becoming a rout by the arrival of reinforcements for the Allies, and the need of the Axis units to return to Mareth.

The Allied forces now forming 8th Army and Desert Air Force were greatly streamlined and reduced since the Alamein battle. Montgomery fielded the 2nd New Zealand Division, 50th and 51st Infantry Divisions, 4th Indian Division, 1st and 7th Armoured Divisions and 201st Guards Brigade. All were 'crack' units, the two British infantry divisions each including their own supporting armored

brigade as additional firepower. Desert Air Force had left behind all its Hurricane fighter units for rear defense, and had available one Spitfire wing of four squadrons plus a single Hurricane night intruder unit; two wings of Kittyhawk fighter-bombers with seven squadrons between them; a USAAF P-40F Warhawk group of three squadrons; one wing of light bombers with three squadrons of Douglas Bostons and Martin Baltimores (plus part of a US group of B-25 Mitchells); and a single tactical reconnaissance squadron which was just converting from Hurricanes to Spitfires. A further US P-40F group, another RAF light bomber wing and a single squadron of Hurricane IID anti-tank aircraft would soon join this force, to be supported by a photo-reconnaissance squadron and a flight, both with Baltimores, but also with two De Havilland Mosquitos which had been provided at the personal request of Montgomery for the forthcoming Mareth operations. Finally, four squadrons of Vickers Wellington night bombers had been moved forward to Gardabia for night raids on the Axis positions.

The Afrika Korps comprised the 10th, 15th and 21st Panzer Divisions, the 90th Light Division, the Italian Young Fascists, Sahar, Pistoia and Centauro Armoured Divisions. The air forces supporting this army included a full Geschwader of Messerschmitt Bf109Gs — JG77 — which had arrived in Africa from the Soviet front during October and November 1942, a single Gruppe of Bf109E fighter-bombers, two Gruppen of Ju87D dive-bombers and three reconnaissance Staffeln; the Italian component now included only a single Gruppo of Macchi C 202 fighters and a liaison squadriglia. Assistance from the air forces in the north was available, but in practise Afrika Korps' air force had itself frequently to deal with attacks from the Allied air forces supporting US II Corps, and by heavy bombers from Algeria.

Although 8th Army would not be ready to begin its direct assault on the formidable Mareth defenses until late March 1943, the air offensive against the Axis line began on 26 February. The operations were typical of what had gone before. Overwhelming numbers of fighter-bombers and light bombers raided firstly the Axis airfields in an effort to

win early air superiority so that positions in the line and supply dumps behind the front could be hit with impunity. The Germans struck back hard at the attackers and inflicted heavy losses, but it was to be the last time they were to enjoy such success.

Fighter-bomber attacks begin

As the Axis forces in the north under General Jurgen von Arnim launched an abortive offensive — Operation *Ochsenkopf* — against the British 1st Army, Desert Air Force began a series of fighter-bomber attacks on airfields at Gabes, where the units of JG77 were based. Six strikes were made between 0700–1200 hours on 26 February during which the pilots of JG77 claimed 18 Kittyhawks shot down against an actual RAF loss of 14 and several damaged. The Germans retaliated with two attacks on British airfields during both of which combats were fought with Spitfires, so that by the end of the day Allied claims against the German fighters totalled 12 and four probables, although actual losses were somewhat lower. While a certain amount of damage had been inflicted on the Gabes airfields, the balance on the first day was with the Luftwaffe — and it had been a good day for two of JG77's great 'Experten'; in I Gruppe Hauptmann Heinz Bär had claimed five of the victories, whilst II Gruppe's Oblt Ernst-Wilhehm Reinert had claimed four.

The fighter-bomber attacks were resumed next day, the Italian airfields at El Hamma also being attacked and several of their Macchi fighters destroyed. The two following days remained fairly quiet after the initial attacks, but with the evening of 1 March came an unpleasant surprise for Desert Air Force — and particularly for the squadrons of 244 Spitfire Wing. At 1650 hours artillery fire from the Mareth Line suddenly crashed down on Hazbub Main airfield where 601 Squadron had recently arrived. The unit's aircraft were rapidly scrambled, but one was hit and crashed soon after it had taken off. The rest flew to El Assa and Zuara. Half an hour later the shells began falling on Medenine where 92 and 145 Squadrons were also forced to flee under fire. The Wing reassembled next morning at Ben Gardane.

As if in revenge Axis airfields suffered further attacks on 3 March, B-25s of Desert Air Force being joined by B-17 Flying Fortresses from Algeria in delivering heavy raids on I/JG77's base at Fatnassa, and on the Italian airstrip K.41 at El Hamma where a considerable number of MC 202s were lost. Fighter-bomber attacks on targets throughout the Mareth area continued through this and the next day.

In an effort to catch 8th Army off balance before they were ready to attack Mareth, an offensive was launched by Axis forces on 6 March. Sick and dispirited after the withdrawal of his forces from Kasserine, Rommel had returned to Europe and would not be seen again in Tunisia, where Von Arnim became Axis Supreme Commander. The Afrika

WESTERN DESERT AIR FORCE LIGHT BOMBERS OFF TO ATTACK TARGETS AROUND MARETH. IN THE FOREGROUND AND LEFT BACKGROUND ARE NORTH AMERICAN B-25C MITCHELLS OF THE US 12TH BOMB GROUP, WHICH ARE FOLLOWING MARTIN BALTIMORES OF THE RAF'S 232 WING. AN ESCORTING KITTYHAWK FIGHTER CAN JUST BE SEEN IN THE FAR LEFT BACKGROUND.

Korps, renamed I Italian Army, had been taken over by Generale Giovanni Messe, and it was he who launched 10th, 15th and 21st Panzer Divisions in a three-pronged 'spoiling' attack from Tojane and Hallouf against the British positions at Medenine. Here the 100 000 men, 700 guns and 200 tanks ran up against the well dug-in troops of 201st Guards Brigade, 131st Lorried Infantry Brigade and 2nd New Zealand Division. Montgomery adopted Rommel's own tactics, drawing the attackers onto a screen of anti-tank guns, and by midday they had been halted. After regrouping, they attacked again at 1530 hours, but made no progress and were forced to retreat, leaving behind 52 wrecked tanks that could ill be spared.

Bad weather had reduced the part that Desert Air Force could play, but for this operation the Axis forces had been temporarily reinforced from the north by III/ZG1, equipped with twin-engined Messerschmitt Me210 Zerstörer aircraft, and by III/SKG10, equipped with the latest Focke-Wulf FW190 fighter-bombers. Eighteen of the

Me210s attacked Neffatia airfield, achieving complete surprise. One of the escorting Bf109 pilots from I/JG77 recorded:

> 'This morning we intended to join the army in an attack, but the weather was bad. At midday we made a start. We escorted a formation of (Me) 210s and FW190s to the airfield at Neffatia, east of Medenine. We carried out a sequence of attacks with the 109s also joining in as fighter-bombers. It was marvellous to see German aircraft once again in the sky over Africa. It was certainly a surprise for the British. Our force was so big and so strongly protected that the Spitfires looking on did not come down. But the Flak over the airfield was the heaviest I have seen for a long time.'

The Spitfires did, however, meet 28 Ju87Ds of III/StG3 with an escort of Bf109s, but were only able to claim one of the dive-bombers shot down and one probable on this occasion. The Luftwaffe launched a maximum effort to

---

MAIN AIRCRAFT TYPES EMPLOYED DURING THE MARETH BATTLE

ROYAL AIR FORCE

Most main types were versions of aircraft already described. Supermarine Spitfire V, as used over Malta, and Spitfire IX, a development of the basic design generally similar in appearance but featuring a more powerful Rolls Royce Merlin 61 engine of 1660 hp, which slightly lengthened the nose of the aircraft, but substantially increased the performance to a maximum speed of 408 mph at 25 000 ft and a service ceiling of 44 000 ft.

Curtiss Kittyhawk IA, II and III
The Kittyhawk IA was basically the USAAF's P-40E fighter fitted with British equipment. The Kittyhawk III was the RAF's version of the P-40K, powered by a 1325 hp Allison V-1710-73 engine which increased maximum speed to 362 mph at 15 000 ft. Visually the aircraft differed only in having a small curved fillet at the base of the fin's leading edge. Used in smaller numbers than the Mk IA and III by the RAF was the Mk II, which was the British version of the P-40F Warhawk – see below.

Hawker Hurricane IID
The basic Hurricane II fitted with a pair of 40 mm Vickers anti-tank cannon in 'gondola' fairings beneath the wings. The cannon installation reduced the top speed of the aircraft to about 300 mph and rendered the aircraft less manoeuvreable. It was employed only in the specialist anti-tank role.

Martin Baltimore
A fast American-built bomber monoplane of low-mid wing configuration powered by a pair of Wright R-2600–A5B engines of 1660 hp each. The bomber was heavily armed with four wing-mounted 0.303 in Browning machine guns, a power-operated dorsal turret armed with either four 0.303 in or two 0.50 in Brownings, and two more 0.30 in guns for use downwards and to the rear through a hatch in the underside of the fuselage. Up to 2000 lb of bombs could be carried and maximum speed was 302 mph at 11 000 ft. Service ceiling was 24 000 ft, and range 950 miles.

Douglas Boston III
Another fast American light bomber, the Boston featured a high-mid wing and was powered by a pair of Wright Double Row Cyclone R-2600-A5B engines of 1600 hp. Very similar in performance and armament to the Baltimore, the Boston reached 304 mph at 13 000 ft, a service ceiling of 24 250 ft and had a range of 1020 miles. It was armed with four fixed forward-

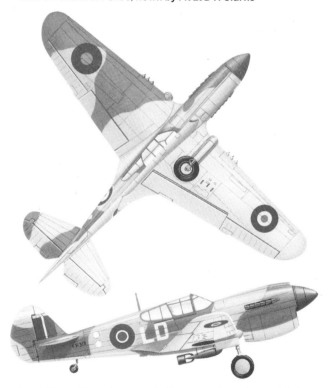

Curtiss Kittyhawk III of 250 Squadron, 239 Wing, Western Desert Air Force, flown by Flt Lt D H Clarke

firing 0.303 in Browning guns in the nose with twin hand-held guns of similar calibre in dorsal and ventral positions for rear defense.

UNITED STATES ARMY AIR FORCE

Curtiss P-40F Warhawk
The P-40F differed from the P-40E employed in the Philippines in being powered by a Packard-built Rolls Royce Merlin V-1650-1 engine of 1300 hp. This provided a better performance at altitude, the top speed of 364 mph being reached at 20 000 ft and service ceiling being increased to 34 400 ft. The aircraft could carry a 500 lb bomb beneath the

reduce British aerial activity next day (7 March) as the Germans returned to their own lines, and there was fierce fighting over the Medenine area throughout the day. The German pilots claimed seven or eight Spitfires and a Kittyhawk shot down, two of them by pilots of II/JG51 from central Tunisia which operated briefly over Medenine on this date. Two were claimed by Reinert to raise his personal score to 130, while Bär also claimed his 170th personal victory.

The claims, made in cloudy conditions and in fierce combats, seem to have considerably overestimated British losses, which were minimal. The Spitfires had very much the best of the day in fact, their pilots claiming five Bf109s, two MC 202s and a Fiat G.50 fighter-bomber, while the Kittyhawks added a further Bf109. Two of the Messerschmitts were credited to Flt Lt Neville Duke, a flight commander in 92 Squadron who emerged as Allied topscorer of the Tunisian Campaign.

Far to the south in Chad a force of Free French troops had been gathered by General LeClerc, and had been waiting for months for the right moment to join the Allies. Now they were ordered to motor across the Sahara to the region of Ksar Rhilane. Here they would take up position to the left of 8th Army's extreme flank. It was hoped that from here they would soon be able to link with US II Corps' right flank, completing the cordon round the Axis forces in Tunisia. Von Arnim could see the threat at once, despatching a column of motorized troops supported by fighter-bombers and dive-bombers to intercept and stop them.

'Tank-busters' at work

Desert Air Force was tasked with supporting the Free French, and the Hurricane IID 'tank-busters' of 6 Squadron were ordered to fly their first operational sorties since Alamein. The hard-hitting cannon aircraft made two attacks, during the first of which 12 of 20 vehicles were put out of action; more were claimed in the next attack, while others were destroyed by Kittyhawk fighter-

---

fuselage as well as its normal armament of six 0.50 in Browning machine guns.

North American B-25 Mitchell

The B-25 was a high-mid wing monoplane medium bomber fitted with twin fins and rudders and powered by two Wright R-2600-13 engines of 1700 hp each. The aircraft was armed with six 0.50 in Browning guns, two in the dorsal power turret and two in a retractable ventral turret in the belly, while one was fixed to fire forward in the nose, a second being available as a flexible gun for the bombardier's use. It could carry 3000 lb of bombs over a range of 1500 miles. Maximum speed was 284 mph at 15 000 ft, and service ceiling was 21 200 ft.

GERMAN

The Luftwaffe employed the G variant of the familiar Messerschmitt Bf109. With a more powerful Daimler-Benz DB 605A-1 engine of 1475 hp, the aircraft featured a maximum speed of 387 mph at 22 970 ft – virtually the same as the lighter Bf109F. Service ceiling was increased to 38 500 ft and range to 450 miles, which could be substantially increased if lower throttle

settings were employed. A heavier armament was fitted, comprising two 13 mm MG131 machine guns and one 20 mm MG151/20 cannon in the nose.

The FW190A fighter-bomber and Ju88A bomber were types which have been described elsewhere.

Messerschmitt Me210A

A relatively unsuccessful Zerstörer heavy-fighter aircraft of very clean design. Powered by two Daimler-Benz BD601F engines of 1395 hp each, it was armed with two 20mm MG151 cannon and two 7.9 mm MG17 machine guns in the nose. Rear armament comprised a 13 mm MG131 gun in a remotely controlled barbette on each side of the fuselage, operated by the gunner. Up to 4400 lb of bombs could be carried, half in an internal bomb bay. Maximum speed was 385 mph, service ceiling was 22 965 ft and range 1491 miles.

ITALIAN

The Italians employed the same Macchi MC 202 fighter over Mareth as had been employed throughout 1942 over Malta.

Messerschmitt Bf109G-2 Trop of I/Jagdgeschwader 77, flown by the Gruppenadjutant, Lt Heinz-Edgar Berres

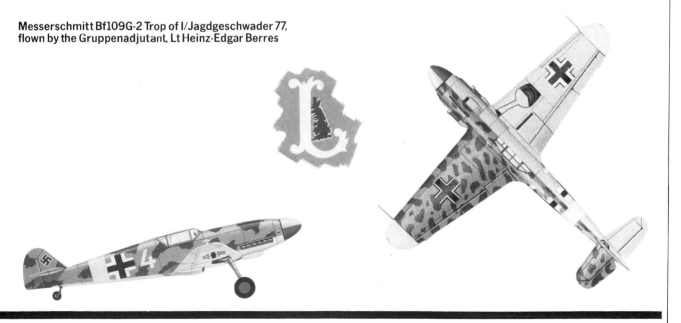

EVEN IN THE DESERT THERE COULD BE MUD! PERSONNEL OF
THE US 57TH FIGHTER GROUP TRY TO FREE ONE OF THE
UNIT'S CURTISS P-40F WARHAWK FIGHTER-BOMBERS FOR A
MISSION.

bombers. Twenty-four of the latter from 239 Wing were
making their attack when their escort — more Kittyhawks
of 112 Squadron — saw a formation of StG3 Ju87Ds
approaching, covered by JG77 Bf109s. The 'Shark'
Squadron pilots attacked at once, claiming two Stukas and
a Messerschmitt shot down, but paid the price for doing so.
Six Kittyhawks were also shot down, two of them by
JG77's highly experienced Kommodore, Major Joachim
Müncheberg. Müncheberg's second victim was eight-
victory ace, Canadian Flt Lt Robert R Smith DFC, who was
taken prisoner.

Preparations for the offensive were continuing apace,
and on 11 March, 2nd New Zealand Division began moving
forward to Ben Gardane in conditions of great secrecy. At
the same time, 244 Wing at the airfields in this location
received a most unusual reinforcement with the arrival of
the Polish Fighting Team. This was an all-volunteer unit of
17 experienced Polish fighter pilots commanded by Wing
Commander T H Rolski, to be led in the air by the great
Squadron Leader Stanislaw Skalski, top-scorer of the
September 1939 fighting, whose personal total now stood at
13¼. The Team was attached for operations to 145
Squadron — a unique unit in RAF history!

The equally gifted pilots of JG77 enjoyed more success
on 13 March during two combats. In the morning Maj
Müncheberg led II/JG77 to intercept 57th Fighter Group
P-40Fs escorted by 244 Wing Spitfires. Five of the Warhawks were claimed (actual losses were four), the American
pilots claiming three Messerschmitts in return, the Spitfires
adding one more. In the afternoon came an attack from the
Axis 'rear', as units of XII ASC launched one of the growing number of raids they were now directing on the Gabes
area in support of the 8th Army. This time the Messerschmitts intercepted a formation of Bell P-39 Airacobra
fighters from the 81st Fighter Group, escorted by
American-flown Spitfires of the 31st Fighter Group, as
these were approaching La Fauconnerie airfield. Against
eight claims, seven Airacobras were actually lost — more
than half the formation! In these two fights Ernst-Wilhelm
Reinert had added six more victories to his total,

Müncheberg claiming one in each fight, and Oblt Siegfried
Freytag (JG77's top-scorer over Malta) two Airacobras to
bring his score to 87.

On 17 March, US II Corps bgan to press towards the
coast in the rear of the Mareth Line, Gafsa swiftly falling
into their hands, although they made little progress beyond
this point. Air fighting and fighter-bombing attacks continued daily, but on 18 March bad weather rendered most
Axis airfields in the area unserviceable.

All was now ready. Gen Mezze had been forced to split
his forces as a result of recent actions. In the line at Mareth
were the 15th and 21st Panzer Divisions, part of the 10th
Panzer, the 90th Light and the Italian Young Fascists. The
rest of 10th Panzer with the Centauro Armoured Division
were held back facing the Americans south-east of Gafsa,
while the Sahar and Pistoia Divisions were at the Tebaga
Gap. The Gap is situated between the Djebels (mountains),
Tebaga and Melab to the north-west of Mareth. The Mareth
Line spanned the coastal strip between the sea at Zarat and
the Matmata Hills. These hills cut southern Tunisia off
from Libya up to the great salt flats of the Chott Djerid, and
were easily passable only at the Gap.

The New Zealand Division had by now moved on from
Ben Gardane, and during the night of 19–20 March was
ordered to move with all speed around the south of the
Matmata Hills to attack the Tebaga Gap in an effort to take
I Italian Army in the flank. They reached the Gap during 20
March only to find the defenders already being reinforced
by the German 164th Light Division which Messe had with-
drawn from reserve. He drew 21st Panzer Division back to
Gabes from Mareth ready to follow if necessary.

Air support for the offensive

Desert Air Force efforts were now redoubled, light bombers
appearing over the Mareth defenses in formations 18 strong
throughout the day. Other bombers attacked Fatnassa,
where I/JG77's 1 Staffel had all its aircraft destroyed by the
end of the day. However, at K.41 airfield the Italian 16°
Gruppo CT was reinforced with nine new MC 202s. At
2030 hours that night 8th Army opened a heavy artillery
bombardment on the Mareth positions, falling first on the
positions of the Young Fascists, who were defending the
Wadi Zigzaou. It was into this defile that 50th Infantry
Division began the assault soon afterwards. Recent rains
had filled the wadi with much more water than had been
anticipated, however, and although a bridgehead was
secured on the northern side, this was swept by murderous
fire which quickly brought the advance to a halt.

Daylight on 21 March brought a new threat to the New
Zealanders passing to the south of the Matmata Hills from a
group of 40 tanks. Consequently, Hurricane 'tank-busters'
and Kittyhawks were called in to break this up. Meanwhile,
in support of the main attack the air forces in the north
began a major series of attacks on the Axis airfields
supporting the Mareth defenses, putting the units operating
here under great pressure.

'About 0900, 18 Boeings made their attack. Fires started
at the Italian jetty. The 88 mm Flak position has seven
dead and several wounded. Another heavy gun protects
our site. An Italian 120 mm gun position receives a
direct hit. An hour later comes a second attack. A
German 88 mm Flak opens fire. About 1600 another air
raid alarm. 54 four-engined bombers with 49 fighters
attack our ill-fated airfield. There is no escape from the

bombs. One must only trust to luck. The effect on the nerves is indescribable. Every single man, from airman to Staffel Commander is utterly exhausted by the incessant bombing. In addition, not a wink of sleep. An hour later came the fourth attack of the day. That was the beginning of Spring in Tunisia!'

So recorded one of JG77's pilots to his diary.

Air activity at the front was again affected by the weather on 22 March, however, as I Italian Army launched a counter-attack by 15th Panzer Division against the 50th Division positions along the Wadi Zigzaou. At the same time Messe moved 21st Panzer Division west to join the fighting at the approaches to the Tebaga Gap. Fighter-bombers ranged over the front when rain allowed, concentrating their activities particularly against 21st Panzer's column. Overhead there was considerable fighting, the Poles with 244 Wing seeing their first actions on this date.

Axis reverses

In the early afternoon 13 of 6 Squadron's Hurricane IIDs were sent off after the German armor as it arrived to the south of El Hamma, and nine tanks were claimed immobilized. Bf109s attacked and three of the 'tank-busters' were shot down. Six returned to the attack two hours later, but one was hit and force-landed.

The next day (23 March) proved to be a bad day for the Axis fighters in more than one way. In the morning Maj Müncheberg and his wingman, Lt Strasen, took off from La Fauconnerie to fly down to Mareth looking for targets. Before they had gone far, however, they spotted a pair of XII ASC Spitfires from the US 52nd Fighter Group and dived to the attack. Müncheberg shot down one for his 135th victory, but was either rammed by the stricken aircraft, or flew into the wreckage, crashing to his death alongside his victim. During the same day 244 Wing took delivery of a dozen Spitfire IXs, a significant strengthening of their forces. Six of these superior fighters were made available to the Poles, four to 92 Squadron and two kept in reserve.

The Mark IX had the edge over most German fighters: others had already gone to squadrons in the north, and some would soon reach XII ASC. Their arrival gave the Allied fighter pilots an edge which they had not enjoyed before. Soon they would be giving the Axis fighters a bad time, and the days when the high flying 'Experten' ruled the skies were fast approaching their end.

By the evening of 23 March 1st Armoured Division had come up behind the New Zealanders at Tebaga ready to exploit any breakthrough they might achieve, and by night Montgomery began quietly to withdraw 50th Division from their dangerous bridgehead. Next day Desert Air Force continued its attacks on the forces opposing the New Zealand infantry with increased intensity, particular attention being paid to 21st Panzer, 164th Light and the Italian La Spezia Divisions. Hurricane IIDs from 6 Squadron were again involved both morning and afternoon, but during their first attack ran into fierce ground fire which shot down one 'tank-buster' and caused a second to crash-land at 200 mph.

LEADING FIGHTER PILOTS OF THE MARETH BATTLE

The Luftwaffe

Major Heinz 'Pritzl' Bär had flown in action since the beginning of the war. During 1940 he had been the top-scoring NCO pilot of the Luftwaffe (with 13 victories by the end of the year) and had been commissioned before the invasion of the Soviet Union in June 1941. By the end of June 1942 his score had reached 113, 96 of them in the USSR, and he had been awarded the Knight's Cross with Oak leaves.

Posted from JG51 with which he had served for three years, he took command of I/JG77 and led the unit to Sicily at the start of July, gaining a further five victories in the skies over Malta. At the end of October 1942 he took his unit across the Mediterranean to Libya. In North Africa alone he claimed 61 further victories before the fall of Tunisia in May 1943, 19 of them during the Mareth operation. Ill with malaria and a stomach ulcer, he was rested until late 1943, when he began flying

HPT HEINZ BÄR, I/JG77.

on Home Defense duties with II/JG1 in Germany, reaching his 200th victory during April 1944.

He later commanded JG3 and then flew Me262 jet fighters during 1945, emerging as the Luftwaffe's top-scoring jet pilot with 16 of his 220 victories claimed while flying these aircraft. He died in a light aircraft accident some years after the war.

JG77's second great 'Experte' was Oberleutnant Ernst-Wilhelm Reinert of II Gruppe. He joined this unit in the Soviet Union during the first days of the Eastern Campaign, and, taking advantage of the conditions there, by October 1942 had already gained 100 victories. His unit then moved to North Africa where between January and April 1943 he claimed 51 further victories. Following service in Sicily, he led a Gruppe of JG27 on Home Defense, finishing the war with 174 victories. He was awarded the Knight's Cross with Swords and Oak Leaves.

The Desert Air Force

Allied top-scorer in Tunisia was Flt Lt Neville Duke. After brief service in England in 1941, where he gained two victories whilst flying Spitfires with 92 Squadron, he was posted to the Western Desert, where he flew Curtiss Tomahawk and Kittyhawk fighters through late 1941 and early 1942. At the end of his first operational tour he spent some weeks as an instructor before rejoining 92 Squadron — now also in North Africa — as a flight commander late in 1942. During the first four months of 1943 he claimed 14 victories over Tunisia, the highest total for any Allied pilot during the campaign.

With his personal score at 21 and two shared, he was again rested until March 1944 when he took command of 145 Squadron in Italy. Here he claimed a final six victories during and after the advance on Rome, finishing his third tour during September 1944 as Desert Air Force's top-scorer of the war.

Awarded a DSO, DFC and two Bars, he then attended a test pilot's course, subsequently leaving the RAF to join Hawker Aircraft. He eventually became Chief Test Pilot, and gained fame internationally when he captured the World Air Speed Record in a specially modified Hunter fighter on 7 September, 1953.

FLT LT N F DUKE, 92 SQUADRON.

This gave the Hurricane a chance to yet again demonstrate its great structural strength with the pilot stepping out unscathed!

A unit of Hurricane fighter-bombers, 241 Squadron, had been sent down to the USAAF's Thelpte airfield in central Tunisia from 242 Group in the north, to aid DAF's efforts at Tebaga. During the afternoon 12 of the unit's aircraft followed 6 Squadron's second attack near El Hamma. Although JG77's fighters were much engaged with XII ASC aircraft during the day I Gruppe pilots were nevertheless able to intercept, shooting down two of the 'tank-busters' and one fighter-bomber Hurricane. Generally, however, the Kittyhawks, Warhawks, Bostons, Baltimores and B-25s were able to operate unscathed under an 'umbrella' of Spitfires, causing much disturbance and loss to the Axis forces.

TOP: CURTISS KITTYHAWK II FIGHTER-BOMBERS OF 3 RAAF SQUADRON.

ABOVE: THE RAF'S FIRST GENUINE ANTITANK AIRCRAFT, THE HURRICANE IID, WHICH SAW MUCH SERVICE OVER SOUTHERN TUNISIA IN EARLY 1943. THE BIG 40 MM VICKERS 'S' ANTI-TANK CANNON CAN BE CLEARLY SEEN BENEATH THE WING. THIS WAS A PRESENTATION AIRCRAFT.

ABOVE RIGHT: ARMORERS PREPARE TO SHACKLE 250 LB BOMBS BENEATH THE BELLY OF A CURTISS P-40F WARHAWK ON A NORTH AFRICAN AIRFIELD. THIS IS AN AIRCRAFT OF THE 64TH (SCORPIONS) SQUADRON, OF THE 57TH FIGHTER GROUP, USAAF.

Generale Messe was now well aware that the focus of the 8th Army's attack was changing and during 24 March he ordered 15th Panzer Division to cease its counter-attacks on 50th Division's positions on the Wadi Zigzaou and move to a central position as a mobile reserve which he could swing west or south as the threats developed. The air attacks on the growing forces in the El Hamma area continued throughout 25 March, but Spitfire pilots now encountered both Ju88s and Me210s, indicating that the Luftwaffe was again being reinforced from the north due to the scale of the British threat.

Fighter-bombers as battlefield support

The level of reinforcement of the Tebaga area was making a breakthrough more unlikely day by day, unless very high losses were to be suffered. Numbers of the deadly dual-purpose 88 mm Flak guns had been dug in, to ensure that any attempt at breakthrough by the armor would be very costly (as it had been at Alamein) unless some new method of neutralizing them could be found. Consequently, the decision was taken to employ the fighter-bombers in direct close battlefield support of the army spearheads in a manner that had never been attempted by the British before, but was redolent of the *Blitzkrieg* employment of Stukas and Schlacht aircraft by the Luftwaffe. The wings were put on notice to be ready for special operations next day.

Meanwhile, 6 Squadron had again launched its hard-working Hurricane IIDs against the Axis tanks during the early afternoon of 25 March. The aircraft, flying slow and straight at low altitude to get their sights on the armor, flew into a veritable storm of light flak, directed at their relatively vulnerable undersides. Five went down at once and one more force-landed on return — yet not one pilot was hurt.

JG77 was on the move during the day; the constant attacks on the Gabes airfields had taken their toll and the Geschwader was moving back to airfields at La Fauconnerie and Bou Thadi. The unit's patrols were constantly harried next morning as Spitfires swept over the Tebaga battle area seeking to gain local air supremacy before the operations in support of the army began. Fighter battles raged overhead throughout the day, but all was clear by the afternoon when the first wave of bombers appeared. This comprised six Baltimores and 12 Bostons of 3 SAAF Wing, 12 Baltimores of 232 Wing and 12 B-25s of the US 12th Bombardment Group which passed over in tight, closely-escorted formations to rain bombs on strongpoints at the funnel-shaped entrance to the Gap.

Next came the first of the fighter-bombers, 21 bomb-carrying Kittyhawks of 250 and 3 RAAF Squadrons escorting 11 Hurricane IIDs from 6 Squadron to the area. The Hurricanes made a quick sweep over the sector looking for any tanks, but none were seen, although two of the 'tank-busters' were hit by Flak and shot down. The Kittyhawks then came down to attack gun positions and dugouts: two 250 Squadron aircraft failed to return, while two of the Australian fighters force-landed.

As the fighter-bombers completed their initial attack, 2nd New Zealand Division and 8th Armoured Brigade opened the attack from the ground, but found themselves held up by a concentration of 88mm guns south of El Hamma. The delay was only temporary, for minutes later the next wave of air support arrived as 11 Kittyhawks of 260 Squadron and elements of all four squadrons of the US 79th Fighter Group swept in to take-out the guns. Flak and defending Messerschmitts took their toll, four of the American P-40s being lost, including that flown by the commanding officer of the attached 316th Squadron, while two more came down in Allied lines; a 260 Squadron Kittyhawk also failed to return.

Behind came yet a third wave, this time aircraft of 7 SAAF Wing which lost one Kittyhawk with three more badly damaged and one slightly damaged. But the overall tactic had been successful. At 1800 hours the Sherman tanks of 1st Armoured Division burst through the hole which the air assault had torn in the defenses, followed by the New Zealanders — both divisions virtually unscathed. Throughout the afternoon the Axis fighters, hunted by Desert Air Force Spitfires and attacked on their own airfields by the XII ASC units, had scarcely been effective at all. Only once during the second wave attacks had some of I/JG77's Messerschmitts been able to intervene briefly, Heinz Bär and his pilots claiming four of the fighter-bombers shot down.

The cost to Desert Air Force had been moderately heavy, but nonetheless amounted on average to less than one aircraft per squadron of the 17 fighter-bomber and ground-attack squadrons that took part in the assault. However, 6 Squadron had now lost so many aircraft in such a short space of time that it was withdrawn at the end of the day to await the arrival of replacement Hurricanes.

The threat that the breakout posed to I Italian Army — of being outflanked and cut off in the Mareth Line — caused Messe to order a precipitate withdrawal northwards. Even this might not have been enough had it not been for the desperate efforts of the Panzers during 27 March to hold

1st Armoured Division at El Hamma just long enough to allow the main body of troops to escape up the coastal highway. To the north the US 34th Infantry Division launched an attack on the Fondouk Pass in an effort to close the trap further up the coast, but this petered out in the face of heavy artillery fire. Now the fighter-bombers could turn their attention to their more familiar prey — the fleeing columns of Axis vehicles — but still they continued to suffer losses to both Flak and the hard-pressed fighters of JG77. Overhead, Spitfires of 145 Squadron met a rare daylight formation of ten Junkers Ju88 bombers — an indication of the special efforts being expended by the Luftwaffe to aid their comrades on the ground — and two of these were claimed shot down while others were damaged. A few of the new specialized Henschel Hs129B anti-tank aircraft of 8(Pz)/SG2, which had recently arrived in Africa, also made an appearance, attacking the pursuing British armor.

Next day 145 Squadron again saw Ju88s, catching two bombers of KG30 taking off from Gafsa and shooting both down. The Polish Fighting Team then spotted seven more of these aircraft near Sfax, Sqn Ldr Skalski and Flt Lt Horbaczewski despatching a further pair. During 28 March the New Zealanders took El Hamma and had reached Gabes by nightfall, but already the first elements of I Italian Army were entering their next defensive positions at Wadi Akarit where they began digging in on 29 March. The first land battle in which Allied airpower had played a decisive role was at an end.

The value of air supremacy

That the battle on land and in the air had been a hard one barely needs saying. Despite the depredations inflicted upon them by constant air attacks, the pilots of JG77 had done their utmost to protect the ground forces. That they failed should not detract from the magnitude of their personal efforts, and the losses they had inflicted on their opponents had at times been grievous. In a period of just one month Heinz Bär had claimed 19 victories and Ernst-Wilhelm Reinert another 18. Bär's adjutant, Heinz-Edgar Berres had made nine claims, while the Geschwader Kommodore, the great Müncheberg, had been credited with six in the short period before his death.

Against the outnumbered Axis air forces, the Allied pilots enjoyed less opportunities to build up big scores, but the Spitfires were steadily whittling away the opposition on the road to aerial supremacy, and 92 Squadron's Neville Duke had confirmed his position as the outstanding Desert Air Force fighter pilot, claiming six victories over Messerschmitts and Macchis during this brief period.

It was the beginning of the final phase in Africa for the Axis. Soon after the victory at Mareth, 8th Army joined hands with US II Corps, and the Allied cordon was complete. Now with a preponderance of airpower, the Allied armies drove the German and Italian forces into north-eastern Tunisia like a piston up a cylinder — but there was no exhaust valve at the top! Evacuation to Sicily or Sardinia was impossible due to the Allied domination of the sea, and of the air above it. During early May the Axis defenses crumbled away in the face of a final massive offensive, and nearly a quarter of a million troops surrendered, including all the splendid, battle-hardened veteran divisions of the Afrika Korps. Coming so soon after the equally costly loss of the 6th Army at Stalingrad, it was a major blow to the Axis — a blow which left the way open for an early invasion of Southern Europe.

FIERCE CLASHES AT KURSK

JULY 1943

Overleaf

On 7 July, 1943, with the fighting in the Kursk Salient at its height,
Ilyushin Il-2m3 Shturmovik aircraft make sustained attacks on the German Panzers. Here such an assault
is being pressed home against PzKw IV and V tanks of one of the Wehrmacht's divisions.

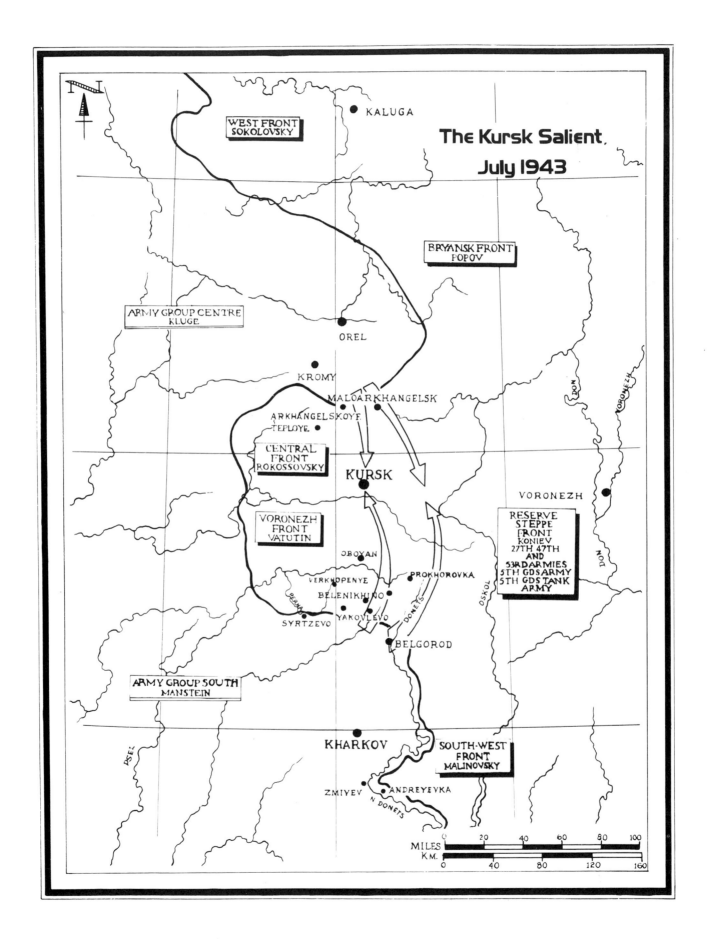

Asked which was the greatest battle of World War II, few in the Western world other than the knowledgeable student of history would mention the name Kursk. Yet here was undoubtedly a battle of epic proportions between Nazi Germany and the Soviet Union that deserves to be considered the greatest and most important battle of that war, if not of all wars in history. The sheer numbers of men, tanks, guns and aircraft involved were on a scale without precedent. It was Adolf Hitler's last great gamble before the war in the East was irrevocably lost to him — and the first day of this great clash of Titans was also the most costly single day of aerial warfare of all time.

Operation *Barbarossa* — the great invasion of Soviet Russia by the German Wehrmacht which began in mid summer 1941 — had almost succeeded in achieving total victory that year. But the great Soviet commanders, 'General Mud' and 'General Winter' had stalled the thrust of the Panzers short of Moscow, and fierce Soviet counter-offensives in the winter had stabilized the line. With a return to good weather, the Germans had tried again. Once more the onset of autumn and winter prevented a complete Soviet collapse, and then at Stalingrad a stubborn Soviet defense was developed into an annihilating victory which totally destroyed the German 6th Army, while shattering and demoralizing their Italian and Rumanian allies.

Coupled with the great British victory at El Alamein in North Africa, and the Anglo-American landings in French North-West Africa, which coincided with the Stalingrad disaster, the tide seemed to have turned fully against Germany and her allies. Early in 1943 the Soviets exploited their success with a new offensive which drove the Germans back in the whole southern sector. Yet even then the resilience, experience and sheer fighting quality of the German elements of General Von Manstein's Army Group South allowed them to hold the assault and then drive it back at least part of the way. By the end of March 1943 the line had stabilized, Kharkov and Stalino falling back into German hands. Kursk, however, remained in the Soviet grasp, and around the city, from just below Orel in the north to just above Kharkov in the south, a great salient bulged into the German line.

Hitler had high hopes that the Panzers could repeat their magic yet again in the summer of 1943. Indeed, they had to! Soviet power at the front and her production of tanks, guns and aircraft was now rapidly overtaking that of Germany. This could well be the last chance!

True the Wehrmacht had lost some of its aura of invinc-ibility as a result of its recent defeats, but in terms of experience and combat-worthiness it still enjoyed considerable superiority. And new equipment was at last appearing — the mighty Tiger tank with its 88 mm gun was coming into service in increasing numbers, while the new Panther was about to enter service, and would be a match for anything the Soviets could field.

In the sky above the steppes the Luftwaffe certainly still ruled supreme. Its fighters already enjoyed a marked predominance over their Soviet opposite numbers, particularly in respect of pilot quality and experience, but now the elderly Ju87 dive-bombers were at last beginning to be joined by ground-attack versions of the superb Focke-Wulf FW190 fighter, and by a new generation of specialized 'tank-busting' aircraft.

A fatal German flaw

Yet as Soviet strength had grown, so the demands of the war in the air elsewhere were having a deleterious effect on the proportion of the Luftwaffe that could be retained in the East. During 1942 the calls of the Mediterranean had drained away two complete Jagdgeschwadern (JG53 and 77), together with substantial numbers of bomber and dive-bomber Gruppen. Late in the same year the Anglo-American advance into Tunisia led to the withdrawal of more units to the area, while simultaneously US heavy bombers began appearing over the borders of the Reich.

Initially, only two further Jagdgruppen were withdrawn to face this threat, but a large percentage of new fighter aircraft and pilots had to be held back from the war zones to form new air defense units to meet not only this danger but the growing weight of attack by the RAF's heavy bombers at night.

Nevertheless, despite these withdrawals, the Luftwaffe was still able to gather together a force of over 2000 aircraft in two Luftflotten for the Kursk operations, representing nearly 70 per cent of the air force's total available operational strength. Only in the north around Leningrad and the Arctic regions was any worthwhile element of air power left with Luftflotten 1 and 5, the rest of the Eastern Front being denuded for the forthcoming offensive.

It was in bombers that the force gathered was particularly strong. There were more than a dozen Kampf-gruppen in the Mediterranean, together with three Stuka-gruppen, but there were few such units left in Western Europe or the Reich. Around Kursk, however, the Germans enjoyed a substantial numerical superiority in bomber aircraft over the Soviets, although the latter fielded nearly twice as many fighters and ground attack aircraft.

As in previous years it had been the German plan to attack in late May or June, as soon as the ground was dry enough to allow full movement by the Panzers. However, Hitler was unwilling to allow Operation *Zitadel* (Citadel) to start until the arrival of the new equipment on which the Germans were counting to renew their superiority — particularly the Panther tanks. The Germans suffered from a major disadvantage, however, — that of security. The German High Command had been infiltrated by a Swiss-based spy network, while the ability of the British Intelligence service to break German cypher signals with the 'Ultra' machine meant that the Allies were fully aware of plans for *Zitadel*. Only the date for the start of the offensive was unknown, but both the knowledge and the delays had allowed the Soviet Union to prepare defenses in unprecedented depth.

APPROXIMATE GERMAN AIR STRENGTH	
Bombers	1200
Fighters	600
Ground-attack	100
Reconnaissance	150
Total	2050

APPROXIMATE SOVIET AIR STRENGTH	
Day Bombers	500
Night Bombers	400
Fighters	1060
Ground-attack	940
Total	2900

RED AIR FLEET ORDER OF BATTLE, JULY 1943

Northern Sector		Air Divisions identified	
16th Air Army	Col Gen S I Rudenko	1st Guards Fighter Air Division	Lt Col I V Krupenin
Southern Sector		2nd Guards Air Division	Col G I Komarov
		3rd Guards Fighter Air Division	Col Vilukhov
2nd Air Army	Col Gen S A Krasovsky Oboyan area	4th Guards Fighter Air Division	Gen Maj V A Kitayev
17th Air Army	Col Gen V A Sudets Karocha area	4th Assault Air Division	
Approximate strength – 2900 aircraft		8th Guards Fighter Air Division	Gen D P Golunov
Both sectors were reinforced throughout by units from AFLRO and other air armies. Notably, the Northern Sector was reinforced during the later part of the fighting by elements of the 1st and 15th Air Armies. No full breakdown of the units forming the three main Air Armies was available to the author, but a considerable number have been identified, as follows:		8th Guards Assault Air Division	
		8th Bomber Air Division	
		9th Guards Assault Air Division	Gen F A Agaltsov
		10th Guards Fighter Air Division	
		10th Guards Assault Air Division	
		11th Guards Assault Air Division	
		12th Guards Fighter Air Division	
Air Corps identified		30th Air Division	
		225th Assault Air Division	
1st Guards Fighter Air Corps		233rd Assault Air Division	
1st Bomber Air Corps	Gen Maj I S Polbin	234th Assault Air Division	
1st Assault Air Corps	Gen Lt V G Ryazanov	256th Fighter Air Division	
3rd Bomber Air Corps	Gen A Z Karavatsky	282nd Fighter Air Division	Col S P Danilov
5th Air Corps	Gen Maj D P Galunov	283rd Fighter Air Division	Gen Sergei P Denisov
5th Assault Air Corps	Gen Maj N P Kamanin	288th Fighter Air Division	
6th Fighter Air Corps	Gen N Y Yerlykhin	291st Assault Air Division	Col A N Vitruk
6th Composite Air Corps	Gen I D Antoshkin	299th Assault Air Division	Col I V Krupsky

To the north of the Salient, facing the main front of Army Group Center, based on Orel and Bryansk, was the Soviet Bryansk Front which comprised three armies. Within the Salient, to the north of Kursk itself, was the Central Front with five armies in the line and the 2nd Tank Army in reserve; the south sector of the Salient was held by the six armies of the Voronezh Front, while south of the Salient, behind the River Donets, was the 57th Army of the South-West Front. Behind these front-line forces was the Reserve (or Steppe) Front which had five armies held in reserve around Voronezh.

Impressive Soviet air back-up

To support these land armies, the Soviets had to hand three air armies — the 16th with the Central Front, 2nd with the Voronezh Front, and 17th with the South-West Front. These were to be supported by substantial elements of AFLRO — the Stavka's strategic reserve — while elements of 15th Air Army with the Bryansk Front could be called upon if needed. This added up to a Soviet strength immediately available of some 2900 aircraft.

The importance of the Kursk Salient had ensured that these air forces were equipped with the latest products of the Soviet factories — Lavochkin La 5 and Yakovlev Yak 9 fighters, and Petlyakov Pe 2 twin-engined bombers. They also had the latest two-seat version of the Ilyushin Il-2 'Sturmovik' ground-attack aircraft, now fitted with highly-effective 37 mm cannon in the wings; these heavily armored machines were the most feared of all Soviet aircraft by the German ground forces, to whom they were known as the *Zementer* (Cement Bomber) due to their apparent invulnerability to ground fire. The Soviets also used their new PTAB hollow-charge anti-tank bomb for the first time during this battle.

While Army Group Center's 2nd Army held the line of the Salient directly opposite Kursk, the force gathered for the strike from the north comprised 9th Army. On the other side of the Salient, Army Group South had gathered 4th Panzer Army behind Belgorod to strike northwards, and Army Detachment Kempf near Kharkov, ready to move across the Donets on the right flank of the advance.

Although Hitler finally set the date for the opening of *Zitadel* as 5 July, 1943 and while the Soviet Union remained alert, and aware from preparations on the other side of the line that the attack must come at any moment, the Soviets remained ignorant of the actual date.

For two months before *Zitadel*, however, the Red Air Force had been undertaking a campaign of interdiction against the Luftwaffe airfields in an effort to take the edge off the force that was gathered ready for the big day. This series of attacks failed to make much impact on the opposition, but did result in some fairly substantial losses for the Soviets. Indeed, during this period the Germans claimed to have destroyed some 2300 Soviet aircraft, 1257 of them in May alone, against Luftwaffe losses of about 10–15 per cent of that number.

Prior to the main offensive beginning, 4th Panzer Army launched a limited attack on the afternoon of 4 July to take a line of hills to the north of Belgorod, from where it was to launch its main thrust on the morrow. *Zitadel* began at 0330 hours on 5 July — with massive artillery barrages launched simultaneously on both fronts, with 9th Army in the north making the initial movements on the ground — this despite the fact that at 0110 hours the Northern front of the Salient had been shattered by the opening of a concentrated and unexpected Soviet artillery barrage. In the south, Army Group South's units followed behind a massive assault launched by Luftflotte 4's VIII Fliegerkorps.

In the north Feldmarshal Von Kluge's forces had available 15 divisions in one Army Corps and three Panzer Corps — more than 200 000 men — but at first it was infantry and assault guns that he employed, holding the armor in reserve to exploit any breach of the line. The defenses proved surprisingly obdurate from the start, being well dug-in and of much greater depth than had been expected, or indeed, met before. Some ground was taken, but the Soviets held particularly firm on the left flank, the Germans failing to reach Maloarkhangelsk.

Overhead Luftflotte 6 was strong in its support from first light, when Stukas of III/StG1 led by their

		Air Regiments identified		
IAP (REGIMENTS)	IAD (DIVISIONS)	IAK(CORPS)	AIR ARMY	REGIMENTAL COMMANDER
Istrebitelnyi Aviacionnyi Pulk (Fighter Air Regiments)				
5th Guards	295th			
8th Guards				
32nd Guards	4th Guards	1st Guards		Lt Col Aleksandr F Semenov
32nd	256th			
40th				
41st Guards	8th Guards		2nd	
54th Guards	1st Guards		16th	
63rd Guards	4th Guards	1st Guards		Lt Col Nikolai P Ivanov
64th Guards	3rd Guards	1st Guards		Lt Col Nikolai P Ivanov
65th Guards	3rd Guards	1st Guards		Lt Col Mikhail N Zvorygin
66th Guards	3rd Guards	1st Guards		Lt Col A A Surkov
67th Guards			16th	Lt Col Aleksei B Panov
88th Guards	8th Guards		2nd	
127th			16th	Capt F V Khimisch
152nd	8th Guards		2nd	
160th	4th Guards	1st Guards		Maj V A Yamanov
166th				
171st				
179th				
240th			16th	
270th				
427th				Maj A D Yakimenko
438th				Maj Konstantin P Oborin
283rd			17th	Maj Andrei I Giritsch
512th				
519th				
581st				
728th				Lt Col V S Vasilyaka
774th	282nd		17th	
866th	288th		17th	Capt A I Koldunov
Shturmovyi Aviacionnyi Pulk (Assault Air Regiments)				
58th			16th	
62nd	233rd		2nd	
90th Guards	4th Guards		2nd	
93rd			17th	
140th				Maj Yakovitsky
141st	9th Guards		2nd	
142nd	8th Guards		2nd	
143rd	8th Guards		2nd	
165th	10th Guards		2nd	
166th	10th Guards		2nd	
175th				Lt Col M D Zakharchenko
176th Guards	11th Guards		17th	
198th	233rd		2nd	
218th	299th			
241st				
525th			17th	I M Dolgov
614th	225th		17th	
667th				
672nd	30th		2nd	
812th	225th		17th	
948th				
955th				

Kommandeur Maj Friedrich Lang, a holder of the Knight's Cross with Oak Leaves, howled down to attack gun emplacements on the fringe of a wood. Other dive-bombers hit convoys and supply routes, as well as defensive localities, while the Panzerjäger units employed their heavy cannon against Soviet tanks. The powerful Focke-Wulf FW190 fighters from the Gruppen of JG51 and 54 were also conspicuous, engaging the Yaks and Lavochkins of General Yerhykin's 6th Fighter Air Corps and the 1st Guards Fighter Air Division, as these units rose to give battle over the fighting below.

Heavy losses — on both sides

In fierce combat on this front during the day the Russians claimed 106 victories in 76 different engagements for an admitted loss of 98. 1/Lt Stepan K Kolesnichenko of the 519th IAP was the Russian 'star' here, claiming three victories on this date, while 2/Lt Vitalii K Polyakov from the Guards unit (54th Gu IAP) shot down one aircraft and then rammed a second — the first of at least six deliberate ramming attacks to be made by Russian fighter pilots during the battle.

The outstanding performer of the day was undoutedly

the Luftwaffe's Oberfeldwebel Hubert Strassl of III/JG51 who had flown four times by dusk, during which sorties he claimed the almost unbelievable total of 15 aircraft shot down! Targets were available to him and his fellow pilots in plenty, for the Soviet 16th Air Army launched all its major units into the battle during the day, including the 3rd Bomber and 6th Composite Air Corps, and the 2nd Guards and 299th Ground Attack Divisions. The Russian pilots roamed over the battlefield in groups of six to eight aircraft, seeking targets of opportunity amongst the German troops and vehicles near Yasnaya, Polyana, Ozerok and Arkhangelskaye. Subsequently, however, the Soviet command admitted that the Red Air Force fighters had allowed themselves to be drawn off into combats with the FW190s, allowing the German bombers, Stukas and Panzerjägern to find their targets free of interception.

If the fighting in the air over von Kluge's forces was heavy, that in the south was of almost cataclysmic proportions. It had been planned that Army Group South's assault should be spearheaded by a massive air attack, which would go in at dawn as the artillery barrage lifted. Consequently, at airfields throughout Luftflotte 4's area some 800 Stukas, bombers and escorting fighters were preparing for take-off. Suddenly came the alarm! The Soviets were attempting a pre-emptive strike, designed to cripple the Luftflotte's power on its airfields before the battle had even been fully joined.

Fortunately for the Germans, they had established a number of 'Freya' radar sets close to the front, and these provided just sufficient warning for decisive action to be

A FORMATION OF FAST, EFFECTIVE PETLYAKOV PE-2 DIVE-BOMBERS OF THE SOVIET AIR FORCE HEAD FOR THE FRONT. THESE AIRCRAFT APPEARED IN CONSIDERABLE STRENGTH AT KURSK.

taken to save the day. At once all the units standing ready were ordered to take off and clear the area of the airfields, while 270 fighters from JG3 and 52 were scrambled to intercept the approaching raiders. Thus when at 0430 hours the Soviet force approached the airfields at Mikayanovka, Sokoniki, Pomerki, Osnova, Rogan, Barvenkuro and Kramatorskaya, it was to find only a handful of unserviceable machines present there — and it was 60 of these types which were later claimed destroyed by the Soviets.

The Soviets lose control
Their plan had backfired for the Soviet aircraft were now themselves in great danger as the Messerschmitts bored in. The 17th Air Army, which had provided 132 ground-attack aircraft and 285 fighters to make up the bulk of the attacking force, took the brunt of the reverse as the German pilots enjoyed a field day, claiming 120 victories for minimal loss.

This rebuff had an immediate effect on the rest of the day's actions, for now the German bombers and assault aircraft undertook their planned attack in face of little opposition. Indeed, on the Voronezh Front, the responsibility of the hard-hit 17th Air Army, the troops were without air support of any kind until 0900 hours.

LUFTWAFFE ORDER OF BATTLE JULY 1943

UNIT	AIRCRAFT
SOUTH OF SALIENT	
Luftflotte 4 Belgorod and Kharkov	
I,III/JG52	Bf109G (Croat Staffel attached)
II,III/JG3	Bf109G
I,II/KG3	Ju88A (6 Staffel with Ju88C-6 Zerstörer)
I,II,III/KG27	He111H
I,II,III/KG55	He111H
I,II,III/StG2	Ju87D (Plus experimental Panzerjägerstaffel with Ju87G)
I,II,III/StG77	Ju87D
I/SchG1	FW190F
4,8/SchG1	Hs129B
4,8/SchG2	Hs129B
Ten tactical reconnaissance Staffeln	Bf109 & FW190
One NSGr	Various light aircraft
2nd Hungarian Air Corps	
5/1 Fighter Group	Bf109G
102/2 Dive-Bomber Squadron	Ju87D
Bomber Group	Ju88A
1 independent long-range Reconnaissance Group	Ju88D
3/1 Reconnaissance Squadron	FW187
NORTH OF SALIENT	
Luftflotte 6 – Orel	
I,III,IV/JG51	FW190A (Spanish Staffel attached)
I/JG54	FW190A
I/ZG1	Bf110F
II,III/KG51	Ju88A (7 Staffel with Ju88C-6 Zerstörer)
KG4 KG53 Four Gruppen	He111H
I,II,III/StG1	Ju87D
PzJäg St/JG51	Hs129B (ex-Versuchskommando fur Panzerbekämpflug)
PzJäg St/St/G1	Ju87G (ex-Versuchskommando fur Panzerbekämpflug)
PzJäg St/ZG1	Bf110G (ex-Versuchskommando fur Panzerbekämpflug)
Several tactical reconnaissance Staffeln FW190 & Bf109	

173 victories by the end of the day, 76 of them credited to General D P Golunov's 8th Guards Fighter Division; three pilots were credited with four victories each — Senior Lieutenants Belikov, Panin and Bulayev.

Yet this total was barely half of what Luftflotte 4's fighters were believed to have achieved. By nightfall the staggering total of 432 Soviet aircraft had been claimed shot down, 77 by II/JG3 alone. This Gruppe included 62 bomber aircraft amongst its total, the Gruppen Kommandeur, Hpt Kurt Brändle personally claiming five to raise his own score to 151, while one of his pilots, Oblt Joachim Kirschner claimed nine. Some of JG52's pilots did even better; Hpt Johannes Wiese, Kommandeur of I Gruppe claimed 12, and Oblt Walter Krupinski of III Gruppe added 11 more to raise his personal tally to 90. Five victories also went to the Hungarian 5/1 Group, which had joined in the initial early morning interception. Losses to the German fighters in achieving this amazing total had amounted to just 26 aircraft. The events of 5 July, 1943 comprised the greatest single day of combat in terms of aircraft claimed shot down; it would never be matched — even by the oft-recorded Marianas 'Turkey Shoot'.

The battle continued unabated next day. In the south the Soviets desperately threw in every possible ground-attack and bomber aircraft to attack the tank formations threatening to break through in the area of the 6th Guards Army. As in the north, groups of six to eight aircraft appeared at first, but as the day wore on they were increased in strength to 30–40, since the larger groups proved somewhat easier for the hard-pressed fighters to protect. Despite their efforts, the power and ferocity of the German attack tore a huge gap in General Chityakov's army, and into this Manstein thrust his reserves, the spearheads taking Luchkit, where the SS Panzer Corps found itself 20 miles inside the evening defenses.

In the north less progress continued to be made, and here von Kluge began feeding in his Panzer reserves in an

On the ground Army Group South now struck its opening blows, Manstein's army having available over 1000 tanks and 300 assault guns, which swept forward, Hoth's 4th Panzer Army driving north-east through Belgorod, while Army Detachment Kempf attacked eastwards across the Donets. In support, I/SchG1's FW190F fighter-bombers rained the deadly new SD-1 and SD-2 bomb containers onto the Soviet anti-tank positions. As the containers opened, hundreds of vicious little fragmentation bombs were scattered over the area, causing the gunners to dive for cover or die. On this front, the penetration into the Salient bit much deeper than in the north, considerably more territory being taken on this opening day.

Overhead the Soviets were soon back in the air, but here too they were forced to admit that they had lost control of their fighters and that 'serious inadequacies' had manifested themselves. Here the Red Air Force claimed at least effort to force the breakthrough. It was here that the first of the Soviet reserves were fed in, and a tank counter-attack was made, beginning a four-day battle. This attack, which went in at 0500 hours in the Pololyan, Saborovka and Butirki areas was supported by an initial strike by 140 aircraft from the 16th Air Army. Two further attacks followed, escorted by the 127th Fighter Regiment, and by the end of the day 113 victories had been claimed for 91 losses on this front.

Pilots of distinction

Over the battle area as a whole Luftwaffe claims totalled 205 on 6 July, many of these going to Luftflotte 6's JG51 whose Ofw Strassl was again to the fore, claiming ten further successes. It was a day of glory for the Russian fighters also, Lt Alexandr K Gorovetz of the 166th IAP reportedly attacked a formation of Ju87s over Zarinskiye Dvory, bringing down nine of them (one by ramming) before he fell victim to an escorting Luftwaffe fighter. He was posthumously named a Hero of the Soviet Union.

Guards Major Alexei Maras'yev had been shot down a year earlier and had made an epic escape to Soviet lines where his damaged legs had been amputated. Now returning to action as the Russian Douglas Bader, this tough and gallant pilot re-opened his score, shooting down two Ju87 Stukas from a formation of 20. Another of these aircraft was claimed by a young La-5 pilot in one of the Stavka's crack fighter units, the 240th IAP; it was the first victory for Ivan Kojedub, subsequently to become the top-scoring Soviet fighter ace of the war.

Maras'yev gained more success next day as the Soviets claimed that 16th Air Army had gained the initiative over the northern sector, where most bomber formations were now being intercepted. Here Maras'yev claimed three FW190s shot down. On both sides of the line the new and more powerful anti-tank aircraft were playing a bigger part in the ground battle than ever before.

The Soviets continued to call in the reserves from the Steppe Front to prevent disaster, but in the south the commander of the 1st Tank Army reported that the new

THE ACES OF KURSK

Around a dozen Soviet fighter pilots were awarded the gold stars of Heroes of the Soviet Union for the Kursk fighting, half of these going to members of the 5th Guards Fighter Air Regiment, whose commander, Colonel V A Zaytsev, received this award for the second time. The fighting in the northern sector involved not only the Free French unit, but also the 73rd Fighter Air Regiment, one of the Soviet Union's all-women units. The 73rd's most successful pilot, 2/Lt Lilya Litvak, was killed over Orel on 1 August 1943 with her personal tally at 13 victories.

The Germans

Amongst the many very successful fighter pilots serving with the Luftwaffe on the Eastern Front, four particularly 'shone' at Kursk. The most successful had been Strassl, who flew with JG51 over the northern sector of the Salient. Strassl had flown in the Soviet Union from late 1941 to early 1943, gaining 19 victories during this time. Returning to II/JG51 after a short period as an instructor, he claimed 18 victories during June, and then 30 between 5 and 8 July before his death in action. He was awarded a posthumous Knight's Cross.

In the southern sector, Johannes Wiese commanded 2 Staffel of the 'crack' I/JG52. Already a Ritterkreuzträger (Knight's Cross holder) with over 50 victories by mid 1943, his 12 victories on 5 July, 1943 was one of the outstanding achievements of the campaign. By early 1944 his score had risen to 125, and in October of that year he took command of JG77 on the West Front. He was shot down and badly wounded on Christmas Day 1944 with his total at 133 plus 75 more unconfirmed. He remained prisoner of the Soviets until 1950.

Walter Krupinski — known as 'Graf Punski' (Count Punski) — had claimed 66 victories in the Soviet Union by the end of 1942, when he was wounded. His 11 on 5 July, 1943 raised the total to 90, and by early 1944 when he was posted home to I/JG5 this score had risen to 177. He later commanded II/JG11 and then III/JG26, adding 20 victories in the West by the end of the war, which found him flying Me262 jets in Galland's JV44.

Joachim Kirshner had joined II/JG3 late in 1941, and apart from a few weeks in Sicily flying over Malta, had operated continually over the Soviet Union since then. His 5 July, 1943 score of nine victories raised his overall total to 150. Posted to command the new IV/JG27 in Greece, he claimed 13 victories in a very short time. On 17 December, 1943 he was shot down over Yugoslavia but succeeded in parachuting to safety. He was, however, captured by partisans of the 29th Communist Brigade, who shot and killed him — his final score at the time of his death being 188. Like Wiese and Krupinksi he had received the Knight's Cross with Oak Leaves.

Germany's most highly-decorated airman was Hans-Ulrich Rudel, a 'Stuka' pilot from the beginning of the war, who first flew a Ju87G anti-tank aircraft during the Kursk battle. Rudel flew over 2500 sorties by the end of the war, losing one leg in February 1945 during one of the several times he was shot down and wounded.

LEFT: III/JG51'S EXTRAORDINARILY SUCCESSFUL 'EXPERTE' OF KURSK, OFW HUBERT STRASSL. ABOVE: HPT GÜNTHER RALL, III/JG53.

Amongst other targets he was personally credited with destroying at least 519 Russian tanks, 16 of which were claimed in two days at Kursk. He was the only recipient of the Golden Oak Leaves to the Knight's Cross with Swords and Diamonds.

Bruno Meyer was another noted German ground-attack and anti-tank pilot of the Luftwaffe who flew in a Schlacht staffel from the beginning of the war. At Kursk he led the Hs129B and FW190 Schlacht units, having previously flown Hs129s in Tunisia.

The Russians

Few Russian Shturmovik pilots had survived long enough to become well-known by July 1943, but the Pe-2 leader, Maj Gen Ivan S Polbin, who organized and co-ordinated the air attacks on German armor by his unit and several of the Il-2 regiments on 12 July, was probably the best-known of all Soviet ground-attack pilots. Insisting on flying regularly throughout the war, he was killed in action in February 1945, by which time he had twice become a Hero of the Soviet Union. Throughout, Polbin commanded the 1st Bomber Air Corps.

Amongst the leading Shturmovik units of the battle, 14 pilots of the 614th SAP claimed seven tanks destroyed on 15 July, while on the next day 23 Il-2s of the 812th SAP were credited with 17 tanks destroyed. During a second strike 19 more aircraft from this unit claimed a further ten. At

Tigers and Panthers were giving his crews considerable problems, while the new ground-support aircraft which the Soviets considered to be virtually flying anti-tank artillery, were proving a particularly unpleasant surprise. One local commander, General Getman, suffered the loss of 12 of his T-34s to just one gun-equipped Ju87G from StG2 — but this aircraft was flown by no ordinary pilot, it was in the hands of Oblt Hans-Ulrich Rudel, Germany's No 1 combat pilot of the war!

However, Rudel's lone exploit paled into insignificance compared to the achievements of General V G Ryazanov's 1st Ground Attack Air Corps in the northern sector, which launched two concentrated attacks on German armor near Syrtsevo and Yakovlevo. Here the up-gunned Ilyushin Il-2m3 'Shturmoviks' first put their new 37 mm cannon to good use. Passing the columns of German tanks to one side, they then swept into a great circle overhead, diving out to shoot at the rear of the armored vehicles where their protection was thinnest. Such tactics could be maintained for 15–30 minutes at a time and proved devastating in the extreme. According to Soviet sources, 9th Panzer Division lost 70 tanks in 20 minutes during one attack, while in nine hours 3rd Panzer suffered 2000 casualties and 220 tanks out of action. Hardest hit of all was 17th Panzer Division which was almost wiped out, having 240 vehicles making unserviceable during four hours of continual assault.

Progress in the south continued to be good on 7 July, but the delays in the north were now threatening the success of the whole offensive. On 8 July more Panzers were thrown in, and supported by Stukas, struck again towards Teploye. On this front during the day III/JG51's successful Ofw Herbert Strassl claimed three further victories to raise his total since the offensive opened to 30, and his overall total to 67. His aircraft was then hit and he was forced to bale out, but he was too low for the canopy of his parachute to deploy, and was killed as his body struck the ground. By 9 July the German advance was progressing well in the south. Verkhopenye was taken, a damaged bridge across the river Pena being seized here. The Germans were now within 12 miles of Oboyan from where they would be able to get on

least 14 of the Shturmovik pilots operating over Kursk subsequently became Heroes of the Soviet Union.

In April 1942, Alexei Petrovich Maras'yev had been shot down over enemy territory after he had in turn shot down two Ju52 transport aircraft as they were taking off. The eight-victory ace injured both feet in the crash which followed. Showing incredible doggedness, he crawled for 19 days towards the Soviet lines, living on berries, insects and hedgehogs. Fitted with artificial feet, he was determined to fly again, and rejoined his unit (63rd Gu IAP in the 1st Guards Fighter Air Corps) just in time for the Kursk battles. Here he got five victories in two days, raising his total to 19 by the end of July, flying a La-5. Not surprisingly, he received the Gold Star of a Hero of the Soviet Union.

Yak-7B pilot Stepan K Kolesnitschenko, who had done so well on the first day of the battle, retained his ascendancy, being credited with 16 victories over the Kursk area by the end of the fighting there. Top scorer for the whole battle was Arsenii V Vorozheikin of the 728th Fighter Air Regiment (IAP), who was credited with 19 victories during the German offensive and the Soviet counter-attack which followed. On 14 July, leading six Yak-7Bs to attack Ju87s over the Bogorodetskoye-Velenikhino area, he personally claimed two. During the next flight he engaged 18 more German aircraft, claiming two more

Ju87s and a Bf109. He claimed four more on 4 August, ending the war with a total of 52 victories. A third Yak-7B pilot to do well was Senior Lt Anatoli L Kozhevnikov of the 438th IAP, who claimed eight victories during the first three days of the fighting, including four Ju88s, three Bf109s and a He111.

Future top-scorer of the Soviet Air Force (VVS) was Ivan Nikitich Kozhedub, who first saw action on the northern sector of the front, over Kursk as an La-5 pilot in the 240th IAP in the 16th Air Army, claiming five victories during July and three more in August. Previous experience as an instructor stood him in good stead and victories came fast. During the autumn of 1943 he claimed 11 in ten days,

and by the end of the war he was deputy commander of the 'crack' 176th Guards IAP, flying La-7 aircraft. One of the very few Russians to be created a Hero of the Soviet Union three times, his final score reached 62 — the highest of all Allied pilots — and included one of the fast Me262 jets.

LEFT: GUARDS COL KIRILL YEVSTIGNEYEV, 240TH IAP. ABOVE: LT IVAN N KOZHEDUB, 240TH IAP.

With Kozhedub in the 240th IAP in July 1943 was another of the Soviet Union's leading aces, Kirill A Yevstigneyev, who claimed at least eight of his 52 victories during that month's fighting, three of them Ju87s in two engagements on 8 July. The following October he claimed 12 in nine combats, ending the war as a double Hero of the Soviet Union.

Amongst other notable pilots, Capt Konstantin A Novikov of the 40th Gu IAP claimed five victories on 5 July, while Nikolai Kotlov was also credited with five in a day two days later, although he was shot down and killed on that date. Next day Maj Moisei S Tokarev claimed four to raise his score for the war to 22, but he too was then killed.

Known aces of the battle were:

Name	Score	Final Score	Unit
Arsenii V Vorozheikin	19	52	728th IAP
Stepan K Kolesnitschenko	16	U/K	519th IAP
Alexei P Maras'yev	10	19	63rd Gu IAP
Alexsandr K Gorovetz	9	10	166th IAP
Andrei Y Barovykh	8	32	U/K
Ivan N Kozhedub	8	52	240th IAP
Kirill A Yevstigneyev	8	52	240th IAP
Georgii A Bayevskii	5	19	U/K
Konstantin A Novikov	5	29	40th Gu IAP
Nikolai Kotlov	5	U/K	U/K

(U/K = unknown)

MAIN AIRCRAFT TYPES EMPLOYED DURING THE BATTLE FOR KURSK

SOVIET

Yakovlev Yak 9
A single -seat low-wing monoplane fighter of conventional design, powered by a single Klimov M-105 in-line engine of 1260 hp. Constructed mainly of wood, the Yak 9 used in 1943 had a top speed of 373 mph at 11 480 ft, a service ceiling of 36 090 ft and a range of 870 miles. It was armed with one 20 mm cannon and one 12.7 mm machine gun, both mounted in the nose, with the cannon firing through the propeller boss.

Lavochkin La-5FN
Developed from the in-line engined LaGG-3, the La-5FN was a low-wing monoplane single-seat fighter of mainly wooden construction, powered by a 1640 hp Shvetsov M-82FN radial engine. Tough and manoeuvreable, the aircraft had a top speed of 403 mph at 20 997 ft, a ceiling of 31 168 ft, and a rang eof 475 miles. It was armed with two 20 mm cannon mounted in the nose and synchronized to fire through the airscrew disc.

Ilyushin Il-2m3
The famous 'Shturmovik' built in larger numbers than any other aircraft of World War II, the Il-2 was a single-engined low-wing monoplane ground-attack aircraft. Built round an armored steel 'bath', which housed the engine and cockpit, it was almost impervious to light ground fire. Originally built as a single-seater, the early Il-2s proved underpowered and lacking in manoeuvreability, while also being vulnerable to fighter attack from the rear. The Il-2m3 used at Kursk had a more powerful engine and a second seat for a rear gunner, armed with a 12.7 mm machine gun on a flexible mounting which cured these problems. The aircraft was also fitted with a pair of newly-developed NS-37 cannon in the wings. These 37 mm weapons were capable of piercing the armor of most German tanks. RS-82 and RS-132 rocket propelled missiles could also be carried beneath the wings, while the aircraft also featured a number of small bomb-bays for the internal carriage of anti-personnel, or PTAB hollow-charge anti-tank bombs. Powered by a 1750 hp Mikulin AM-38F in-line engine which gave a top speed of 251 mph at 4920 ft, the Il-2m3 had a limited service ceiling of 11 480 ft, but for its low level activities it did not need more. Range of this formidable weapon was 475 miles.

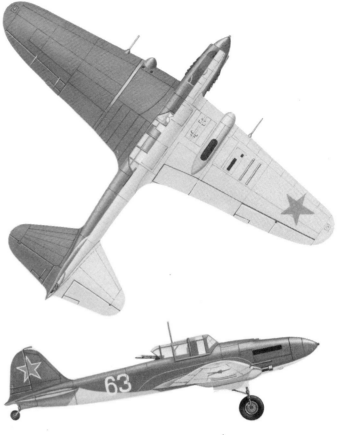

Ilyushin Il-2m3 'Shturmovik' of the Red Air Force

Petlyakov Pe-2FT
A fast, streamlined twin-engined low-wing monoplane bomber with twin fins and rudders, the Pe-2FT was powered by two 1260 hp Klimov M-105PF in-line engines which gave it the very high top speed of 361 mph at 16 400 ft, a service ceiling 29 530 ft, and a range of 1100 miles. The aircraft could carry up to 12

---

the main road to Kursk. However, while 4th Panzer Army's drive was going to plan, Army Detachment Kempf was still held up in the strong, deep defenses which it had found on the other side of the Donets, and as a result had not yet been able to strike deeply north-eastwards into the Salient to protect the right flank of Hoth's forces.

At this point the Soviets attempted to take advantage of this situation and deal Hoth's Panzers a devastating blow. The Soviet II Guards Tank Corps had a combat group positioned near Gartishchevo to block Kempf's advance, but with the latter still held up further south, this force was swinging westwards to take Hausser's SS Panzer Corps, which formed the right arm of 4th Panzer Army, in the flank. Such an attack would help save XXXI Tank Corps of 1st Tank Army which seemed on the point of total collapse.

As the columns of infantry-supported T.34s crept through the morning mists they were spotted by Hpt Bruno Meyer of Schlachtgeschwader 1 as he led three Henschel Hs129 Panzerjäger aircraft on a reconnaissance over the area. Realizing at once the import of what he was seeing, he returned to Mikoyanovka to report, and to organize

appropriate action. It was almost a carbon copy of the Soviet 1st Ground Attack Air Corps' success of two days earlier; the four Staffeln of Henschels took off in rotation, 16 at a time, to keep up a steady attack on the tanks, the armor-piercing shells of the heavy MK 103 30mm cannon biting into the thinner armor on the back of the tanks. In support of their 'tank-busting' comrades, the pilots of I/SchG1, led by their Kommandeur, Major Alfred Druschel, swept overhead in their Focke-Wulfs to shower SD-1s and SD-2s onto the infantry and mobile Flak guns to reduce resistance to the attack. After an hour of this, more than 50 tanks had been destroyed and the Soviet thrust defeated. Despite this success in the air, on the ground

THE SPECIALIST ANTITANK HENSCHEL HS 129B PLAYED A MAJOR PART IN THE FIGHTING AT KURSK, PROVING TO BE AN UNPLEASANT SHOCK FOR SOVIET TANK CREWS. THIS AIRCRAFT OF 4(PZ)/SCHGl IS FLOWN BY ONE OF THE LUFTWAFFE'S FUTURE 'TANK-BUSTERS', OBLT GEORG DORNEMANN.

bombs each of 100 kg, half in a fuselage bomb-bay, four under each wing center section and one in a bay in the rear of each engine. It was armed with two fixed 12.7 mm BS machine guns in the nose, one flexible gun of similar calibre in a rear turret, and one in a ventral position for defense of the underside. Two 7.62 mm ShKAS guns could be fitted in the side panels of the cockpit for additional defense. The Pe-2 could operate equally well as a level or dive-bomber, or for high-speed reconnaissance.

GERMAN

Messerschmitt Bf109G	
Junkers Ju87D	
Junkers Ju88A	See earlier chapters.
Heinkel He111H	
Messerschmitt Bf110D	

Focke-Wulf FW190A

One of the finest fighters of the war, the FW190A was a low-wing monoplane powered by a 1700 hp BMW801D-2 radial engine. This tough fighter was armed with two 7.9 mm MG17 machine guns in the nose, two 20 mm MG151 cannon in the wing roots and two 20 mm MG/FF cannon in the wings. Capable of 413 mph at 20 400 ft and a service ceiling of 36 800 ft, the aircraft had a range of 565 miles. The fighter-bomber, or Schlacht version, had the outer cannon removed to make way for the underwing bomb racks, while an additional rack was situated under the fuselage. A variety of bombs or bomb-containers could be carried.

Henschel Hs129B

The Luftwaffe's first and only specialist anti-tank aircraft, the Hs129B was a twin-engined, low-wing single-seat monoplane which was constructed around a very heavily armored nose and cockpit section. Powered by a pair of French Gnome-Rhone 14M 4/5 engines producing 700 hp each, the aircraft, when fitted to carry a full complement of anti-tank cannon, had a top speed of 199 mph at 9845 ft, a service ceiling of 24 600 ft and a range of 384 miles. Armament in this guise comprised two 7.9 mm MG17 machine guns and two 20 mm MG151 cannon in the fuselage and a 30 mm MK101 gun in a 'gondola' fairing fitted beneath the fuselage. The cannon aramament could be deleted to allow various alternative bombloads to be carried.

Junkers Ju87G

This special anti-tank version of the classic 'Stuka' was a conversion of the D Model to carry a 37 mm Flak 37 cannon

beneath each wing in addition to the basic machine gun armament. With the fitting of the cannon, the speed of the aircraft was considerably reduced, and as it was also lacking in heavy armor, it was generally accompanied on operations by standard dive-bomber Ju87Ds which attacked and suppressed the AA gunners while the cannon aircraft attacked the tanks and other vehicles.

Henschel Hs129B of 8(Pz)/Schlachtgeschwader 2

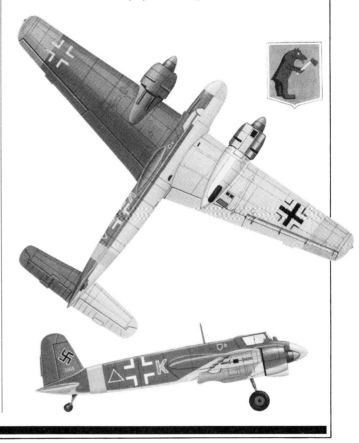

Political Commissar Nikita Kruschev (in later years the charismatic Soviet Premier) managed to dispel the panic in XXXI Tank Corps and to re-organize the defense to prevent a precipitate collapse until further reinforcements could be brought forward.

Still the Germans continued to batter their way forward, but with painful slowness and at great cost — there were still none of the great, sweeping tank thrusts through the open steppe which had so marked previous summer offensives. Overhead the air battles continued at an extraordinary level of ferocity. Nearly all the action took place within an area 60 kilometres long and 20 kilometres deep, where frequently 100–150 aircraft at a time were involved.

By 10 July the Soviets were reporting that their 16th Air Army alone had flown over 7600 sorties since the battle had begun, while AFLRO (Stavka) units operating with them had added another 800 with 517 aerial victories claimed.

2nd Air Army was also racking up successes, claiming 330 victories against losses of 153 since 5 July. Having now had the opportunity to re-organize, 2nd and 17th Air Army and AFLRO bomber units were beginning to make frequent

ABOVE: SCOURGE OF THE PANZERS: THE ILYUSHIN Il-2M
'SHTURMOVIK' ANTITANK AND GROUND-ATTACK AIRCRAFT
WAS BUILT IN GREATER NUMBERS THAN ANY OTHER AIRCRAFT
OF WORLD WAR II.
RIGHT: PETLYAKOV PE-2 DIVE-BOMBERS IN FLIGHT.

attacks by night on the Wehrmacht columns and supply lines, adding an additional dimension.

However, during 10 July the 6th SS Panzer Grenadier Regiment of the 'Totenkopf' Division formed a bridgehead over the River Psel at Krasuyy Oktyabr, and on 11 July Hausser's SS Panzer Corps as spearhead of Hoth's 4th Panzer Army, pushed on strongly towards Prokhorovka. In the north Model's Army was ready to burst through the last defenses at Teploye, and at last it looked as if *Zitadel* had reached the moment of decision and that the breakout might come at any moment.

Soviet forces at risk again

Despite all the Soviet efforts in the air and on the ground, their new equipment and their massive defense preparations in such depth, suddenly they were once again in apalling danger. In the south 6th Guards Army had been knocked out and 1st Tank Army badly battered; 5th Guards Army had been thrown in piecemeal to try and fill the gaps as they appeared, and its strength dissipated. Now 5th Guards Tank Army was brought up from the Steppe Front reserve, and headed for Prokhorovka to try and block 4th Panzer Army.

It was at this point that the first of two fateful decisions which eventually decided the outcome of the battle was made. Although much of the front was in confusion and disintegration, General Vatutin courageously decided to throw every reserve into the coming battle at Prokhorovka, regardless of the situation elsewhere. It was a finely-balanced situation; 5th Guards Tank Army had three armored corps with approximately 850 tanks and heavy self-propelled guns. If 4th Panzer Army arrived alone, it would have only 600 available, but if the long-awaited advance of Army Detachment Kempf could come up on the right in time, his 300 tanks would swing the balance in the German's favor. All was set for the greatest clash of armor in history. But there were jokers in the pack.

Even as the battle was at its height on 10 July came news of a major Anglo-American invasion of Sicily, and quickly it became obvious to the German High Command that Italian resistance was crumbling away. Suddenly Hitler was faced with the spectre of an Allied advance through Southern Europe — possibly a drive into the Balkans. Both ground and air forces in Italy would therefore require

urgent reinforcement. If *Zitadel* was to succeed it must do so quickly.

Then on the morning of 12 July the Soviets went onto the offensive. In the northern sector 17th Air Army's 213th Night Bomber Air Division and AFLRO units, reinforced by the 313th Night Bomber Air Division from the 15th Air Army, had attacked all night, flying 362 sorties and dropping 210 tons of bombs. With the dawn 70 Pe.2 bombers and 48 Il-2 'Shturmoviks' from General M M Gromov's fresh 1st Air Army struck at 9th Army as the overture to a counter-attack by 11th Guards Army into the rear of Model's forces.

At once Stukas and Schlacht aircraft were thrown into the fray, many pilots making up to six sorties during the

THE SECOND NEW SOVIET FIGHTER TYPE TO APPEAR IN STRENGTH OVER KURSK WAS THE YAKOVLEV YAK 9.

day. Coupled with the concentrated fire of the German artillery, these efforts held the Soviet attack, but Model was forced onto the defensive, and was unable to complete the breakthrough at Teploye. Soviet activity in the air in support of these moves was at an even higher level, three Air Armies operating over the Orel region during the day, and flying a tremendous total of 2174 sorties. A staggering 72 air battles with the Luftwaffe were recorded, many of them by 1st Guards Fighter Air Corps, during which 86 victories were claimed for 59 losses. Included in these victories were at least eight by the 32nd Gu IAP, seven by the 66th Gu IAP and six by the 240th IAP. Involved in these actions were the Yak 9 fighters of the Free French 'Normandie' fighter group, which operated under Soviet command.

To the south 2nd Air Army also launched a strike by 200 aircraft on Hausser's Panzer spearheads, followed 40 minutes later by the opening of Lt Gen Rotmistrov's powerful tank counter-attack at Prokhorovka. The critical battle within-a-battle had been joined. Without the benefit of Model's expected thrust from the north, Hoth's forces were forced onto the defensive by the strength of the Soviet attack, while overhead Luftflotte 4 and 2nd Air Army fought a series of violent pitched battles for air superiority. Everything now depended on Kempf, whose III Panzer Corps was making good progress in its efforts to join Hoth. Next day the Corps began passing through a bridgehead at Rzhavets which had been captured overnight, its arrival threatening to trap the Soviet 69th Army and two tank corps in a pocket between itself and 4th Panzer Army, in the area Rzhavets-Belenikhino-Gostishchevo.

Hitler loses his nerve

It was at this point, however, that Adolf Hitler's nerve failed. The Soviet counter-offensive at Orel was the last straw. Against the advice of his generals, just as there seemed a real chance that the Panzers might again burst forth to ravage Central Russia, he ordered that the offensive be ceased. A few days of virtual stalemate followed, and then on 17 July he ordered the immediate withdrawal from the line of Hausser's 'crack' SS Panzer Corps for despatch

to Italy to stop the rot there. Two other Panzer Divisions were transferred from 4th Panzer Army to Army Group Center to aid in stabilizing the situation at Orel. It was the end of *Zitadel* and the Kursk offensive.

For the Germans the results were catastrophic. The hard-pressed Soviets were allowed to regroup and counter-attack, and by 23 July they had regained all the ground lost. True they had lost 85 000 men in the southern sector of the Salient alone, but the Red Army was now growing at a faster rate than the Wehrmacht, and Soviet war production had overtaken that of Germany. Hitler's reserves had melted away on the furnace of the Salient. There would be no more grand offensives; from now on the war would be one long, hard, costly retreat. Kursk had been the turning point; the initiative had now passed irrevocably to the Allies.

Even as the battles in USSR and Sicily drew all eyes to the east and south, the city of Hamburg was almost totally destroyed in the most devastating series of air raids yet experienced. Civilian morale plummeted; if the war was to continue, the Reich would need to be much more heavily and effectively defended against the growing Allied bombing offensives by day and night, and it would have to be the war fronts which were robbed for the fighter units and Flak batteries necessary. *Zitadel* was the last major action in the east for Luftflotte 4's JG3 — within a few weeks the remaining Gruppen were withdrawn for home defense as was Luftflotte 6's I/ZG1 and many of the units in Italy. In the Soviet Union the Luftwaffe fighters would never lose their ascendency — when they were available: but increasingly the Red Air Force was left alone to harrass the Wehrmacht and increase its work of carnage on the shrinking force of Panzers.

Despite the deficiencies which were found still to exist, the defense of the Belgorod-Kursk area had been the most successful exercise of their air power to date for the Soviets and reflected the beginning of a new phase of operations for the Red Air Force. Between 5 and 23 July they had flown some 19 263 sorties — an average of 1000 per day. Pilots had claimed over 1500 aerial victories while losses were admitted to be 'about 1000', but were probably higher. German losses on the other hand, are known to have been much lower, not even totalling 1000 aircraft.

CHAPTER EIGHT

THE NIGHT BOMBER OFFENSIVE

FEATURING THE LEIPZIG RAID
19-20 FEBRUARY 1944

Overleaf

Junkers Ju88C-6 nightfighter of the Luftwaffe prepares to attack a
Handley-Page Halifax of No 6 (RCAF) Bomber Group as it approaches Leipzig during the night of
19-20 February, 1944.

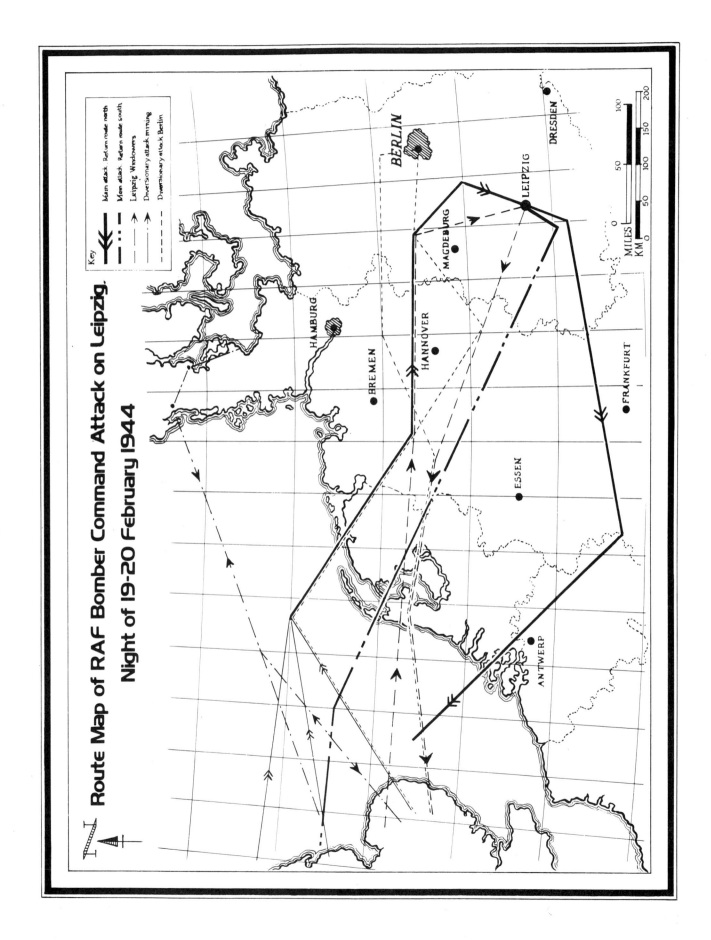

Route Map of RAF Bomber Command Attack on Leipzig.
Night of 19-20 February 1944

The ethos of the Royal Air Force since its formation in 1918 had always been offensive action — and, if possible, independent offensive action. The threat posed by Nazi Germany during the 1930s had required much priority to be given to the modernization and strengthening of Fighter Command and its associated radar. Those parts of the air force concerned mainly with co-operation with the other services — Coastal Command, and particularly Army Co-operation Command — were somewhat neglected, but this was not the case with Bomber Command. If Fighter Command was the shield, the bombers were the sword, and every effort had been made to develop new and effective types for this role.

At the outbreak of the war the RAF was the only air force in the world to have in service quantities of bombers equipped with power-operated gun turrets. While these carried only .303in rifle-calibre machine guns, this armament represented a major advance on what had gone before, and it was firmly and fondly believed that tight, mutually-supporting formations of the faster and more modern bombers so armed would be able to fight their way to their targets by day even in the face of hostile fighter interception. While units flying the older types such as the Whitley had been trained in night operations, little serious thought had been given to this tactic as a major element of future strategy.

In 1939 Bomber Command appeared on paper to be a relatively effective and strong force. The Command was divided into five geographically-separated operational groups, each one of which employed different equipment in terms of aircraft. The ten squadrons of No 1 Group, equipped with single-engined Fairey Battle light bombers, were at once despatched to France to form the Advanced Air Striking Force of the British Expeditionary Force. This was not in fact a great loss to the strength of the Command, for the poorly-armed, slow Battle had neither the range nor bombload to be considered anything more than a tactical support aircraft in real terms. No 2 Group had available seven squadrons of Bristol Blenheim IVs — twin-engined light bombers which were also earmarked for eventual service in France, but in the meantime were considerably more effective and useful than the Battles.

The main striking force comprised the three groups of medium bombers; No 3 Group had six squadrons of Vickers Wellingtons — the best aircraft available, and the most heavily armed; No 4 Group had six squadrons of the older, but reliable and long-ranging Armstrong-Whitworth Whitleys, which were suitable for use only by night due to their low speed; finally No 5 Group also comprised six squadrons, which flew Handley-Page Hampdens, the lightest and fastest of the three types of 'medium' in use.

Early operations

On the second day of the war Blenheims had attacked Wilhelmshaven, whilst Wellingtons raided Brünsbuttel, both sorties being made in the hope of inflicting damage on the major German warships anchored in these ports. The Blenheim's low-level attack achieved little, five bombers being lost to the Flak defenses, whilst two Wellingtons fell to Bf109 fighters — a graphic illustration of the dangers facing future operations by day.

By night, activity was limited to dropping propaganda leaflets over Germany, since the French and British governments had agreed that no bombs should be dropped on inland targets in an effort not to provoke a similar response from the Luftwaffe. For the time being the Germans tacitly recognized this 'truce' and limited their own bombing actions to shipping and coastal targets also. For Bomber Command the only legitimate targets were German naval vessels, either at anchor or underway, and many 'armed reconnaissances' were flown in search of this elusive prey.

In late September 1939 a complete flight of Hampdens vanished without trace, shot down by Luftwaffe fighters during one of these reconnaissances over the North Sea. Still confident of the correctness of its 'self-defending formation' concept, Bomber Command Headquarters decided to disregard the German claims which were broadcast after this interception, treating them as propaganda; the armed reconnaissances continued.

On 3 December, by extraordinary good fortune rather than anything else, a formation of Wellingtons escaped almost unscathed from intercepting fighters. This encouraged the operational planners to increase such activity, and on 14 December five Wellingtons were lost in a vicious day engagement off Heligoland. Although all five had fallen victim to the fighters, No 3 Group Staff still decided to believe that they had been shot down by ships' Flak. This was proved to be a fatal miscalculation four days later when a strong formation of Wellingtons flew out to Wilhelmshaven and was cut to pieces in a savage battle over the German Bight. Twelve bombers failed to return and nearly all the others were damaged; at last the danger of the cannon-armed fighter began fully to be appreciated.

The offensive emphasis was subtly altered thereafter towards night operations, but when the Wehrmacht, ably supported by the Luftwaffe, invaded Scandinavia, Bomber Command was once again plunged into a daylight battle which reinforced the lessons learned in December 1939 — that unescorted bomber formations could expect heavy casualties when opposed by strong fighter defenses. The campaign in Norway also demonstrated again the effectiveness of air support in a tactical situation. But for the Luftwaffe, the Germans might well have failed in their attempt to secure the north of the country and would have had to face a continued British presence there.

Germany in the ascendancy

Even before this battle was over, however, the Germans had struck again, the hammer-blow falling on 10 May, 1940. Swiftly German forces overran Holland, Belgium and France, rolling back the Western allies, despite the suicidal gallantry of the defending air forces — not least the Blenheim and Battle crews of the RAF.

Bomber Command operated in a tactical role for the first few days, but on the night of 15 May targets in Germany became legitimate objectives although still within a tight framework of rules. U-Boat factories, troop concentrations and, especially, oil installations all became targets. The strategic air offensive had begun.

The Germans, never slow to react to events, now gave urgent consideration to their air defense. 'Dammerungseinsatze' (twilight operations) had begun in 1939, using selected Bf109 units, but these were clearly unsuitable for the task now on hand. In late June 1940 Hitler appointed General Josef Kammhuber to form a new nightfighter force. The latter chose Hpt Wolfgang Falck to command the new Nachtjagdgeschwader 1, which was itself formed from various Bf110-equipped Zerstörergruppen, together with the Bf109s mentioned above and also the long-range Ju88C fighters from Kampfgeschwader 30, which had enjoyed considerable success in Norway. Slowly Kammhuber and Falck began to weld the new unit into a fighting force.

Meanwhile, Bomber Command had been presented with a new problem. Operation *Seelöwe*, the projected German invasion of England, was in its initial stages of preparation, and the Battle of Britain was about to begin. The Wehrmacht's invasion fleet was to consist in large part of motorized barges, which were beginning to arrive at all the Channel ports from Rotterdam to Le Havre. Whilst the RAF had to destroy these at all costs, the pressure had to be maintained against other military objectives. Therefore the remnants of the Battle squadrons, withdrawn to England before the Dunkirk evacuation, were hastily re-equipped to assist in this task, and nightly sorties began against the Channel ports whilst the daylight battles raged over the southern counties of England.

The Battle of Britain has generally been regarded as a purely Fighter Command affair, and Bomber Command's contribution is normally overlooked. The fact is that between 1 July and 31 October, 1940, a total of 185 bombers failed to return from night operations, while a further 57 Blenheims were lost by day. Perhaps its greatest contribution to the battle came on 25 August, when bombers attacked Berlin as a reprisal for an (accidental) bombing of London by German aircraft a few nights earlier. This had the result of causing the German command to miscalculate and redirect the main Luftwaffe effort against London with the eventual result that *Seelöwe* had to be postponed indefinitely.

In November, though the second phase of the assault on England commenced with the beginning of the night 'Blitz'. On 14 November the factories of Coventry were attacked by the Luftwaffe, and despite an average 100-yard bombing error, every single briefed target was hit and much damage was done to the city. As a direct reprisal, Mannheim was selected as Bomber Command's target on the night of 16 December, 1940; for the first time crews were ordered to 'aim at the centre of the town'. All pretence of military objectives was abandoned, for this was the first 'area attack' — known colloquially as 'carpet bombing'. Paradoxically perhaps, the attack was a dismal failure.

Bomber Command tactics change

Until 1941 Bomber Command tactics had consisted in the main of sending out very small numbers of aircraft in 'Penny Packet' attacks on a variety of targets over a large area. The object of these tactics was to cause large-scale disruption of German industry by widespread air raid alerts. Their great disadvantage lay in the fact that little material damage could be inflicted by the small number of bombers briefed to attack each target. The Germans soon became accustomed to this, and in fact, little disruption was caused.

So, with the heightening of the Battle of the Atlantic being waged by U-Boats, surface raiders and Focke-Wulf FW200 maritime bomber aircraft against shipping carrying

---

OUTSTANDING PILOTS OF THE NIGHT BOMBER OFFENSIVE

The Royal Air Force

Unlike the US 8th Air Force, Bomber Command produced a number of notable bomber pilots. These were the 'Bomber Barons', the best-known of whom were Group Captains Guy Gibson and Leonard Cheshire, both recipients of the Victoria Cross. Many of the 'Bomber Barons' undertook three, or even four, operational tours, most ending up in the Pathfinder Force — and all with multiple decorations.

Gibson and Cheshire were in many respects representative of most of these men, both having received pre-war training and been with squadrons at the outbreak of war, Gibson with 83 Squadron flying Hampdens and Cheshire flying Whitleys with 102 Squadron. At the end of his first tour, Gibson's 'rest' involved a period as a Beaufighter nightfighter pilot, during which he shot down four German bombers and was himself shot down over his own airfield by a German intruder. He subsequently commanded 106 Squadron in 1942, first flying Manchesters and then Lancasters, but in 1943 was the first commander of the new 617 Squadron formed specially to breach the Ruhr dams. Leadership of this attack gained him the Victoria Cross, but also a further rest from operations. He returned in 1944 as a Master Bomber, flying a Mosquito, but was shot down and killed by Flak on the night of 19 September, 1944 while returning from what was to have been his last sortie.

Cheshire's second tour took him to 35 Squadron on Halifaxes, and then as commander of 76 Squadron for a third tour. Promoted to Group Captain in early 1943, he subsequently dropped rank to return to operations as commander of 617 Squadron in the precision bombing role, later directing operations in a Mosquito, and subsequently a Mustang fighter. He received the VC on 8 September, 1944 for his sustained outstanding performance.

Other great night bomber pilots included the Australian Don Bennett, a highly-

GP CAPT L CHESHIRE VC, 617 SQUADRON.

experienced pre-war pilot, who after two tours on Whitleys and Halifaxes, became the youngest commander of a group in the RAF when he formed the Pathfinder Force, which he led for the rest of the war, rising to the rank of Air Vice-Marshal. Another Australian who was one of the greatest of all bomber pilots was H B 'Mick' Martin, DSO and Bar, DFC and Bar, who flew Wellingtons and Hampdens before serving in 617 Squadron with Gibson during the Dams raid. He ended the war as a No 100 Group Mosquito fighter-bomber pilot.

Several other notable airmen eventually became Mosquito pilots after long spells with the heavy bomber units, some flying with the Light Night Striking Force, and others with No 2 Group in 2nd Tactical Air Force. These included Gp Capt P C Pickard, DSO and 2 Bars, DFC, who led the attack on the Gestapo prison in Amiens on 18 February 1944, but was then shot down and killed on the way back to base by an FW190. It also included pilots like Wg Cdr John DeL Wooldridge, DSO, DFC and Bar, DFM and J Roy Ralston DSO, AFC, DFM. Amongst those who failed to survive the war like Gibson and Pickard, were Wg Cdr Fraser Barron, DSO and Bar, DFC, DFM, a New Zealander lost on the night of 19–20 May 1944, and Wg Cdr Alex Cranswick DSO, DFC, shot down by Flak in his Pathfinder Lancaster on 4–5 July, 1944.

Like Fighter Command, the bombers also had their resident Americans, most of whom came via the RCAF. The most notable of these was Maj Nick Knilans, who transferred to the USAAF, but remained with Bomber Command. Awarded DSO and Bar, DFC and the US DFC, he flew Lancasters in 619 and then 617 Squadron, taking part in the successful raid on the *Tirpitz* late in the war.

When the No 100 Group

---

vital supplies, war materials and food to Britain, the bomber force was directed to employ all its means to destroy the U-Boat factories and the industrial complex at Bremen which was producing the FW200. For the first time the weight of Bomber Command was turned against a single specific military objective, and soon raids by more than 100 aircraft were being concentrated on this type of target.

Newer aircraft were now entering service; these included notably the ill-fated Avro Manchester with 207 Squadron, the Short Stirling with 7 and 15 Squadrons, and the Handley-Page Halifax with 35 and 76 Squadrons. The two latter types were the first of the new generation of four-engined 'heavies' which served with distinction throughout the war. However, the Manchester proved a great disappointment. Its two powerful engines were of a revolutionary design, but insufficient time had been spent on their research and development. Thus its relatively short service life was dogged by engine failure — and the bomber would not fly on only one powerplant. The Stirling too had its drawbacks. Designed to fit pre-war hangar doors, its wingspan was short, giving it a low service ceiling; and its bomb bay was designed to the principle that nothing heavier than a 500lb bomb would be carried in each of the cells.

During 1941 Bremen, Hamburg, the Ruhr complex and Berlin became regular targets for ever-increasing numbers of bombers per night, until attacks by more than 100 aircraft became commonplace. By day too, Bomber Command began to venture forth on 'Circus' operations, heavily escorted by fighters. At first only the Blenheims were used, but subsequently these were replaced on occasion by Stirlings or Hampdens. The 'heavies' also operated unescorted occasionally and in small numbers, but the main business was undoubtedly the 'Circus'. The heaviest such raid occurred on 29 July, 1941 under the codename Operation *Sunrise*.

The German battlecruisers *Scharnhorst* and *Gneisenau* had arrived in Brest earlier in the year after a successful raiding cruise in the Southern Atlantic and these were joined by the cruiser *Prinz Eugen*, former consort of the *Bismarck*. A large daylight operation was planned with almost 100 bombers employed to attack these warships. Fighter escort was limited, however, and a large number of the bombers were shot down, including five Halifaxes. The attack was repeated in December, but although the losses were lighter, little damage was done to the ships.

At this time the effectiveness of Bomber Command's operations was being brought into question — particularly by the Admiralty, who considered that the use of four-engined bombers in the Battle of the Atlantic was preferable to their expensive raids on the Reich. Doubts as to the profitability of such raids were fully justified for it was becoming widespread knowledge that only one bomber crew in six was finding an inland target, and bombing within 75 square miles of the aiming point. Raids against coastal targets — easier to find — resulted in one crew in three finding the objective.

Mosquito escort fighters began to appear during the last stages of the campaign, one RAF pilot particularly shone. This was Sqn Ldr Branse Burbridge of 85 Squadron, who in seven months added 16 victories to five claimed earlier on defensive duties over England. His total included three Ju88Gs and a Bf110 during the night of 4–5 November, 1944.

The Luftwaffe

The bombers' opponents, the German nightfighter crews, fought a long, hard battle against the raiders. Until the appearance of the No 100 Group Mosquitos, their successes were frequent and their losses relatively small. From humble beginnings the Nachtjagdwaffe became a formidable force with many proponents who enjoyed unequalled opportunities to increase their skills as the bombers returned night after night, year in, year out.

Perhaps the greatest of all was Oberstleutnant Helmut Lent, who began the war with I/ZG76 as a Zerstörerflieger (heavy fighter pilot). In late 1940 his unit became one of those amalgamated into the new nightfighter force, where Lent became the first pilot to claim 50 night victories, and then the first to achieve 100, a total he reached during the night of 15–16 June 1944, at which time he was Kommodore of NJG3. Awarded the Knight's Cross with Diamonds, Swords and Oak Leaves, he had claimed 110 victories, all but eight of them by night, when he was killed in a landing accident on 3 October 1944.

Lent's pre-eminence was often challenged by Oberst Werner Streib, who like Lent flew initially with NJG1. Streib it was who made the first operational tests of the new 'Lichtenstein' airborne radar in 1942, and of the new Heinkel He219 nightfighter a year later, in one of these claiming five Lancasters shot down in one sortie.

The total scores of both these 'Experten' were eclipsed late in the war by Maj Heinz-Wolfgang Schnauffer, who had 42 victories by the end of 1943, claiming nine more Lancasters during early 1944. His 100th victory was recorded on 9 October 1944, days after Lent's death, and he was posted from NJG1 to command NJG4. On 21 February, 1945 he claimed two Lancasters during the early hours of the day and then seven in 17 minutes in the pre-midnight hours of the following night. Awarded the same 'full house' of decorations as Lent, he survived the war with 121 victories, but died a few years later in a road accident.

Amongst other outstanding pilots were Hpt Manfred Meurer of NJG1 and 5 with 65 victories, Oberst Günther Radusch who served with NJG 1,2,3 and 5 with 64, Maj Paul Zorner with 59 and Maj Egmont Prinz zur Lippe – Weissenfeldt with 51, both the latter gaining successes during the Leipzig battle on February 19–20, 1944. Hpt Wilhelm Herget held the record for victories in a single night, claiming eight during 20–21 December 1943, while Oblt Kurt Welter, one of the leading 'Wilde Sau'

HPT WOLFGANG SCHNAUFFER (MIDDLE) WITH HIS CREW, OFW WILHELM GÄNSELER (GUNNER) AND LT FRITZ RUMPELHARDT (RADAR OPERATOR), IV/NJG1

pilots, later led the first unit of Me262 jet nightfighters, gaining several victories against Mosquitos over Berlin.

Throughout the long night battles, Luftwaffe units claimed some 5000 victories over Europe, 2311 of which were credited to NJG1.

MAJ EGMONT PRINZ ZUR LIPPE-WEISSENFELD, NJG2.

MAJ WERNER STREIB, NJG1

The Admiralty became considerably more vociferous following the breakout of the German battlecruisers from Brest harbor in February 1942. Despite all efforts of the RAF and Royal Navy, the ships fled up the Channel protected by an 'umbrella' of fighters, and after negotiating the Straits of Dover, safely reached Kiel in North Germany. The only bright spot in a gloomy episode was provided by the success of Bomber Command minelayers, since air-laid mines caused minor damage to both capital ships. Indeed, since the war there has been an element of military opinion which has held that these minelaying operations actually achieved more to shorten the war than did the bomber offensive itself.

Harris takes over
Shortly after this 'Channel Dash' leadership of Bomber Command passed into the dynamic hands of Air Marshal Arthur Harris, who was given the unenviable task of restoring official faith in the bomber force as an effective weapon. A new radio position-finding aid known as 'GEE' was coming into service at this time, and Harris determined that within six months he would be able to put 1000 bombers over a specific target — which at a stroke would redeem official favor and boost public morale. In the meantime the newest of the heavy bombers was about to enter squadron service. This was the Avro Lancaster, developed from the earlier Manchester by replacing the two unreliable Vulture engines by four tried and trusted Rolls Royce Merlins.

By late May 1942 conditions were right for Harris' raid; several squadrons were now equipped with 'GEE', and by adding to the force aircraft and crews from the training units, and borrowing some from Coastal Command, the requisite number of aircraft could be found. The date chosen for Operation *Millenium I* was 30 May, and the target was Cologne. Until this time no specific 'bomber stream' concept had been employed, aircraft having been allowed to make their own way to the target over a wide front and a very loose timescale. This had given the German nightfighters a greater chance of interception, since each fighter occupied a strictly-controlled 'box' of airspace. If aircraft could be sent in a close-knit stream through a single one of these boxes, the likelihood of interception would be reduced theoretically to a ratio of 1000 to one. In practice, to avoid mid-air collision, the stream was quite wide, and on this first occasion 41 bombers were lost, representing 3.8 per cent of the attacking force — a substantial reduction on previous figures. The bomber stream had been born.

This first really big attack was an outstanding success and the case for strategic bombing had been vindicated as far as the War Cabinet was concerned. Two further 'Thousand Plan' attacks followed in June, the first against Essen being a costly failure, while that on Bremen on 25 June proved rather more successful.

In an effort to increase the accuracy of Main Force attacks, a new No 8 Group was formed in August 1942 to act as a Pathfinder Force. After a less than successful start, this new elite force, which was initially unpopular with the other Groups and to an extent with Harris himself as it tended to 'poach' the best crews from other units for its specialist activities, began to prove its worth.

New developments aid Bomber Command
Early in 1943 Harris decided upon a concerted effort against the industrial towns of the Ruhr Valley, opening his 'Battle of the Ruhr' in March. By now two new navigational and bombing aids had been introduced, and a radical new aircraft, the De Havilland Mosquito, had entered service. The first of the new aids was known as 'Oboe'; it was a system which employed signals emitted from ground stations to enable Mosquitos to lay target-marker flares with remarkable accuracy. The only drawback was range, which was less than 300 miles for an aircraft flying at 28 000 feet due to the effect of the curvature of the earth; range decreased proportionally at lesser altitudes. The second aid was codenamed 'H2S', and was an airborne ground-sweeping radar, which gave a 'moving picture' of the landscape below. Both devices proved invaluable in the hard months to come.

The Ruhr was well within Oboe range, and despite the perpetual haze that cloaked the factories, the opening attack on 5 March caused great damage to the Krupps armaments complex at Essen. It was the first time that the new device had been used to spearhead a Main Force attack.

However, losses proved heavy over the Ruhr. Such had been the improvement in the night air defenses of the Reich that between 5 March and 28 June 1943, during which 27 Main Force attacks were directed against the Ruhr (including two raids on Cologne and the famous breaching of the Mohne and Eder dams by 617 Squadron), no less than 640 bombers were reported missing. These raids were not the total of the Command's effort, however, for the period also included several raids on Berlin, and others on targets in Munich, Stuttgart, Mannheim and locations as far away as La Spezia in Italy, together with considerable mining.

Bomber Command was now able to make use of another secret device, however. Scientists had discovered that strips of metal tinfoil, cut to precise lengths could confuse the German radar system, whether the airborne sets in fighter aircraft or the ground control stations linked to both the air and Flak defenses. Use of this had been delayed, since the Germans could equally well employ it in raids against Britain. Fighter Command first needed a radar capable of 'seeing' through this countermeasure (codenamed 'Window'). So when the new Mark X radar was tested and found to be immune, the way was clear for Operation *Gomorrah*, an all-out attack on Hamburg.

On 24 July, 1943 this plan was put into operation. The German defenses, blinded by Window, could only fumble in the dark, and the satisfactorily low loss rate confirmed Bomber Command's hopes and expectations. During this series of raids, which covered several nights of concentrated bombing, Hamburg experienced its first firestorm, a raging furnace equalled only by the subsequent stupendous fire-raids inflicted on Tokyo by the Americans in 1945. Hamburg was gutted, and such was the awesome power of RAF attacks, and the helplessness of the defenders, that Reichminister Albert Speer admitted after the war that if Bomber Command could have repeated the operation on another three or four cities, Germany would have had little option but to capitulate.

As it was, for the moment, Bomber Command had to an extent 'shot its bolt'. The Germans, always quick to learn, overcame the problems set by Window to a large degree in quite a short time. In the meantime, however, another threat had emerged which Bomber Command would have to try and combat — German 'secret weapons'.

For some time British Intelligence had been aware that development was underway of pilotless aircraft and

A PAIR OF AVRO LANCASTER BOMBERS WHICH BOTH
COMPLETED OVER 100 SORTIES. NEAREST IS QR-N (SERIAL
ED860 OF 61 SQUADRON, WHILE BEYOND IS VN-S (ED588)
OF 50 SQUADRON—BOTH TYPICAL OF AIRCRAFT TAKING
PART IN THE LEIPZIG RAID.

missiles, and that this was now being carried out at
Peenemünde, on the Baltic coast. These new weapons were
in fact of two types — the Fieseler Fi103, or V-1, and the
A-4 supersonic rocket, also known as the V-2. Photo reconnaissance had indicated that these weapons were now reaching operational capability, and thus on 17 August, 1943
Bomber Command Headquarters despatched a 'maximum
effort' order to neutralize this research facility.

The attack was an outstanding success, much of the
complex being totally destroyed, while many of the German
scientists were killed. This was due in no small part to the
'Master Bomber' technique which was used for the first
time during a Main Force raid. The scheme had been introduced by Wing Commander Guy Gibson of 617 Squadron
during the dams raid. Fighter-type VHF radios had been
fitted in each aircraft of his force of Lancasters, allowing
him to communicate verbally with his crews. This system,
used over Peenemünde by Gp Capt Searby, was
instrumental in concentrating the bombing on the vital
areas. However, development of the rockets was already
too far advanced for the long-term effects to be great, and it
was later estimated that production of the V-2 rocket had
been halted for only two months.

Pointblank or Berlin?

In the meantime, the Joint Chiefs of Staff of the US and
British forces had issued their *Pointblank* bombing
directive which required that a major bombing effort be
directed against the German aircraft industry by the Allied
Strategic Air Forces. Air Marshal Harris disagreed with the
directive, claiming that an all-out assault against the
German capital would have more far-reaching effects. He
stated that: 'If the Americans will come in on it, we can
wreck the city from end to end. It will cost us between four
and five hundred aircraft. It will cost Germany the war'.

The Americans did not 'come in on it' until the battle
was almost over. However, the Battle of Berlin was opened
by Bomber Command on the night of 18 November, 1943,
nearly 450 aircraft being sent to the 'Big City'. The bomber
stream was preceded by a 'spoof' attack by four Mosquitos
of the Pathfinder Force (PFF) which attempted a double
bluff against the defenses. It was by now standard practice
to mount a feint attack on one target in order to draw away
the fighters from the main raid, and consequently, a second
force of nearly 300 aircraft was briefed to bomb Mannheim
during the same night.

The bluff worked well; fighters were drawn towards
Berlin initially as the PFF Mosquitos approached. When it
was realized that this was a feint, they were diverted to meet
the force heading for Mannheim. This allowed the Main
Force to get through to Berlin and return with a loss of only
nine aircraft. The Mannheim diversionary attack paid more
heavily, 23 bombers failing to return from this. Four nights
later Berlin was the sole target for 630 aircraft which lost 26
of their number.

By late March 1944 when the battle petered out, 15
major attacks had been made. Harris's estimate of losses
had been accurate; 492 bombers had failed to return, while
nearly 100 more had been destroyed in crashes on return,
due mainly to damage suffered. He had been wrong in other
respects, however, the war was not over and Berlin still
stood, battered but unbowed.

While the Battle of Berlin was still underway an
important addition had been made to Bomber Command.
This was the formation of No 100 (Bomber Support)

OFW KURT WELTER, A SUCCESSFUL 'WILDE SAU' PILOT OF I/JG302, SITS ON THE WING OF HIS FOCKE-WULF FW190.

Group in November 1943. The group was intended to undertake three major roles:-

1 To provide suitably equipped aircraft to confuse and jam the German radar
2 To attack German nightfighter bases with low-level fighter-intruder aircraft
3 To provide high-altitude fighter patrols to intercept Luftwaffe nightfighters approaching, within, and departing the bomber stream.

In the hard months still to come, this new formation proved its worth many times over.

While the destruction of Berlin remained the Command's primary objective during the opening months of 1944, it was still obliged to make some contribution to the *Pointblank* directive. As a result attacks were also made on the Ruhr, Stettin, Stuttgart and Magdeburg. One important target on the *Pointblank* 'shopping list' was the Junkers factory at Leipzig, to the south of Berlin, and an attack on this target was planned to coincide with the opening of the USAAF's Operation *Avalanche* — the series of daylight attacks which came to be known as 'Big Week'. The raid was planned to take place during the night of 19 February, 1944 and an elaborate series of feint attacks were planned in order to confuse the defenses.

Preliminaries to the Leipzig Raid

The initial thrust was to be a minelaying force comprising 50 aircraft from No 3 Group, despatched towards the Baltic Sea. The crews of these aircraft had the unenviable task of acting as decoys to draw the nightfighters away northwards.

A feint attack would then be mounted by Mosquitos on Berlin, which on this occasion had been chosen as the 'spoof' objective — a good choice, as it seemed to be the likely target, given the recent scale of assault on the capital. The Main Force too would head towards Berlin, but would then swing half-south towards Dresden, before turning again for the run-up to the target. Three more Mosquitos from the PFF would make a 'nuisance' raid on Aachen, while another 16 from the Light Night Striking Force were to bomb a number of Luftwaffe bases. In support of these operations No 100 Group would send out a dozen intruder Mosquitos together with a handful of similar aircraft from Fighter Command squadrons to attack aircraft found around the German airfields. It was a typical plan of the period, comprised of many parts linked to a tactical whole. Unfortunately, like so many well-devised plans, there was always something to go wrong.

The minelaying operation went like clockwork; the 50 Lancasters headed out across the North Sea in the direction of Denmark, the absence of any radar counter-measures giving the Luftwaffe fighter controllers ample time to get their interceptors airborne. The first of 294 available fighters began to roll down the dimly-lit runways of airfields in North Germany, Holland and Denmark. Probably first off were elements of Maj Werner Husemann's NJG3, based around Schleswig, but with detached Gruppen as far north as Westerland, and Aalborg in Denmark. Oberstlt Werner Streib's NJG1 was also on full alert in Holland, as was NJG2, commanded by Maj Egmont Prinz zur Lippe-Weissenfeld, here and in North-West Germany.

As the minelayers, keeping low, got underway, the first of the No 100 Group radar counter-measures aircraft had also departed ahead of the Main Force, these heading almost due east from Essex direct for Berlin. Behind them came the 113 flare-carrying aircraft of the Pathfinders, while 741 more bombers of the Main Force, drawn from all five heavy bomber groups, waited their turn to thunder down the murky runways to lurch heavy-laden, into the black depths of the night sky.

The first mishap occurred just as the Main Force was departing when for no apparent reason Halifax 'S-Sugar' of 158 Squadron suddenly became uncontrollable in cloud soon after take off and plunged into the ground near Catfoss, Plt Off Jennings and his crew being killed. The rest of the stream ploughed on towards the first turning point mid-way across the North Sea, where the 'heavies' were joined by the Berlin-bound Mosquitos of the Light Night Striking Force.

Main Force is engaged

In the meantime, the intruders, which had left a little earlier, were already approaching the Luftwaffe's nightfighter airfields. Contacts were at once made, and in engagements with unidentified German aircraft, one was claimed shot down at St Hubert by Flt Lt Scherf of 418 Squadron and one at Handorf by Flt Sgt Chapman. The confusion caused by the arrival of the Mosquitos resulted in the German controllers panicking, and they began recalling the fighters to defend their bases. It was at this point that the Main Force, having turned south-eastwards, was crossing the North German coast near Emden, following the radar counter-measures aircraft, which were now cascading Window across the countryside. Here the Luftwaffe nightfighters, returning south at full throttle in answer to the controllers' urgent summonses, suddenly found themselves amongst the bomber stream. The results were catastrophic.

The German controllers had by this time realized their basic error, and had ordered more fighters into the air, including NJG5 and the single-engined 'Wilde Sau' aircraft of JG300 and JG302 — the latter to patrol in the area between Vechta and Hanover. The Wilde Sau (Wild Boar) were a new addition to the defenses, introduced as a result of the disastrous Hamburg raids. The 'brainchild' of former bomber pilot Hajo Herrmann, the units were equipped with Bf109G and FW190 day fighters, but without the benefit of radar equipment.

They were directed to, and fed into the bomber stream, by the ground controllers, and then relied on eyesight, proximity and luck to pick up the British bombers in the searchlights, against the glare of the fires on the ground, and by the glint of moonlight. Although a relatively 'hit-and-miss' expedient, at times they enjoyed remarkable success. Apart from these units, NJG6, based far to the south, was put on alert, for the RAF had made many long-penetration raids during previous weeks.

The first interceptions occurred at the coast, the initial loss probably being a Lancaster of 626 Squadron which was shot down into the sea off Schiermonnikoog with the loss of F/Sgt Matheson and his crew. Within minutes another Lancaster, this time from 576 Squadron, fell into the Ems Estuary off De Lokk.

The main body of nightfighters struck the bomber stream to the south of Bremen, the twin-engined Bf110s and Ju88s joining with the nimble Messerschmitts and Focke-Wulfs of the Wilde Sau to form a defensive line through which the bombers had to pass — fortuitously for the defenses, they had selected the bombers' next turning point for their patrol area; already the area was illuminated by route marker flares released by PFF aircraft, indicating that from this point the route lay due east, towards Berlin. One of the bombers to fall here was a 10 Squadron Halifax, shot down by Fw Franke of 6/NJG3, a pilot who was later to claim five bombers shot down during this night.

Between Bremen and Hanover a dozen more bombers were brought down by the fighters. One Wilde Sau pilot, Lt Kurt Welter of I/JG302 claimed two bombers here, but probably his opponent on both occasions was a Lancaster of 625 Squadron flown by Sqn Ldr Dovetil, whose bomber was twice attacked by a single-engined fighter before crashing on the outskirts of Hanover. Four more claims were submitted by Hpt Paul Zorner of 8/NJG3, and it would seem that the first of these was another 10 Squadron Halifax, this one flown by F/Sgt Walker, which went down near Wesendorf. Another of his victims has been identified as Flg Off Sidebotham's Lancaster from 100 Squadron; some of the crew from this aircraft managed to bale out near Gardelegen, and became prisoners.

This was the point where the greatest number of casualties occurred, for again it was a turning point, well-marked by the Pathfinders' flares. From here the No 8 Group Mosquitos continued straight on to Berlin to execute a first-class 'spoof' attack, dropping four tons of bombs; one Mosquito flown by Flt Lt Thomas DFC of 692 Squadron was shot down to the south of the city.

The controllers were indeed taken in by the 'spoof', calling urgently for fighters to defend the capital from the expected Main Force attack. This did little to take the pressure off the hard-pressed bombers, however, for the fighter pilots, already in contact with the bomber stream, were loath to depart. It was at this moment too that the

fresh reserve aircraft from NJG6, flying up from the south, joined the fray. As a result at least 15 more bombers fell here as the stream turned south-east towards Dresden. One 77 Squadron Halifax blundered on, directly over that city, where F/Sgt Dalzell and his crew were shot down, either by Flak or a fighter, and crashed into a residential area. About six more bombers fell during this final leg, and around the last turning point near Treuenbreitzen; here Lt Wilhelm Engel of I/NJG6 intercepted and shot down one of the Pathfinder aircraft, an 83 Squadron Lancaster flown by Flg Off Field.

At risk from Flak and fighter

The bombers were now on the dangerous straight-and-level run-up to the target, and here Flak became their main enemy as the nightfighters stood off to allow Leipzig's gunners to blaze away uninterrupted. No evasive action was possible as the target markers showered down, and it was now that the radar-predicted guns had their best chance of the night of achieving other than a random chance hit. As the Main Force neared the aiming point the Flak struck home, Flt Off Yates' 630 Squadron Lancaster falling flaming into the city.

Then the bombs were falling, 2291 tons of high explosives and incendiaries raining down in a remarkably accurate attack which, despite the losses and confusion of the flight to the target, caused great damage to the Junkers factory — a plant which was in no small measure a contributor to the nightfighter force which was tormenting the raiders. Including the Pathfinders, 730 bombers actually attacked the primary target, and as the great bomber stream droned slowly out of range of the Leipzig heavy Flak batteries, the fighters were lurking to the south, waiting to

TOP: JUNKERS JU88G NIGHTFIGHTER. PART OF THE AERIAL ARRAY FOR THE FUG220 LICHENSTEIN SN-2 RADAR CAN BE SEEN PROTRUDING FROM THE NOSE, AS CAN THE PAIR OF 20 MM MG 151 'SCHRAGE MUSIK' CANNON IN THE UPPER FUSELAGE.

ABOVE: A PAIR OF MESSERSCHMITT BF110G-4 NIGHTFIGHTERS OF 7/NJG4.

RAF BOMBER COMMAND ORDER OF BATTLE, FEBRUARY 1944

Headquarters High Wycombe, Bucks, Air Marshal A T Harris		
UNIT	**BASE**	**AIRCRAFT**
No 1 (Heavy Bomber) Group	**Bawtry, Yorks**	**Air Vice-Marshal E A B Rice**
12 and 626 Squadrons	Wickenby, Lincs	Lancaster I & III
100 & 550 Squadrons	Waltham, Lincs	Lancaster I & III
101 Squadron	Ludford Magna, Lincs	Lancaster I & III
103 & 576 Squadrons	Elsham Wolds, Lincs	Lancaster I & III
166 Squadron	Kirmington, Lincs	Lancaster I & III
300 (Polish) Squadron	Ingham, Lincs	Wellington X
460 Squadron, RAAF	Binbrook, Lincs	Lancaster I & III
625 Squadron	Kelstern, Lincs	Lancaster I & III
No 3 (Heavy Bomber) Group	**Exning, Suffolk**	**Air Vice-Marshal R Harrison**
15 & 622 Squadrons	Mildenhall, Suffolk	Lancaster I & III
75 (New Zealand) Squadron	Mepal, Cambs	Stirling I & III
90 Squadron	Tuddenham, Suffolk	Stirling I & III
115 Squadron	Witchford, Cambs	Lancaster II
138 Squadron	Tempsford, Bede	Halifax II (Special Duties)
161 Squadron	Tempsford Bede	Halifax II/Hudson III (Special Duties)
149 Squadron	Lakenheath, Suffolk	Stirling I & III
	Tempsford Bede	(detachment for Special Duties)
218 Squadron	Downham Market, Norfolk	Stirling I & III
514 Squadron	Waterbeach, Cambs	Lancaster II
No 4 (Heavy Bomber) Group	**Healington Hall, Yorks**	**Air Vice-Marshal C R Carr**
10 Squadron	Melbourne, Yorks	Halifax II
51 Squadron	Smith, Yorks	Halifax III
73 Squadron	Holme-on-Spalding Moor, Yorks	Halifax V
77 Squadron	Elvington, Yorks	Halifax V
78 Squadron	Breighton, Yorks	Halifax V
102 Squadron	Pocklington, Yorks	Halifax II
158 Squadron	Lisset, Yorks	Halifax III
466 Squadron RAAF and		
640 Squadron	Leconfield, Yorks	Halifax III
578 Squadron	Burn, Yorks	Halifax III

No 5 (Heavy Bomber) Group	**Swinderby, Lincs**	**Air Vice-Marshal The Hon R Cochrane**
44 Squadron	Dunholme Lodge, Lincs	Lancaster I & III
49 Squadron	Fiskerton, Lincs	Lancaster I & III
50 Squadron	Skellingthorpe, Lincs	Lancaster I & III
57 & 630 Squadrons	East Kirkby, Lincs	Lancaster I & III
61 & 619 Squadrons	Coningsby, Lincs	Lancaster I & III
106 Squadron	Metheringham, Lincs	Lancaster I & III
207 Squadron	Spilsby, Lincs	Lancaster I & III
463 & 467 Squadrons RAAF	Luddington, Lincs	Lancaster I & III
617 Squadron	Woodhall Spa, Lincs	Lancaster I & III
627 Squadron	Oakington, Cambs	Mosquito IV
No 6 (Heavy Bomber) Group	**Allerton Park, Yorks**	**RCAF Air Vice-Marshal G E Brookes**
408 & 426 Squadrons RCAF	Linton-on-Ouse, Yorks	Lancaster II
419 & 428 Squadrons RCAF	Middleton St George, Durham	Halifax II
420 & 425 Squadrons RCAF	Tholtorpe, Yorks	Halifax III
424 & 433 Squadrons RCAF	Skipton-on-Swale, Yorks	Halifax III
427 & 429 Squadrons RCAF	Leeming, Yorks	Halifax III & V
431 & 434 Squadrons RCAF	Croft, Durham	Halifax V
432 Squadron RCAF	East Moor, Yorks	Lancaster II (converting to Halifax III)
No 8 (Pathfinder) Group	**Castle Hill House, Hunts**	**Air Vice-Marshal A C T Bennett**
7 Squadron	Oakington, Cambs	Lancaster I & III
9 Squadron	Bardney, Lincs	Lancaster I & III
35 Squadron	Graveley, Hunts	Halifax II
692 Squadron	Graveley, Hunts	Mosquito IV
83 Squadron	Wyton, Hunts	Lancaster I & III
97 Squadron	Burn, Cambs	Lancaster I & III
105 & 109 Squadrons	Marham, Norfolk	Mosquito IV & XI
139 Squadron	Upwood, Hunts	Mosquit IV & XI
156 Squadron	Warboys, Hunts	Lancaster I & III
405 Squadron RCAF	Gransden Lodge, Beds	Lancaster I & III
No 100 (Bomber Support) Group		
141 & 239 Squadrons	West Raynham, Norfolk	Mosquito FII & VI
169 & 515 Squadrons	Little Snoring, Norfolk	Mosquito FII
192 Squadron	Feltwell, Norfolk	Wellington X/Mosquito IV
199 Squadron	North Creake, Norfolk	Stirling III
214 Squadron	Sculthorpe, Norfolk	Fortress II
BSDU*	Swanton Morley, Norfolk	Mosquito FII
(*Bomber Support Development Unit)		

pounce again during the long homeward flight.

It was as the bombers started their return journey that Oblt Martin Becker of I/NJG6, who had pursued the stream all the way from Hanover, claimed his fourth victim of the night when he shot down F/Sgt Kingston's Lancaster from 166 Squadron to the south-west of the city. A few minutes later Sgt Mackrell's 460 Squadron Lancaster fell near Troglitz, shot down by Oblt Helmuth Schultz of II/NJG5 for his second victory of the night; he had already despatched a bomber near Brandenburg. The gunners in the turrets of the Lancasters and Halifaxes continued to defend their bombers to the best of their ability, enjoying rather more success at this point, where they claimed a Ju88, Bf110 and a Do217 shot down.

The ferocity of the battle was lessening now, as the fighters began to run low on fuel and ammunition, and were obliged to break off and return to their bases. Meanwhile, the 'Windowing' force, which had taken a shorter route into the target than the Main Force, had turned north-west on reaching Leipzig; after a slight course change, they headed out across the Zuyder Zee. The Main Force continued on south for a while, then turned in a more westerly direction too.

Here the force split into two distinct streams; the southerly of these headed west, passing well to the south of Aachen before turning north-west across Belgium and out over the coast near Schouwen Island; the northern stream made direct for North Holland. These routes prevented the southerly stream from blundering over the formidable defenses of the Ruhr, while the northern stream was routed well to the north of the main Luftwaffe defenses in Holland.

There were few further engagements as the bombers put on the best possible turn of speed on the 'downhill leg'. A few more aircraft were lost over Holland, where a 408 Squadron Lancaster was shot down by Hpt Eckart-Wilhelm von Bonin of II/NJG1 over Holst, near Antwerp. On the southerly route a Halifax of 77 Squadron strayed far off track and was lost near Hesdin in France. As the exhausted bomber crews reached the English coast, their vigilance beginning to relax at last, two Lancasters of 103 Squadron collided in the landing circuit at Elsham Wolds, both crashing.

LUFTWAFFE NIGHTFIGHTER ORDER OF BATTLE, FEBRUARY 1944

UNIT	BASE	AIRCRAFT
LUFTFLOTTE 3		
Nachtjagdgeschwader 4		
Stab	Florennes	Messerschmitt Bf110
I Gruppe	Florennes and Laon/Athies	Messerschmitt Bf110/Do217/Ju88
II Gruppe	St Dizier	Messerschmitt Bf110/Dornier Do217
III Gruppe	Juvincourt	Messerschmitt Bf110/Dornier Do217
LUFTFLOTTE REICH		
Nachtjagdgeschwader 1		
Stab	Bonninghardt	Messerschmitt Bf110
I Gruppe	Venlo	Messerschmitt Bf110/Heinkel He219
II Gruppe	St Trond	Messerschmitt Bf110/Dornier Do217
III Gruppe	Laon/Athies	Messerschmitt Bf110
IV Grupe	Leeuwarden	Messerschmitt Bf110
10 Staffel	Quackenbrück	Messerschmitt Bf110
Nachtjagdgeschwader 2		
Stab	Deelen	Messerschmitt Bf110/Junkers Ju88
I Gruppe	Kassel	Messerschmitt Bf110
II Gruppe	Deelen	Junkers Ju88
III Gruppe	Twente	Messerschmitt Bf110/Junkers Ju88
Nachtjagdgeschwader 3		
Stabl	Stade	Messerschmitt Bf110/Junkers Ju88
I Gruppe	Vechta and Wittmundhafen	Messerschmitt Bf110/Dornier Do217
II Gruppe	Schleswig & Werneuchen	Junkers Ju88/Dornier Do217
III Gruppe	Stade, Nordholz & Luneburg	Messerschmitt Bf110
IV Gruppe	Westerland & Aalborg	Messerschmitt Bf110/Junkers Ju88
Nachtjagdgeschwader 5		
Stab	Doberitz	Messerschmitt Bf110
I Gruppe	Stendal	Messerschmitt Bf110
II Gruppe	Parchim	Messerschmitt Bf110
III Gruppe	Königsberg/Neumark	Messerschmitt Bf110
IV Gruppe	Erfurt & Brandis	Messerschmitt Bf110
V Gruppe	Insterburg & Powunden	Messerschmitt Bf110
Nachtjagdgeschwader 6		
Stab	Schleissheim	Messerschmitt Bf110
I Gruppe	Mainz/Finthem	Messerschmitt Bf110/Dornier Do217
II Gruppe	Schleissheim	Messerschmitt Bf110
Nachtjagdgeschwader 7		
I Gruppe	Handorf & Hopsten	Junkers Ju88
Nachtjagdgruppe 10	Werneuchen	Various
Jagdgeschwader 300 'Wilde Sau'		
Stab	Krefeld	Focke-Wulf FW190A
I Gruppe	Hangelar	Messerschmitt Bf109G
II Gruppe	Rheine	Focke-Wulf FW190A
III Gruppe	Wiesbaden	Messerschmitt Bf109G
Jagdgeschwader 301 'Wilde Sau'		
Stab	Schleissheim, Neubiberg, Zerbst and Leipheim	Messerschmitt Bf109G
III Gruppe	Zerbst	Messerschmitt Bf109G
Jagdgeschwader 302 'Wilde Sau'		
Stab	Doberitz	Focke-Wulf FW190A/Messerschmitt Bf109G
I Gruppe	Brandis/Juterborg	Focke-Wulf FW190A/Messerschmitt Bf109G
II Gruppe	Ludwiglust	Focke-Wulf FW190A/Messerschmitt Bf109G
III Gruppe	Oldenburg	Focke-Wulf FW190A/Messerschmitt Bf109G
Nachtjagdgeschwader 101 (Operational Training)		
Stab	Ingolstadt	Various
I Gruppe	Ingolstadt	Various
II Gruppe	Parndorf	Various
Nachtjagdgeschwader 102 (Operation Training)		
Stab	Kitzingen	Various
I Gruppe	Kitzingen	Various
II Gruppe	Echterdingen	Various
Minor Units within Luftflotte Reich		
Erprobungskommando 410	Venlo	Messerschmitt Me410
Additional Units which saw some service during the Battle were:		
LBeoSt 1	Neuruppin	
LBeoSt 2	Stade	
LBeoSt 3	Venlo	
LBeoSt 7	Echterdingen	
BehBelSt 1	Rhein/Main	
BehBelSt 2	Celle	

The Luftwaffe had suffered its own losses too. Of nearly 700 nightfighters airborne during the night, 17 were shot down by gunners in the British bombers, or by the intruders. This total included three Wilde Sau Bf109Gs, one from each of the three Gruppen of JG302, one pilot being killed. Hpt Ernst Zechlin of I/NJG2 who had himself claimed a Lancaster during the fighting, was shot down near Halle, his radar operator being killed when his parachute became entangled in the tailplane of the Bf110.

The Luftwaffe hailed this battle as a great victory for the defenders. Seventy-nine victories were claimed in all, 74 of them by the nightfighter units of I Jagdkorps; at least 63 of these claims are known to have been confirmed by the High Command. There had been several multiple victories claimed by pilots of various units, and these included five

each by Hpt Erhard Peters of 9/NJG3 and Off Heinz Vinke of 11/NJG1. British losses had indeed amounted to precisely 79 aircraft (ten Pathfinders and 69 Main Force aircraft). Not all these were to fighters and Flak, as has been seen, but the official Bomber Command summary recorded 155 separate engagements with fighters resulting in 58 combats and the loss of 73 bombers to fighter action — thus the Luftwaffe claims were virtually 100 per cent accurate!

But worse was to come. Six weeks later Harris ordered an attack to be made on Nuremberg. On this occasion the customary feint was dispensed with, the bomber stream heading direct for its target. This seemed a worthwhile change of tactic for the German defenses were now quite

BOMBER COMMAND LOSSES BY SQUADRON, LEIPZIG RAID, NIGHT OF 19–20 FEBRUARY, 1944

7 Squadron	2	78 Squadron	3	207 Squadron	2	463 Squadron, RAAF	1
9 Squadron	1	83 Squadron	2	408 Squadron, RCAF	4	466 Squadron, RAAF	1
10 Squadron	2	100 Squadron	1	419 Squadron, RCAF	2	514 Squadron	1
12 Squadron	3	101 Squadron	1	426 Squadron, RCAF	1	550 Squadron	1
15 Squadron	1	102 Squadron	2	427 Squadron, RCAF	1	576 Squadron	1
35 Squadron	4	103 Squadron	2	428 Squadron, RCAF	1	625 Squadron	3
49 Squadron	2	106 Squadron	1	429 Squadron, RCAF	3	626 Squadron	1
51 Squadron	1	115 Squadron	1	431 Squadron, RCAF	2	630 Squadron	2
57 Squadron	1	156 Squadron	2	433 Squadron, RCAF	1	640 Squadron	2
61 Squadron	2	158 Squadron	2	434 Squadron, RCAF	3	692 Squadron	1
77 Squadron	4	166 Squadron	3	460 Squadron, RAAF	2	(Mosquito)	

used to 'guessing' where an attack would actually fall. They would expect the thrust suddenly to deflect elsewhere.

On this occasion, however, things went sadly wrong. A full moon, few clouds and a low condensation layer which caused the bombers to trail the familiar flowing white 'tails' behind them, made the stream readily visible. To make matters worse the course took the bombers directly over two nightfighter beacons around which the airborne Bf110s and Ju88s were orbiting, waiting direction onto the stream. The result was carnage! Ninety-five bombers failed to return that night, with the loss of more than 600 aircrew.

To add to the RAF's tale of woe, the raid was singularly unsuccessful; target markers were dropped slightly short of the aiming point, and the inevitable 'creep back', as bombs

MAIN AIRCRAFT TYPES EMPLOYED IN THE NIGHT BOMBER OFFENSIVE, 1944

BRITISH

Avro Lancaster
A mid-wing monoplane with twin fins and rudders, the Lancaster was the most successful of Bomber Command's heavy bombers. The Mk I and III were powered respectively by four Rolls Royce Merlin 20, 22 or 24 in-line engines of 1460 or 1640 hp, and by Packard-built Merlin 28, 38 or 224 engines of similar power. The Mk II was powered by four Bristol Hercules VI radial engines of 1650 hp. By 1944 most were armed with power-operated turrets in nose, dorsal and tail positions, the nose and dorsal turrets each fitted with two 0.303 in Browning machine guns, while the tail turret carried four of these weapons. Some early Mk Is also had a ventral gun position with two more Brownings. Top speed of a typical model was 281 mph at 11 500 ft, service ceiling 24 500 ft, and range up to 1660 miles with 14 000 lb of bombs. Up to 22 000 lb could be carried if the dorsal turret was deleted.

Handley Page Halifax
The Halifax was of very similar general design to the Lancaster, but differed in armament arrangement. Power turrets were fitted only in the dorsal and tail positions, each of these being fitted with four 0.303 in Brownings. A similar calibre hand-held Vickers 'K' gun was fitted in the glazed nose of the aircraft. The models in service in early 1944 included the Mk II Series IA, and Mk V, both fitted with Rolls Royce Merlin engines, and the Mk III with Bristol Hercules XVI radials of 1615 hp.

Typical performance included a maximum speed of 260 mph at 19000 ft (280 mph at 13 500 ft for the Mk III). The Merlin-powered versions could carry 13 000 lb of bombs for 600 miles, or 4000 lb for 1900 miles; the Mk III carried 13 000 lb for 1077 miles. Service ceiling was 24 000 ft.

De Havilland Mosquito
Built as a private venture, the Mosquito was designed as a high-performance unarmed light bomber, relying for protection from interception on its high speed. In the event the aircraft proved to be one of the most versatile of the war, seeing service not only as a bomber, but for photo-reconnaissance, coastal strike, nightfighting, night intruder and fighter-bomber operations. As a fighter the aircraft carried an armament of four 20 mm Hispano cannon and four 0.303 in Browning machine guns in the nose. Later nightfighters had the Brownings removed to allow larger

Avro Lancaster I of 619 Squadron, No 5 Group, Bomber Command

airborne radar sets to be carried. An exceptionally clean twin-engined monoplane with a high-mid wing, the two-seat Mosquito was constructed mainly of wood. It was powered by two Rolls Royce Merlin engines. Main types used by Bomber Command in early 1944 were the unarmed Mk IV bomber and the eight gun armed fighter Mk II, the latter in No 100 Group. The bomber had a top speed of 380 mph at 17 000 ft, a service ceiling of 28

were released as quickly as possible to get out of the dangerous straight and level phase, resulted in the bombing doing little significant damage. It was the worst night Bomber Command ever suffered. Allegations in recent years that the Germans had foreknowledge of the target have brought forth strong denials from the German commanders involved. No evidence has been found to substantiate this claim; the disaster of Nuremberg was undoubtedly the result of a tragic combination of coincidence.

Another change of tactics

The spring of 1944 brought a major change in tactical policy. Hitherto Harris had attempted both to break civilian morale and to shatter German industry. On 14 April, in preparation for the projected invasion of France, Bomber Command was transferred temporarily to the tactical role with the US 8th Air Force, both under the overall direction of the Supreme Allied Commander for the invasion, General Dwight D Eisenhower. Targets would now be road and rail transport, military encampments in the occupied territories, coastal defenses and coastal radar stations — the latter targets being left until the very last moment.

One such attack was launched against Mailly-le-Camp early in May 1944. Although a high percentage of the aircraft despatched were lost, an important Panzer training base was destroyed with the loss to the Germans of many irreplaceable personnel. Particularly successful during this period were the attacks against rail targets, the most profitable of these proving to be those directed against marshalling yards where much rolling stock was destroyed. This would subsequently greatly hinder the passage of reinforcements when the battle for Normandy began.

Bomber Command was also heavily engaged during the night prior to the invasion attacking gun positions, dropping dummy parachutes as a diversion, and particularly by creating a phantom 'Invasion Fleet' in the Pas de Calais area by the carefully-planned release of a continuous curtain of the radar-reflecting Window. Following the successful landings during June, several massive daylight raids were made to assist the army in breaking through strong German defenses at Caen, but the command was

---

000 ft and a range of 1370 to 1795 miles depending on bombload, which could be up to 2000 lb. The fighter reached 370 mph at 14 000 ft, but had a service ceiling of 34 500 ft and a range of 1520 miles. Because of its basically wooden construction, the Mosquito presented a weak image on German radar screens which, coupled with its fine performance, rendered it a very difficult aircraft to intercept.

GERMAN

The two main Luftwaffe nightfighters in use in 1944 were versions of types which have already been described in earlier chapters — the Messerschmitt Bf110 Zerstörer and the Junkers Ju88 bomber.

Messerschmitt Bf110G
The nightfighter version of this aircraft differed from the Zerstörer only in being fitted with airborne radar in the nose with associated aerial display, and with flame-damping shrouds to the engine exhaust stubs. Armed with two 30 mm MK108 and two 20 mm MG151 cannon in the nose, the three-seater aircraft had two hand-held 7.9 mm MG81 machine guns for rear defense. The two DB605B engines provided a maximum speed of 342 mph at 22 900 ft, a service ceiling of 26 000 ft and a range of 1305 miles. The armament of these aircraft was on occasion augmented with a belly pack of additional cannon, or two extra MG151s mounted in the fuselage behind the cockpit to fire forwards and upwards for attack from behind and below unsuspecting bombers. This latter arrangement, known as 'Schräge Musik' (Jazz Music) proved very effective and was increasingly favored as the war progressed.

Junkers Ju88C and G
The Ju88C was a direct fighter conversion of the Ju88A bomber, with three 20 mm MG FF cannon and three 7.9 mm MG17 machine guns in a new solid nose which also carried airborne radar — FuG220 by early 1944. The three-seater aircraft carried a single 13 mm MG131 for rear defense; its two annular-cowled Jumo 211J engines of 1410 hp each gave a top speed of 311 mph at 19 685 ft, and a service ceiling of 32 480 ft. Thus although of lower overall performance than the Bf110G, it offered a better high altitude performance. This was improved considerably in the purpose-built G model, which had a completely redesigned forward fuselage. A four-seater powered by two 1725 hp Jumo 213E engines, the aircraft had a speed of 363 mph at height, which could be temporarily boosted to 389 mph by application of MW50 boost. Ceiling remained in excess of 30 000 ft, but armament was improved to four 20 mm MG151s. It retained the rear-firing MG131 for defense. Either model could also be fitted with the twin MG151 'Schräge Musik' arrangement.

A similar conversion to the Ju88C had been made to the Dornier Do217 bomber, but this nightfighter, although still in limited service in early 1944, had a disappointing performance and was already being phased out.

Messerschmitt Bf110G of Nachtjagdgeschwader 3

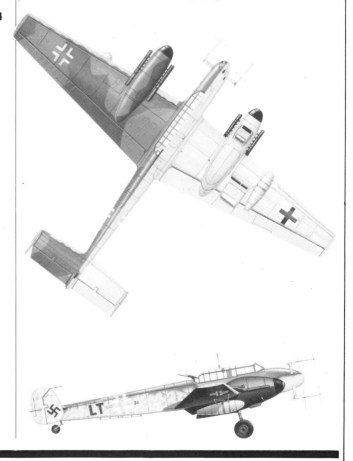

then ordered to assist in the neutralization of the German missile programme.

The first of the V-1 flying bombs had been launched against England on 12 June, and the bombing campaign against the launching sites for these along the French coast would continue until 6 September by which time most had fallen into the hands of the advancing Allied armies. These attacks were frequently made in daylight, for the crushing air superiority achieved by the Allied Air Forces now allowed the lightly-armed RAF 'heavies' to operate by day with relative impunity as far as the Ruhr; the main enemy was now Flak.

Other raids were made on the missile storage depots in France while on 27 August the first major penetration beyond the Ruhr by day was made, a successful attack under heavy escort being made on oil plants at Hamburg.

Night operations still predominated, however, and although Bomber Command was ably supported by the intruder and escort Mosquitos of No 100 Group, which were taking an increasing toll of the German nightfighters, the Luftwaffe's nocturnal defenses were by no means defeated. Indeed, many were the hard-fought engagements that took place in the night skies over the Reich before the final surrender of the German forces. For example, during the night of 19 October, Bomber Command despatched 1576 aircraft on all duties, including a record 1294 against targets in Germany. A total of 4547 tons of bombs fell on Duisberg during the night — the heaviest attack on a single objective throughout the war.

With a few significant exceptions, Bomber Command had never been regarded as a precision bombing force, but during the period 23 September–21 November, 1944 the Dortmund-Ems Canal was breached three times, this important waterborne highway thus being cut by a most impressive display of precision bomb-aiming. Based around the Lancaster's quite extraordinary load-carrying capabilities — and a new generation of high-penetration bombs of very great weight — the 12 000 lb 'Tallboy' and the 22 000 lb 'Grand Slam' which had been designed by that engineering genius, Barnes Wallis — a small specialist force for high-precision daylight bombing had been formed, including the original 'Dam Busters' Squadron 617. On 12 November this unit and 9 Squadron succeeded in sinking the oft-bombed battleship *Tirpitz* in Tromso Fjord, Norway, employing the incredible power of the Tallboys.

HANDLEY PAGE HALIFAX III BOMBER OF 425 (RCAF) SQUADRON PREPARING TO TAKE OFF. THIS AIRCRAFT, KW-M (SERIAL MZ954) FEATURES A VENTRAL DEFENSIVE POSITION FORWARD WITH A SINGLE 50″ BROWNING MACHINE GUN; THIS WAS A LOCAL MODIFICATION UNDERTAKEN BY NO 6 GROUP.

With the liberation of the occupied nations achieved and with the Allied armies moving into Germany, the Luftwaffe threw in all they had in a last ditch attempt to gain a negotiated peace. Berlin again became a priority target for the RAF bombing effort, and on 20 February, 1945 Mosquitos commenced a night-by-night assault which continued uninterrupted until 27 March. On 3 March the Main Force was taken by surprise when the Luftwaffe launched Operation *Gisella*; a large force of German nightfighters followed the returning bomber stream to the area of their bases, shooting down more than 20 of them over Eastern England. It was their last major effort against the RAF.

A month later during the night of 9–10 April, the battle cruiser *Admiral Scheer* was sunk at her moorings in Kiel harbor, and two more heavy naval units were damaged beyond repair. On the night of 25 April the last Main Force attack was made, 100 aircraft bombing an oil refinery at Tonsberg. Bomber Command's last sorties of the war were made on 2–3 May when Kiel was attacked by 303 aircraft, three of which failed to return. The longest campaign of World War II had at last ended.

A high price to pay

The cost had been terrible — to both sides. Bomber Command had lost 8655 aircraft on operations (the majority of these by night), and nearly 500 more had been written off due to battle damage. Some 47 000 aircrew — all amongst the 'brightest and the best' of the Commonwealth's young men — had died (67 per cent of total RAF casualties during the war), and a further 4200 were wounded. Bomber Command aircrew had enjoyed less than a one in three chance of surviving the war; only service in the German U-Boat force had offered a worse chance of survival! Almost a million tons of bombs had been dropped; and not surprisingly perhaps, given these figures, the Command had been fertile ground for acts of great gallantry or supreme self-sacrifice.

In consequence, 22 Victoria Crosses had been received by members of the Command, precisely half of these for operations by night. Of these 22, ten were posthumous awards, a further three recipients were subsequently killed in action, or while flying operationally.

In the years since the war much controversy has surrounded both the effectiveness and the morality of the RAF's night-bombing offensive. It warrants repeating that for much of its duration there was little alternative. A nation smaller than the German Reich and initially at least, less well equipped with weapons of war, still smarting under the terrible loss and waste of life little more than 20 years before in the trenches of Flanders, could not even consider an invasion of Western Europe. The lack of escort fighters prevented major bombing by day; the lack of navigational aids prevented precision bombing by night.

After 1941 a substantial expeditionary army and air force could have been sent to Russia to fight alongside the Red Army — always supposing the Soviets had been agreeable. However, to support and maintain this effort without some major action against Germany in the West would have posed problems of a gigantic nature. By 1943, when other options became available and viable, the investment had already been made. Recall too that the British were faced by a foe in the Nazi regime which was perceived to be implacably evil — and the towns and cities of Britain had been bombed without mercy. There *was* no realistic alternative.

CHAPTER NINE

THE DAYLIGHT BOMBER OFFENSIVE

FEATURING 'BIG WEEK'
20-25 FEBRUARY 1944

Overleaf

Although 'Big Week' began the destruction of the German fighter force
in February, 1944, a year later the Luftwaffe could still hit back — particularly after the introduction of
the radical Messerschmitt Me262 jet fighter. Here one of these advanced aircraft dives to
attack Consolidated B-24 Liberators of the US 8th Air Force in March, 1945, as
these head for one of the few remaining targets in the
stricken Reich.

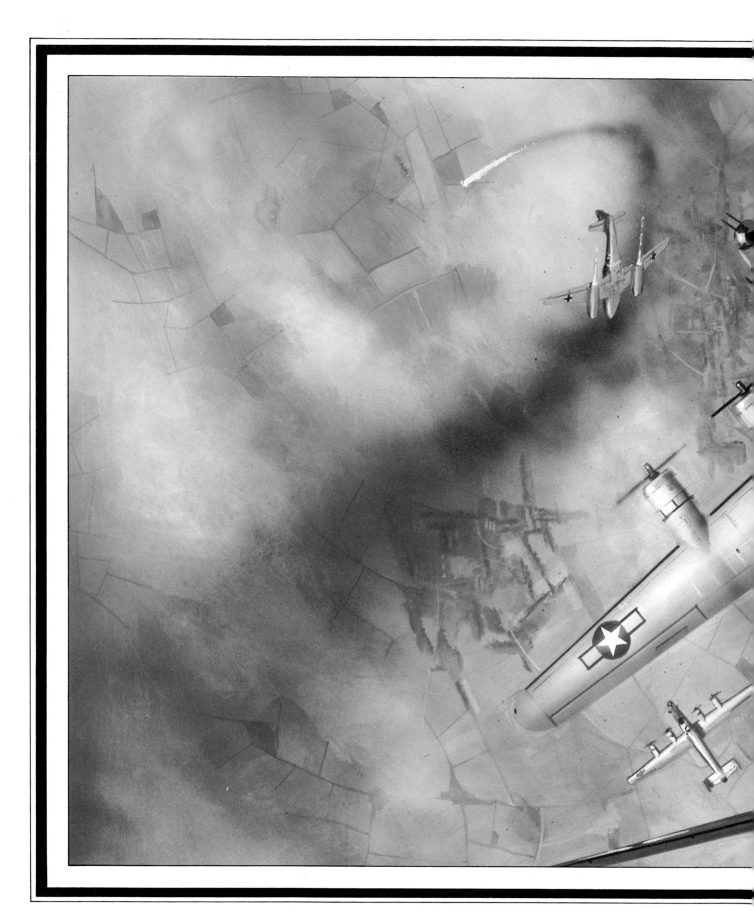

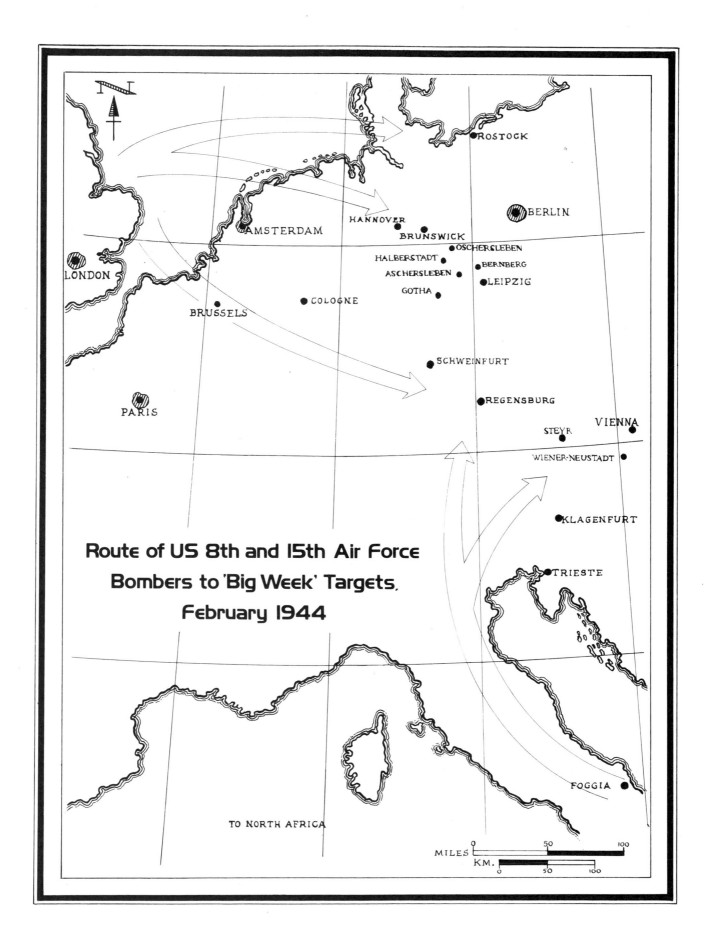

Route of US 8th and 15th Air Force
Bombers to 'Big Week' Targets.
February 1944

While the Royal Air Force had turned its back on a major day bombing offensive as a result of its early experiences, and particularly due to the lack of any viable long-range escort fighter, the entry of the United States into World War II in December 1941 brought a resurrection of such plans.

Although the leaders of the US Army Air Force accepted the desirability of adequate fighter escort as soon as suitable aircraft could be developed, they believed that tight formations of their heavily-armed four-engined bombers could be fought through to their targets, flying at high altitude. True, because of the heavy load of armor and guns they carried, the American bombers could not carry nearly such a large bombload, or such large bombs as their more lightly loaded British counterparts. Nevertheless, it was believed that the newly-developed Norden bombsight would allow such accurate bomb-aiming that lesser weights of bombs would achieve the same results.

US plans to establish a massive air striking force in England to carry the war to Germany at the earliest possible date was, however, to be affected substantially by the demands of circumstance. By the time sufficient resources had been despatched to the South and South-West Pacific areas to stop the rot the war there was already six months old. The need to support the British 8th Army in North Africa also ensured that the first heavy bombers to be sent across the Atlantic had Egypt as their destination. It was a dozen of these aircraft — Consolidated B-24D Liberators — which undertook the first bombing raid of the European war by US aircraft with an attack on the Ploesti oil refineries in Rumania on 11 June, 1942.

First strikes
Even as this initial — and one-off — strike was underway, the first three groups of Boeing B-17 Fortress bombers were beginning their journey to the United Kingdom where the fledgling US 8th Air Force was being formed. With the heavy bombers came a group of Lockheed P-38 Lightning fighters and two other fighter groups leaving behind in the US their Bell P-39 Airacobras to be equipped instead with ex-RAF Spitfire Vs.

Settling in took a little time, but at last on 17 August, 1942 six B-17Es of the 97th Bombardment Group (H) undertook the first 8th Air Force heavy bomber raid — on Rouen-Sotteville marshalling yards, carried out under a protective 'umbrella' of RAF Spitfires. At this time the Luftwaffe's fighter defenses in the West amounted only to two Geschwadern in France and Belgium and a third in Holland and North Germany.

But at this stage the small US presence presented no more than the beginnings of a threat which existing German resources could deal with. Nevertheless, the German pilots were initially wary of the new American bombers, which arrived on the scene with a reputation for toughness and heavy armament. Consequently, the first clash took place on 21 August without loss, but already the experienced pilots of Jagdgeschwadern 2 and 26 had spotted the weak point of the bombers — frontal defense. Clearly, they believed, the difficult head-on attack offered the best chances for success without unacceptable loss levels.

Meantime, bomber strength was steadily building-up and on 6 September, 54 B-17s attacked the Meaulte aircraft production plant in France, still close enough to England to ensure an escort of Spitfires. This time, however, the Luftwaffe broke through, shooting down two of the bombers. A month later an even more ambitious effort was undertaken, when 108 bombers — including the first B-24s to operate from England — attacked Lille Steelworks. FW190s from JG26 intercepted, shooting down four heavy bombers for the loss of two of their number.

By November 1942 8th Air Force was becoming a formidable force, however. Four more groups of B-17s, and one of the B-24s had arrived since August as had two more groups of P-38s. The three squadrons of American volunteer pilots in the RAF had been transferred to the USAAF with their Spitfires to form the 4th Fighter Group, while the first group of the new Republic P-47C Thunderbolt fighters was due to arrive soon. At this stage, however, the 8th was greatly weakened by a major diversion of effort elsewhere.

On 8 November, 1942 Anglo-American forces landed in French North-West Africa in an effort to bring the campaign in Libya to a speedy end. To support this effort all the 8th's fighter groups bar the 4th, and two of its original B-17 groups (the 97th and 301st) were despatched to Algeria. The 8th was left with four groups of B-17s, two of B-24s, and a single group of Spitfires.

The 8th planners were not to be deterred, however, and on 27 January, 1943 64 B-17s at last penetrated Reich territory with a raid on the port of Wilhelmshaven on the north coast. Jagdgeschwader 1 intercepted, but failed to employ the head-on attacks of the units further south. Flying into the fire of the massed half inch machine guns of the formation's defenses, they were successful in shooting down three Fortresses — but at a high cost of seven of their own aircraft. They soon learnt, however. A raid on Hamm on 7 February brought only four losses to the force of 86 bombers, but the deepest raid yet tried on 17 April, 1943, which took 106 B-17s to attack a Focke-Wulf plant at Bremen cost 16 Fortresses.

During December 1942 one of the 8th's two B-24 groups, the 93rd, had been detached to Africa where the 9th Air Force had already reinforced its B-24 force to two groups; it would return in February 1943. In April, two more B-17 groups flew directly to Algeria from the US, but these were the last diversions to the Mediterranean for the time being, as the campaign in Tunisia was almost at an end. This allowed the 8th to be strengthened once more, five new bomber groups being sent to England during April, followed by nine more over the next three months, together with three more fighter groups with P-47s.

All-out assault begins
From the spring of 1943 the 8th Air Force was ready to begin a sustained campaign against Germany's industry and war potential which lasted for the next two years. With some 500 bombers now available, up to half this number could regularly be put into the air, and in April the P-47s began to operate. After initial sweeps to familiarize themselves with the European coastline they undertook their first escort on 4 May, accompanying the bombers to Antwerp in Belgium.

The threat posed by the US bombers was now forcing the Luftwaffe to strengthen its defense, notably in the North German area where the 8th Air Force had directed its first penetrations into the German homeland. Here JG1 was split to form the nucleus of a new Jagdgeschwader, JG11. The fighters of these units made their increased strength felt in telling style on 13 June, 1943 when they shot down 26 bombers from a force raiding Kiel and Bremen; 22 of these were from newly-arrived and still inexperienced groups.

Deeper penetrations into Germany were undertaken during the dependable summer weather of July, but now the Americans found themselves up against the most intense fighter opposition yet encountered, 128 B-17s being lost in action during the month. The gunners, however, believed that they were making interception of the bombers a devastatingly expensive business for the Luftwaffe, claiming no less than 545 fighters shot down during the same month. But the massed fire of hundreds of individual gunners directed at every fighter coming within range led to (well-intentioned) multiple overclaiming; actual German losses amounted to a more modest 40 aircraft.

The reasons for the growing toll of US aircraft were several. With the fall of Tunisia some German units were recalled from the Mediterranean, and after the Allied invasions of Sicily in July 1943, more returned. To combat the bombers the Zerstörergeschwadern were reformed and brought up to strength, recalled from the Southern and Eastern Fronts for this purpose. These heavily armed, stable twin-engined heavy fighters proved devastatingly effective against unescorted bombers. Fighter units were also withdrawn from the Soviet Union — initially III/JG54 and I/JG3 but subsequently the whole of the latter Geschwader. Better tactics and more heavily armed aircraft also played their part.

However, the major reason for the rapid improvement in the German air defenses was the spur provided by the devastatingly successful series of Allied bombing raids on Hamburg during July, which almost totally destroyed the city. These had been undertaken mainly by night by RAF Bomber Command, but the fires had been 'stoked' by day by the 8th Air Force.

The efforts to increase the US bombers' protection were consequently redoubled. A number of B-17s were up-armed as YB-40 gunships, but as these were still tied-in to the formations, their employment was not a success. Fighters were the answer, but sufficient range still eluded the P-47s, which, when employed to maximize on their high altitude and dive performance, were beginning to take the measure of the opposition. At last 100-gallon drop tanks became available which enabled them to carry sufficient fuel to reach the Dutch/German border; but as yet the 200-gallon tank, although available, was not pressurized. As a result it could not be used at altitude making it all but useless for escort purposes. Thus the Luftwaffe were still left with plenty of time to inflict great damage to the bombers over German territory, and they generally left well alone, until the escorts reached the limit of their range and turned back.

Meanwhile, in the Mediterranean, where the heavy bombers of the 12th Air Force enjoyed P-38 escort throughout their missions, this sizeable force was gradually stretching out its tentacles to more strategic targets. On 19 July all four B-17 groups there bombed Rome for the first time from bases in Tunisia, joined by five groups of B-24s from Libya. Three of the latter were 8th Air Force units which had flown out to Africa on detachment. The prime reason for their presence became obvious on 1 August, when 178 8th and 9th Air Force B-24s carried out a low level maximum effort attack on Ploesti. Without escort, the Liberators were attacked into, over and out of the target, which they bombed in a hurricane of Flak. Fifty-seven failed to return and many others were damaged. The 8th's three groups did not return to England until October 1943.

The most ambitious effort to date came on 17 August,

1943, the first anniversary of the initial B-17 sorties over Europe. The 3rd Bombardment Division's B-17s were to attack the Messerschmitt factory at Regensburg, then fly on direct to airfields in North Africa. Behind them would come the 1st Division's Wings, which would hit nearby Schweinfurt and then return to England. The raid was little short of a disaster. The Regensburg formation was intercepted well before it reached the target, and by the time it cleared the Alps to the Mediterranean, 24 B-17s had gone down. The following Schweinfurt attacks were delayed in setting off by low cloud over their bases; the defenders had enjoyed the time necessary to land and refuel, and mauled these Fortresses even more severely, 36 failing to return; 60 in a day was an unbearable rate of attrition.

While the losses were being made good, the bombers raided Luftwaffe fighter fields in France and the Low Countries, under large escorts of P-47s, and Spitfires, but the Germans were rarely caught on the ground and joined combat only on their own terms. Results were poor. With the late summer the deep penetration raids were resumed — and so were the US losses.

A raid on the ball-bearing plant at Stuttgart on 6 September cost 45 bombers, while an attack on Bremen — Vegesack on 8 October brought another 30 losses, with an additional 26 damaged. After 17 August there had been those who had maintained that the main reason for the heavy losses had been the division of the force into two separate formations. Now, however, the Luftwaffe hammered home the true reason — lack of proper escort. Twenty-eight losses were incurred over Poland on 9 October, and 30 more ten days later during an attack on Munster, including all 12 aircraft sent out by the 100th Bombardment Group. A return visit to Schweinfurt later in the month matched the losses of that dreadful August anniversary, 60 B-17s failing to return although 67 per cent ball-bearing production was lost.

The need for protection and escorts

It was now becoming increasingly obvious to all concerned that, until effective escort could be provided, deep penetration raids would have to cease. However, steps were being taken, for during the last three months four more P-47 groups had reached England, as had two new groups of the longer-ranging P-38s. In the Pacific, and to a lesser extent in the Mediterranean, the P-38 had been a big success, but its fortunes over Western Europe were to be at best mixed. The aircraft lacked adequate heating and in the extremes of temperature met at high altitudes during a European winter, it was beset by problems. The 55th Fighter Group began operating during October, but on 13 November the unit was hard hit over Bremen, losing seven Lightnings, with 16 more damaged. A little over two weeks later another seven were shot down by German fighters: in all 18 P-38s were lost in action during November. It did not seem that the P-38 was the answer to the 8th's problems.

Another long winter of overcast weather and fog loomed ahead to reduce the 8th's efforts once again. It appeared that opinion in US military circles was beginning to swing against the 8th; to them the English base from where the US participated in the joint bomber offensive seemed to be taking an inordinately long time to build up and bear fruit. The constant interference of the unreliable Northern European weather particularly had been noted. In addition, the swift fall of Sicily to Allied invasion, and the early capture of Southern Italy raised attractive alternatives.

B-17Fs OF THE 569TH SQUADRON, 390TH BOMB GROUP (H) OF THE 3RD BOMBARDMENT DIVISION FROM FRAMLINGHAM, SUFFOLK, RELEASE STRINGS OF BOMBS OVER THEIR TARGET IN GERMANY.

On 27 September, 1943 the Foggia Plain, on the east coast of Southern Italy had passed into Allied hands, and within days the B-17 and B-24 groups of the 9th and 12th Air Forces had flown in, launching their first attack into mainland Europe on 1 October with a raid on Wiener Neustadt, Austria. Here it seemed was a base free from the vagaries of England's weather and the transfer of a major part of the 8th's future expansion to this area began.

On 1 November the new 15th Air Force was set up, the four B-17 and two B-24 groups being transferred in, together with three P-38 groups and a further fighter group which was just converting from P-40Fs to P-47Ds. A Wing of B-26 medium bombers was also allocated to the 15th on a temporary basis, but was soon released when six more B-24 groups, originally earmarked for the 8th, arrived. In the event Italy and the Alps proved to have just as many weather problems as did Western Europe, while the maintenance problem of supporting two major strategic air forces at widely separated bases was less than ideal.

In an effort to increase striking power by other than the formation of ever more new units, squadron strength was raised from nine to 12 bombers during October 1943, while during December the 8th was further reinforced with four more new B-24 groups, despite the recent diversions to Italy. However, the weather had again deteriorated in late 1943, and faced with the almost total overcast on most days, raids were greatly reduced.

Now use was made of the bombing aids recently developed for RAF Bomber Command — H2S and H2X radar and 'Oboe' radio direction guidance systems; pathfinder units were also set up. Until early 1944 these remained the major type of mission undertaken, with pathfinder-led attacks through cloud on ports and industrial areas. Although the cloud also reduced Luftwaffe interceptions, some successes were still being chalked up by the German fighters. Flying to attack targets in South Germany during the last two days of the year, on 30 December 23 bombers were lost over Ludwigshafen, while next day 25 more went down and 18 others were damaged to a point where they had to be written off on return; this was despite fighter cover provided all the way to the target by P-38s and the new P-51Bs.

It was in the latter fighter type that salvation lay, however. The North American P-51B Mustang was a fighter which had come about almost by chance, and had not been ordered originally by the USAAF. Initially, the Mustangs had come to England for the new tactical air force which was being set up for the forthcoming invasion of Europe.

A 2ND BOMBARDMENT DIVISION CONSOLIDATED B-24J
LIBERATOR HEADS OUT UNDER THE COMFORTING PROTECTION
OF ESCORT FIGHTERS WHICH LEAVE THEIR CONDENSATION
CONTRAILS HIGH ABOVE. THE BOMBER IS AN AIRCRAFT OF THE
491ST BOMB GROUP WHICH FIRST SAW SERVICE DURING THE
SPRING OF 1944.

The first group, the 354th, was loaned to the 8th Air Force
for escort duties late in the year, flying its first sorties on 5
December.

Some very heavy air fighting took place during January
1944 between the growing force of escort fighters and the
increased defensive strength of the Luftwaffe. Well-
impressed with the high performance and great range
potential of the Mustang, 8th Air Force attempted to have
the 354th transferred from the 9th Air Force, now England-
based. The latter would not play, however, but were
prepared to exchange the newly-arrived P-51B-equipped
357th Fighter Group for one of the 8th's experienced P-47
units, the 358th.

During January, although plagued by some gun
stoppages caused again by the intense cold at high altitude,
and to various other minor teething troubles resulting from
the aircraft's rapid entry into service, the Mustang started to
come into its own. On 5 January the 354th claimed 18 for no
loss, while on 11 January, again without loss, the group
claimed 15 of the 28 victories recorded, ten of the remainder
being credited to Zemke's 'Wolfpack' — the 56th Fighter
Group, at this time 8th Air Force's top scorer by a wide
margin. The P-47s were also about to receive a major and
welcome boost in range, attachments for drop tanks under
each wing, rather than for a single tank under the fuselage,
being installed. Towards the end of the month the Luftwaffe was hit really hard, 45 victories being claimed for 14
losses on 29 January, and another 45 for only four lost next
day. Even the P-38s were successful on 29 January, ten
claims being made by the Lightning pilots against only four
losses.

Conditions right for 'Big Week'

The 8th Air Force was now ready to launch a new offensive
when the weather allowed, but this time its target was to be
its main opponent — the Luftwaffe fighter force.
Operation *Argument* was planned as a major series of raids
on the German fighter aircraft production facility, con-
ducted by way of precision bombing under the maximum
possible fighter escort. There was not long to wait, for on 19
February, 1944 the meteorological experts detected an
extensive high pressure area approaching Germany; this
would allow the clear skies and fine weather necessary for
Argument to be implemented.

The series of attacks later known as 'Big Week' were
about to begin. At airfields in Eastern England a mighty
force comprising 21 groups of B-17s, nine groups of B-24s
and 17 fighter groups, five of them borrowed from the 9th
Air Force, stood ready. In Italy, on the Foggia Plain, a further four groups of B-17s, eight of B-24s and four of
fighters were available to add their weight to the assault. To
face this huge aerial armada the Luftwaffe had in mainland
Europe some 28 day fighter Gruppen with FW190As and
Bf109Gs, seven Gruppen of Bf110G and Me410 heavy
fighters, and over 20 smaller Stabschwarme,
Einsatzstaffeln, and other such units. Also available
between 15th Air Force and targets in the Reich were the
eight fighter Gruppen, one Staffel and two Stabschwarme
of Luftflotte 2 situated in Italy. This represented a total
force of over 1000 interceptors.

Bomber Command effectively opened 'Big Week', however, with its heavy attacks on the Junkers factory at
Leipzig during the night of 19–20 February. Next morning,
with good weather predicted over Germany, the US
formations began to gather. A massive force of 417 B-17s
and 272 B-24s from the 1st and 2nd Bomber Divisions set
out on the route which the RAF had followed the night
before, the single long column which they formed being
escorted by nearly all the available long-range fighters. As
the force formed up and headed out, some 117 B-17s and 28
B-24s returned to base due to one problem or another, but
the balance, still 544 strong, headed on into Central
Germany.

Here they split up and headed for various targets, 239
B-17s attacking Leipzig's Mockau airfield and aircraft factories at Hesterblink and Abtnaundorf. Thirty-seven more
hit a plant at Bernburg and 44 attacked Oschersleben. This
target was also hit by 13 B-24s, while 87 more of the
Liberators attacked Gotha, 76 Wilhelmtor, Brunswick and
Neupetritor, and 58 Helmstedt. The remaining 30 aircraft
released their bombs on targets of opportunity. The Messerschmitt Bf109 production plant at Leipzig was particularly
well hit by the 401st Bomb Group, although several of this
unit's bombers were damaged severely during the attack.

Meanwhile, 319 more B-17s from the 3rd Division had
set off on a diversionary raid on a more northerly line, 105
getting through to attack Tutow airfield, 176 bombing
Rostock, with 115 releasing on opportunity targets. Most of
the German fighters which had been scrambled were
directed against this northern thrust, so losses suffered by
the main attack were not heavy, amounting to seven B-17s
and eight B-24s. Despite their role as decoys, the 3rd
Division also lost only six B-17s, although in the force as a
whole 242 more bombers were damaged, five of them
critically.

One B-17 of the 351st Group was hit by a cannon shell
which killed the co-pilot and seriously wounded the pilot

himself. Some members of the crew baled out, but two others, 2/Lt Walter Truemper (navigator) and Staff Sgt Archie Mathies (engineer) took over the controls and flew the aircraft back to England. Sadly, their attempt to land ended in disaster, for the bomber crashed and all aboard were killed; both men were awarded posthumous Congressional Medals of Honor.

In the 305th Group another B-17 was hit during a head-on attack by fighters and fell away with an engine blazing, the pilot wounded, co-pilot dead and seven other members of the crew hit. 1/Lt William Lawley, the pilot, managed to right the aircraft and ordered that the crew abandon it. However, one of the gunners was too badly wounded, so despite severe facial injuries, Lawley jettisoned the bomb-load and despite the loss of a second engine, managed to accomplish the long journey back to England. As he at last reached the English coast, a third engine ran out of fuel, but Lawley nonetheless managed to make a good crash-landing at the first airfield seen, saving his crew's lives. He too was awarded a Medal of Honor — the only time three were to be awarded to the 8th Air Force for a single day's action.

Germans incur heavy losses

While the bombers had been making their attacks, overhead a force of 668 P-47s, 94 P-38s, and 73 P-51s had been giving the Luftwaffe a very hard time indeed. For the loss of two P-47s, one P-38 and one P-51 the American pilots claimed 61 victories, with seven more probables and 37 damaged (the bombers' gunners submitted a further 65 claims for aircraft destroyed, but they were notorious for their high over-claiming — usually in a ratio of at least ten to one).

The aggressive pilots of Zemke's Wolfpack — the 56th Fighter Group — spotted 24 Bf110Gs of III/ZG26 near Minden, just about to attack the bombers, and jettisoning the 150-gallon drop tanks that the P-47s were using for the first time on this mission, hit the Zerstörern hard, claiming nine shot down, three of them by Capt Leroy Schreiber and two each by Lts Bob Johnson, Fred Christensen and Don Smith, while Lt Col Francis Gabreski claimed two Me410s.

Other units then joined the fight, pilots of the 352nd Fighter Group claiming five more Bf110s and other groups a further four to bring the losses suffered by III/ZG26 to 18. The Wolfpack's 16 victories on this day were equalled by the 354th 'Pioneer Mustang' Group, while the second P-51 unit to begin operating, the 357th Group, opened its scoring with two Bf109s. Even the P-38s did better on 20 February. Seven victories were claimed, two of them by Capt C E Jackson before he was shot down himself. Of the two P-47s lost, one fell to Maj Gunther Specht, Kommodore of Jagdgeschwader 11 — but it was a quite devastating victory for the US fighters.

Far away in the south another 126 B-17s had been des-patched by the 15th Air Force's 5th Bombardment Wing to attack the aircraft plant at Regensburg-Obertraubling but icy conditions over the Alps resulted in an abort of this mission. Meanwhile, B-24s from this air force operated locally in Italy, bombing tactical targets at Anzio.

Continued bad weather in this area prevented the 15th playing its part again next day, but from England almost as strong a force as on 20 February was again despatched to North Germany, Brunswick being the main target designated. All three divisions put up a force of 617 B-17s and 244 B-24s, 99 of which proved none-effective. The other 518 proceeded to their targets escorted by a force of 69 P-38s, 542 P-47s and 68 P-51s.

On this occasion Brunswick and many of the alternative targets were found to be under a thick layer of cloud and much of the bombing was undertaken by reliance on radar-directed pathfinders, which marked Brunswick for general rather than pinpoint attack. A number of aircraft depots and airfields were also attacked, the best bombing of the day being recorded at the depot at Diepholz, which received a well-concentrated bomb carpet. Hanover, Lingen and Caerorden also received bombs, the airfields attacked including Alhorn, Verden, Hopsten, Rheine, Quackenbruck, Bramsche, Achmer and Hesepe.

Once again the defenders were alert, but due both to the cloud conditions and the strength of the escorts, US losses were again light, only 13 B-17s and three B-24s failing to get back, though seven more were written off on return, including two B-17s which collided in cloud, and in all 105 suffered damage. The B-24s of the 2nd Division escaped with the lightest casualties, while the 1st Division suffered the greatest proportion of losses and damage. Nineteen vic-tories and 16 probables were claimed by the gunners, 12 of the former by the harder-hit units of the 1st Division.

The fighters again had something of a field day, claim-ing 33 victories for five losses (two P-47s and three P-51s) although another three were written off on return — two of them P-47s — and three more Thunderbolts were damaged. Again, the 56th Fighter Group was in the lead with 13 vic-tories — though the strength of this unit now allowed it to send out two group-strength formations, which no other fighter unit could do. Two of the claims credited on this date, which included ten Bf109s, were made by Flt Lt Mike

TOP: REPUBLIC P-47D THUNDERBOLT OF THE US 8TH AIR FORCE'S 78TH FIGHTER GROUP IN EARLY 1944. 'SPOKANE CHIEF' WAS FLOWN BY MAJOR EUGENE ROBERTS, THE 8TH'S SECOND FIGHTER ACE OF THE WAR.
ABOVE: THE SUPREME ESCORT FIGHTER OF THE WAR, THE NORTH AMERICAN P-51B. THIS EARLY EXAMPLE WAS FLOWN BY THE 356TH SQUADRON OF THE 354TH FIGHTER GROUP — THE 'PIONEER MUSTANGS' — DURING FEBRUARY 1944.

US ARMY AIR FORCE ORDER OF BATTLE, FEBRUARY 1944

UNIT	BASE	AIRCRAFT
VIII BOMBER COMMAND		
1st BOMBARDMENT DIVISION		
1st Bombardment Wing		
91st Bombardment Group(H)		
322nd, 323rd, 324th, 401st Sqn	Bassingbourn, Cambs	B-17
381st Bombardment Group(H)		
532nd, 533rd, 534th, 535th Sqn	Ridgewell, Essex	B-17
398th Bombardment Group(H)		
600th, 601st, 602nd, 603rd Sqn	Nuthampstead, Herts	B-17
40th Bombardment Wing		
92nd Bombardment Group(H)		
325th, 326th, 327th, 407th Sqn	Podington, Beds	B-17
305th Bombardment Group(H)		
364th, 365th, 366th, 422nd Sqn	Chelveston, Northants	B-17
306th Bombardment Group(H)		
367th, 368th, 369th, 423rd Sqn	Thurleigh, Beds	B-17
41st Bombardment Wing		
303rd Bombardment Group(H)		
358th, 359th, 360th, 427th Sqn	Molesworth, Hunts	B-17
379th Bombardment Group(H)		
524th, 525th, 526th, 527th Sqn	Kimbolton, Hunts	B-17
384th Bombardment Group(H)		
544th, 545th, 546th, 547th Sqn	Grafton Underwood, Northants	B-17
94th Bombardment Wing		
351st Bombardment Group(H)		
508th, 509th, 510th, 511th Sqn	Polebrook, Northants	B-17
401st Bombardment Group(H)		
612th, 613rd, 614th, 615th Sqn	Deenthorpe, Northants	B-17
457th Bombardment Group(H)		
748th, 749th, 750th, 751st Sqn	Glatton, Hunts	B-17
2ND BOMBARDMENT DIVISION		
2nd Bombardment Wing		
389th Bombardment Group(H)		
564th, 565th, 566th, 567th Sqn	Hethel, Norfolk	B-24
445th Bombardment Group(H)		
700th, 701st, 702nd, 703rd Sqn	Tibenham, Norfolk	B-24
453rd Bombardment Group(H)		
732nd, 733rd, 734th, 735th Sqn	Old Buckenham, Norfolk	B-24
14th Bombardment Wing		
44th Bombardment Group(H)		
66th, 67th, 68th, 506th Sqn	Shipdham, Norfolk	B-24
392nd Bombardment Group(H)		
576th, 577th, 578th, 579th Sqn	Wendling, Norfolk	B-24
20th Bombardment Wing		
93rd Bombardment Group(H)		
328th, 329th, 330th, 409th Sqn	Hardwick, Norfolk	B-24
446th Bombardment Group(H)		
704th, 705th, 706th, 707th Sqn	Bungay, Suffolk	B-24
448th Bombardment Group(H)		
712th, 713th, 714th, 715th Sqn	Seething, Norfolk	B-24
96th Bombardment Wing		
458th Bombardment Group(H)		
752nd, 753rd, 754th, 755th Sqn	Horsham St Faith, Norfolk	B-24
3RD BOMBARDMENT DIVISION		
4th Bombardment Wing		
94th Bombardment Group(H)		
331st, 332nd, 333rd, 410th Sqn	Rougham, Suffolk	B-17

UNIT	BASE	AIRCRAFT
385th Bombardment Group(H)		
548th, 549th, 550th, 551st Sqn	Great Ashfield, Suffolk	B-17
447th Bombardment Group(H)		
708th, 709th, 710th, 711th Sqn	Rattlesden, Suffolk	B-17
13th Bombardment Wing		
95th Bombardment Group(H)		
334th, 335th, 336th, 412th Sqn	Horham, Suffolk	B-17
100th Bombardment Group(H)		
349th, 350th, 351st, 418th Sqn	Thorpe Abbotts, Norfolk	B-17
390th Bombardment Group(H)		
568th, 569th, 570th, 571st Sqn	Framlingham, Suffolk	B-17
45th Bombardment Wing		
96th Bombardment Group(H)		
337th, 338th, 339th, 413th Sqn	Snetterton Heath, Suffolk	B-17
388th Bombardment Group(H)		
560th, 561st, 562nd, 563rd Sqn	Knettishall, Suffolk	B-17
452nd Bombardment Group(H)		
728th, 729th, 730th, 731st Sqn	Deopham Green, Norfolk	B-17
VIII FIGHTER COMMAND		
4th Fighter Group		
334th, 335th, 336th Sqn	Debden, Essex	P-47
56th Fighter Group		
61st, 62nd, 63rd Sqn	Halesworth, Suffolk	P-47
78th Fighter Group		
82nd, 83rd, 84th Sqn	Duxford, Cambs	P-47
352nd Fighter Group		
328th, 486th, 487th Sqn	Bodney, Norfolk	P-47
353rd Fighter Group		
350th, 351st, 352nd Sqn	Metfield, Suffolk	P-47
355th Fighter Group		
354th, 357th, 358th Sqn	Steeple Morden, Herts	P-47
356th Fighter Group		
359th, 360th, 361st Sqn	Martlesham Heath, Suffolk	P-47
359th Fighter Group		
368th, 369th, 370th Sqn	East Wretham, Norfolk	P-47
361st Fighter Group		
374th, 375th, 376th Sqn	Bottisham, Cambs	P-47
20th Fighter Group		
55th, 77th, 79th Sqn	Kings Cliffe, Northants	P-38
55th Fighter Group		
38th, 338th, 343rd Sqn	Nuthampstead, Herts	P-38
357th Fighter Group		
362nd, 363rd, 364th Sqn	Leiston, Suffolk	P-51B
Attached 9th Air Force Fighter Units		
354th Fighter Group		
353rd, 355th, 356th Sqn	Boxted, Suffolk	P-51B
358th Fighter Group		
365th, 366th, 367th Sqn	Raydon, Suffolk	P-47
362nd Fighter Group		
377th, 378th, 379th Sqn	Wormingford, Essex	P-47
363rd Fighter Group		
380th, 381st, 382nd Sqn	Rivenhall, Suffolk	P-47
365th Fighter Group		
386th, 387th, 388th Sqn	Gosfield	P-47
XV BOMBER COMMAND		
5th Bombardment Wing		
2nd Bombardment Group(H)		
20th, 49th, 96th, 429th Sqn	Amendola, Italy	B-17
97th Bombardment Group(H)		
340th, 341st, 342nd, 414th Sqn	Amendola, Italy	B-17
99th Bombardment Group(H)		
346th, 347th, 348th, 416th Sqn	Tortorella, Italy	B-17
301st Bombardment Group(H)		
32nd, 352nd, 353rd, 419th Sqn	Lucera, Italy	B-17

UNIT	BASE	AIRCRAFT
47th Bombardment Wing		
98th Bombardment Group(H)		
343rd, 344th, 345th, 415th Sqn	Lecce, Italy	B-24
376th Bombardment Group(H)		
512nd, 513rd, 514th, 515th Sqn	San Pacrazio, Italy	B-24
449th Bombardment Group(H)		
716th, 717th, 718th, 719th Sqn	Grottaglie, Italy	B-24
450th Bombardment Group(H)		
720th, 721st, 722nd, 723rd Sqn	Manduria, Italy	B-24
451st Bombardment Group(H)		
724th, 725th, 726th, 727th Sqn	San Pacrazio, Italy	B-24
304th Bombardment Wing		
454th Bombardment Group(H)		
736th, 737th, 738th, 739th Sqn	San Giovanni, Italy	B-24
455th Bombardment Group(H)		
740th, 741st, 742nd, 743rd Sqn	San Giovanni, Italy	B-24
456th Bombardment Group(H)		
744th, 745th, 746th, 747th Sqn	Stornara, Italy	B-24

XV FIGHTER COMMAND

UNIT	BASE	AIRCRAFT
1st Fighter Group		
27th, 71st, 94th Sqn	Salsola, Italy	P-38
14th Fighter Group		
37th, 48th, 49th Sqn	Triolo, Italy	P-38
82nd Fighter Group		
95th, 96th, 97th Sqn	Vincenzo, Italy	P-38
325th Fighter Group		
317th, 318th, 319th Sqn	Foggia, Italy	P-47

OBERST WALTER OESAU, KOMMODORE OF JAGDGESCHWADER 1, IN THE COCKPIT OF HIS FW190A FIGHTER PRIOR TO TAKE-OFF TO INTERCEPT US BOMBERS OVER NORTHERN GERMANY.

Gladych, a Polish pilot flying with the 56th on attachment. Again the 'Pioneer Mustangs' were not far behind with ten victories, three credited to 2/Lt Don McDowell, while others went to Don Beerbower, Glen Eagleston, later the group's (and the 9th Air Force's) top-scorer, and to Lt Charles Gumm, the unit's first ace.

For the second day running the Luftwaffe's II/JG26 was amongst the successful units intercepting, but the outstanding performance was recorded by II/JG1's Kommandeur, Maj Heinz Bär, who claimed two B-17s, a P-47 and a P-51.

While the weather had not allowed all the objectives of *Argument* to be achieved during these opening days, the attacks made had been by no means unsuccessful, and now the weather forecasters promised more clear weather over the target areas. Considering it was February, the Americans' luck was in.

Consequently on 22 February the 8th Air Force's three divisions were once more ordered off, forming up in vile local weather conditions and fighting their way through towering clouds, rain, snow and murk to get to the promised fair weather beyond. The 1st and 2nd Divisions were again targeted with North Germany, but the 3rd was sent south to attack Schweinfurt in co-ordination with the 15th Air Force's first strike of the week, which was to hit nearby Regenburg.

All did not go according to plan, however. The forecasters were wrong and continued bad weather prevented the 333 B-17s of the 3rd Division getting through to Schweinfurt. Indeed, the bombers received the abandonment order even before enemy territory had been reached. Of 177 B-24s sent off by the 2nd Division to attack targets on the Dutch-German frontier, no less than 103 were forced to turn back. Seventy-four bombed Enschede, Arnhem and Nijmegen-Deventer, but two of these mistook Nijmegen for a German town and released their bombs on it, killing 200 Dutch civilians. Few German fighters were seen by the Liberator crews in the dreadful weather conditions they were encountering, and only two were claimed shot down by the gunners; three B-24s failed to return and three more were damaged.

Luftwaffe defense strength

The 1st Division on the other hand had a real fight on its hands as 289 B-17s headed for North Germany again. As with the 2nd Division, there were many aborts, no less than 128 bombers failing to reach their targets. Of the remaining 161 only 99 hit their primary targets, 47 bombing Bernburg, 34 Aschersleben and 18 Halberstadt, at each of which locations aircraft factories were hit.

The defenders were on their toes, and at Bernburg the 306th Bomber Group was hit hard as it attacked the Ju88 factory, seven B-17s being shot down and 33 more damaged. Altogether 38 Fortresses were lost by this division and 145 more were damaged, four of which were write-offs. Two of the bombers were shot down by Heinz Bär of II/JG1, one by Maj Specht of JG11 for the 31st of his 32 victories and one by Oblt Heinz Knoke, one of Specht's pilots in the Geschwader's II Gruppe. II/JG26 was once again successful claiming five B-17s and two P-47s, three of the bombers and one of the fighters being credited to Lt Adolf Glunz, who had already claimed a B-17 on 21 February. However, the unit lost two pilots killed including 23 victory 'Experte' Hpt Horst Sternberg.

Once again, the US fighters enjoyed the day's greatest success, claiming 57 victories, but suffering heavier losses than on previous days, including eight P-47s out of 535 and three P-51s from 57. Twelve more P-47s, six P-38s and three P-51s were damaged. Yet again, it was the 56th Fighter Group which led the way, 15 more victories being claimed to raise the group's total past the 250 mark — far in excess of the totals credited to any other 8th Air Force unit, while the 61st Squadron became the first in the USAAF to claim 100. Again, also, the 354th's Mustangs were close behind with 12 claims, the two groups having between them shot down nine Bf110s — the Zerstörern had again taken a beating. Six more claims had been made by pilots of the 353rd Fighter

LUFTWAFFE DAY FIGHTER ORDER OF BATTLE, FEBRUARY 1944
(UNITS AVAILABLE FOR DEFENSIVE OPERATIONS AGAINST US 8TH AND 15TH AIR FORCES)

UNIT	BASE	AIRCRAFT
1 JAGDDIVISION, DÖBERITZ, BERLIN		
Jagdgeschwader 3 'Udet'		
Stab	Salzwedel	Messerschmitt Bf109G
I Gruppe	Burg	Messerschmitt Bf109G
II Gruppe	Gardelegen	Messerschmitt Bf109G
IV Gruppe	Salzwedel	Messerschmitt Bf109G
Jagdgeschwader 300 'Wilde Sau'		
III Gruppe	Zerbst	Messerschmitt Bf109G
Jagdgeshwader 302 'Wilde Sau'		
Stab	Döberitz	Focke-Wulf FW190A/ Messerschmitt Bf109G
I Gruppe	Jüterborg	Focke-Wulf FW190A/ Messerschmitt Bf109G
II Gruppe	Ludwigslust	Focke-Wulf FW190A/ Messerschmitt Bf109G
Sturmstaffel 1	Salzwedel	Focke-Wulf FW190A
Zerstörergeschwader 26 'Horst Wessel'		
I Gruppe	Braunschweig-Völkenrode	Messerschmitt Me410
II Gruppe	Hildesheim	Messerschmitt Me410
III Gruppe	Wunstorf	Messerschmitt Me410
Einsatzstaffeln (sections only)		
Ago	Oschersleben	Focke-Wulf FW190A
Erla	Delitzsch	Messerschmitt Bf109G
Arado	Tutow	Focke-Wulf FW190A
Air Observation Staffel 1	Neurupin	Junkers Ju88
2 JAGDDIVISION, STADE, HAMBURG		
Jagdgeschwader 11		
Stab	Rotenburg	Messerschmitt Bf109G
I Gruppe	Rotenburg	Focke-Wulf FW190A
II Gruppe	Wunstorf	Messerschmitt Bf109G
III Gruppe	Oldenburg	Focke-Wulf FW190A
10 Staffel	Aalborg, Denmark	Focke-Wulf FW190A/ Messerschmitt Bf109G
11 Staffel	Lister, Norway	Messerschmitt Bf109G
Jagdgeschwader 54 'Grünherz'		
III Gruppe	Lüneburg	Messerschmitt Bf109G
Erprobüngsgruppe 25	Parchim-Rechlin	FW190A/Bf109G/ Me410/Ju88
Einsatzstaffeln (sections only)		
Neumunster	Neumunster	Messerschmitt Bf109G
Fieseler	Kassel-Rothwesten	Focke-Wulf FW190A
Focke-Wulf	Langenhausen	Focke-Wulf FW190A
Air Observation Staffel 2	Stade	Junkers Ju88/ Messerschmitt Bf110
3 JAGDDIVISION, DEELEN, ARNHEM, HOLLAND		
Jagdgeschwader 1		
Stab	Rheine	Focke-Wulf FW190A
I Gruppe	Twente	Focke-Wulf FW190A
II Gruppe	Rheine	Focke-Wulf FW190A
Jagdgeschwader 300 'Wilde Sau'		
Stab	Deelen	Messerschmitt Bf109G
I Gruppe	Bonn-Hangelar	Messerschmitt Bf109G
II Gruppe	Rheine	Focke-Wulf FW190A
Air Observation Staffel 3	Venlo	Junkers Ju88
4 JAGDDIVISION, METZ, FRANCE		
Jagdgeschwader 2 'Richthofen'		
Stab	Cormeilles	Messerschmitt Bf109G
II Gruppe	Creil	Messerschmitt Bf109G
III Gruppe	Cormeilles	Focke-Wulf FW190A
Jagdgeschwader 26 'Schlageter'		
Stab	Lille-Nord	Focke-Wulf FW190A
I Gruppe	Lille-Nord, Florennes, Wevelghem	Focke-Wulf FW190A
II Gruppe	Epinoy, Grevilliers	Focke-Wulf FW190A
III Gruppe	Vendeville, Denain, St Dizier	Messerschmitt Bf109G
7 JAGDDIVISION, SCHLEISHEIM, MUNICH		
Jagdgeschwader 3 'Udet'		
III Gruppe	Wiesbaden-Erbenheim	Messerschmitt Bf109G
Jagdgeschwader 5 'Eismeer'		
I Gruppe	Herzogenaurach	Messerschmitt Bf109G
Jagdgeschwader 27		
I Gruppe	Fels am Wagram	Messerschmitt Bf109G
II Gruppe	Wiesbaden-Erbenheim	Messerschmitt Bf109G
Jagdgeschwader 53 'Pik As'		
II Gruppe	Frankfurt-Eschborn	Messerschmitt Bf109G
Jagdgeschwader 300 'Wilde Sau'		
III Gruppe	Wiesbaden-Erbenjeim	Messerschmitt Bf109G
Jagdgeschwader 301 'Wilde Sau'		
I Gruppe	Leipheim	Messerschmitt Bf109G
II Gruppe	Seyring	Messerschmitt Bf109G
Zerstörergeschwader 1 'Wespen'		
II Gruppe	Wels	Messerschmitt Bf110G
Zerstörergeschwader 76		
Stab	Ansbach	Messerschmitt Bf110G
I Gruppe	Ansbach	Messerschmitt Bf110G
II Gruppe	Ansbach	Messerschmitt Bf110G
III Gruppen	Öttingen	Messerschmitt Bf110G
Einsatzstaffeln (sections only)		
Messerschmitt	Regensburg-Obertraubling	Messerschmitt Bf109G
Messerschmitt	Wiener Neustadt	Messerschmitt Bf109G
Jagdschulen (instructors' units)		
Jagdgruppe 104	Fürth	Messerschmitt Bf109G
Jagdgruppe 108	Vöslau	Messerschmitt Bf109G
LUFTFLOTTE 2, ITALY		
Jagdgeschwader 2 'Udet'		
1 Gruppe		Focke-Wulf FW190A
4 Staffel		Messerschmitt Bf109G
Jagdgeschwader 4		
I Gruppe		Messerschmitt Bf109G
Jagdgeschwader 51 'Mölders'		
II Gruppe		Messerschmitt Bf109G
Jagdgeschwader 53 'Pik As'		
Stab		Messerschmitt Bf109G
I Gruppe		Messerschmitt Bf109G
III Gruppe		Messerschmitt Bf109G
Jagdgeschwader 77 'Herz As'		
Stab		Messerschmitt Bf109G
I Gruppe		Messerschmitt Bf109G
II Gruppe		Messerschmitt Bf109G
1° Gruppo CT, Republica Sociale Italiana		Macchi C 205

Group, which lost two of its Thunderbolts to the German fighters.

As the group headed for home, a detour was made to strafe an airfield near Bonn, but here as Maj Walter Beckham led his formation down to attack, his aircraft was hit by light Flak and he baled out — the 8th's top-scorer to date had been lost to the scourge of all pilots, and which was to bring down all too many leading USAAF fighter pilots. It was not real air combat as skill and experience were of little use against the coldly impersonal fire of the deadly light Flak at low altitude. Beckham was not alone, for two more of the unit's Thunderbolts were lost in this attack. The 22 February had cost the 353rd five P-47s!

The most successful US pilot of the day had been Maj Jack Oberhansley of the 354th who was credited with three victories to raise his score to five. One of the victories claimed by the 'Pioneer Mustangs' had been an Me410 — the only one claimed on this date. There is little doubt that this was the aircraft flown by Maj Edward Tratt, Kommandeur of II/ZG26, who was killed. Tratt had been the most successful Zerstörerflieger of the war, with 38 victories; he was also the only one to be awarded the Oak Leaves to his Knights' Cross (posthumously). The 1st Division's gunners had also blazed away at their tormentors, their claims on this date amounting to 32 and 18 probables.

This was not all, however, for the 15th Air Force had despatched 118 B-24s to attack the Regensburg-Obertraubling aircraft assembly factory, while 65 B-17s were sent to the nearby Prüfening Messerschmitt component factory. This raid was supposed to coincide with the 8th's attack on Schweinfurt, and when this was abandoned, the 15th's formations found the whole of the Luftwaffe's southern defenses waiting for them.

Bf109s from I/JG5 and I/JG27 were amongst those which were involved in the interception, as were the Macchi C205s of the 1°Gruppo CT of the RSI, which rose to the attack over Klagenfurt, Austria. One hundred and twenty fighters launched into the B-24 formations, 14 of the big Liberators going down, while the B-17s lost five. P-38s and P-47s arrived (122 of them) to provide withdrawal support, one of each type being lost, although no victories could be claimed. The 15th Air Force launched secondary attacks on Peterhausen marshalling yards, and on targets in Yugoslavia. It was by now realized that 22 February had proved an altogether less satisfactory and more costly day than the first two days of the battle.

On 23 February, it was the 8th Air Force which was grounded by adverse weather (not a bomber or fighter from England crossed the Channel) with the assault being maintained by the 15th Air Force. It launched a heavy raid against the Daimler-Benz aero-engine works at Steyr in Austria. Again, the Luftwaffe's southern defenses were ready for them, I/JG27, III/JG3, and some of the Zerstörergruppen taking part in the interception. Seventeen B-24s were lost, with the 376th Bomb Group being particularly hard hit, losing eight of its aircraft as 120 fighters again pressed home their attacks.

Two of the bombers were claimed by III/JG3's Kommandeur, Maj Walther Dahl, who also claimed one of the escorting P-38s. None of the latter were in fact lost, although they were able to claim only one Zestörer shot down (claimed as an Me210) and two probables. However, fire from the US bombers brought down several of the single-engined fighters including at least two from I/JG27,

in one of which five victory budding, Experte' Fw Otto Haas was killed.

The fighting intensifies

Argument was now approaching its climax and some of the heaviest fighting of the week was about to take place. Better weather on 24 February allowed both air forces to deploy their full striking power jointly for the first time. From England, the 3rd Division's B-17s headed unescorted for the North German/Polish border, 295 of the 304 bombers which took off attacking Rostock or a variety of targets of opportunity. The primary target was hidden under a blanket of cloud, so again radar aids were used, and no precision bomb-aiming was possible. Resistance was relatively muted, only five B-17s being lost, though 60 more suffered damage — frequently to Flak. The gunners defended the formation with vigor and in their own inimitable fashion claimed 23 shot down and 11 probables.

The Main Force headed into Central Germany on this occasion; 238 1st Division B-17s (out of a force of 266 despatched) bombed factories at Schweinfurt, while 169 of 239 B-24s raided a Bf110 plant at Gotha, and 44 more bombed Eisenach. The Fortresses suffered the moderately light loss of 11 aircraft, but 160 more suffered damage; the gunners claimed a modest ten and one probable in return. It was the Liberators which took the brunt of the defenders' efforts, meeting constant determined fighter attacks from a point 80 miles out from their targets until well into the return journey.

The 2nd Division's raid had gone wrong from the start as winds were being met of a speed and direction totally different from those forecast. As a result, the leading 'boxes' of B-24s approached the area well ahead of the rest of the force — including the substantial fighter escort. To compound the error, the bombardier in the lead aircraft of the leading formation which comprised the 389th Bomb Group suffered a failure of his oxygen supply and collapsed over his instruments, accidentally tripping the bomb release. The rest of the group at once bombed on his release.

Realizing that there had been a mistake, the following 445th Bomb Group continued alone to the target, as a result gaining the specific attentions of the interceptors, which continued to attack for an hour into the homeward leg. The results were catastrophic, 13 of the unit's 25 aircraft being shot down and nine damaged. Now also alone, the 389th paid for its error with six losses. The rest of the force were able to place their bombs accurately and effectively, but they too suffered constant attack, the 392nd Bomb Group alone losing seven aircraft with 13 damaged, total casualties to the 2nd Division amounting to no less than 33 B-24s (nearly 14 per cent of the force despatched).

Claims by gunners totalled 50 destroyed and ten probables, but the 767 escorting fighters, arriving late on the scene, were able only to claim 34 victories on this occasion, losing four P-38s, four P-47s and two P-51s, with 11 other fighters damaged; the Luftwaffe was beginning to 'claw back' the differential. All the P-47s lost seem to have fallen to I and II/JG26, these Gruppen enjoying a relatively good day with claims for four B-24s, two B-17s, four P-47s and a P-51 for the loss of six pilots. As usual, most of the victories went to the 'Experte' Oblt Waldemar Radener (36 victories) claimed a B-24 and the P-51, also cutting a B-17 out of the formation and leaving it alone and damaged. Fw Gerd Wiegand (32 victories) was credited with a B-17 and two P-47s, while other successful pilots included Walter

Matoni, Wolfgang Neu, Karl Borris, Wilhelm Mayer and Karl Willius — all big names in the Geschwader. Amongst the other defending Gruppen, JG1 was as always in the forefront of the fray, Heinz Bär adding further to his recent successes with claims for two of the B-24s.

15th Air Force in action
To the south 87 B-17s from the 15th Air Force airfields on the Foggia Plain set out for the Daimler-Puch component plant at Steyr in Austria, while 27 more began a diversionary attack on an oil refinery and torpedo works at

Fiume at the head of the Adriatic Sea. Eighty-seven P-38s and 59 P-47s provided withdrawal escort to the main force, which was led by the veteran 97th Bomb Group, and the rear was brought up by the equally experienced 2nd Bomb Group.

As had happened in Central Germany, the Luftwaffe were quick off the mark, the first interception coming 100 miles out from the target when 20 Bf109's attacked aggressively. Over the target an estimated 110 fighters appeared, including Messerschmitts from I/JG5, I/JG27, III/JG3 and II/JG53. These concentrated on the tail of the

---

MAIN AIRCRAFT TYPES OPERATING DURING 'BIG WEEK', FEBRUARY 1944

AMERICAN

Boeing B-17F and G Fortress
The more numerous of the two heavy bombers employed by the US 8th Air Force, the B-17 was a clean and graceful four-engined low-mid wing monoplane of conventional design. The engines were Wright R-1820-97 radials of 1200 hp each, these providing a high performance which featured a maximum speed of 299 mph at 25 000 ft and a tremendous service ceiling of 37 500 ft. Normal war range was 1300 miles, over which distance 6000 lb of bombs could be carried. Armament was very heavy, comprising pairs of 0.50 in Browning machine guns in dorsal, ventral and tail turrets, two or three hand-held guns in the nose and another of these weapons in each of two waist openings in the sides of the fuselage. Finally, another hand-held gun of 0.30 in or 0.50 in was available in the radio operator's compartment, to fire through a hatch in the top of the fuselage.

During early 1944 the B-17F was being supplemented by the G model. Similar in most respects to the earlier aircraft, the G featured an additional power-operated 'chin' turret under the nose with a pair of Brownings for more effective defense against head-on attack. The additional weight and drag reduced top speed to 287 mph and ceiling to 35 600 ft.

Consolidated B-24H and J Liberator
The second US heavy bomber, the B-24 was of later design than the B-17, but offered no increase over the performance of the Fortress. It was more numerous than the B-17 in the 15th Air Force, though less so in the 8th. Of slab-sided appearance, the B-24 featured a long, high aspect ratio shoulder-mounted wing and a twin fin and rudder tailplane. Power was provided by four Pratt and Whitney R-1830-65 radials of 1200 hp each which gave a top speed of 290 mph at 25 000 ft and a service ceiling of 28 000 ft. Up to 5000 lb of bombs could be carried over the very good range of 2100 miles. Armament comprised pairs of 0.50 in Browning in power-operated turrets in nose, tail, dorsal and ventral 'ball positions', plus two more hand-held guns in waist openings. In combat the B-24 tended to burn more easily than the B-17, and when damaged was inclined to break up if a wheels-up landing was attempted.

Lockheed P-38J Lightning
The oldest design amongst the US escort fighters was the unconventional P-38. A mid-wing monoplane, the P-38 possessed no fuselage as such; the nose section, carrying an armament of one 20 mm cannon four 0.50 in Browning machine guns, and the cockpit formed a 'pod' mounted on the wing center section, while the housings for the two 1425 hp Allison V-1710 in-line engines were extended into long 'booms' behind the wings which terminated in twin fins and rudders, carrying between them the single tailplane. These booms carried turbo-superchargers which boosted the power of the engines at altitude to give an excellent ceiling of 44 000 ft. When employed by an experienced pilot, differential throttling of the engines allowed the aircraft to turn very sharply, while the power available provided a very high climb rate. Top speed was 414 mph at

25 000 ft and range was 450 miles upwards, depending on the additional jettisonable fuel tanks carried, and the speed maintained.

Republic P-47D Thunderbolt
The big, heavy Thunderbolt was a low-wing monoplane featuring a semi-elliptical wing planform. Powered by a massive 2300 hp Pratt and Whitney R-2800-59 twin-row radial engine to which was fitted a very large four-bladed 'paddle'-type propeller, the aircraft reached a top speed of 428 mph at 30 000 ft, aided by a turbo-supercharger in the fuselage. Service ceiling was 42 000 ft, and range 475 miles upwards to 1700 miles. The P-47 performed best at altitude, and could generally be out-performed and outmanoeuvred by Luftwaffe fighters at lower altitudes; it was able to employ its massive seven-ton weight to outdive any fighter extant, while its massive armament of eight wing-mounted 0.50 in Brownings provided an incredible 'punch'. Later in the war it was to become the most numerous and successful US fighter-bomber — a role to which it was relegated by the supreme P-51.

Consolidated B-24J Liberator of the 93rd Bombardment Group (Heavy), US 8th Air Force

---

formation where a complete 'box' of ten of the 2nd Bomb Group's B-17s were shot down. As the bombers turned for home, Bf110s of ZG1 attacked with rockets, and when the fighters arrived to escort them home, they were directed to the rear to aid the hard-pressed 2nd.

All the three groups of 15th Air Force's P-38s swept into the attack, claiming eight Zerstörern shot down — all but two by the 82nd Fighter Group, this latter unit also adding a couple of Bf109s. Three P-38s were lost including that flown by the 1st Fighter Group's Operations Officer, Lt Col Burton McKenzie, but the force of the assault had at least

been broken. The shattered 2nd Bomb Group had lost 14 of the 16 Fortresses which failed to return, while the 97th Bomb Group in the van had suffered damage to 18 of its aircraft, though all returned. During this long and ferocious fight the gunners had claimed 25 shot down and ten probables.

Their fire had certainly had some effect, for while Luftwaffe casualties in all but the Zerstörergruppen were light, three pilots of I/JG27 had been hit, as had one in I/JG5. Oblt Alfred Hammer (26 victories), Staffelkapitän of 6/JG53, was also wounded and carried out a crash-landing

North American P-51B Mustang
Designed initially to meet a British requirement, the Mustang proved to be the best fighter of the war when fitted with a licence-built Packard V-1650-3 Rolls Royce Merlin in-line engine of 1595 hp. A slim, low-wing monoplane of clean conventional design, featuring an angular wing of laminar flow section, and an engine radiator mounted beneath the fuselage below the cockpit, the P-51B was armed with four wing-mounted 0.50 in Brownings. Although basic range was only 400 miles, when fitted with underwing drop-tanks the Mustang could accompany the bombers to Berlin and back, or could stay with them on 'shuttle' missions to Italy or Russia. With a top speed of 440 mph at 30 000 ft and a service ceiling of 41 800 ft, the Mustang out-performed most models of the Bf109 and FW190 by which it was opposed, in almost all respects, including top speed and manoeuvrability. Late in 1944 the P-51D appeared which featured a cut-down rear fuselage and a clear 'teardrop' or 'bubble' cockpit canopy, and an increased armament of six Brownings. Similar cockpit modifications were made to later models of the P-47D at this time.

GERMAN

In early 1944 the main German interceptors were still developed versions of the Messerschmitt Bf109G and the Focke-Wulf FW190A. During 1943 units engaging the unescorted US bomber formations had been equipped with versions of these aircraft featuring heavier cannon armament and increased armor protection, but these improvements to their effectiveness against the B-17s and B-24s reduced their performance and manoeuvreability, rendering them more vulnerable to the escort fighters when these appeared. Eventually it became necessary for some Gruppen to be equipped with more lightly-armed aircraft to protect the bomber-destroyers. The G-6 version of the Messerschmitt could carry an additional 20 mm MG 151 cannon in a 'gondola' fairing under each wing, or alternatively a launching tube for a 21 cm rocket to fire into the bomber 'boxes'. Performance remained basically unchanged since the introduction of the G to service in late 1942.

The FW190A-4, powered by a 2100 hp BMW 801D-2 radial, could now reach 416 mph at 20 600 ft for a brief period by fuel injection as a boost. The MG FF cannon in the wingroots had been replaced by an additional pair of faster-firing MG 151s, so that four of these cannon and two 7.9 mm machine guns were carried. The A-8 bomber-destroyer had the nose-mounted MG 17s replaced by 13 mm MG 131s, while the outboard MG 151s could be replaced by 30 mm MK 103s in underwing 'gondolas', or alternatively with 'trays', each carrying a pair of MG151s. The increased armament of even the basic A-8 reduced top speed to 408 mph, or lower if the underwing weapons packs were fitted.

The Zerstörergeschwadern were largely equipped with the Messerschmitt Bf110G, which differed little in appearance from the earlier C and D versions, but had been re-engined with more powerful 1475 hp DB605B in-line engines. Nose armament had been upgraded to a pair of 30 mm MK 108 cannon and a pair of 20 mm MG 151s, while rear defense comprised a pair of 7.9 mm MG 81s. The more powerful engines had done nothing to improve performance of the much heavier G, while service ceiling had fallen to 26 000 ft. However, the Bf110G could carry

Focke-Wulf FW190A-4 of II/Jagdgeschwader 1

additional weapons in under-fuselage packs, and up to four rocket launchers beneath the wings. When not opposed by escort fighters, the aircraft was a formidable bomber destroyer.

Messerschmitt Me410 Hornisse
Developed from the unsuccessful Me210, the Me410 was powered by a pair of 1750 hp Daimler-Benz DB 603A in-line engines. A very clean low-wing monoplane, the aircraft enjoyed a good performance with a top speed in its 'clean' version of 388 mph, at 21 980 ft and a service ceiling of 32 800 ft. The Me410A carried a forward-firing armament in the nose of four 20 mm MG 151 cannon and two 7.9 mm MG 17 machine guns, while 13 mm MG 131s were fitted in controllable 'barbettes' on the fuselage sides for rearward defense. The later B version carried six MG 151s and two MG 131s firing forward, while the A could be modified to carry an additional four MG 151s under the fuselage, or alternatively a pair of 30 mm or a single 50 mm BK 5 cannon. With a range of up to 1450 miles, the Me410 could pursue the bomber formations for as long as ammunition lasted. Despite the aircraft's high performance, it was still no match for any of the US escort fighters, and soon disappeared from service once these were able to accompany the bombers all the way to their targets. The Me410 was also quite widely used as a high-speed light bomber, as a fast reconnaissance aircraft, and occasionally as a nightfighter.

OUTSTANDING PILOTS OF THE DAY BOMBER OFFENSIVE

Because of the involvement of the escort fighters, much of the publicity for 8th Air Force personnel went to the fighter pilots, whose more glamorous and easily quantifiable achievements seized the public imagination to a greater degree than did the more mundane, but no less dangerous and admirable achievements of the bomber crews. The 8th's offensive — and even more so that of the 15th Air Force — was considerably shorter than that of Bomber Command, and as a result there were fewer pilots who returned for a second or third tour.

Consequently, it was some of the earlier group commanders, several of whom later rose to lead Bombardment Wings or even Divisions of the 8th Air Force, whose names are amongst the best known of the US bomber men.

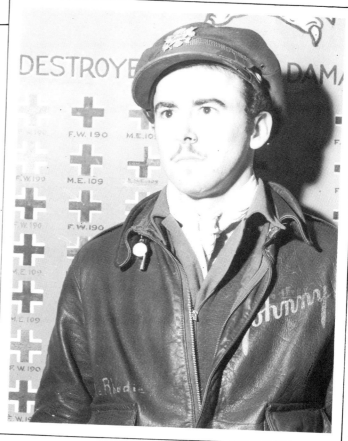

Americans

Leaders like Frank Armstrong who headed the first 8th Air Force B-17 raid on 17 August, 1942 as commander of the 97th Bomb Group. Remaining in England when his unit was transferred to North Africa, he then commanded the 306th Group until early 1943, when he joined the staff of the 1st Bombardment Wing as a Brigadier General.

Another of the 8th's first officers was Fred Castle, who volunteered to take over the 94th Bomb Group in June 1943 after service as a staff officer at the 8th's Headquarters. Promoted to lead the 4th Wing in April 1944, he became a Brigadier General in November. On 24 December, 1944, leading a major attack on targets connected with support of the German Ardennes offensive, his B-17 was hit by fighters and badly damaged. Castle took over the controls, allowing the crew to bale out, but a further attack severed one wing and he was unable to follow. He received a posthumous award of the Medal of Honor — the last such made to a member of the 8th Air Force before the war's end.

Castle was not the only senior officer to receive the supreme award. Leon

Johnson, a career West Pointer, and another 'original' of 1942, commanded the 44th Bomb Group, leading his Liberators on detachment to North Africa in summer 1943. He received his Medal of Honor for leading the unit into the inferno at Ploesti, Rumania, on 1 August — a raid which he survived. Returning to England, he took command of the 2nd Division's 14th wing, a post he held until the end of the war.

Probably the 8th's most notable operational bomber pilot was Curtis LeMay. Reaching England in December 1942 as commander of the 305th Bomb Group, his great ability ensured a swift promotion to command the 4th Bombardment Wing, which he led during the costly Regensburg raid on 17 August, 1943. Early in 1944 he moved up to command the 3rd Division, but in May 1944 was posted to the Pacific to head the fledgling

MAJ WALTER C BECKHAM, 353RD FIGHTER GROUP.

CAPT DON GENTILE, 4TH FIGHTER GROUP.

B-29 Superfortress force in the new 20th Air Force. LeMay later became famous during the 1950s as commander of the USAF's Strategic Air Command – a brilliant but abrasive leader.

Another pilot of note was Russell Wilson, who commanded the 385th Bomb Group during 1943, rose to lead the 3rd Wing in early 1944, but lost his life during the 8th Air Force's first raid on Berlin on 6 March of that year.

Amongst the US fighter pilots, by February 1944 Walter Beckham and Walker Mahurin were joint top-scorers with 16 victories each. After Beckham's loss to Flak, Mahurin regained his position as the 8th's No 1, but on 15 March was overtaken by another 56th Fighter Group pilot, Lt Bob Johnson, who pushed his own total to 19. Mahurin was shot down on 27 March by the gunner of a Do217 bomber, baling out into hostile territory. He subsequently made good his escape to England, but saw no more action over Europe, later gaining additional successes in the Pacific area, and then over Korea in the early 1950s.

LT JOHN T GODFREY, 4TH FIGHTER GROUP.

The heavy air fighting of the spring and early summer of 1944 brought a plethora of new aces, particularly as more Mustangs became available to units like the 4th Fighter Group, whose Don Gentile had gained over 21 victories by 8th April (including two with the RAF in 1942), plus seven destroyed on the ground. He then crashed his P-51 while stunting for Press photographers, and was went home on a Bond-raising tour as a hero, but in some disgrace. With him went Johnny Godfrey, his frequent wingman, who had claimed 14 and a shared plus several on the ground. Godfrey later returned for a second tour, gaining further victories, but was shot down by Flak while strafing and became a prisoner like Beckham.

Meanwhile in the 56th Johnson's score had continued to rise, and on 8 May he became top-scorer with 27 — later corrected to 28 by confirmation of a 'probable'; he too was shipped home at that stage. One of the 56th's senior pilots, Lt Col Francis 'Gabby' Gabreski, equalled

COL HUBERT 'HUB' ZEMKE (MIDDLE) WITH LT ROBERT S JOHNSON (LEFT) AND CAPT WALKER MAHURIN, 56TH FIGHTER GROUP.

Johnson's score on 5 July, but no one in the 8th ever exceeded it. Gabreski became another Flak victim shortly afterwards, but survived as a prisoner, later flying with considerable success in Korea, where he shot down several MiGs.

The 56th produced several more leading fighter pilots — not least its great commander, 'Hub' Zemke (17½ victories); others included David Schilling, who had 14½ victories by August, raising that total to 22½ and 10½ on the ground by the end of his second tour, while Fred Christensen claimed 21½.

In the rival 4th, Don Blakeslee, the unit commander, was another talented leader, who also claimed 14½ victories. Duane Beeson brought his score rapidly to over 19, while James 'Goody' Goodson claimed 15 in the air and an equal number on the ground; both became prisoners after being shot down by Flak while strafing. The 4th's Ralph 'Kid' Hofer was shot down and killed over Hungary during one of the shuttle raids to the Soviet Union on 2 July 1944; with a score of 16½, he was the highest-scoring 8th Air Force pilot to be lost in aerial combat.

The 352nd Group's George Preddy had over 25 aerial victories, including six Bf109s in one day on 6 August 1944, but was killed on Christmas Day 1944 when shot down by mistake by US anti-aircraft gunners whilst in pursuit of a Bf109 over an airfield in Western Europe. Leading his group at this time was one of the 8th's other top-scorers of the war, John C Meyer, who claimed 24 in the air and 13 on the ground. Like Gabreski, he later shot down MiGs in Korea.

For the 8th Air Force, the situation regarding supreme awards was very similar to that in the RAF. While 17 Medals of Honor went to bomber men, only one was awarded to a fighter pilot. This went to Lt Col James H Howard of the 354th Fighter Group — not even a unit of the 8th, but one attached to it from the 9th Air Force! Howard gained the award for single-handedly driving off attacking fighters from a formation of B-17s and escorting them to safety on 11 January, 1944. He had flown earlier as one of Claire Chennault's 'Flying Tigers' in Burma, with a personal score including 7¼ victories against the Japanese, and 6 against the Luftwaffe.

Germans

When the US bombers first appeared over Western Europe, they were met initially by the 'resident' Luftwaffe fighter units, JG2 and 26. These experienced and battle-hardened units were quick to find the weak points of the bombers and to develop the head-on attack. It was Obstlt Egon Mayer, the Kommodore of JG2, who did much to develop anti-bomber tactics, and who was initially the leading 'slayer' of these aircraft. Mayer, the first Luftwaffe pilot to claim a total of 100 victories entirely on the tough West

MAJ WALTER DAHL, III/JG3.

European front, a total he reached on 5 February 1944, was killed in action with US fighters less than a month later on 2 March with his score at 102, including 25 four-engined types.

Mayer's opposite number at the head of JG26, Oberst Josef Priller, had raised his score in the West to 101 by the end of 1944. However, once the 8th Air Force began attacking targets in Germany, their route to the target frequently lay further north, into the area defended by JG1, and the second North German-based Geschwader formed from it, JG11. Although initially less experienced than the units in France, these Geschwadern were soon building up big scores of B-17s and B-24s shot down. Indeed immediately after Mayer's death II/JG11's Lt Hugo Frey moved into the 'top spot' with 26 four-engined aircraft shot down out of 32 victories; he too was killed in action before March was through.

First units to be brought back from other fronts for Home Defense were the Gruppen of JG3, and it was this Geschwader which produced many of the leading 'Experten' against the

OBERSTLT JOSEF 'PIPS' PRILLER, KOMMODORE OF JG26.

bombers. JG53, which reached South Germany after service in Italy and Tunisia, where its pilots had already fought the Mediterranean-based US bombers, also did well, as did the ex-'Wilde Sau' JG300, which with JG301 and 302 became Home Defense day units during the spring and summer.

Oberst Walter Dahl, who had returned from Russia with III/JG3, subsequently formed a special composite anti-bomber Geschwader before becoming Kommodore

of JG300. He ended the war with 36 heavy bombers amongst his 128 victories, a total equalled by Maj Georg-Peter Eder (78 victories), but bettered by JG53's Lt Herbert Rollwage, top-scorer against the big bombers. Rollwage included 44 of these amongst his 102 victories, many of which had been claimed over Malta, Tunisia and Italy with the Geschwader's II Gruppe. Other top-scorers in this particular area of combat included Oblt Konrad Bauer of JG3 and 300 (68 victories) and Maj Anton Hackl (192 victories) who served in many units, replacing Dahl as the head of JG300 at the end of the war; both these pilots claimed 32 'heavies'. Four more pilots claimed 25 or more four-engines, while another eight claimed more than 20, amongst them Obstlt Heinz Bär of JG1, who included 21 amongst his 220 victories, as well as a considerable number of 8th Air Force fighters.

LT HERBERT ROLLWAGE, II/JG53.

During the first nine months of 1944 about 50 leading 'Experten' fell on the West Front and on Home Defense, many of them to the escort fighters of the 8th. These included the leading Zerstörer Experten, Tratt and Kiel, as already mentioned, and such Geschwader-kommodore as JG3's Oberst Wolf-Dietrich Wilcke (162 victories) and his successor, Maj Friedrich-Karl 'Tutti' Müller (140 victories), Maj Kurt Ubben (110 victories) who had replaced Mayer at the head of JG2, and JG1's Oberst Walter Oesau (123 victories). The loss of such pilots illustrates clearly the extent to which the US fighters had gained the ascendancy over the Jagdwaffe during 1944.

near Vienna, while several other losses were suffered by the attacking units.

This day (24 February) had cost the combined American air forces 65 bombers and 13 fighters — heavy losses, but acceptable as the attacks seemed to have been in the main effective. Next day dawned clear with good visibility and the first fully co-ordinated attack was launched from England and Italy on the aircraft industry in Southern Germany. Regensburg was again the main target, 267 of 290 3rd Division B-17s raiding this town and its environs, while 46 more B-17s and 103 B-24s headed for the same target from the south, effectively splitting the effort of the more immediately-placed defending units. A further 268 B-17s were despatched by the 1st Division to nearby Augsburg, 196 reaching this target and 50 more bombing Stuttgart, while the 2nd Division's 196 B-24s were targeted with Fürth, 172 making the attack.

It was the thrust from Italy which took the brunt of the defensive effort on this occasion, as it headed for the Prüfening factory complex yet again. The B-17s led (31 from the 301st Bomb Group and ten from the 2nd) but they were first attacked before they had even crossed the Alps, some 100 Italy-based fighters intercepting near Fiume. Ten of the 301st's aircraft had already aborted, and now 11 more were shot down. The remaining 24 reached the target and bombed through Flak, but were then attacked by more fighters for a further half-hour, three 2nd Bomb Group aircraft going down. During this ordeal, the 301st Group's gunners claimed 31 attacking fighters shot down and six probables, whilst those of the 2nd claimed nine more.

Behind them came the B-24s which also came under heavy attack, the leading 450th Bomb Group encountering the first 15 interceptors while still 300 miles from the target. In a long running fight, the group's gunners claimed three of the attackers shot down before going in to bomb the Prüfening factory with a fair degree of accuracy. Two of the Liberators were shot down while over the target, 20 more were damaged by Flak, and two severely crippled. As the unit turned for home, the fighters struck again and the two

limping stragglers were also shot down. Behind came the 449th Group, which suffered three more losses.

One of the missing aircraft was 'Pistol Packin' Mama', which had two engines put out of action before going in and making her bombing run. As this Group also turned for home, the gunners in 'Pistol Packin' Mama' continued to fight off the Messerschmitts until the crew had claimed a record 15 shot down in one action. Sgt Paul Biggart was credited with four of these before he was killed, but the rest of the crew survived to bale out, and to make their way safely to Allied lines. Twelve more B-24s were lost by other units, half of them by the 451st Bomb Group, whose gunners claimed 16 and three probables from the 91 and 17 probables credited to 15th Air Force gunners on this date.

The escorting fighters (85 P-38s and 40 P-47s) again had relatively little part to play, 1st Fighter Group Lightning pilots claiming two Bf110s shot down and one probable against a loss by the three groups involved of three P-38s and a single P-47. The raid had been very effective, however, and the Prüfening factory was totally smashed, with full production not being resumed there for four months.

The factory had received further bombs from the 8th Air Force's 3rd Division bombers, which also attacked the Obertraubling plant. These Fortress crews met considerably less opposition than their 15th Air Force counterparts (only 12 B-17s being lost) although 83 were damaged; they claimed 13 and one probable in return. The Augsburg force suffered one more loss at 13, but had 172 bombers damaged, while the B-24s lost only six on their raid to Fürth, with some 45 more damaged. Claims by gunners in these two divisions were much more modest, their combined total amounting only to ten destroyed and six probables.

VICTORY CLAIMS BY USAAF FIGHTER GROUPS DURING 'BIG WEEK'

8th Air Force		15th Air Force	
56th Fighter Group	52	82nd Fighter Group	8
354th Fighter Group	45	14th Fighter Group	5
357th Fighter Group	21	Total	13
78th Fighter Group	19		
4th Fighter Group	16		
352nd Fighter Group	14		
353rd Fighter Group	11		
20th Fighter Group	8		
355th Fighter Group	8		
361st Fighter Group	8		
359th Fighter Group	7		
55th Fighter Group	2		
356th Fighter Group	1		
362nd Fighter Group	1		
Total	153		

USAAF LOSSES DURING 'BIG WEEK'

8TH AIR FORCE

BOMBERS		FIGHTERS	
44th Bomb Group	6	4th Fighter Group	2
91st Bomb Group	10	20th Fighter Group	3
92nd Bomb Group	10	55th Fighter Group	2
93rd Bomb Group	3	56th Fighter Group	1
96th Bomb Group	5	78th Fighter Group	1
100th Bomb Group	5	353rd Fighter Group	5
303rd Bomb Group	6	354th Fighter Group	3
305th Bomb Group	13	356th Fighter Group	1
351st Bomb Group	5	357th Fighter Group	8
379th Bomb Group	6	358th Fighter Group	2
381st Bomb Group	8	359th Fighter Group	1
385th Bomb Group	2	361st Fighter Group	2
388th Bomb Group	2	362nd Fighter Group	1
389th Bomb Group	13		
390th Bomb Group	1	Total	32
392nd Bomb Group	1	(5 P-38s, 16 P-47s, 11 P-51s)	
401st Bomb Group	3		
445th Bomb Group	16		
446th Bomb Group	3		
447th Bomb Group	2		
448th Bomb Group	3		
452nd Bomb Group	1		
453rd Bomb Group	3		
457th Bomb Group	4		
482nd Bomb Group	1		
Total	132		

15TH AIR FORCE (INCOMPLETE)

BOMBERS		FIGHTERS	
2nd Bomb Group	17	1st Fighter Group	4
301st Bomb Group	16	14th Fighter Group	0
376th Bomb Group	8	82nd Fighter Group	3
449th Bomb Group	3	325th Fighter Group	2
450th Bomb Group	4		
451st Bomb Group	6	Total	9
454th Bomb Group	4	(7 P-38s, 2 P-47s)	
Other losses	34		
Total	92		

Totals for both air forces: 224 Bombers, 41 Fighters

Total	265

The escort force, massively strong again at 73 P-38s, 687 P-47s and 139 P-51s, made 28 confirmed claims, losing a P-47 and two P-51s, with six more Thunderbolts damaged. Honors for the day went to the Mustang units, the 354th and 357th Fighter Groups each claiming seven victories. In the former unit, Lt Charles Gumm, the group's first acc, gained his sixth and last success: he was killed in a take-off accident a few days later. One of the higher-scoring units on this occasion was the 4th Fighter Group, the pilots of which claimed five FW190s shot down, three of these being credited to rising 'stars' Duane Beeson, Vermont Garrison and Don Gentile.

Amongst the defending units II and III/JG26 had both intercepted the 8th Air Force formations, as had II/JG1. In the latter unit, Heinz Bär was again to the fore, adding a B-24, a B-17 and two more Fortresses as probables to bring his 'Big Week' score to ten and two probables. In II/JG26 Oblt Waldmar Radener had another good day, being credited with a B-24 and a probable B-17. Other pilots of this Gruppe added two more B-17s.

Throughout this period, RAF fighters and elements of the US 9th Air Force in England had been raiding airfields and coastal targets along the Channel and North Sea coasts in support of the bombing efforts. On 24 February, 9th Air Force Martin B-26 Marauder medium bombers attacked targets on the Belgian coast, losing four of their number in the process, three of them to I/JG26; two of these were credited to Oblt Karl Willius. JG26 lost only two pilots on this date, but one of these was a III Gruppe 'Experte', Hpt Rudolf Leuschel (eight victories).

Against the Regensburg and Augsburg attacks, I and II/JG27, III/JG3 and I/JG5 were amongst those units involved, the JG27 Gruppen losing at least five Bf109s, but in III/JG3 Maj Walther Dahl had added four more of the bombers and a P-38 to his score during these two days of heavy fighting to raise his tally for the week to eight. The Italians also became engaged with the 15th Air Force effort, 12 Macchi C205s engaging B-24s over the Alps; one bomber was claimed for the loss of Sottotenente Tombolini, who was shot down and killed.

From Italy too, 15th Air Force formations were making diversionary raids, 27 B-17s attacking Pola and Klagenfurt, Austria while B-24s attacked several marshalling yards. These secondary strikes suffered an additional six losses, including one Fortress shot down over Klagenfurt by Oberst Johannes Steinhoff, Kommodore of JG77, for his 166th victory.

Assessing 'Big Week'
Next day the weather clamped right down with winter grimness, and 'Big Week' was at an end. In the five days of operations, the combined US Air Forces and RAF Bomber Command had undertaken 8148 bombing sorties, dropping 19 177 tons of bombs. Of these the 8th Air Force had contributed 3300 sorties and 6000 tons. Sixty-eight per cent of the factory buildings associated with the German aircraft industry had been destroyed or damaged, and the ball-bearing industry had also been damaged. These results were not as devastating as the figures may indicate, however, for the bombs carried by the Americans were not large and powerful enough to destroy the all-important machine tools; when the debris and rubble was cleared, most of these were still useable. German production of fighters was indeed sub-

stantially disrupted, and during the month following 'Big Week' fell way below targets. However, at the time, dispersal of production was already underway, and was greatly speeded thereafter; and by early summer aircraft were again flowing off the production lines in full spate.

It was the fighting in the air which was most noteworthy and significant. Already in January, the number of Luftwaffe defending fighters lost to the US escorts had reached worrying levels. In February, as the American fighters penetrated even deeper into Reich airspace, they rose alarmingly. As throughout 1943, the gunners in the bomber formations had claimed massively — well over 400 during 'Big Week' alone — but it was the Mustangs, Lightnings and Thunderbolts that were taking the real toll. During February as a whole, there were 12 major US bomber incursions against which the Luftwaffe fighters flew 4399 sorties, 808 by the twin-engined Zerstörern, the rest by the single-engined Gruppen.

A total of 529 of the US raiders were claimed shot down with another 154 probables, while the Flak defenses added claims for a further 120 shot down and 17 probables. But 355 fighters were lost in return for these claims, and 155 more were damaged; amongst the losses were several lesser 'Experten' — pilots of experience and training, actual or potential formation leaders who became increasingly rare as the year wore on.

During February, it had been the Zerstörergruppen which had suffered particularly heavily. Already Tratt, their most successful exponent had been a victim of 'Big Week'; on the last day of the month Hpt Johannes Kiel, Kommandeur of III/ZG76 was lost. Credited with 21 four-engined bombers and a holder of the Knights' Cross, he had been second only to Tratt in successes. With his death his unit was disbanded, so heavy had been its losses — and the survivors were amalgamated into I Gruppe. The Zerstörern were then withdrawn to South Germany and Austria, beyond the range of most 8th Air Force fighters — just as the strength of 15th Air Force fighter escorts became fully effective. By mid-year, the cost had been just too high and most of the survivors had to be converted to single-engined types.

By the close of 'Big Week', another milestone was passed, for with the addition of further units, 8th Air Force had at last overtaken RAF Bomber Command in numbers, if not in load-carrying capacity. Following the attacks on the ball-bearing and aircraft industries, the oil and synthetic oil industries became a priority target. This was particularly so for 15th Air Force, which began a sustained campaign against the Ploesti oilfields in Rumania. With increasing numbers of P-51s becoming available, the US fighters began a sustained battle against the German fighters which lasted throughout the spring and early summer. Not only did Luftwaffe losses rise, but the numbers of its really great fighter pilots were increasingly depleted.

Helping the land campaign

In the last weeks prior to the Normandy invasion, much of the 8th Air Force's efforts were diverted to tactical and transportation targets in France in support of the forthcoming cross-Channel operations. The actions of June and July 1944 threw many Luftwaffe fighter units into the battle zone where their losses were severe in the extreme. General-leutnant Adolf Galland, Inspector of the Day Fighters, constantly attempted to build up a force of fighters to make a really sustained attack on the bombers and inflict devastatingly severe casualties.

Each time the needs of the front and the orders of his superior, Göring, frustrated his plans. Everything was tried by the Luftwaffe; special attack units of heavily armed and armored Sturm (assault) fighters (usually FW190s) were formed to make head-on attacks on the bomber 'boxes', while supporting Gruppen of more lightly-armed Bf109s attempted to hold off the escorts. Sometimes these tactics achieved success, but steadily their losses rose; also, some units were formed of pilots in disgrace, who were given the opportunity to redeem themselves with close attacks dedicated to end by ramming if necessary — anything to obtain the objective of downing the bombers.

After the invasion the massively strong 8th Air Force resumed the strategic role, bombing armaments factories, synthetic fuel and chemical plants and other war industries throughout Germany. Some raids were made from both England and Italy which landed at airfields in the Soviet Union before shuttling back to their bases, further raids being undertaken during the return flight. During Summer 1944, the 15th Air Force concentrated much of its efforts against targets in Hungary, Rumania, Bulgaria and Czechoslovakia and in supporting the invasion of Southern France in August.

However, as the Red Army advanced inexorably from the East, most of these targets disappeared, and from September raids were concentrated on Austria and South Germany. With the reduction in Luftwaffe fighter activity following the Normandy invasions, the USAAF was joined with growing frequency by big formations of RAF heavy bombers, now operating by day in the less dangerous skies. At first escorted as far as was possible by Spitfires, these were soon replaced by RAF-flown Mustangs as a growing number of squadrons were re-equipped with these longer ranging aircraft, and new wings were formed specifically for bomber-escort duties.

By late 1944 the Luftwaffe fighter arm had been all but defeated by day, and could do little to disrupt the attacks which were devastating every corner of the Reich. The three Allied strategic air forces could now put up to 3000 heavy bombers into the air if they so wished. Towards the end of 1944, though the radical new German jet fighter, the Messerschmitt Me262, began to appear — an aircraft with a performance so high that the Allied escorts had the greatest difficulty in countering it. Not until February 1945 did the jets start to operate in strength however, but then they began to take an increasing toll of Allied bombers, the loss ratio rising alarmingly during March. But it was too late. A few days before the final unconditional surrender, the bombers stopped operating. It had been a long, costly war; the chances of survival for US bomber crews had been little better than that of their counterparts in RAF Bomber Command — but the battle was over; there were no worthwhile targets left.

To employ the idiom of the war years, for the American bomber force the arrival of the long-range escort fighters had been the end of the beginning; 'Big Week' had been the beginning of the end. Much was claimed at the time and subsequently for the achievements of the strategic bombers. Certainly they had played their part in the overall progress of the war. Certainly some of their activities — notably the campaign against oil — had been tellingly effective. But in Europe at least they had undoubtedly failed to live up to the independently war-winning hopes of the more sanguine of their proponents.

CHAPTER TEN

THE GREAT MARIANAS 'TURKEY SHOOT'

JUNE – JULY 1944

Overleaf

During the afternoon of 19 June, 1944, the First Battle of the Philippine
Sea is already well advanced. A fourth and final strike has been launched by the Japanese carriers, but part
of this force comprising aircraft of the 601st Kokutai from the carrier *Zuikaku*, have spotted a
passing search flight of VT-16 Grumman TBF Avengers and escorting F6F-3 Hellcat fighters from
VF-16. Ten elderly Mitsubishi A6M2 Zero fighter-bombers
break off to attack. In the next few minutes seven will be claimed shot
down and two more probably so for no loss to the American aircraft involved.

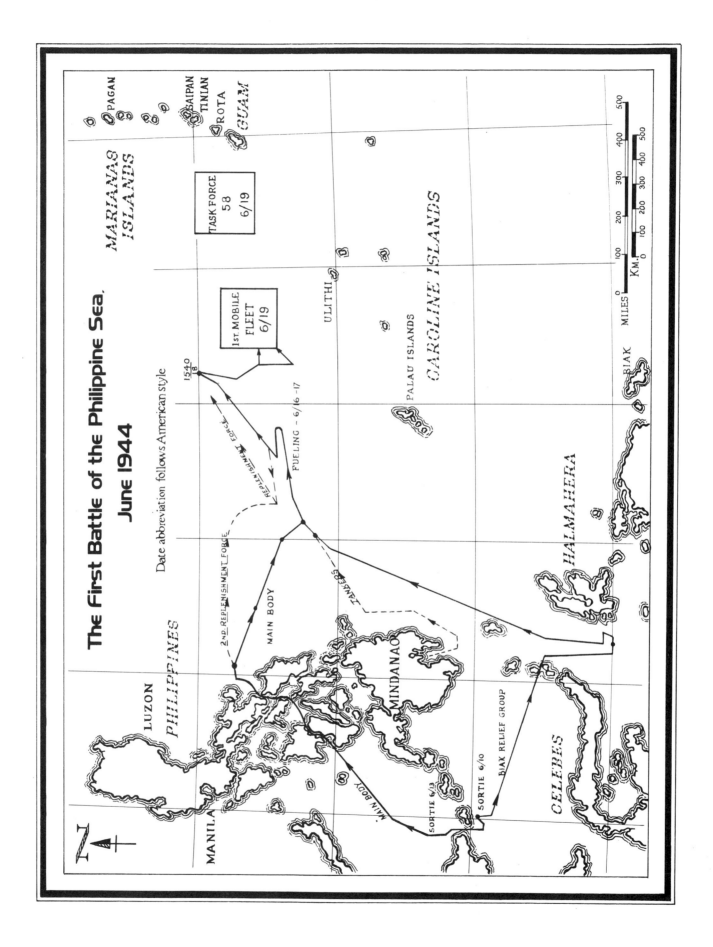

The First Battle of the Philippine Sea,
June 1944

Date abbreviation follows American style

MARIANAS
ISLANDS

PAGAN

SAIPAN
TINIAN
ROTA
GUAM

TASK FORCE
58
6/19

1st. MOBILE
FLEET
6/19

154-0
8

ULITHI

CAROLINE ISLANDS

PALAU ISLANDS

BIAK

REPLENISHMENT FORCE

FUELING ~ 6/16-17

2ND REPLENISHMENT FORCE

MAIN BODY

TANKERS

HALMAHERA

LUZON

PHILIPPINES

MINDANAO

BIAK RELIEF GROUP

SORTIE 6/10

MANILA

MAIN BODY

SORTIE 6/13

CELEBES

N

KM.

MILES

500

400

300

200

100

0

500

400

300

200

100

0

June 1944 proved one of the high points of the war for the Allies, both in the West and the East. On the fifth day of the month, in Italy Rome fell while next day saw the great Anglo-American landings in Normandy. Before the month was out the mighty Soviet summer offensive was launched, crushing the German Army Group Center, and driving the Axis forces from their remaining hold on Soviet soil. In Burma the fighting at Kohima and Imphal was going well for the British, while in the main Pacific zone the initiative had passed firmly to the Americans — particularly to their far-ranging force of fast new aircraft carriers.

After initial action in late 1943, the carrier task groups had — with some trepidation — launched an air strike on the main Japanese Pacific Fleet base of Truk during February 1944. The results had exceeded expectations, leading to a repeat attack in April, followed by sorties over Marcus and Wake Islands during May, while a US Army force landed on Biak on 27 February. Attacks on bases in the Marianas Islands were also made during the month, following which Consolidated B-24 Liberator bombers of the 7th Air Force, joined on occasions by others from 13th Air Force, began regular attacks on the Carolines and Marianas, and on Truk.

The very success of these daring raids encouraged the US High Command to take a great gamble. Raids on the Japanese Home Islands were about to be commenced by the new Boeing B-29 Superfortress bomber from bases in China. However, the problems of supply and base security here meant that alternative bases on Pacific islands offered a better alternative.

Consequently, it was planned to leap forward 1000 miles, bypassing Truk and the Carolines, and to land in the Marianas which was well-suited for US purposes. It was appreciated that such an operation would undoubtedly bring out the main Japanese fleet in force, but now the Americans felt confident in their strength to meet, bring to battle and defeat this threat. As a result Operation *Forager* was put in train, designed to carry out the invasion and it led directly to the greatest carrier battle of the war.

The operation takes shape

The great naval force assembled to undertake the operation — Task Force 58 — was commanded by Vice Admiral Marc Mitscher, and overall command of the venture was in the hands of Admiral Raymond Spruance, US Fifth Fleet. Mitscher's force was split into five Task Groups numbered 58.1–4 and 58.7, all but the last of these being formed around groups of carriers; TG 58.7 had as its nucleus seven fast battleships. This striking force thus comprised in total seven fleet carriers (CVs), eight light carriers (CVLs), seven battleships, four heavy cruisers, nine light cruisers, four anti-aircraft cruisers and 65 destroyers — a truly formidable armada of fighting ships. In addition to provide close support and anti-submarine patrol for the main convoy of invasion transports were two groups of escort carriers (CVEs), which carried 28 Grumman FM-2 Wildcats and 71 TBM-1C Avengers.

The carriers had aboard a total of 470 Grumman F6F-3 Hellcat fighters, 165 Curtiss SB2C Helldiver and 57 Douglas SBD-5 Dauntless dive-bombers, 199 Grumman TBF and TBM Avenger torpedo-bombers, and three Vought F4U-2 Corsair nightfighters. Also present were four further escort carriers, two loaded with replacement aircraft and two which carried the 73 Republic P-47D Thunderbolt

fighters of the 19th and 73rd Squadrons of the 318th Fighter Group, US 7th Air Force, which were to be flown off as soon as landing grounds were available ashore. In reserve at Eniwetok Atoll were five more CVEs with 68 F6F-3s, 28 FM-2s and 39 TBMs; and over 100 more replacement aircraft were also to hand.

The units aboard the carriers of Task Force 58 were well trained and led by experienced leaders. The F6F-3 Hellcat of the fighter units (VF) was now thoroughly battle-tested, and was in many respects superior to its main adversary, the Mitsubishi A6M5 Zero (Allied codename 'Zeke 52'); it was certainly faster, harder-hitting and much more rugged. It also had an excellent range, and good bomb-carrying capabilities.

The dive-bomber squadrons (VB) had now been re-equipped to a large extent with the big SB2C Helldiver — a powerful aircraft carrying its bombload internally, but difficult to fly; its nickname 'The Beast' accurately reflected the pilots' view of it. TG 58.3's fleet carriers still deployed the older, slower, but handy and well-beloved SBD Dauntless in its final Mark -5 version. All carriers had aboard the excellent and reliable Grumman TBF-1 Avenger (or its TBM version, built by General Motors). Capable of level or torpedo bombing with this aircraft, the torpedo-bomber (VT) crews were well satisfied with their mount. Most fleet carriers included a detachment of radar-equipped F6F 3N nightfighters, but on *Enterprise* alone were based a handful of the similarly equipped F4U-2 Corsair.

The fighters were greatly aided in their tasks by a radar controlled system adopted by the US Navy directly from that employed by the RAF during the Battle of Britain. Equipment of the escort carriers differed in that their VF units flew the latest General Motors-built version of the older F4F Wildcat — the FM-2.

Whilst the US Navy realized it would face the bulk of the Japanese carrier forces, the size of the land-based air force in the area had been considerably underestimated. Vice

LATE MODEL SBD-5 DAUNTLESS SERVED WITH TASK GROUP 58.3 IN THE MARIANAS, THIS FAITHFUL OLD DIVE-BOMBER PROVING TO BE ONE OF THE MOST RELIABLE CARRIER-BORNE AIRCRAFT OF THE BATTLE.

US TASK FORCE 58, JUNE 1944 COMMANDER ADMIRAL MARC MITSCHER		
Task Group 58.1 **Commander Rear Admiral J J Clark**	**Task Group 58.2** **Commander Rear Admiral Alfred Montgomery**	**Task Group 58.3** **Commander Rear Admiral John Reeves**
CARRIER	**CARRIER**	**CARRIER**
USS *Hornet* (CV-12) Air Group 2 – 36 Grumman F6F-3 and F6F-3N; 33 Curtiss SB2C; 19 Grumman TBF, 1 TBM	USS *Bunker Hill* (CV-17) Air Group 8 – 37 Grumman F6F-3 and 3 F6F-3N; 33 Curtiss SB2C; 13 Grumman TBF, 5 TBM	USS *Enterprise* (CV-6) Air Group 10 – 31 Grumman F6F-3; 3 Vought F4U-2; 23 Douglas SBD-5; 8 Grumman TBF, 7 TBM
USS *Yorktown* (CV-10) Air Group 1 – 41 Grumman F6F3 and 5 F6F-3N; 31 Curtiss SB2C; 1 Grumman TBF, 17 TBM	USS *Wasp* (CV-18) Air Group 14 – 34 Grumman F6F-3 and 5F6F-3N; 32 Curtiss SB2C; 18 Grumman TBF	USS *Lexington* (CV-16) Air Group 16 – 37 Grumman F6F-3 and 4 F6F-3N; 34 Douglas SBD-5; 19 Grumman TBF, 1 TBM
USS *Belleau Wood* (CVL-24) Air Group 24 – 26 Grumman F6F-3, 3 Grumman TBF, 6 TBM	USS *Monterey* (CVL-26) Air Group 28 – 34 Grumman F6F-3; 8 Grumman TBM	USS *Princeton* (CVL-23) Air Group 27 – 24 Grumman F6F-3; 9 Grumman TBM
USS *Bataan* (CVL-29) Air Group 50 – 24 Grumman F6F-3; 9 Grumman TBM	USS *Cabot* (CVL-28) Air Group 31 – 24 Grumman F6F-3; 1 Grumman TBF, 8 TBM	USS *San Jacinto* (CVL-30) Air Group 51 – 24 Grumman F6F-3; 8 Grumman TBM
Supported by:	Supported by:	Supported by:
3 Heavy Cruisers 2 Anti-aircraft Cruisers 14 Destroyers	1 Heavy Cruiser 3 Light Cruisers 1 Anti-aircraft Cruiser 12 Destroyers	3 Light Cruisers 12 Destroyers

Task Group 58.4 **Commander Rear Admiral William Harrill**		
CARRIER	To provide close support and anti-submarine patrol for the main convoy of invasion transports were two groups of escort carriers, which carried 98 Grumman FM-2 Wildcats and 71 Grumman TBM-1C Avengers. These were:	
USS *Essex* (CV-9) Air Group 15 – 38 Grumman F6F-3 and 6 F6F-3N; 36 Curtiss SB2C; 15 Grumman TBF,5 TBM	**Task Group 52.11**	**Task Group 52.14**
USS *Cowpens* (CVL-25) Air Group 25 – 23 Grumman F6F-3; 3 Grumman TBF, 6 TBM	USS *Gambier Bay* (CVE-73); USS *Kitkun Bay* (CVE-71); USS *Nehenta Bay* (CVE-74)	USS *Fanshawe Bay* (CVE-70) USS *Kalinin Bay* (CVE-68) USS *Midway* (CVE-63) USS *White Plains* (CVE-66)
USS *Langley* (CVL-27) Air Group 32 – 23 Grumman F6F-3; 2 Grumman TBF, 7 TBM	**Task Group 58.7**	
Supported by:		
3 Light Cruisers 1 Anti-aircraft Cruiser 14 Destroyers	7 Fast Battleships 4 Heavy Cruisers 13 Destroyers	

Also present were USS *Brenton* (CVE-23) and USS *Capabee* (CVE-12), carrying replacement aircraft, and USS *Manila Bay* and USS *Natona Bay* carrying 73 Republic P-47D Thunderbolt fighters of the 318th Fighter Group USAAF.

Admiral Kakuji Kakuta, Commander of the 1st Air Fleet, controlled some 1000 aircraft based in the Marianas, Carolines, on Iwo Jima and at Truk; his headquarters were located at Tinian in the Marianas. This formidable force — most of it had arrived in the past two months — included the 201st, 202nd, 203rd, 253rd, 261st, 263rd, 265th, 321st and 343rd Kokutais. However, the US landings at Biak in late May had resulted in 118 fighters, 40 bombers and 8 reconnaissance aircraft from this force being ordered down to north-western New Guinea and Halmahera Island to launch attacks on the beachhead area, leaving several units crucially weakened by their departure.

Task Force 58 sailed from Majuro on 6 June (the day of the Normandy landings) while USN PB4Y Liberators stepped up reconnaissance sorties over the Marianas, their USAAF B-24 counterparts redoubling their attacks on Truk by night.

Since a dawn sweep was now recognized by the Japanese to be a prelude to an invasion, allowing them the rest of the hours of daylight to find the American vessels and launch counter-strikes, Mitscher decided upon an afternoon attack with which to open proceedings. Thus at 1300 hours on 11 June, 1944, the first of 211 Hellcats and eight guiding Avengers took off on a counter-air sweep, an action designed either to bring up the enemy air force to fight, or to destroy its aircraft on the ground. To this purpose, TG

THE JAPANESE MOBILE FLEET, JUNE 1944

CARRIER DIVISION 1	CARRIER DIVISION 2	CARRIER DIVISION 3
Carrier	**Carrier**	**Carrier**
Shokaku	*Hiyo*	*Chitose*
Taiho	*Junyo*	*Chiyoda*
Zuikaku	*Ryuho*	*Zuiho*
Air Units	**Air Units**	**Air Units**
601st Kokutai	652nd Kokutai	653rd Kokutai
70 Mitsubishi A6M5	45 Mitsubishi A6M5	45 Mitsubishi A6M5
70 Yokosuka D4Y	27 Mitsubishi A6M2	45 Mitsubishi A6M2
51 Nakajima B6N	27 Yokosuka D4Y	9 Nakajima B6N
	27 Aichi D3A	17 Nakajima B5N
	18 Nakajima B6N	
Supported by:	**Supported by:**	**Supported by:**
1 Battleship	1 Battleship	4 Battleships
1 Light Cruiser	1 Heavy Cruiser	4 Heavy Cruisers
7 Destroyers	8 Destroyers	1 Light Cruiser
		8 Destroyers

58.1's aircraft made for Guam Island, TG 58.2's for Saipan and TG 58.3's for Tinian, while TG 58.4 was also targeted for Tinian, and for the smaller island of Pegan.

These attacks proved devastatingly effective. The Hellcat pilots swept in over their targets between 60 and 90 minutes after taking off, catching the Japanese interceptors at a disadvantage as they attempted to gain altitude to oppose the strike. The greatest execution was made around Guam; here VF-2's pilots claimed 23 fighters shot down, sweeping the board so clean that the following aircraft of VF-24 were able to claim only a single A6M. Cdr William A Dean, VF-2's CO, was credited with three victories, as was Lt (jg) John T Wolf.

Over Tinian VF-10 encountered the ten A6Ms of Sento 316 of the 301st Ku, plus two other fighters identified as Army Nakajima Ki43s (Oscars). The American pilots claimed eight of these, three by Ensign Les Gray alone; Sento 316 was composed of ex-floatplane pilots, hastily retrained to fly the Zero *at night*. They had only arrived on the island nine days earlier, and paid dearly for their lack of experience. None of them returned. Straying from their designated target area of Saipan, TG 58.2's VF-28 also found 'trade' over Tinian, claiming to have shot down six Mitsubishi G4M (Betty) bombers here, while over Saipan VF-31 claimed 13 and two probables, plus four destroyed on the ground.

In the same area Cdr David McCampbell, the Air Group Commander (CAG) from *Essex* who was flying with VF-15, spotted a lone A6M which he shot down for his first victory. Most of the victims here were from the 265th Ku, which reported the loss of nearly all its 12 A6Ms over Saipan. VF-51's Hellcats caught and shot down two 'snoopers' (reconnaissance aircraft searching for the American vessels). Later in the afternoon more of VF-2's fighters on defensive patrol (CAP — Carrier Air Patrol) over the Fleet intercepted and shot down three more G4M bombers.

This unit subsequently flew a second sweep over Guam, claiming on this occasion seven more A6Ms and two Army Ki44s (Tojos), plus a Nakajima J1N1 (Irving) twin-engined heavy fighter; these latter aircraft were being operated from the island by the 321st Ku, a second of their fighters being claimed by VF-2 late in the evening during a further CAP. This brought total US claims for the day to 81 shot down

and 29 destroyed on the ground for the loss of 21 Hellcats; six of the US pilots had been recovered.

During the next three days relatively little opposition was met; on 12 June a small convoy was seen leaving Saipan for Japan by scouting aircraft; two air attacks were launched against this during that day and one on the next. Ten cargo vessels, a torpedo-boat and three submarine chasers were sunk. After one attack early on the same day, fighters of VF-10 from *Enterprise* spotted two twin-engined 'snoopers' identified as a G4M and a Kawasaki Ki48 (Lily) and both were claimed shot down, but the day was to bring only about a dozen victories in total.

Sweeps and strafes were flown against the various Japanese airfields, but not without cost. Over Saipan's Aslito airfield on 13 June, *Enterprise* lost two VT-10 Avengers and a VF-10 Hellcat to AA, while VT-16 Avengers from *Lexington* attacking the island with some of the first rocket projectiles to be employed in the Pacific, lost their commanding officer, Cdr Robert H Isley to the same cause. To back up the efforts of the carrier aircraft, 26 Air Force B-24s raided Truk in daylight on this date.

The Japanese retaliate

It was not until 13 June that the Japanese reacted fully to the US presence in the Marianas. The Mobile Fleet appeared to be very powerful, and plans for Operation *A* — a sustained battle with the US fleet — had long been in preparation. Although Admiral Soemu Toyoda was Commander-in-Chief, he was aboard his flagship in Hiroshima Bay. The battle would rest in the hands of Vice Admiral Jisaburo Ozawa, Commander of the 1st Mobile Fleet and 3rd Fleet. His command included all nine available aircraft carriers and 64 other vessels, including the mighty battleships *Yamato* and *Musashi*, each of 74 000 tons displacement and mounting nine 18.1 inch guns as main armament — the biggest and most powerful battleships ever built. Ozawa was required to co-ordinate his action with Vice Admiral Kakuta's land-based air power — unaware that this was already being devastated by the Hellcats.

Ozawa divided his force into two parts: Van Force, under Vice Admiral Takeo Kurita, which was to lead the way and draw on itself any incoming air attacks, and Main

Force. Van Force included Rear Admiral Sueo Obayashi's Carrier Division 3 (CarDiv 3). This was indeed a formidable force, and Ozawa was confident that if he could bring the Americans to battle, he could win, providing he found them first. This was because his lighter, unarmored aircraft enjoyed a longer range than their US counterparts, and could hit the opposition before they could hit him. It was, however, in the air that he was at his weakest. Now the Japanese would suffer for the attrition inflicted on their highly trained carrier groups during the long, costly Solomons campaign.

Following the Japanese withdrawal from Rabaul earlier in 1944 all the carrier air groups had had to be reformed, and they were full of new and inexperienced men. There had been little time for training, and apart from a few experienced formation leaders most crews could do little more than fly their aircraft and land on the carriers. This was particularly the case with the newer 652nd and 653rd Ku, which were based on the carriers of CarDivs 2 and 3 respectively, and which had been formed only in the last three–four months. Only CarDiv 1's 601st Ku was fully equipped with the most modern types available; the Yokosuka D4Y (Judy) dive-bomber and Nakajima B6N (Jill) torpedo-bomber were excellent aircraft, but the Mitsubishi A6M5, the latest version of the Zero, was not a match for the Hellcat in other than manoeuvrability. Of the D4Ys available to the 601st Ku, nine were of the earlier D4Y1 reconnaissance version.

In the other two units the situation was less satisfactory. Large numbers of old A6M2 Zeros (Zeke 32s) had been pressed back into service, modified as fighter-bombers, while much of the remaining strength was made up of the elderly Aichi D3A (Val) dive-bombers and Nakajima B5N (Kate) torpedo-bombers with which the IJNAF had entered the war.

During 13 June the Japanese Mobile Fleet sailed from its

ONE OF THE NEW JAPANESE TYPES APPEARING DURING THE MARIANAS FIGHTING WAS THE HIGH PERFORMANCE NAKAJIMA B6N ('JILL') TORPEDO-BOMBER. WITH MORE EXPERIENCED CREWS, THESE AIRCRAFT COULD HAVE POSED A DEADLY THREAT TO TASK FORCE 58.

base at Tawi Tawi, which was located to the east of Borneo in the Sulu Archipelago. Its departure was spotted immediately by US submarines, and reported to Mitscher. Mobile Fleet was due to rendezvous with the battleship force 400 miles east of Samar on 16 June, but on the first day, as it headed towards the San Bernadino Strait to pass through the Philippines, its first setback occurred. While landing-on from an anti-submarine reconnaissance, a B6N crashed, hitting another of these aircraft and bursting into flames; the conflagration destroyed two fighters and two D4Ys as well.

Mitscher takes the offensive

Now with full knowledge of the whereabouts and likely time of arrival of his main enemy, Mitscher decided to take action to reduce further the threat of interference from land-based Japanese aircraft. During the night of 14 June he despatched Task Groups 58.1 and 4 under the overall command of Rear Admiral 'Jocko' Clark, to raid the islands of Iwo Jima and Chichi Jima, respectively 635 and 755 miles north of Saipan. These were important staging bases for reinforcements from the Japanese Home Islands. 'Jocko' Clark's task groups were in range of their targets by midday on 15 June, and at 1430 hours 44 Hellcats, together with Helldivers and Avengers swept over Iwo.

VF-1 and -2 arrived first, reporting that 38 Japanese aircraft were in the air to meet them, 18 of which were the A6Ms of Sento 601 of the 301st Ku, which had arrived on the island on 11 June. The Hellcats swarmed all over the Zeros, claiming to have shot down nearly all of them in a few minutes — 25 being claimed by VF-2 alone! Lt Lloyd G Barnard of this unit claimed five A6Ms, three of which exploded and two crashed into the sea. Outstanding performances were also put in by Lts (jg) Myron E Noble and Charles H Caroll, who claimed three apiece, while four other pilots claimed six between them.

At the same time a single division of four Hellcats from VF-1, led by Lt Paul M 'Pablo' Henderson, claimed ten victories, Henderson and Lt (jg) J R Meharg being credited with four apiece. Henderson was hit, however, and failed to return while a second VF-1 Hellcat was shot down by AA; VF-2 suffered no casualties but Myron Noble's Hellcat sustained severe damage. When VF-15's aircraft arrived over the island it was to find only three A6Ms in the air, and all these were claimed shot down, other pilots then strafing aircraft on the ground.

Sento 601 was virtually wiped out, 16 of its aircraft being shot down and one more force-landing in a damaged condition. Over on Chichi Jima the 203rd Ku's A6Ms were caught on the ground by shelling from 'Jocko' Clark's warships. Eight of the Zeros were destroyed and 23 more damaged, seven of them seriously. Meanwhile in the Marianas the invasion of Saipan had begun at 0840 hours on 14 June, and by evening nearly 20000 American troops were ashore. On the same day 48 China-based B-29s launched the first raid over the Japanese Home Islands since the Doolittle Raid of 1942; this time the steel-producing plant at Yawata was bombed.

In response to the US action in the Marianas, Japanese Army Air Force units from the Carolinas were rushed to Guam, while those Navy units which had been despatched to New Guinea for action over Biak were called back to Tinian and Peleliu with all speed. Both the 263rd and 265th Kokutais were in action on 15 June, joining other units in attacks on the American shipping anchored around the

MAIN AIRCRAFT TYPES EMPLOYED IN THE MARIANAS CAMPAIGN

AMERICAN

Grumman F6F-3 Hellcat
A manoeuvreable mid-wing monoplane fighter powered by a 2000 hp Pratt and Whitney R-2800-10 radial engine, which built up one of the best kill/loss ratios of the war. With a top speed of 376 mph at 17 300 ft, a service ceiling of 38 400 ft and a range of 1090 miles, the Hellcat was heavily armed with six 0.50 in Browning machine guns in the wings. The –3N nightfighter version carried an Airborne Interception radar scanner in a pod on the port wing.

Curtiss SB2C Helldiver
The Helldiver was a powerful two-seat, single-engined low-wing monoplane dive-bomber. It carried a 1000 lb bombload in an internal bomb bay and was armed with four wing-mounted 0.50 in Brownings and two 0.30 in guns on a flexible mounting in the rear cockpit. Powered by a 1700 hp Wright R-2600-8 radial, it had a top speed of 281 mph at 12 400 ft, a service ceiling of 24 700 ft, and a range of 1110 miles.

Other US aircraft employed included the Douglas SBD-5 Dauntless; this was a development of the aircraft used at Guadalcanal. The Grumman TBF/TBM Avenger was also described in that chapter, as was the Grumman F4F Wildcat, of which the FM-2 was a slightly refined version with a taller tail.

Grumman F6F-3 Hellcat flown by Cdr David McCampbell, Commander of Air Group 15, USS *Essex*

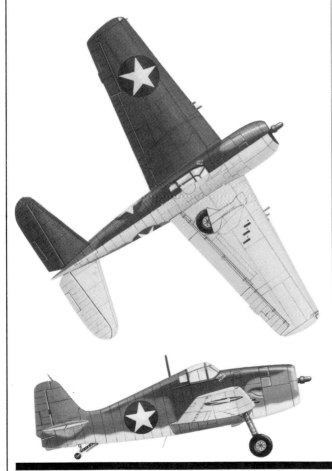

Yokosuka D4Y2 ('Judy') of Carrier Division I

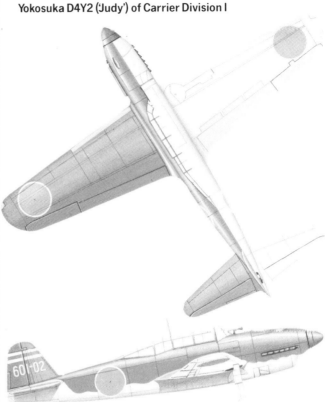

JAPANESE

Mitsubishi A6M5 Zero-Sen
A late development of the basic Zero, the –5 model was powered by a 1100 hp Nakajima Sakae 21 radial engine which gave a top speed of 351 mph at 19 685 ft and a ceiling of 38 520 ft, together with a superlative range of 1171 miles. Armed with two 20 mm cannon in the wings and two 7.7 mm machine guns above the engine, the A6M5 retained the Zero's incredible manoeuvreability, but was in all other respects inferior to the US Navy's F6F.

Nakajima B6N2
A very clean low-wing three-seat monoplane powered by a single 1850 hp Mitsubishi MK4T Kasei 25 Radial engine. Built as a torpedo-bomber and reconnaissance scout, the B6N reached 289 mph at 15 750 ft and had considerable range at 2142 miles; service ceiling was 28 380 ft. Armament remained as for the B5N at a single rear defence 7.7 mm machine gun, while the bomb/torpedo load was also unchanged.

Yokosuka D4Y2
The Yokosuka D4Y dive-bomber, developed as a replacement for the Aichi D3A, was an exceptionally fast and clean mid-wing monoplane, powered by a single 1010 hp Aichi Atsuta 12 in-line engine, which gave it a speed of 343 mph at 15 585 ft – nearly as fast as a contemporary fighter. With a crew of two, it was armed with two 7.7 mm fixed forward-firing guns, and a single flexible 7.92 mm gun for rearward defense. It carried one 551 or 1102 lb bomb and two of 66 lb for the relatively short range of 978 miles.

Other Japanese aircraft employed included the Mitsubishi A6M2 and A6M2-N fighters, Nakajima B5N and Aichi D3A carrier bombers, and the Mitsubishi G4M and Ki21 medium bombers as already described in earlier chapters.

invasion area. During the course of such attacks, defending F6Fs from VF-51 claimed seven aircraft shot down and one probable, three Army Kawasaki Ki61 (Tony) fighters being credited to Lt W R Maxwell.

Pre-battle skirmishes

As evening approached, seven twin-engined bombers, identified as Mitsubishi Ki21 (Sally) Army aircraft came in very low to attack TG 58.3, but achieved no hits; six of the attackers were shot down by the gunners; and as the sun set two of VF(N)-101's F4U-2 Corsairs from *Enterprise* made the first night interceptions, but despite two engagements no definite results could be achieved.

Clark's two task forces were still in the vicinity of Iwo Jima on 16 June, but weather on this date proved too bad for an effective strike to be laid on. The skies cleared sufficiently for a fighter sweep to be flown during the afternoon, but little was seen and no opposition was encountered in the air. Anti-aircraft fire was fierce, however, and 12 US aircraft were shot down. At this point Clark received orders from Mitscher to rejoin the Task Force pending the approach of the Mobile Fleet. While en route 35 aircraft were flown off to make a small attack on Pagan Island in the northern Marianas. TG 58.3 was also undertaking some offensive action in the invasion zone while awaiting the return of Clark's carriers. Air Group 10 bombed Guam's Orote airfield, while Air Group 16 from *Lexington* attacked Agana airfield on the same island.

There was more effective action by Japanese land-based aviation on 17 June as B5N torpedo-bombers from Truk sank an infantry landing craft (LCI) between Eniwetok and Saipan. At evening 17 D4Ys, two P1Y1 twin-engined (Frances) bombers, and 31 escorting A6Ms attacked the invasion transports and their escorts, obtaining a hit on the CVE *Fanshawe Bay* and near-missing two more. Forty-six FM-2 Wildcats on CAP handled the raid poorly, claiming only eight shot down, while the AA defenses claimed seven more. *Fanshawe Bay* was forced to withdraw as a result of the damage suffered.

FREQUENTLY MET BY USN COMBAT AIR PATROLS, THE AICHI E13A ('JAKE') WAS THE COMMONEST OF THE JAPANESE BATTLESHIP AND CRUISER FLOATPLANES TO BE SENT OUT SEARCHING FOR THE US SHIPS.

It was partly as a result of this attack that Mitscher took a decision next day for which he was later to receive some criticism — unjustified, many historians feel. The Mobile Fleet was about 660 miles west of Saipan, only some 400 miles from the Task Force. Instead of sailing west with all speed to reduce the range and join battle, Mitscher elected to remain close to Saipan to afford protection to the landings. He feared that the Japanese may well have split their forces, and that his departure might be followed by an attack which the covering force of escort carriers and old battleships would not be able to contain.

First sighting was made by the Japanese, the crew of one of their aircraft spotting the carriers at 1514 hours, some 420 miles from the Mobile Fleet. Ozawa waited for a confirmatory second sighting which came at 1600 hours, then turned away south-west to prepare his units for action next morning.

Even as the two fleets groped blindly for each other's whereabouts, Kakuta's remaining land-based units in the Marianas resumed their attack on the American shipping. On one occasion during the day 15 A6Ms 'bounced' eight VF-24 Hellcats; these were probably aircraft of the 261st Ku on their way back from Halmahera, during which flight Warrant Officer Minpo Tanaka, one of the unit's leading pilots, claimed two F6Fs shot down off Saipan before going in to land on Guam. However, the Hellcat pilots turned the tables on their attackers, claiming seven of them shot down, of which three were credited to Lt (jg) Robert Thelen.

Towards the end of this day a further attack was made on the landing fleet by Japanese aircraft. Five attackers were claimed by the Wildcat pilots and AA gunners, but darkness had fallen by the time these fighters came in to land, and 31 of them were lost in accidents and ditchings. *Kalinin Bay* at once steamed for Eniwetok to bring replenishment supplies of aircraft.

Tension mounts

The night of 18–19 June was one of great tension for the Americans. The Task Force was at instant readiness for the great engagement, but still no sign of the Japanese carriers had been found. At last at 0115 hours a Martin PBM Mariner flyingboat established radar contact, reporting 40 ships in two groups. At once a further search was launched, 15 scouts going out at 0218 hours; however, they found nothing and turned back — only 40–50 miles short of the Mobile Fleet, as it transpired.

Meanwhile, Ozawa ordered his first searches off at 0445 hours, 16 floatplanes being launched from the catapults of the cruisers and battleships, soon followed by more floatplanes (B5Ns and D4Ys) the latter from *Shokoku*. The first sighting of the US ships was made just as a second wave of searchers was despatched. At the same time, however, came the first engagement of the day as Lt (jg) W T Fitzpatrick of VF-28 intercepted two D4Ys and shot one down. A few minutes later some half dozen Zero fighter-bombers attacked the Fleet — probably land-based aircraft from Guam. They did no damage, and one was claimed shot down by gunners in a destroyer.

About an hour later a division of F6Fs of VF-24 was diverted from CAP duties to sweep over Guam following a radar report of activity there. The Hellcat pilots saw many aircraft over Orote and radioed for help before attacking a formation of A6Ms (probably 13 aircraft of the 253rd Ku) which was just coming in to land when the US fighters attacked. The Japanese unit, which had been despatched

FINAL MODEL OF THE FAMOUS ZERO, THE A6M5 ('ZEKE 52')
WAS THE MAJOR LAND AND CARRIER-BASED FIGHTER USED BY
THE IJNAF DURING THE MARIANAS CAMPAIGN. ALTHOUGH
STILL A POTENT FIGHTER, IT WAS OUTCLASSED BY THE USN'S
F6F-3 EXCEPT IN THE HANDS OF AN EXCEPTIONAL PILOT.

from Truk to provide escort for the attack aircraft on Guam, suffered the loss of five of their Zeros shot down, the rest being destroyed on the ground. Wt Off Sadamu Komachi, one of the unit's aces, was amongst those shot down, but he was rescued from the sea, suffering from slight wounds. The victorious pilots of VF-24 claimed ten shot down, suffering no losses themselves. Meanwhile, 33 of 40 other Hellcats which were in the air reacted to the squadron's call for aid, and fighting over the island continued until 0930 hours, by which time 30 Zeros and five bombers had been claimed. More were seen, but at 1001 hours the fighters were called back to meet a new threat.

Aboard the Japanese carriers feverish preparations had followed the initial sighting of the Americans, as the first strikes were prepared. At 0830 hours Carrier Division 3 in Van Force launched 43 A6M2 fighter-bombers, seven or eight B6Ns (accounts vary), and 14 escorting A6M5s, the whole force being led by Lt Kenji Nakagawa. The incoming raid was first detected just after 1000 hours by the battleship USS *Alabama* while the Japanese formations were still 130–150 miles from the American shipping. Fifty-nine F6Fs were up on CAP and as already recorded, 27 more were recalled urgently from over Guam. About 30 of the fighters in the air were low on fuel, and recovery of these began at once, while a further 140 Hellcats were launched with all speed to add their weight to the defenses.

To the amazement of the waiting Americans, the strike force temporarily halted its inexorable approach when still 75 miles out and began to orbit over the sea while the leader briefed the inexperienced aircrews of the 653rd Ku with the details of how the attack was to be carried out. This almost unbelievable delay was fortuitous for the defenders, providing the intercepting fighters with an extraordinary opportunity to reach the attackers well before they reached their targets — the carriers.

The great battle begins

First on the scene at 1035 hours were eight VF-15 aircraft led by Cdr Charles W Brewer, and as these opened fire on the A6M2 dive-bombers, the First Battle of the Philippine Sea

had at last been joined. In this first devastating 'pass', which was to set the pattern for what was to follow, Brewer's pilots claimed 19 of the elderly Zeros shot down; three of these were credited to Brewer himself, who then also claimed a lone D4Y (presumably one of the reconnaissance aircraft), while four more were claimed by Ens Richard E Fowler. Other Hellcats were close behind: elements of VF-2 and VF-27 were on the scene three minutes later followed by 20 more from VF-25 and VF-31. Six of the VF-25 fighters went after the B6Ns which had gone into a dive, but found them too fast for the Hellcat and could only shoot one down.

After 25 minutes of constant combat, VF-8 and VF-28 joined the fray, but when six of VF-51's F6Fs reached the area it was to find the Japanese attack force in tatters. These late arrivals intercepted ten survivors which were still 30 miles west of the Task Force, and six of these were claimed shot down. Five minutes later the first of the attackers reached the area of the ships, where one more of the 'last ditch' sections of F6Fs (these being aircraft of VF-10) saw four A6M2s about to attack the battleships of TG 58.7 and shot down two of them. Another of this unit's divisions spotted two of the B6Ns coming in low on a torpedo run and shot down one, just outside the AA barrage.

About 20 scattered remnants got through to attack the ships, one 550lb bomb gaining a direct hit on the battleship *South Dakota*, but doing only superficial damage to the armored colossus. The gunners of the Fleet claimed 17 shot down, and then the attack was over. For the loss of three F6Fs and their pilots, two of them from VF-27 and one from VF-25, actual losses inflicted on the Japanese amounted to 32 A6M2s, eight A6M5s and two B6Ns. The survivors reported that hits had been gained on a carrier and a cruiser, but because of the heavy losses which had been sustained, a second strike planned for this Carrier Division was suspended.

Raid 2 was not far behind. CarDiv 1 had started launching 53 D4Ys, 27 B6Ns and 48 A6M5s of the 601st Ku at 0856 hours from their position 100 miles behind (west) of CarDiv 3. This raid seemed ill-fated from the start; as the formation headed away at 0910 hours the US submarine *Albacore* launched a salvo of six torpedoes at *Taiho*. Wt Off Sakio Komatsu, a B6N pilot, saw one heading straight for the ship and with suicidal courage dived his aircraft directly onto this deadly missile, exploding it. Despite his sacrifice, a second torpedo struck the carrier, although the damage caused was not critical — or so it seemed. Within the next

THE GRUMMAN F6F-3 HELLCAT ENJOYED THE EDGE OVER
ALL THE JAPANESE AIRCRAFT IT ENGAGED DURING THE FIRST
BATTLE OF THE PHILIPPINE SEA.

few miles eight more aircraft were forced to turn back, and
then as the rest passed over Van Force, the gunners below
opened fire on them. Two aircraft were shot down and eight
others badly damaged, all being obliged to return; already
the Japanese strike force had been reduced to 108.

This raid was picked up by TG 58's radar at a distance of
115 miles at 1107 hours, but a shadowing aircraft released
'Window' (the aluminium foil strips designed to create false
images on the radar screens) and TG 58.1 despatched its
fighters to intercept this 'spoof'. However, at 1126 hours
the first dozen fighters from VF-15 reached the 601st Ku aircraft as they too went into a briefing orbit 90 miles out. For
six minutes Cdr David McCampbell, Air Group 15's CAG,
and his pilots had the enemy all to themselves, McCampbell
personally downing five of the D4Ys, whilst the others kept
the fighters off his back.

One hundred and twenty F6Fs were still in the air
following the initial Japanese attack, and none of these aircraft had yet engaged. Thirty-three more were scrambled to
join them, and from 1132 hours onwards these aircraft
began joining VF-15 in their assault on the 601st Ku as its
formations closed from 55 to 30 miles range. Twelve VF-14
Hellcats were first on the scene, followed by 23 from VF-16
and eight from VF-27. VF-1 was close behind, flying in
three separate formations of six, ten and five aircraft.

The Japanese suffer greatly

VF-16 went after the dive-bombers which had already been
mauled by VF-15, and Lt Alex Vraciu claimed a further six
of the D4Ys shot down, while the rest of his squadron added
claims for 16 more during a 25-minute running battle. VF-1
and VF-27 took on the escorts, the former unit alone claiming 32 out of one formation of 35 A6Ms; Lt R T Eastmond
claimed four, while four other pilots claimed three apiece.
Four F6Fs and three pilots were lost during this fight, but as
a result of the defenders' efforts, only 20 attackers survived
to break through to the ships, two more being chopped
down by VF-50 as they too headed for the battleships of
TF 58.7.

The remainder of the Japanese aircraft had broken into
two streams during the fight, the survivors of one formation
reaching the battleships where a B6N crashed into the
armored belt around the hull of *Indiana*. The others

reached TF 58.2. Six D4Ys attacked *Wasp* and *Bunker Hill*,
slightly damaging the former and starting fires aboard the
latter with near-misses; three of the dive-bombers escaped.
TG 58.3 was also hit, B6Ns near-missing *Enterprise* and
Princeton with torpedoes.

Again Japanese losses were catastrophically high for no
material success. They amounted to 41 D4Ys, 32 A6M5s
and 23 B6Ns. Yet still the worst was not over for CarDiv 1.
Even as the survivors headed for home, another American
submarine, the USS *Cavalla*, which had already spotted the
battleships of Van Force, but had waited for the carriers,
saw CarDiv 1 following and attacked *Shokaku*, obtaining
three direct torpedo hits on the carrier. Fumes from the
dangerously volatile unrefined Borneo fuel oil in the ship
spread throughout the hull, and at 1500 hours she blew up
and sank, taking nine aircraft and 1263 men down with her.

Because of similar fuel fumes on *Taiho* resulting from
the earlier torpedo damage, an inexperienced officer had
opened the ventilation ducts, allowing these to spread
throughout this carrier too. No danger was expected as the
damage suffered had not been particularly serious, but at
1532 hours a violent explosion suddenly ripped the vessel
apart and she too went down, taking 13 aircraft with her;
about 500 members of her crew of 2150 were saved.

Before these disasters had befallen him, Ozawa had
launched a third strike at 1000 hours on receipt of the sighting report of his second wave of reconnaissance aircraft.
Now CarDiv 2's 652nd Ku launched 15 A6M5s, 25 A6M2s
and seven B6Ns, but the search reports had not been
corrected for a compass error, and this force headed off in
two groups in the wrong direction. One group found
nothing and returned, but the other, about 20 strong, continued to search and was detected by *Hornet*'s radar, about
90 miles out; 17 F6Fs from VF-1 and -2 were vectored onto
them. VF-2 claimed 14, but losses actually amounted to five
A6M2s, one A6M5 and a B6N. The remainder of the
Japanese force attacked TF 58.4, which they had at last
found, near-missing *Essex*.

An hour later, as Raid 1 was ending, and just before the
torpedo attack on *Shokaku*, a fourth strike had flown off.
This comprised two more groups from the 652nd Ku from
CarDiv 2; the first of these comprised nine D4Ys and six
A6M5s, which had orders to land at Rota after the attack,
while the second (and larger) force of 27 D3As, 20 A6M5s
and two B6Ns, was to land on Guam, since it was likely that
darkness would have fallen before they reached the carriers
if a return flight were attempted. This force was joined by a
third group of 601st Ku aircraft from *Zuikaku*, comprising
four A6M5s, four B6Ns and ten A6M2 fighter-bombers —
apparently transferred to the ship from one of the other
CarDivs.

The *Zuikaku* force proved unable to find any US ships,
but did pass a small scouting section comprised of two
Avengers from VT-16 and escorting VF-16 Hellcats which
were out searching for the Japanese Fleet. The ten A6M2s
broke off to attack these, but failed to hit any of the US aircraft; one Hellcat pilot claimed two of the B6Ns shot down,
while two others claimed five of the Zeros between them, the
Avenger crews claiming two more and two probables. This
force reportedly lost a total of eight A6M2s and four
B6Ns on this operation, so it is possible that the survivors of
this brief engagement flew on to Guam to land, and became
involved with other US fighters there.

The 652nd Ku's smaller group of D4Ys and A6M5s
actually managed to escape interception and found TG

58.2, attacking *Wasp* and *Bunker Hill* again, but without success; five D4Y dive-bombers fell to AA fire from the ships.

The air battle intensifies

The second group found nothing, and headed for Guam; their approach to the island was noted on radar, however, and the US fighter controller was able to divert Hellcats to catch them. The first section of VF-10 aircraft arrived here at 1606 hours, just as the Japanese formation was preparing to land. More F6Fs from VF-2, -15 and -25 were close behind as Lt Rod Devine led the VF-10 section down to attack. The Japanese were yet again caught at a hopeless disadvantage, and in minutes Devine and two of his wingmen claimed 11 between them. The fourth member of his division had become separated and joined two other VF-10 aircraft; and these three pilots added a further six claims to the tally.

As this action was at its height, elements of VF-15 led by Cdr McCampbell arrived and added greatly to the execution, claiming two D3As and a dozen A6Ms in a single pass. Many of the Japanese aircraft were still in the air some time later when a formation of VF-2 fighters reached the area; included in this new formation were three nightfighter F6F-3Ns from *Hornet*'s VF(N)-76 detachment. This time 19 D3As were claimed, together with eight Zeros; VF-2's Ens Wilbur Webb claimed six of the dive-bombers, while one of the nightfighter pilots, Lt Russ Reiserer, claimed five more. At 1645 hours VF-16 claimed another five A6Ms over the airfield, while at 1825 hours VF-15 flew a final interception there, making claims for another eight A6Ms to raise total claims over Orote airfield during the afternoon and evening to 40 fighters, 27 dive-bombers and five other types.

During this last sweep by VF-15, Cdr Brewer's division pursued a lone D4Y, which was shot down by Lt John Strane, but the Hellcats were then bounced by 12 A6Ms. In the worst reverse for the US fighters of the day, Brewer and two of his wingmen were shot down and killed. This raised to seven the number of F6Fs lost in combat over or near the island on 19 June; one SBD was also shot down by fighters,

---

OUTSTANDING PILOTS OF THE FIRST BATTLE OF THE PHILIPPINE SEA

Americans

Lt Cdr Alex Vraciu served with VF-6 on USS *Intrepid* during late 1943 when the new F6F Hellcat fighter saw its first actions. During strikes on Truk and Kwajalein Atoll, seven claims in two days brought his score to nine by February 1944. Posted to VF-16 aboard USS *Lexington*, Vraciu had added two more victories during April before the Marianas battle began. Then in three combats, including that on 19 June when he claimed six

LT CDR ALEX VRACIU, VF-6.

CDR DAVID McCAMPBELL, AIR GROUP 15.

Yokosuka D4Y dive-bombers in one sortie, he became the current US Navy top-scorer with a total of 19. His combat tour was quite eventful as he twice had to ditch in the sea and was twice present on aircraft carriers when they were torpedoed. Cdr David McCampbell was a very experienced naval aviator, who had served on USS *Wasp* during the summer of 1942 when the carrier ferried Spitfires to Malta for the RAF. Despite the ship's brief foray to Guadalcanal in late 1942, he had gained no aerial victories before it was sunk. Early in 1943 he became Air Group Commander on the flagship of the new class of fleet carriers, USS *Essex*, but when the Marianas fighting began had still to gain his first aerial victory. This was not long in coming however, with the first claim being made on 11 June. When on 19 June he claimed seven and a probable in one day his total grew quite considerably. The Philippines during September were the scene of his next run of successes, four in a day on 12 September being but the highlight of a month which brought his score to 19 — equal to Vraciu.

McCampbell's greatest day came on 24 October when he and his wingman found a large formation of ineptly flown fighters. Following these, aircraft after aircraft was picked off until nine and two probables had gone down to his guns, five more being claimed by the wingman, Roy Rushing. Several more successes came during November, the last on 14 November which brought a grand total of 38, making him the US Navy top-scorer of the war by a wide margin.

His record nine in one sortie was never equalled by any other American pilot, and for this came the award of a Congressional Medal of Honor.

LT (JG) KANEYOSHI MUTO, YOKOSUKA KOKUTAI.

Japanese

Lt (jg) Kaneyoshi Muto had flown in China in 1937, and then in the Philippines in December 1941 with the 3rd Kokutai. He later served over the Solomons from Rabaul, but from March 1943 to June 1944 served in Japan with the Yokosuka Kokutai. After outstanding service on Iwo Jima during the summer of 1944, he joined the 343rd Ku on home defense, claiming for a second time four US Navy fighters in one combat on 26 February, 1945. In June 1945 Muto moved with his unit to Okinawa where on 24 July he was shot down and killed by a P-51 Mustang. His score of 28, claimed between December 1937 and July 1945, included four of the giant B-29 Superfortress bombers over the Japanese Home Islands.

while two more fighters and six bombers had fallen to AA.

The 652nd Ku formations which had provided the bulk of the targets over Guam had lost 20 of their 27 D3As, all but one of the 20 A6Ms, and one of the two B6Ns. The Japanese fighter pilots had done what they could to protect their charges, but had been almost entirely wiped out. Amongst those killed were two aces, Ens Kazaburo Yasui (11 victories) and Wt Off Tetsuo Kikuchi, whose score of about 20 included two F6Fs which it was believed he had shot down during this last fight. It is likely that other aircraft, possibly including the survivors of the 601st Ku formation, were involved in some of this action, while the final fight in which VF-15 lost its commanding officer, was probably with one of the land-based units.

One other success enjoyed by the Japanese had occurred earlier in the day when two VF-10 Hellcats and two F4U-2s of VF(N)-101 were despatched from Enterprise on ResCAP — a patrol in support of air-sea rescue aircraft. At 1420 hours the controller directed them to the aid of a Curtiss SOC rescue floatplane which was reported in trouble, and they soon found the little biplane down on the water, being strafed by two 343rd Ku A6Ms. Lt Hank Clem dived down low and then pulled his Hellcat up vertically to attack one of the Zeros from below. The Japanese leader was ace Lt Shimazu Ozaki, who turned to meet Clem head-on and shot him down. Lt Cdr Richard 'Chick' Harmer, the VF(N)-101 CO fired at Ozaki's Zero, which made off, trailing smoke.

Although no claim was made, Harmer's fire had mortally wounded Ozaki, who died after landing. He was credited with victories over both the Hellcat and the SOC, but in fact the latter was able to take off again, and was escorted to safety by the Corsairs. By night the F6F-3Ns took up the patrol over Guam and Rota, and two pilots from Essex's VF(N)-77A claimed three aircraft shot down as they attempted to take off.

So ended 19 June, a day which had seen some of the most intense fighting of the entire war. For the loss of 16 F6Fs and 13 pilots, the US fighters had claimed 378 victories in a single day; 15–17 more had been claimed on the ground, while the AA defenses had added claims for a further 19. VF-16's Alex Vraciu had increased his personal score to 18, to become top navy ace at the time, and other pilots had made impressive claims also. One Hellcat pilot described the actions as resembling a 'country turkey shoot', and this description stuck; indeed, 19 June went down in US military and aviation history as 'The Great Marianas Turkey Shoot'.

The Japanese had achieved nothing. No US ship had been lost, or even seriously damaged, although at times the Task Force had been in great danger from the small percentage of attackers that did break through. Only the inexperience of their pilots preventing serious damage being inflicted. On those ships which had been attacked, 31 men had been killed and 108 wounded. Of 450 aircraft available to the Mobile Fleet, 328 had been launched, together with 24 search aircraft from the carriers and 19 floatplanes from the battleships and cruisers. A total of 220 Japanese attack force aircraft and 23 search planes had been shot down, or had been lost with the two sunk carriers, while 12 more reconnaissance aircraft from Guam had also been lost. Total casualties among land-based aircraft amounted to nearly 60 in combats, accidents and to strafing.

Carrier search is resumed
Again a major diversionary effort had been launched by the USAAF during the day, with 56 7th and 13th Air Force

B-24s bombing targets at Truk. But still, despite this victory, the American air groups had not found the Japanese carriers. The search was resumed next morning, while a dawn sweep was flown over Orote airfield. Here the fighters claimed another 18 shot down and many destroyed or damaged on the ground, which prevented the last Japanese attempt at a further strike against the Task Force.

Guam's air strength was now exhausted, with 58 aircraft having been shot down and 52 destroyed on the ground, and many others damaged beyond repair during these operations. However, the seven remaining carriers of the Mobile Fleet still had 68 A6M2 and A6M5 fighters, three D4Y dive-bombers and 29 B5N and B6N torpedo-bombers serviceable.

As the US searches continued, Japanese scouting aircraft were frequently encountered and several were shot down; eight VF-2 Hellcats which were on a search with four SB2Cs accounted for two E13A floatplanes and a B5N, while another B5N fell to a pilot of VF-10. Lt Charles Henderson a VT-10 Avenger pilot, shot down a B6N with his front gun, while one of this unit's turret gunners claimed an A6M.

Finally at 1540 hours on 20 June came the first sighting of the Japanese carriers by Lt Robert S Nelson of VT-10 from Enterprise. An additional report gave confirmation at 1610 hours, and 11 minutes later the first of 216 aircraft took off to strike at the opposing fleet. This force comprised 85 F6Fs, 77 SB2Cs and SBDs, and 54 TBFs and TBMs, most of the latter with bombs rather than torpedoes. Sightings had indicated that the Mobile Fleet was 220 miles away — optimum range for the US aircraft — but a subsequent report indicated that this was an underestimate, and the ships were in fact 60 miles further on. Despite the late hour the strike was not recalled, although a second follow-up launch was cancelled.

The first ships of the Mobile Fleet were spotted at 1840 hours, but some 40 A6Ms were up and fought well in defense of their parent vessels. The formation from TG 58.3 came under particularly severe attack as 15 SBDs of VB-16 and ten of VB-10, accompanied by five Avengers and 12 F6Fs, approached. The dive-bombers headed for CarDiv 2, but over Junyo VB-10 was attacked, and one SBD was badly damaged before it managed to fight clear. At that point VF-10 Hellcats arrived, shooting down two of the attackers and driving off the rest. Zeros shot down a TBM of VT-16; Lt Alex Vraciu and Ens H W Brockmeyer of VF-16 went to its aid but were pressed hard themselves. Brockmeyer was shot down, Vraciu despatching the fighter responsible from his wingman's tail for his 19th and last victory. VB-16's SBDs were also under fierce attack, several being hit and damaged, and one flown by Lt (jg) Jay A Shields, was shot down.

With only four of VF-16's Hellcats defending them, things were looking bad for the Americans, even though the Dauntless crews were able to claim two 'Zekes' shot down and nine damaged. Rescue arrived here too, however, more Hellcats joining the fight and driving off the opposition. Much of the fighting was done by VF-10, which turned in the best score of the day with seven claimed shot down for the loss of one Hellcat. Six more were claimed by VF-8, and five by VF-14 which lost one pilot when Lt M F Cotton collided head-on with one of the A6Ms.

Over Zuikaku (CarDiv 1's remaining carrier) VF-24 and -50 claimed seven between them, but lost three F6Fs to bring Hellcat losses to a total of six. One further claim was submitted by Lt (jg) Albert Voris of VF-1. Apart from the Hellcats and the Dauntlesses, ten SB2Cs and four Avengers were lost to the defending fighters at a cost to the Japanese of 25 A6Ms shot down and nine badly damaged.

From *Zuikaku* eight A6M5s had taken off, led by ace Ens Yoshio Fukui, and had claimed 15 victories. Two of these were claimed by Wt Off Yoshijiro Shirahama, who had also claimed one on the previous day — his first — and would end the war with a score of 11. It was dark by the time the 601st Ku fighters came in to land and most force-landed in the sea. Other A6Ms of the 652nd and 653rd Kokutais jointly claimed about 20 victories. The former unit put 26 aircraft into the sky to claim seven TBFs and two probables, and two F6Fs, but 11 were shot down and three force-landed in the water; the 653rd also suffered heavy losses amounting to most of its remaining aircraft. Indeed, after this fight CarDiv 3 was left with just two A6M5s, three A6M2s and six torpedo-bombers.

Japanese losses increase

Although optimistic claims were made by the American bomber crews for the results of their attacks on the ships, these were not as in fact as impressive as they believed, considering the strength of the strike force — possibly because of the failing light as dusk approached. However, *Zuikaku* had suffered one direct hit and several near-misses and was fairly badly damaged, and all CarDiv 2's carriers suffered attacks, *Hiyo* sinking after two torpedo hits, while *Junyo* was damaged by two hits and six misses by bombs; *Ryuho* escaped with a few near-misses. In CarDiv 3 *Chiyoda* was also struck by a single bomb. Quite a few Japanese aircraft were destroyed on the carriers, or went down with *Hiyo*. Their total losses during this attack amounted to 65, including the A6Ms lost in combat. More effective for the Americans was a dive-bombing attack on the oilers of the fleet replenishment units; two were so badly damaged that subsequently they had to be sunk by Japanese destroyers, while a third also suffered severe damage, but survived.

Now the US aircraft set course for the long flight back to Task Force 58, and the pilots were faced with distances of 250–300 miles as they set off into the gathering darkness. The first of them arrived back at 2245 hours, by which time all were desperately short of fuel. So much so that Marc Mitscher now took a calculated gamble which made him beloved of all his aircrews, issuing the order, 'Turn on the lights'.

In total violation of all security, every vessel in the Fleet — not just the carriers — lit up. Most pilots had no chance to find the right ship, so they landed wherever they could, and in the darkness some (dazzled by the sudden brilliance of the lights) attempted to land on vessels that were not aircraft carriers at all! Already Avengers, Helldivers and Hellcats were flopping into the sea all around the Fleet as the last vestiges of fuel in their tanks were exhausted; but many did get down safely. Most successful were the reliable old SBDs as all but three of the 26 returning made safe landings. Seventy-five per cent of the Hellcats also got aboard, but 20 of the Avengers and 35 of the 40 SB2Cs were lost.

By 2300 hours all were down one way or another, but 104 aircraft had been lost, 80 of them due to fuel exhaustion or landing accidents. Aircrew recovery was excellent, however, and of the 209 airmen who did not get aboard, all but 49 were saved — and of those lost at least 36 had gone down in the attack on the Japanese ships.

Following this costly night recovery, Mitscher resumed his pursuit of the Japanese carriers, but again was not able to catch them. Consequently, the Task Group finally returned to the Marianas. Here on 22, 23 and 24 June the P-47Ds of the 318th Fighter Group were launched from the escort carriers, flying ashore to Aslito airfield. From here they were at once in action, giving close support to the ground forces fighting their way inland. Not until 23 June did the carrier air groups see anything of note, but on that day Hellcats of VF-15 sweeping over Guam's Orote airfield found 18 A6Ms in the air, claiming 14 shot down and three probables for the loss of two F6Fs and one pilot.

Following this engagement TGs 58.2, 3 and 4 were ordered to Eniwetok to rest, but for TG 58.1 it was back to Iwo Jima for another series of neutralization strikes to prevent any reinforcement of Guam or Tinian. As many as 122 IJNAF aircraft were on Iwo on 24 June as the carriers launched their air groups for another bad weather assault. Over half of these were from the Japanese carriers, but the force also included the Yokosuka Kokutai, which had arrived four days earlier. This unit had been formed from the Navy's oldest aircraft test unit, and included on its strength many successful and highly-experienced pilots.

In the first engagement on 24 June VF-1 and -2 encountered over 60 incoming A6Ms and about 20 D4Ys, which had been ordered off when the US ships had been spotted by a 'snooper'. Most of the attackers jettisoned their bombs and gave battle, VF-1 claiming 18 and five probables for one loss, while VF-2 claimed 25 A6Ms and eight D4Ys, for one loss and one Hellcat badly damaged. VF-2's Lt (jg) Everett C Hargreaves claimed four victories and one probable and Lt (jg) M W Vineyard four, while

'THE BEAST'—THE EPITHET BESTOWED ON THE BIG, HEAVY CURTISS SB2C HELLDIVER DIVE-BOMBER INDICATED THAT ITS CREWS HAD NO GREAT LOVE FOR THIS POWERFUL AIRCRAFT. NONETHELESS, IT PLAYED A WORTHWHILE PART DURING THE OPERATIONS OF 1944.

VF-1's Lt (jg) T Schroeder claimed three.

Twenty-seven A6Ms of the Yokosuka Ku had been led off by Lt Sadao Yamaguchi, together with nine from the 301st Ku and others from the 252nd. The Yokosuka pilots claimed 11 F6Fs and six probables for nine losses, including 11-victory ace Wt Off Kiyoshi Sekiga who was killed, and Wt Off Tomita Atake (10 victories) who was shot down and wounded. Four of the victories were claimed by the unit's leading pilot, NAP 1/C Kinsuke Muto, and two by the one-eyed Saburo Sakai in his first combat since being wounded so badly over Guadalcanal in August 1942. Four 301st aircraft were lost against five claims, while the 252nd claimed 19 (!) but lost ten of its own, including the Sento 302 CO Lt Nobuo Aiwa. NAP 1/C Masao Sugawara claimed three of the victories, but his aircraft was hit and he baled out.

Futile gestures
Twenty unescorted B5N torpedo-bombers were then sent out to attack the carriers. They were met by the CAP and destroyed, VF-2 claiming 14 shot down while Lt John Dear of VF(N)-76 added three more. The rest fell to the guns of the Fleet, none returning; they achieved nothing. Later in the afternoon nine B6Ns, three D4Ys and 23 A6Ms (nine of them from the Yokosuka Ku) took off to search for the carriers, but could find nothing in poor weather. VF-2 and -50 were vectored onto them, however, claiming seven B6Ns and ten Zeros — on this occasion exactly the losses admitted by the Japanese.

At evening, 16 of the modern twin-engined P1Y1 bombers went out, but these did not come within sight of the ships either, and seven of them failed to return. Total USN claims came to 116, 62 of them credited to VF-2 alone. Japanese records show that, apart from the P1Y1s, 34 fighters, 27 torpedo-bombers and five dive-bombers had been lost — all at a cost of just six F6Fs in combat.

Over the Marianas only the nightfighters now saw any

action. The new P-61 Black Widows which had just flown in, made their first claim on 27 June for a B5N probable, but during the same night *Enterprise*'s Corsairs gained their first confirmed success, Lt Robert F Holden claiming a Ki21 army bomber shot down. Next night, taking off at 1940 hours, Holden added two G4Ms, while a couple of hours later his commanding officer, Lt Cdr 'Chick' Harmer, claimed another. The USAAF pilots had to wait until the night of 6 July before Lts Franklin C Eaton and Jerome Hansen were able to claim a G4M apiece, Lt Dale F Haberman shooting down one more on 14 July.

Meanwhile, TG 58.1 had again returned to Iwo Jima joined now by an additional carrier, USS *Franklin* (CV-13) with Air Group 13 aboard. VF-13 was equipped with the very latest F6F-5 Hellcats, fitted with zero-length rocket launching stubs beneath the wings which were well used against Japanese shipping before the campaign finally closed. On 3 July, 43 F6F-3s from VF-1 and -2 swept over the island, finding approximately 40 A6Ms in the air. Seventeen VF-1 pilots claimed 11 and five probables for one loss and three Hellcats damaged, while VF-2 again grabbed the biggest part of the action, 11 of the unit's 26 aircraft bombing targets on the ground before joining the fight. Thirty-three claims were then made, Lt Cdr Dean and four others each claiming three; three of the squadron's Hellcats failed to return. Five more Zeros were claimed by VF-50.

The Yokosuka, 252nd and 301st Kokutais were all heavily involved, the latter unit suffering particularly severely. Thirty-one A6Ms of the 301st took off, led by Lt Fujita, but they were 'bounced' as they struggled to gain height, losing 17 against claims for seven Hellcats and three probables. Losses were also suffered by the Yokosuka Ku, although NAP 1/C Muto and Ens Matsuo Hagire were each able to claim two F6Fs shot down.

Most accounts indicate that the strike on 3 July was the last made, and that the remaining Japanese aircraft set out to attack the US Fleet next day. Detailed study of the records shows this not to be the case. Early on 4 July a further sweep over Iwo Jima was made during which 14 fighters were claimed shot down by VF-14, 13 by VF-31 — four of them by Lt (jg) Cornelius Nooy — and three as the first claims of VF-13.

Meanwhile even earlier radar-equipped F6F-3N Hellcats from VF(N)-76 and -77 had approached Chichi Jima, where nine Nakajima A6M2-N float-fighters detached to the island from the Sasebo Ku took off to intercept them. During the next 30 minutes the US fighters claimed eight of these shot down, three of them by Lt John W Dear Jr and four by Lt Fred Dungan; six were actually lost, together with four of their pilots. Only NAP 1/C Teruyuki Naoi, a veteran of the Aleutians campaign in 1942 was able to claim one and two probables. No US losses were in fact suffered, but Dungan landed back on the *Yorktown* with one bullet in his shoulder and his aircraft damaged.

During these three days of fighting the 252nd Ku lost 14 aircraft while making claims for 13 victories; on 4 July the 301st Ku's Sento 601 undertook 14 sorties, claiming six victories but losing three of its Zeros in combat and all the rest which were available on the ground. The unit's outstanding pilot had been Lt (jg) Akio Matsuba, who was credited with shooting down six F6Fs in the 48-hour period. The Yokosuka Ku too had lost virtually all its aircraft and pilots during the three days of fighting, including such veterans as Lt Sadao Yamaguchi (12 victories). Altogether 22 losses were suffered although against this the unit's pilots had

A TRIO OF THE VERY FAST YOKOSUKA D4Y ('JUDY') DIVE-BOMBERS, EMPLOYED IN NUMBERS BY THE CARRIERS OF THE MOBILE FLEET, HEAD OUT ON A TRAINING FLIGHT. THESE PARTICULAR AIRCRAFT ARE FROM THE YOKOSUKA KOKUTAI.

US NAVY FIGHTER PILOTS CLAIMING 5 OR MORE VICTORIES, 11 JUNE–8 AUGUST 1944

NAME	UNIT	CLAIMS	TOTAL FOR WAR
Cdr David McCampbell	VF-15	10½	38
Cdr William A Dean Jr	VF-2	9	11
Lt Landis E Doner	VF-2	8	8
Lt(jg) Richard T Eastmond	VF-1	8	9
Lt(jg) Everett C Hargreaves	VF-2	8	8½
Lt Russell L Reiserer	VF(N)-76	8	9
Lt Arthur Van Haren Jr	VF-2	8	9
Lt(jg) Alexander Vraciu	VF-16	8	19
Lt(jg) John L Banks	VF-2	7	8½
Lt(jg) Daniel A Carmichael Jr	VF-2	7	12
Cdr Charles W Brewer	VF-15	6½	6½ KIA 19 6 44
Lt Lloyd G Barnard	VF-2	6	8
Lt(jg) George R Carr	VF-15	6	11½
Lt(jg) Charles H Carroll	VF-2	6	6
Lt(jg) John W Dear Jr	VF(N)-76	6	7
Lt(jg) Fred L Dungan	VF(N)-76	6	7
Lt Richard J Griffin	VF-2	6	8
Lt Cdr Leroy E Harris	VF-2	6	9¼
Lt(jg) Byron M Johnson	VF-2	6	8
Lt William R Maxwell	VF-51	6	7
Lt(jg) Daniel R Rehm Jr	VF-50	6	9
Lt Roy M Voris	VF-2	6	7
Ens Wilbur B Webb	VF-2	6	7
Lt(jg) John T Wolf	VF-2	6	7
Ens Claude W Plant	VF-15	5½	8½
Lt Oscar C Bailey	VF-28	5	5
Lt Bruce M Barackman	VF-50	5	5
Lt(jg) Daniel B J Driscoll	VF-31	5	5
Lt(jg) Franklin T Gabriel	VF-2	5	8
Lt(jg) Dwight B Galt Jr	VF-31	5	5
Lt Paul McR Henderson Jr	VF-1	5	5 KIA 15 6 44
Ens Kenneth B Lake	VF-2	5	6
Lt William E Lamb	VF-27	5	5
Ens William A McCormick	VF-50	5	7
Lt William C Moseley	VF-1	5	5 KIA 4 7 44
Lt(jg) Myrvin E Noble	VF-2	5	7
Lt(jg) Eugene D Redmond	VF-2	5	9¼
Ens Leroy W Robinson	VF-2	5	5
Ens Ross F Robinson	VF-2	5	5
Lt(jg) Robert W Shackford	VF-2	5	5
Lt(jg) Warren A Skon	VF-2	5	7
Lt John R Strane	VF-15	5	13
Lt Cdr Johnnie C Strange	VF-50	5	5
Lt Charles H Turner	VF-31	5	6
Lt(jg) Merriwell W Vineyard	VF-2	5	6
Lt(jg) John L Wirth	VF-31	5	14

VICTORIES CLAIMED BY US NAVY FIGHTER SQUADRONS, 11 JUNE–8 AUGUST 1944

SQUADRON	NUMBER	SQUADRON	NUMBER
F6F SQUADRONS			
VF-2	197	VF(N)-76	28
VF-15	100½	VF-28	24
VF-1	97	VF-51	22½
VF-31	67½	VF-24	21
VF-50	59	VF-25	20
VF-16	48	VF-32	9
VF-10	40	VF-13	7½
VF-27	36	VF(N)-77	7
VF-14	35½	Others	11
VF-8	30	Total	860½
FM-2 SQUADRONS			
VC-5	10	VC-41	9
VC-33	10	Others	16
		Total	45

vessels as the only effective way remaining of achieving any really damaging results.

Amongst the pilots selected for this mission were the Yokosuka aces, Sakai and Muto. This first officially-ordered suicide mission preceded the well-known 'Kamikaze' attacks on the Allied fleets around the Philippines and Home Islands by several months.

Whilst it has long been reported that this attack was made following the combats over Iwo Jima on 4 July, in fact the mission seems to have actually taken place early in the morning of 8 July, four days later. The small formation took off into conditions of thick cloud, struggling to keep together and to find the American ships in very poor visibility. Radar spotted them, however, and suddenly a swarm of Hellcats were upon them. Their attackers were aircraft of VF-31 from *Cabot* which shot down all but one of the bombers and five of the nine fighters. With no chance of breaking through the fighter cordon, the four surviving Zero pilots had no option but to return to Iwo alone. Kinsuke Muto landed first, believing that he was the sole survivor; but he was followed in by Saburo Sakai and his two wingmen, and the last bomber.

This series of battles virtually brought the campaign to an end, although several more strikes were made against bases in the Palaus, Carolines and Bonins. Saipan was secured on 9 July after heavy US casualties, and on 21 July US landings were made on Guam; troops went ashore on Tinian too, three days later, and both islands were secured by early August. The official close of the campaign occurred on 8 August by which time US Navy aircraft had claimed 922 victories for the loss of 65 of their own in combat — mainly F6Fs; 306 more had been claimed on the ground. Actual Japanese losses were about 60–70 per cent of these figures.

However, the effect on Japan, coupled with the appearance of the B-29s in home skies, was devastating. Told only a story of Japanese victory until this point, suddenly the harsh truth of the situation was revealed. The fall of Saipan coincided with the fall of General Hideki Tojo's government. But perhaps the most poignant epitaph occurred on 6 July when Vice Admiral Choichi Nagumo, the victor of Pearl Harbor, now trapped ignominiously in a cave on Saipan, shot himself. The wheel had turned full circle.

claimed 52 victories — a far higher figure than total TG 58.1 losses for this operation, but an indication of the intensity of the fighting. Sakai later recorded that the force of fighters which had flown into the island a couple of weeks earlier had lost 80 Zeros in combat during this period alone.

A last Japanese effort

TG 58.1 remained in the area for several more days, attacking shipping and intercepting the occasional 'snooper' or bomber attempting lone attacks. All that now remained serviceable on Iwo Jima were eight torpedo-bombers and nine A6Ms. There was little that these could achieve against the hordes of US aircraft available to attack the island or defend their ships, so they were ordered to fly a desperate no-return mission against the American carriers; each pilot was ordered to try and crash his aircraft into one of these

INDEX

Aachen, Germany 162, 173
Aalborg, Denmark 47, 162
Abe, Pty Off Kenichi, 253rd Ku, 110
Abtnaundorf, Germany 176
Adams, Lt Dudley H, VS-71 99
Adler Tag (Eagle Day) 46
Admiral Scheer, German battlecruiser, 168
Admiralty, the 159, 160
Adolph, Hpt Walter, 48
Adriatic Sea, 182
Aegean Sea, 90
Aeronavale, French, 44
Agana, Guam, Marianas, 198
Ahlhorn, Germany, 177
Aichi D3A ('Val') 98-100, 103, 112, 113-5
Specification 117, 118, 196-7, 200-2
Aichi E13A 75, 198, 202
Aioi, Lt Takahide, *Ryujo* 67
Aliwa, Lt Nobo 204
Akarit, Wadi Tunisia 136
Akizuki, Japanese destroyer 113
Alabama USS battleship 199
Alamein, El, Egypt 125-6, 135,141
Albacore, USS submarine 199
Albacore, Fairey 53, 84
Albania, 81
Alam el Halfa, Battle of, Egypt 126
Aleutians 204
Alexandria, Egypt 81
Algeria 92, 126-7, 129, 173
Allard, Flt Lt G 49, 57
Allen, Plt Off J 39
Alps 174-5, 186
Amerine, Lt Richard, VMF-224 108
Andreas, Maj Werner 45
Antwerp, Belgium 164, 173
Anzio, Italy 177
'A' Operation, Japanese 195
Aparri, Philippines 72, 73-5
Argument, Operation 179, 181
Argus, HMS aircraft carrier 81, 83, 90
Arkhangelskoye, Soviet Union 144
Ark Royal, HMS aircraft carrier 82-4
Armstrong, Brig Gen Frank, 184
Arnhem, Holland 179
Arnim, Gen Jurgen von 129
Aschersleben, Germany 179
Ashigawa Japanese cruiser 73
Asigiri Japanese destroyer 105
Aslito, Saipan, Marianas 195, 203
Assa, El, Tunisia 129
Atake, Wt Off Tomita, 204
Atimonen, Philippines 74
Atlanta, USS cruiser 119
Atlantic, Battle of 159
Augsburg, Germany 186-7
Australia 75-6, 97
Austria 188
'Avalanche', Operation 162
A-27, North American 68

Baagoe, Lt Sophus 49
Baatan Peninsula, Philippines 74, 76
Bader, Sqn Ldr D R S, 36, 49, 57, 146
Baguio, Philippines 67, 75
Bailey, Lt Oscar C 205
Baldinus, Lt Lawrence, 105, 108
Balkans 60
Balthasar, Hpt Wilhelm 34, 48
Baltic Sea 161-2
Baltimore, Martin 127, 128-9, 134, 136
Banks Lt (jg) John L 205
Bär Maj Heinz 48,129,179, 182,185,187
Profile 136
Barackman, Lt Bruce M 205
'Barbarossa' Operation, Soviet Union 141
Barker, F/Sgt F 49, 57
Barnard, Lt Lloyd G 196, 205
Barovykh, Andrei Y 147
Barron, Wg Cdr F 158
Barton, Flt Lt R A 56
Barvenkuro, Soviet Union 144
Batan Island, Philippines 72
Batangas, Philippines 74-5
Battle, Fairey 28, 33,157
Battle of Britain, statistics 54
Baver, Lt Col Harold 110,113,118,120
Baver, Oblt Konrad 185
Beamish, Wg Cdr F V 49
Beaufighter, Bristol 56,82-3, 85-6
Specification 86,90-1,92
Becker, Oblt Martin 164
Beckham, Maj Walter 181,184,185
Beechcraft, light aircraft 68
Beerbower, Capt Don 179
Beeson, Maj Duane 184, 187
Belenikhino, Soviet Union 152
Belgium 33-4,56,60, 157,164,173
Belgorod, Soviet Union 142,145,152
Belikov, Sen Lt 145
Bell, Maj, 111
Belser, Hpt Helmut 89,91
Ben Gardane, Tunisia 129
Benghazi, Libya 126
Bennett AVM D, No 8 Gp 158
Berlin, Germany 50, 158-163,168,185
Bernburg, Germany 179
Berres, Lt Heinz-Edgar 89,91,126, 136
Bertram, Hpt Otto 48
Beurling, Flg Off G F 88,89,91
Biak, New Guinea 194,196
Bicol Peninsula, Philippines 74
Biggart, Sgt Paul 186
Biggin Hill, England 47, 50-1
Birmingham, England 57
Bismarc German battleship 159
Blair, Flg Off K H 44
Blakeslee, Col Don 185
Blenheim, Bristol, 33-5
Specification 37,45-7,53,55, 56,82-83,85,157-9
Bob, Oblt Hans-Ekkehard 48
Bogorodetskoye, Soviet Union 147
Boltenstern, Hpt 51
Bonin, Hpt Eckart-Wilhelm von 164
Bonin Islands 205
Bonn, Germany 181
'Booty' convoy 46
Borchers, Walter 48
Borneo 75, 200
Borris, Hpt Karl 182
Boston, Douglas 127,134,136
Bou Thadi, Tunisia 136
Box, England 39
Boyd, Sqn Ldr A H 46,57
Boyd Flt Lt R F 57
Bramsche, Germany 177
Brand, AVM Sir Christopher, No 10 Group 39
Brandenburg, Germany 164
Brändle, Hpt Kurt 145
Brandt, Ofw Walter 89,91
Brannon, Capt Dale D 101,105,118
Brauschitz, Hpt von 46
Bremen, Germany 159-60, 163,173-4
Brest, France 159,160
Bretnutz, Hpt Heinz 48
Brewer, Cdr Charles W 103, 199, 201, 205
Bright, Ens Mark K 100,118
Bristol Aircraft 53
British Army,
1st Army 126,129
8th Army 84,90,125-7, 134,136,173
1st Armoured Div 127,136
7th Armoured Div 127
50th Infantry Div 127,135
51st Infantry Div 127
2nd New Zealand Div 127,136
4th Indian Div 127
201st Guards Brigade 127
British Expeditionary Force, France, 1940 157
Brittany, France 34
Brockmeyer, Ens H W 202
Brooklands, Weybridge, England 51
Brown, Lt Ben 68
Brünsbuttel, Germany 157
Bryansk, Soviet Union 142
Buka Island, Solomons 105,110
Bulayev, Sent Lt 1AP 145
Bulgaria 188
Burbridge Sqn Ldr, B 85 SQN 158
Burma 184,193
Burrows, USS transport 105
Butirki, Soviet Union 146
Bzura River, Poland 26
B-10, Martin 65,68,75
B-17D, Boeing Fortress 61-3,65,67-8,68
Specification 69,71-5
B-17E-G, 97,105,108, III, 113-4, 119-20,129,173-5,175, 179, 181-3
Specification 182,184-7
B-18A, Douglas 65,68,71,75
B-24, Consolidated Liberator 169-71,173-5,179,181-2, 185-7,193-5,202
B-25, North American Mitchell 125,127,128-9,129,134,136
B-26, Martin Marauder 120,175,187
B-29, Boeing Superfortress 74,185,193,196,201,205

Cabanatuan, Philippines 75
Cabot, USS aircraft carrier 205
Caen, France 167
Cagayen, Philippines 75
Caldwell, Lt Turner 105
Canberra, HMAS, cruiser 100
Cant, Z1007*bis,* 82
Specification 87,90-2
Carbury, Plt Off B J G 49,57
Carl, Capt Marion 100,103,105,110-1,118
Carmichael, Lt (jg) Daniel A Jr 205
Caroline Islands 193-4,196,205
Carroll, Lt(jg) Charles H 196,205
Cartwright, Sgt H 36
Castle, Brig Gen Fred 184-5
Catfoss, England 162
Cavalla, USS submarine 200
Cavite Navy Yard, Luzon, Philippines 67,76
'Chain Home' radar 33
Chapman, F/Sgt 162
Chennault, Brig Gen Claire 184
Cheshire, Gp Capt L 617 Sqn Profile 158,158
Chicago, USS cruiser 100
Chichi Jima, 196,204
Chikuma, Japanese cruiser 115
China 65,74,193,196
Chitose, Japanese seaplane tender 75,103
Chityakov, Gen 145
Chiyoda, Japanese aircraft carrier 203
Chokai, Japanese cruiser 119
Christensen, Capt Fred 184
Church, Lt Russell M 75
Churchill, Rt Hon Winston 33,86,126
'Circus' operations 159
Citizen National Army, Philippines 66
Clacton, England 58
Clark, Rear Adm J J, TG 58-1 196,198
Clark Field, Luzon, Philippines 61-3,67-8,71-5
Claus, Oblt Georg 59
Clausen, Lt Erwin, 1 (J)/L62 26
Clemm, Lt Hank 202
Clouston, Flt Lt W G 57
Clowes, Sgt A V 57
Cologne, Germany 160
Commonwealth Air Training Plan 125
29th Communist Brigade, Yugoslavia 146
Conger, 1/Lt Jack E 118
Congressional Medal of Honor 104,111,120,184-5
Connors, Flt Lt S D P 50,57
Cooley, Lt Col 108
Copahee, USS escort carrier 110
Corregidor Island, Philippines 67,76
Cotton, Lt M F 202
Coventry, England 56-7,158
Cranswick, Wg Cdr A 158
Crete 90
Crook, Plt Off D M 36
Crossley, Sqn Ldr M N 49,57
Croydon, England 47,50,52
Currant, Plt Off C R 57
Cyrenaica, Libya 90
Czechoslovakia 19, 188
Czernin, Flg Off Count M B 57,60

Dahl, Maj Walther 181,185, 186,187
Daly, Ens Joseph 98
Dalzell, F/Sgt 163
'Dammerungseinsatze' 157
Davao, Mindanao, Philippines 67,75
Dilley, Oblt Bruno 19
Dobbin, Maj John 108,118
Doe, Plt Off R F T 57
Donaldson, Lt I B Jack 68
Doner, Lt Landis E 205
Donets River, Soviet Union 142,148
Doolittle Raid 196
Dornemann, Oblt Georg 149
Dornier Do17Z 19,21
Specification 22,24,29,34-9, 46-7,50,52,53,56
Dornier Do215 36,39
Dornier Do217 164,166-7
Dortmund -Ems Canal, Germany 168
Dover, England 36,44-46,60
Straits of, 160
Dovetil, Sqn Ldr 163
Doyle, 2/Lt Cecil J 118
Dresden, Germany 162-3
Driffield, England 47
Driscoll, Lt (jg) Daniel B J 205
Drury, 1/Lt Frank C 118
Druschel, Maj Alfred 148
Duisberg, Germany 168
Duke, Flt Lt N F Profile 136
Dundas, Flt Lt J C 48,57
Dungan, Lt Fred 204,205
Dunkirk, France 33,36,39, 81,153
Durbeck, Hpt Wilhelm
Durwal, 2/Lt Hieronim 26
Dutch East Indies Air Force 65
Dutton, Sqn Ldr R G 46,57
Duxford, England 52-3
Dymond, Sgt W L 51,57
Dzialoszyn, Poland 22

Eagle, HMS aircraft carrier 85-6, 89-91
Eagleston, Lt Glen 179
Eastchurch, England 46-7
East Indies 65,74,97
Eastmond, Lt (jg) RT 205
East Prussia, Germany 19
Eaton, Lt Franklin C, 204
Ebeling, Oblt Heinz 48,50
Eder, Maj Georg-Peter 185
Eder Dam, Germany 160
Efate, New Hebrides 100,110
Egypt 81-2,90,125,173
Eichele, Hpt 44
Eisenach, Germany 181
Eisenhower, Gen Dwight D 167
Eldridge, Lt Cdr John 113,117
Elgin Air Force Base, USA 74
Ellis, Sqn Ldr J 57
Elsham Wolds, England 164
Emden, Germany 162
Ems Estuary, Hoffland 163
Engel, Lt Wilhelm 163
English Channel, 47,53,158,160
Eniwetok Atoll, 193,198,203
Enneccerus, Maj Walter 46,81
Enschede, Holland 179
Enterprise, USS aircraft carrier 97-8,101,103,105,108,114-5, 119-20,193,195,198,200,202
Esperance, Cape, Guadacanal 111
Espiritu Santo, Solomons 113,120
Essen Germany 160
Essex, USS aircraft carrier 195,197,200-2
Everton, Capt Loren, VMF-223 105,118
Ewa, Hawaiian Islands 97

Falck, Hpt Wolfgang 157-8
Falmouth England 39
Fanali, Col Dulio 89
Fitzpatrick, Lt (jg) W T 198
Fiume, Italy 186
Flak 21,26,47,53,135-6, 148,160,163,168,181,184, 186,188
'Flambo', German incendiary bomb 21
Flatley, Lt Cdr James 114
Fletcher, Vice Adm Frank 97,101
'Flying Tigers', AVG, Burma 184
Focke-Wulf FW190 141,143-6
Specification 149,162,163
Focke-Wulf FW200 158-9
Specification 183,187,188
Foggia Plain, Italy 175,182
Folkestone, England 45
Fondock Pass, Tunisia 136
Fontana, Maj Paul J, VMF-112 118
'Forager', Operation, Marianas 193
Ford, England 47
Formosa, 65,67,71-2,73,74,76
Foss, Capt Joseph J 104,111, 117-8,120
Fowler, Ens Richard E 199
Foyle Bank, HMS auxiliary AA vessel 35-6
France 33-6,81,125-6,157, 167-8,173,188
Franke, Fw 163
Franklin, F/Sgt W H 36,57
Franklin, USS aircraft carrier 204
Frantisek, Sgt J, 303 Sqn 42,49,57
Frazier, 2/Lt Kenneth DeF 110,118
Freeborn, Plt Off J C 57
Freeman, 2/Lt William B 118
Frey, Lt Hugo 185
Freya, German radar 144
Freytag, Oblt Siegfried 89
Fujita, Lt 204
Fukui, Ens Yoshio 203
Fuller, Lt W H 110
Fulmar, Fairey 81,85
Fumerton, Flg Off R C 88,91
Furious, HMS aircraft carrier 82,91-2
Fürth, Germany 186
F4F, Grumman Wildcat, 93-5, 97-103, 104,105,108
Specification 116,118-20,197
FM-2, General Motors Wildcat 193,197-8
F6F, Grumman Hellcat 189-91, 193,195-6
Specification 197,198-200, 201,
202-205
F4V-2, Vought Corsair 193, 198,200,204

Gabes, Tunisia 126,136
Gabreski, Lt Col Francis 184
Gabriel, Lt (jg) Franklin T 205
Gabszewicz, Lt Alexsander 19,20
Gafsa, Tunisia 136
Gaines, Cdr Richard 114
Galer Maj Robert VMF-224 105,110,113,118
Galland, Maj Adolf JG26 47-8,48,60,188
Galt, Lt (jg) Dwight B Jr 205
Gänseler, Ofw Wilhelm 159
Gardabia, Libya 127
Gardelegen, Germany 163
Garrison, Maj Vermont, 4th FG 187
Gavutu, Solomons 97
Gazala, Libya 90,125
Gedymin, 2/Lt Wlodzimierz 26
GEE, navigation aid 160
Geiger, Gen Roy, *USMC* 117
Geisshardt, Oblt Friedrich, 89,91
Gentile, Capt Don, 4th FG 184,187
Gentzen, Hpt Hannes 26
George F Elliott, USS transport 100
Germany, Map of North 156, Map 172
Gibraltar 90
Gibson, Wg Cdr Guy, Profile 161
Gibson, Flt Lt J A A 49,57
Gies, Lt Carl, 20th Pursuit Sqn 73
'Gisella' Operation 168
Gizo Harbour, Solomons 108
Gladiator, Gloster (also Sea Gladiator) 81,85
Gladych, Flt Lt B M 177-9
Glowacki, Sgt A 49
Glunz, Lt Adolf, 179
Gneisenau, German battlecruiser 159
Gnys, Lt Wladyslaw 17
Godfrey, Lt John T, 184
Goebbels, Dr Josef 17
Goldsmith, Flg Off A P 88,91
Golunov, Gen D P 145
Gollob, Lt Gordon 26
'Gomorrah' Operation, Hamburg 160
Goodson, Maj James A 184
Göring, Reichmarshal Hermann 34,50,52,60,188
Gorovetz, Lt Alexandr, 146,147
Gostishchevo, Soviet Union 146,152
Gotha, Germany 181
Goto, Lt Hidero 117
Grabmann, Maj Walter, 48
Grand Harbour, Malta 81
'Grand Slam' 22 000lb 168
Gray, Plt Off C F 49,57
Gray, Ens Les 195
Great Britain, Map of 1940 32
Greece, 125
Griffin, Lt Richard J 205
Gromov, Gen M 151
Groth, Erich 48
Gryf, Polish minelayer 23
Guadalcanal, Solomons 74
See also Chapter 5
Guam, Marianas 195-6,198-9, 200-3,205
Gumm, Lt Charles, 179,187

Haas, Fw Otto 181
Haberman, Lt Dale F 204
Haberman, 2/Lt Roger A 118
Hackl, Maj Anton, 185
Hagire, Ens Matsuo 204
Hahn, Oblt Hans, 48
Hahn, Oblt Hans von 48
Halberstadt, Germany 179
Hal Far, Malta 82
Halifax, Handley-Page 159,162-4
Specification 166,168
Halle, Germany 165
Hallowes, F/Sgt H J L 47,57
Halmahera Island 194,198
Halsey, Vice Adm 114
Hamar Plt Off J 44
Hamburg, Germany 152, 159-60, 163,168,174
Hamilton, Gnr Henry B 113,118
Hamlyn, Sgt RF 610 Sqn 49
Hamm, Germany 173
Hamma, El, Tunisia 129,134-6
Hammer, Oblt Alfred 183
Hampden, Handley-Page 45,157,159
Handorf, Germany 162
Hannak, Lt Günther 89,91
Hanover, Germany 163-4
Hanson, Lt Jenne NF Sqn 204
Harada, Lt(jg) Kaname, *Hiyo* 113,118
Hargreaves, Lt(jg) Everett C, 203,205
Harris, AVM Arthur, Bomber Command 110,161,165,167
Harris, Lt Cdr Leroy E 205
Haruna, Japanese battleship 73,111
Harwich, England 44,46,56,59
Hashiguchi, Wt Off Yoshio 113
Haugk, Helmut 49
Hausser, Gen, SS Panzer Corps 148,150,152
Hawaii 66
Hawkinge, England 39,46-7
Hazbub Main, Libya 129
Heinkel He59 23,39,59
Heinkel He100D (He113) 39
Heinkel He111 17,19-21,21
Specification 22,34,36-7, 46-7,50,51,52-7,81,91-2,147
Heinkel He219 159
Heligoland, Germany 157
Heller, Richard, II/ZG26 49
Helmstedt, Germany 176
Henderson, Lt Charles 202
Henderson, Lt Paul McR Jr 196,205
Henderson Field, Guadalcanal 93-5,100,105,108,110-4,118-20
Henneburg, Flg Off Z 49
Henschel Hs123A 21
Specification 23,26,27
Henschel Hs126A
Specification 23,25
Henschel Hs129B 136,148
Specification 149
Herget, Hpt Wilhelm 159
Hermosa, Philippines 74
Hero of the Soviet Union 146-9
Herrman, Oberst Hajo, II/KG30 163
Hesdin, France 164
Hesepe, Germany 177
Hesselyn, Flg Off RB 88,91
Hesterblink, Germany 176
Hiei, Japanese battleship 119
Higginson, F/Sgt F W, 56 Sqn 57
Higgs, Flg Off T P K, 111 Sqn 38
Hintze, Oblt Otto, 56
Hiroshima Bay, Japan 195
Hitler, Adolf 17,34,39, 52-53,125,141-2,150,152,157
Hofer, Capt Ralph, 4th FG 184
Holden, Lt Robert F, VF(N)-101 204
Holland 157,162,164,173
Hollowell, Lt George, 108,118
Holst, Belgium 164
Homma, Lt Gen Masaharu 65,75
Home Guard 47
Homuth, Oblt Gerhard 48
Hopsten, Germany 176
Horbaczewski, Flt Lt E 136
Hori, Mitsuo, Tainan Ku 99
Hornchurch, England 47,50
Hornet, USS aircraft carrier 105,108,114-5
Hornet, USS aircraft carrier (new) 200-1
Hoth, Gen, 4th Pz Army 145,148,150,152
Howard, Lt Col James H 184
Hrabak, Hpt Dietrich 48
Hrubieszow, Poland 27
Hudson, Lockheed 46
Hughes, Flt Lt P C 49,57
Hungarian, 2nd Air Corps, Order of Battle 145
Hungarian 5/1 Group 145
Hungary 184,188
Hurricane, Hawker 28,33-6,36, Specification MKI 37, 38-9, 44,45-7,50,52-6,58-60, 81-6 Specification MKII 86,89-91,121-3,125,127, 134-6,134
Husemann, Maj Werner 162
Hutnicki, Poland 27
H2S, radar navigation aid 160,175
H2X, radar navigation aid 175

Iba, Philippines 67-8,71-2,74-5
Ibel, Oberst Max
Ihlefeld, Oblt Herbert, 48
Illg, Ofw Wilhelm-Friedrich 47
Illustrious, HMS aircraft carrier 81
Ilyushin Il2m3 Shturmovik 137-9,142,146-7,
Specification 148,150,151
Imperial Japanese Army 65,72-4,76,100
Imperial Japanese Army Air Force 65,66,72-3,75-6
Imperial Japanese Navy 65
3rd Fleet 195
1st Mobile Fleet 195,198,202
Carrier Division 1 114,196,197,199-200,202
Carrier Division 2 114,196,200,202
Carrier Division 3 196,199,203
Imperial Japanese Navy Air Force 61-8,71-6,97-100, 105,108,110,113,117-8, 120,189-191,194-205
Italy 81,125,174-5,185-7,193
Iwaki, Pty Off 1/c Yoshio 119
Iwo Jima 74,194,196,203-5

Jabs, Oblt Hans-Joachim 48
Jarvis, USS destroyer 100
Jennings, Plt Off 162
Jintsu, Japanese cruiser 105,108
Jito, NAP 3/c Hisao 113,116
Johnson, Lt (jg) Byron M 205
Johnson, Lt Robert S 184,185
Juppien, Hpt Hermann-Friedrich 48
Juneau, USS cruiser 119

Junkers Ju52/3m 28
Junkers Ju86 59
Junkers Ju87B 13,17,20-6
 Specification 22,27,28,34-7, 44-7,58-9,81,84,90-1
 Ju87D 86 Specification 87,92,127, 141,146
 Ju87G 147
 Specification 149
Junkers Ju88A Specification 37,45,46-7,52-6,81,84-6, 87,90-2, 135 6,147
 Ju88C 157,163,163,164,166
 Specification 167
Junyo, Japanese aircraft carrier 113-6,202-3

Kageneck, Oblt Erbo von 48
Kako, Japanese cruiser 100
Kakuta, Rear Adm Kakuji, CarDiv 2, Vice Adm, 1st Air Fleet 194-5, 198
Kalafrana Bay, Malta 81
Kaldrack, Hpt Rolf 76
Kalinin Bay, USS aircraft carrier 198
Kamikawa Maru, Japanese seaplane tender 100,108
'Kamikaze' 205
Kammhuber, Gen Josef 157-8
Kanekoi, Lt Cdr Tadashi, *Hiyo* 118-20
Kasserine, Tunisia 127,129
Kavieng, New Ireland 110
Kawaguchi, Maj Gen 105
Kawanishi H6K 75,97,101
Kawasaki E7K 75
Kawasaki Ki 48 67
 Specification 69,76,195
Kawasaki Ki 61 198
Keator, Lt Randell B 68
Kelly, Lt Colin Jr 73
Kendrick, 2/Lt Charles 118
Kenley, England 47
Kent, Flt Lt J A 49
Kesselring, FM Albert 84,92
Kharkov, Soviet Union 141-2
Kiel, Hpt Johannes 185,188
Kiel, Germany 160,168,173
Kielce, Poland 24
Kikuchi, Wt Off Tetsuo 202
Kilmartin, Flt Lt JI 57
Kingston, F/Sgt 164
Kinryu Maru, Japanese transport 105
Kirishima, Japanese battleship 115,120
Kirn, Lt Cdr Louis 108,110-1,113
Kirschner, Oblt Joachim Profile 146
Kiser, Lt George, 17th Pursuit Sqn 72
Kittyhawk, Curtiss 121-3,125, 127,129,134,136
Klagenfurt, Austria 181
Kleeberg, Gen 28
Kleis, Maj Maxim, III/KG77 53
Kluge, FM von 142,144-5
Knacke, Heinz 48
'Knikkebein' navigation aid 56
Knight's Cross 34,47,143, 146,181,188
Knilans, Maj N 617,619, Sqn 158
Knoke, Oblt Heinz 179
Kobayashi, NAP1/c Shigeto, Yokohama Ku 97
Koc, 2/Lt Tadeusz 28
Koenigsberg, Germany 22
Kohima, Burma 193
Kokuba, Pty Off 2/c Takaichi, Tainan Ku 119
Kolesnichenko, 1/Lt Stepan K Profile 147
Komachi, Wt Of Sadamu 199
Komatsu, Wt Off Sakio 199
Kongo, Japanese battleship 111
Korea 184
Kotlov, Nikolai 147
Kowalewski, Hpt Robert
Kozhedub, Lt Ivan N Profile 147
Kozhevnikov, Sen Lt Anatoli L 438 IAP Profile 147
Kra Isthmus, Malaya/Thailand 66
Kracow, Poland 19
Krahl, Hpt Karl-Heinz, II/JG3 88
Kramatorskaya, Soviet Union 144
Krasuyy Oktyabr, Soviet Union 150
Krupinski, Oblt Walter, 145 Profile 146
Krupps Works, Essen, Germany 160
Kruschev, Nikita 149
Kucing, Poland 24
Kunz, 2/Lt Charles M 118
Kurita, Vice Adm Takeo 195
Kursk, Soviet Union Map 140
 See also Chapter 7
Kutno, Poland 26
K-41 airfield, Tunisia 129

Lacey, Plt Off J H 49,57
Lae, New Guinea 74
Lake, Ens Kenneth B 205
Lamb, Lt William E 205
Lamon Bay, Philippines 76
Lancaster, Avro 160,162-5
 Specification 166,168
Lang, Maj Friedrich 143
Laoag, Philippines 72
Laricheliere, Flg Off J E P 47
Lavochkin La 5 142-3,145,146-7
 Specification 148
Lavochkin La 7 147
Larsen, Lt Harold 108
Laskowski, Capt Florian 21
La Spezia, Italy 160,161
Latvia 28
Lawley, 1/Lt William 305th BG 177
Lee, Flt Lt R H A 50
Legaspi, Luzon, Philippines 74-5
Le Havre, France 158
Leipzig, Germany 153-5,161,162-3
Le May, Gen Curtis, 305th BG,4th BW,3rd BD 185
Leningrad, Soviet Union 141
Lent, Oberst Helmut 26,159
Leonardi, Maj 46
Leppla, Lt John 114
Leppla, Oblt Richard 44
Lesniewski, Capt Miroslaw 23
Leuschel, Hpt Rudolf 187
Lewis, Flg Off G 49,57
Lexington, USS aircraft carrier 195,198
Libya 81,84,125-6,173-4
Lignitz, Oblt Arnold 48
Lille, France 173
Lingayen Gulf, Philippines 75-6
Lion, Lt 23
Lippe-Weissenfeld, Maj Egmont Prinz zur, 162
Litvak, 2/Lt Lilya 146
Liverpool, England 50
Llewellyn, Sgt RT 57
Lloyd, AVM HP 83,91
Lock, Plt Off E S 59,57
Locy, Poland 20
Lodz, Poland 24
Loesch, 1/Lt Gregory K 118
London, England 60,158
Long Island, USS escort carrier 100
Lublin, Poland 25
Lublin R.XIII
 Specification 22,26,28
Lucchini, Cap Franco 89,91
Ludwigshafen, Germany 175
Luftwaffe. Order of Battle Sep 39 18, Claims in Poland 28, Losses in Poland 28, Order of Battle Aug 40, Orders of Battle, Sicily 1941-2, 83,125 Order of Battle, Tunisia Mar 43 127, Order of Battle Kursk July 43 145,158,162, Order of Battle, Night Defence, Feb 44, 165, Order of Battle Day Defence, Feb 44, 180
Luftflotte 1 19-20,26,141
Luftflotte 2 20,34-5,38,47,50
Luftflotte 3 39,45,50
Luftflotte 4 19,21,26, 142,145,152
Luftflotte 5 34,47-8,141
Luftflotte 6 142,152
 II Fliegerkorps 34,84-6,88,90-1
 VIII Fliegerkorps 34,142
 X Fliegerkorps 81
 Fliegerdivision I 26
 Fliegerfuhrer zbV 20
 I Jagdkorps 165
 Jagdflieger führer 2 34,38,45,50,54
 Jagdffiegerführer 3 50
 For individual units see Chapters 1,2,4,6,7,8,9
Lunga Point, Guadalcanal 113,120
Luga, Malta, 77
Lutz, Hpt Martin 53
Lutzow, Hpt Günther 48
Luzon, Philippines Map 64,66-7,74-5
Lysa Gora, Poland 26

Macchi C200 81-2
 Specification 87
Macchi C202 83,85
 Specification 87,89-92, 125,127,129,132,136
Macchi C205 181,187
MacDonnell, Sqn Ldr ARD 57
Machold, OFw Werner 48,58
Mackrell, Sgt, 460 Sqn 164
Mackrocki, Wilhelm 49,58
Maclachlan, Flt Lt JAF 85
Magara, Pty Off 1/C Koichi 119
Magdeburg, Germany 162
Mahoney, Lt Grant 3rd Pursuit Sqn 68,71-2
Mahurin, Capt Walker 56 FG 184,185
Mailley-le-Camp, France 167
Main Force, Bomber Command 160-5,168
Maisel, Hpt 50
Majuro, 194
Malan, Sqn Ldr AG 44,57
Malaszewicze, Poland 22
Malaya, 65-6
Maloarkhangelsk, Soviet Union 142
Malta, Map 80, Chapter 4, 125,185
Maltzahn, Maj Günther von JG53 48,58,88,89
Manchester, Avro 159-160
Mangrum, Lt Col Richard 100
Manhard, Lt Walter 48
Manila, Philippines 67,70-1,72,73,75,76
Maniques, Philippines 75
Mankin, AP 1/C Lee P Jr 118
Mann, 2/Lt Thomas H Jr 118
Mannheim, Germany 158,160-1
Manstein, Gen von 141,145
Manston, England 45-7
Mantle, Acting Seaman Jack, HMS *Foyle Bank* 36
Maras'yev, Gu Maj Alexei 146, Profile 147
Marcus Island 193
Mareth Line, Tunisia, 127,129,132,136
Margate, England 45
Marianas, 145
 See also Chapter 10
Marontate, Lt William F 104,117-8
Marrett, Lt Samuel 34th Pursuit Sqn 72
Martin, Wg Cdr HB 158
Martinoli Serg Teresio 89,91
Martlesham, England 47
Maryland, Martin 81,83,85
Massenbach, Maj Dipl Ing Dietrich Frhr von 59
Master, Lt (jg) C H, VS-71 113
Master Bomber 161
Matheson, F/Sgt 163
Mathies, Staff Sgt Archie 177
Matmata Hills, Tunisia 132
Matoni, Hpt Walter 181-2
Matsuba, Lt(jg) Akio 204
Matsuki, Pty Off 3/c Susumu 119
Maxwell, Lt William R 198,205
Maya, Japanese light cruiser 119
Mayer, Oberstlt Egon 185
Mayer, Hpt Hans-Karl 48,56,58
Mayer, Lt Wilhelm 182
McArthur, Gen Douglas 65-6
McCampbell, Cdr David, 195,197,200
 Profile 201
McCormick, Ens William A 205
McDowell, 2/Lt Don 179
McElroy, Flt Lt JF 88,91
McFarland, USS destroyer/transport 113
McKekkar, Flt Lt AA 49,57-8
McKenzie, Lt Col Burton 183
McKinley, Fort, Philippines 71
McKnight, Flg Off WL 49,57
McLeod, Flt Lt JF 88,91
McMullen, Flg Off DAP 48,56-7
Meaulte, France 173
Medenine, Tunisia 129
Medway River, England 39,45
Medwecki, Capt Mieczyslaw 17
Meharg, Lt(jg) William R 196
Melab, Tunisia 132
Menge, Uffz 47
Messe, Gen Giovanni 130,132-3,135-6
Messerschmitt BF109D 13,20
 Specification 22,23-51,26
BF109E 22,26,34,35,36-9, 44-6,47, 50-6,58-9,60, 60,81,84,125,127
BF109F 60,84,86
 Specification 86-7,88-9,92,125
BF109G 126,127,132-3,136, 145,163,165,176-7,182-3
 Specification 183,184,186,188
Messerschmitt BF110 19-21,21
 Designation B and C, 22,24,26,34,36-9,44-7, 50-5,60,81,85,157,159,163, 163,164-6
 Designation G 167,179, 181,183
 Specification 183,186
Messerschmitt Me210 135,181
Messerschmitt Me410 177,181
 Specification 183
Messerschmitt Me 262 133,147,159,169-71,188
Meurer, Hpt Manfred 159
Meyer, Hpt Bruno Profile 146,148
Meyer, Lt Col John C 184
Michalski, Hpt Gerhard 89,91
Middle Wallop, England 46-7
Midway Island, 76,100,103
MiG 15, 184
Mikayanovka, Soviet Union 144,148
'Millenium I', Operation, Germany 160
Minagumo, Japanese destroyer 110
Mindanao, Philippines 67,75
Mitscher, Vice Adm Marc 193-4,196,198,203
Mitsubishi A5M 67
Mitsubishi A6M Zero-Sen 61-3,67
 A6M2 Specification 69,72-3 74-5,97-8,100-1,103-5,108, 110-1,113-5,117-8,120, 189-91,193,195-6
 A6M5, Specification 197, 198-9, 199,200-5,
Mitsubishi C5M 69,72
Mitsubishi F1M 75-6,104, 108,113,117
 Specification 117,120
Mitsubishi G3M 69,72,74-6,108
Mitsubishi G4M 69,70-1,72, 74-6,93-5,97-9, 100-1,104-5, 105-7,108,110-1, 113,117, 118,195,197,204
Mitsubishi Ki15 69
Mitsubishi Ki21 67
 Specification 69,72,75-6,197-8
Mitsubishi Ki30 69,76
Mockav, Leipzig, Germany 176
Model, Gen 150-2
Mohne Dam, Germany 160
Mölders, Oberstlt Werner, JG51 34,44,48,59
Mondigo, Lt Antonio 74
Montgomery Gen B 92,125,127
Moore Lt Joseph 73
Moriura, Pty Off 3/c Toyoo 113,119
Morocco, 92,126
Morphie, Camp, Philippines 75
Moscow, Soviet Union 141
Moseley, Lt William C 205
Mosquito, De Havilland 127,158-9,160-3
 Specification 166,168
Mugford, USS destroyer 99
Müller, Maj Friedrich-Karl 185
Müller-Duhe, Lt Gerhard 50
Mümler, Maj Mieczyslaw 26,27
Müncheberg, Oblt Joachim 48,58,81-2,89
 Maj, JG77 132-2,136
Mungo-Park, Flg Off 49,57
Munich, Germany 160
Munster, Germany 174
Murakumo Japanese destroyer 111
Murasame, Japanese destroyer 110
Musachi Japanese battleship 195
Mussolini, Benito Italian Dictator 56,125
Muto, Lt(jg) Kaeyoshi, 3rd/343rd/Yokosukaku, Profile 201,204-5
Mutsuke, Japanese destroyer 105
M-3 Stuart light tank 66
Mk 103 German 30mm Cannon 148

Nacke, Hpt Heinz 59
Naganami, Japanese destroyer 117
Nagumo, Vice Adm Choichi 114,205
Naka, Japanese cruiser 72
Nakagawa, Lt Kenji 199
Nakajima A6M2-N 97,108,110, 113,116-7,197,204
Nakajima B5N 65,101, 103,114-6
 Specification 117,196-8, 202,204
Nakajima B6N 196
 Specification 197,199, 200,202,204
Nakajima J1N1 195
Nakajima Ki27
 Specification 69,72,74-6
Nakajima Ki43 195
Nakajima Ki44 195
Nakaya, Yoshiichi 99
Naoi, NAP 1/c Teruyuki 204
Naples, Italy 89
Narr, 2/Lt Joseph L 118
Nash, Flg Off PA 88,90-1
Natsugumo, Japanese destroyer 111
Neil, Plt Off TF 57
Nelson, Lt Robert S 202
Nelson, Flt Lt W H 58
Neu, Hpt Wolfgang 182
Neuhoff, Lt Hermann 88
Neupetritor, Germany 176
Newcastle, England 47
New Georgia, Solomons 110
New Guinea, 74,76,97-8, 194,196
New Hebrides 97,115
Nicholson, Flt Lt JB 47
Nicholls Field, Philippines 71-2,75
Niclot-Doglio, Cap Furio 155°GrCT 88-9,91
Nijmegen, Holland 179
Nishizawa, NAP 1/C Hiroyoshi, Tainan Ku 98,99
Nisniyawa, NAP 2/c, *KamikawaMaru* 110
Nissin, Japanese seaplane tender 110
Noble, Lt (jg) Myron 196,205
Nooy, Lt (jg) Cornelius 204
Norden, bombsight 173
Normandie, French fighter group 152
Normandy, France 34,125,167,188,194
North Carolina, USS battleship 97,108
North Sea 36,47,157,162
North Weald, England 50,56
Norway, 33-4,36,48,81,157-8
Notomi, Lt Kenjiro, *Ryujo* 101
Novikov, Capt Konstantina, Profile 147
Nuremberg, Germany 167

Obayashi, Rear Adm Sueo 196
Oberhaenser, Maj Jack 181
Obertraubling, Regensburg, Germany 177,181,186
'Oboe' navigation aid 160,175
Oboyan, Soviet Union 147
Ochsenkopf, Operation, Tunisia 129
Oesau, Oberst Walter 48,58, 179,185
Ohio, British tanker 91
Ohishi, Lt (jg) Yashio, *Zuikaku* 115
Ohki, Lt Yoshio, Tainan Ku 98,99
Ohkura, Pty Off 253rd ku 110
Ohmori, NAP 1/C Shigetaka, *Shokaku* 115,119
Ohmura, NAP 2/C Matsutara *Kamikawa Maru* 108
Ohno, Takeyoshi, Tainan Ku 98,99
Ohta, Wt Off Toshio Tainan Ku 98,113,119
Okamoto, Pty Off 1/C Juzo 110,119
Okano, Tainan Ku 99
Okecie, Poland 19
Okumura, Takeo Tainan Ku 99
Olongapo, Philippines 75
Ono, Lt *Kamikawa Maru* 108
Orel, Soviet Union 141-2,146,152
Orkney Islands, UK 35
Orote, Guam, Marianas 198,202-3
Oschersleben, Germany 176
Osnova, Soviet Union 144
Osterkamp, Oberstlt Theo 34-5, 58
Ostermarkflug, Operation, Poland 17
Ott, Maj 46
Ozaki, Lt Shimazu 202
Ozawa, Vice Adm Jisaburo 195,198,200
Ozerok, Soviet Union 144
0-19,46,49,52,OA-9, various observation aircraft Types 68

Paepcke, Oblt Heinrich 59
Pagan, Marianas 195,198
Palau Islands 205
Palestine, 82
Pamula, 2/col Leopold 20
Panin, Sen Lt 145
Panki, Poland 20-1
Park, AVM Sir Keith, Malta, 91
Pas de Calais, France 167
Payne, Maj Frederick R VMF-212,213 118
PBM, Martin Mariner 198
PBY, Consolidated Catalina, 67
 Specification 69,73-5, 100,113-5
PB4Y, Consolidated Liberator (USN version) 194
Pearl Harbour, Hawaiian Islands 66,205
'Pedestal', Operation, Malta 91
Peel, Sqn Ldr J 46
Peenemunde, Germany 161
'Peewit', Convoy CW9 45
Peleliu, Marianas 196
Peltz, Oblt Dietrich 59
Peterhausen, Austria 181
Peters, Hpt Erhard 165
Peterson, Maj Edgar 59
Petlyakov Pe 2 142,146
 Specification 148,150-1,151
Pevensey, England 46
Pflanz, Lt Rudolf JG2 48
Philipp, Oblt Hans 26,48,58
Philippine Air Force 65
 6th Pursuit Squadron 74-5
 7th Advanced Training Squadron 75
 8th Air Base Unit 85
 10th Bomb Squadron 75
Philippines, Chapter 3, Map 64,196,205
Phillips, 2/Lt Hyde 118
Pickard, Gp Capt PC 158
Pilar, Philippines 76
Pingel, Hpt Rolf I/JG26 48,58
Piotrkow, Poland 21,24,26
Plagis, Flt Lt JA 88,91
Plant, Ens Claude W 205
Plewig, Hpt Waldemar 59
Ploesti, Rumania 173-4,185,188
Plymouth, England 35
'Pointblank' Directive 161-2
Poland, Map of 16, Chapter 1 174
Polbin, Maj Gen Ivan S Profile 146
Poling, England 47
Polish Air Force, Order of Battle 18, Claims 28, Losses 28, Bomber Brigade 21-2,24-7, 25 Pursuit Brigade 17,19-22, 24-46,25
 For individual Dyons and Squadrons see 17,19,21-27
Polish Army Forces 13,19-27
Polish/German comparative air strength 17
Polish Navy 23
Pololyan, Soviet Union 146
Polyana, Soviet Union 144
Pomerki, Soviet Union 144
Pond, 2/Lt Zenneth 103,305,118
Portland, England 35,39,46-7,53
Portland, USS cruiser 119
Port Moresby, New Guinea 74,97
Portsmouth, England 46,50,53,56
Preddy, Capt George 184
Preston, USS seaplane tender 67
Priller, Oberstlt Josef 48,58,185
Princeton, USS aircraft carrier 200
Prinz Eugen, German cruiser 159
Prokhorovka, Soviet Union 150,152
Prüfening, Regensburg, Germany 181,186
Psel, River, Soviet Union 150
PTAB, Russian hollow-charge bomb 142
Pultusk, Poland 24
PzKw IV tank 137-9
PzKw V Panther tank 137-9,141,147
PzKw VI Tiger tank 141,147
PZl P7 19,26,28
PZl P.11c 13,17,19,20-1
 Specification 23,24,25, 25-8,27
PZl P.23 Karas 21
 Specification 23,24,26-8
PZL P.24 27
PZL P.37 Los 17,22
 Specification 23,24-28
P-26A, Boeing 65
 Specification 69,74-5
P-35A, Seversky, 65,68
 Specification 68,71-2,74,76
P-38, Lockheed Lightning, 118-9,120,173-78,181-3
 Specification 182,186-8
P-39, Bell Airacobra, 74,101,110-1,113
 Specification 116,117-8,120, 132,173
P-400, Bell Airacobra, 101,108,110-1,113
 Specification 116,118,120
P-40B, Curtiss Tomahawk 61-3,67-81
 Specification 68,70,71
P-40E, Curtiss Kittyhawk 67-8
 Specification 68,71-6
P-40F, Curtiss Warhawk, 125,127,132,135,136,175
P-47, Republic Thunderbolt 173-7,177,179,181-3
 Specification 182,186-8,203
P-51B North American Mustang 158,175-7,177, 179,181
 Specification 183,184, 186-8,201
P-61 Northrop Black Widow 204
P1Y1('Frances')198,204

Quackenbruck, Germany 177
Quincy, USS cruiser 100

Rabagliati, Wg Cdr 85,91
Rabaul, New Britain 97,99,100,108,112,119-20,196
Radar Mk X 160
Radar SN-2, German 163
Radener, Oblt Waldemar 181,182
Radom, Poland 26
Radomsko, Poland 21,24
Radusch, Oberst Günther 159
Rakowice, Poland 19
Ralston, Wg Cdr J R 158
Ramlo, 2/Lt Orvin H 118
Ramsgate, England 56
Rayski, Gen 28
Red Air Force, Order of Battle 142-3
 For Air Armies, Corps, Divisions and units see Chapter 7
Red Army see Chapter 7
Redmond, Lt(jg) Eugene D 205
Regensburg, Germany 174,177,181,185-7
Reggiane Re 2001
 Specification 87,90-2
Regia Aeronautica 56,59-60
 Order of Battle, Malta 84

Order of Battle, Tunisia 127
4° Stormo CT 89-91,125
51°Stormo CT 89-91
9°Gruppo CT 89-91
10° Gruppo CT 89-91
16° Gruppo CT 132
20° Gruppo CT 89-91
153° Gruppo CT 85
155° Gruppo CT 89,91
1° Gruppo CT, RSI 181
Register, Ens Francis R 118
Rehm, Lt(jg) Daniel R Jr 205
Reichenau, Gen von 26
Reichstag, Berlin, Germany 39
Reinert, Oblt Ernst-Wilhelm 129,132-3,136
Reiserer, Lt Russell 201,205
Rekata Bay, Solomons 113,116
Restmeyer, Hpt 47
Rheine, Germany 177
Rhodes 90
Rhodes, Rad El Thomas W 99
Rhodes-Moorhouse, Flg Off W 51
Richard, Maj R H 118
Richter, Oblt Gerhard 59
Richthofen, Gen Maj Wolfram von 20-1, 34
Rickenbacker, Edward 104
Roberts, Maj Eugene 177
Robertson, Sgt FN 85,91
Robinson, Ens Leroy W 205
Robinson, Ens Ross F 205
Rochester, England 47
Rodee, Cdr Walter CAG *Hornet* 114
Rödel, Oblt Gustav 26,48
Rogan, Soviet Union 144
Rollwage, Ofw Herbert 89,91,185
Rolski, Wg Cdr T H 132
Rome, Italy 174,193
Rommel, Feldmarshal Erwin 60,84,90-1,127,129
Roosevelt, Franklin D 86
Rossiger, Oblt Wilhelm-Richard 59
Rossiwall, Theodor 49
Rostock, Germany 176,181
Rota, Marianas 200,202
Rotmistrov, Lt Gen 5th Gu Tank Army 152
Rotterdam, Holland 52,158
Rouen-Sotteville, France 173
Royal Aircraft Establishment, Farnborough 52
Royal Air Force, Order of Battle Aug 40, 40-1,81, Order of Battle, Malta 82-157
Auxilliary Air Force 33,86
Volunteer Reserve 33
AASF 152
2nd Tactical Air Force 158
Desert Air Force 90,125, Order of Battle Tunisia 127,129,133-4,136
Army Co-operation Command 157
Bomber Command 33-7,41,50, 55,82,157-162, Coastal Command 35, Order of Battle 1940 42,46-7, 53,157,160
Fighter Command 33,34,35, 36,39, Order of Battle Aug 40 40-1,46-7,50-4, Scores of Sqns, Jul-Nov 40,55,55-6, List of aces 1940 57,60, 157-8,162
No 1 Group 157
No 2 Group 33-5,37,Order of Battle, 1940 42
No 3 Group 157,162
No 4 Group 157
No 5 Group 157,166
No 6 (RCAF) Group 153
No 8 (Pathfinder) Group 158,160-3,165
No 10 Group 39,53,55
No 11 Group 29,35-6,50,53
No 12 Group 35,36,52-3
No 13 Group 35,39
No 100 (Bomber Support) Group 158,161-2,168
No 242 Group 126,134
Light Night Striking Force 158,162
232 Wing 128-9,136
244 Wing 129,132-3
3 SAAF Wing 136
7 SAAF Wing 136
For individual squadrons, flights and units see Chapters 2,3,4,6,8
Royal Navy 33,46,58,60,86, 90,160,
Rubensdorffer, Hpt Walter 47,59
Rudel, Oblt Hans-Ulrich Profile 146,147
Rumania, 28,173,188
Rummel, Oblt 23
Rumpelhardt, Lt Fritz 159
Runyon, Mech Donald 100,103,118
Rupp, Oblt Walter 56
Russell Island, Solomons 111
RWD 14 Czapla 28
Ryazanov, Gen VG 147
Rye, England 46
Ryujo, Japanese aircraft carrier 67,101,103,203
Rzhavets, Soviet Union 152
R4D, Douglas 108,113

Saborovka, Soviet Union 146
Sailer, Maj Joseph 117
Saipan, Marianas 195,198,205
Sakai, NAP 1/C Saburo 79,98,99,119,204-5
Samar, 196
San Bernadino Strait, Philippines 196
Sanchez, Lt Cdr Henry G 114
San Marcellino, Philippines 71
Santa Cruz Islands, 105,114-6
Santa Isabella Island, Solomons 117
Saratoga, USS aircraft carrier 97-8,101,103,105,108,110-1
Sardinia 90,136
Sasai, Lt Junichi, Tainan Ku 98,105,119
Savo Island, Solomons 100,108,119
Savoia S.79 82
Specification 87
Savoia S.84
Specification 87,90
SBD, Douglas Dauntless, 97,99,101-1,102-3,108,110-6
Specification 116,117-20
SBD-5 193,197,201-3
SB2C, Curtiss Helldiver, 193
Specification 197, 202-3
Schade, F/Sgt PA 87,90
Schalk, Oberstlt Johann 49,58
Scharnhorst, German battle crusier 159
Schellmann, Maj Wolfgang 58
Scherf, Flt Lt CC 162
Scherer, Fw Walter 48
Schiermonnikoog, Holland 163
Schiess, Lt Franz 89,91
Schilling, Lt Col David L 184
Schink, Oblt Bernd von 56
Schleswig, Germany 162
Schlichting, Hpt Joachim 48
Schlichting, Maj 46
Schmidt, Lt Erich 48
Schnauffer, Maj Heinz-Wolfgang Profile 159,159
Schnell, Lt Siegfried 48,58
Schöpfel, Oblt Gerhard 48,50
Schouwen, Island, Holland 164
Schreiber, Capt Leroy 177
Schroeder, Lt(jg) T 204
Schultz-Blanck, Oblt 48
Schultz, Oblt Helmuth 164
Schweinfurt, Germany 174,179,181
Scotland 34
SD1/2, German Fragmentation bomb containers 145,148
Searby, Gp Capt 161
Seebad (Seaside), Operation, Warsaw 19,28
Seelöwe (Sea lion), Operation 34,53,158
Sekiga, Wt Off Kiyoshi, Yokosuka Ku 204
Sfax, Tunisia 136
Shackford, Lt (jg) Robert W 205
Sheppard, Lt William 72
Sherman tank 121-123,136
Shetland Islands, UK 35
Shields, Lt(jg) Jay A 202
Shigemi, Wt Off Katsuma *Zuikaku* 115
Shirahama, Wt Off Yoshijiro 203
Shokaku, Japanese aircraft carrier 103,105,114-5,198,200
Short Brothers, 47
Shortland Islands, Solomons 108
Sicily 81-3,90,126,136,150,174
Sidebottom, Flg Off 163
Sikorsky amphibian 68
Silesia, Germany 19
Simpson, Flt Lt J 39,57
Simpson Harbour, Rabaul 105-107
Sirakumo, Japanese destroyer 105
Skalski, Sqn Ldr S F 21,23,24, 51,132,136, Profile 26
Skon, Lt(jg) Warren A 205
Skua, Blackburn 44
Smith, Lt Don 177
Smith, Maj John L 100,105,109,117-8
Smith Flt Lt R R 132
SOC, Curtiss 202
Solomon Islands 196
Soloniki, Soviet Union 144
Southampton, England 47,53
Southampton, HMS cruiser 81
South Dakota, USS battleship 114,116,119,120,199
Southerland, Lt James 98
Spain 34,48,65
Specht, Maj Günther 177,179
Speer, Reichmarshal Albert 160
Spies, Wilhelm 49
Spitfire, Supermarine, 29,33-5
Specification MKI 36,38,38-9,44-7,50,52-3,55, 60,77,85-6
Specification MK V 8689-92,97,127,129, 132-6,173
Sprick, Oblt Gustav 45,48,58
Spruance, Adm Raymond 193
Stalingrad, Soviet Union 136,141
Stalino, Soviet Union 141
Starkes, Lt(jg) Carl 100,103,118
Stavanger, Norway 36
Steinhoff, Oberst Johannes 187
Stephen, Plt Off HM 49,57
Sternberg, Hpt Horst 179
Stettin, Germany 162
Steyr, Austria 181-2
St Hubert, Belgium 162
Stirling, Short 47,159
Storp, Maj Walter 59
Stout, Lt Robert F 118
Stover, Lt(jg) Elisha 108
Strane, Lt John 201,205
Strange, Lt Cdr Johnnie C 205
Strasen, Lt JG77 133
Strassl, Ofw Herbert 144,146,Profile 146
Streib, Oberstlt Werner 59,162
Strong, Lt S Birney, *Enterprise* 114
Stuttgart, Germany 160,162,174,186
Subic Bay, Philippines
Suez Canal, Egypt 125
Suganami, Lt M 120
Sugawara, NAP 1/C Masao 204
Sulu Archipeligo 196
Sunderland, Short 81,85
'Sunrise', Wt Off Kiyanobu, *Junyo* 115,119
Swanage, England 45
Swansea, Wales 39
Swordfish, Fairey 81,84
Syrtsevo, Soviet Union 147
Szczesny, Lt Henryk 26,27
Szysko, Lt 20

Tacoblan, New Hebrides 108
Taiho, Japanese aircraft carrier 199-200
Takanami, Japanese destroyer 117
Takatsuka, Lt Toraichi 108,119
'Tallboy', 12,000lb bomb 168
Tanaka, Wt Off Minpo 198
Tanambogo Island, Solomons 97
Tangmere, England 47
Taranto, Italy 81
Tarantola, Maj Ennio 89,91
Tassafaronga Point, Guadalcanal 120
Tawi Tawi 196
TBF, Grumman Avenger (also TBM) 101,103,108,110-1,114-6
Specification 116,117-20, 189-91, 195-7,202-3
Tebaga, Tunisia 132-6
Tenaru River, Guadalcanal 100
Teploye, Soviet Union 147,150,152
Terauchi, Gen Count Hisaichi 65
Thailand 66
Thames, River, England 39
Thameshaven, England 51
Thelen, Lt(jg) Robert 198
Thelepte, Tunisia 134
Thomas, Flt Lt 163
Thorn, F/Sgt E 49,57
Thorney Island, England 47
'Thousand Plan', 160
Tiedmann, Oblt Helmut 50
Tietzen, Hpt Horst 48,50,58
Tilbury, England 50
Tinian, Marianas 194-6,203,305
Tirpitz, German battleship 158,168
Tobruk, Libya 126
Tojo, Gen Hideki, Japanese Premier 205
Tokarev, Maj Moisei S 147
Tokyo, Japan 160
Tomahawk, Curtiss (RAF) 125
Tombolini, Sottoten 187
Tone, Japanese cruiser 114
Tonsberg, Germany 168
Toraichi, Takatsuka, Tainan Ku 98
Torun, Poland 25
Toyoda, Adm Soemu Naval C in C 195
Tratt, Maj Eduard 49,181,185,188
Tripoli, Libya 125-6
Tripolitania, Libya 81,84
Troglitz, Germany 164
Tromsofjord, Norway 168
Truenbreitzen, Germany 163
Truk, Caroline Islands 105,114,116,193-5,198-9,202
Tsunoda, Lt(jg) Kazuo 120
Tuck, Sqn Ldr RRS 49,57
Tuguegardo, Philippines 72
Tulagi, Solomons 97,105
Tunis, Tunisia 126
Tunisia, 81,92,Chapter 6, 141,173-4,185
Turner, Lt Charles H 205
Turner, Adm Richard Kelly 97
Tweedale, Plt Off GR 90
T-34 tank 147-8

Ubben, Maj Kurt 185
'Ultra' code 34,141
United States Army
II Corps 126-7,132,136
31st Infantry Division 66
39th Infantry Division 136
Philippine Division 66
Provisional Tank Group 66
200th Coast Artillery Regiment 66
United States Army Air Force
'Big Week' fighter claims 187; losses 187
US 5th Air Force 74,118
US 7th Air Force 193,202
US 8th Air Force 167,173-7, Order of Battle Feb,44,178,179,181,182, 184-5,187-8
US 9th Air Force 174-6,179,184,187
US 12th Air Force 126,174-5
US 13th Air Force 193,202
US 15th Air Force 174,176-7, Order of Battle, Feb 44,178-9,181-2,186-8
US 20th Air Force 185
US Far Eastern Air Force 65, Order of Battle 66
XII Air Support Command 126,132-4,136
Strategic Air Command 185
1st Bomb Division 174,176-7,179,181,186
2nd Bomb Division 176-7,179,181,185-6
3rd Bomb Division 175,176,179,181,185-6
3rd Bomb Wing 185
4th Bomb Wing 185
5th Bomb Wing 177
14th Bomb Wing 185
For Bomb Groups see Chapter 8
For Fighter Groups and Squadrons see Chapters 3,5,9,10
United States Marine Corps
1st Marine Division 99
Marine Air Group 14 108
Marine Air Group 23 97,100,113
Marine Air Group 25 108
VMF-112 118,20
VMF-121 104,108,110-1, 113,116-20
VMF-212 100,110,113,118-20
VMF-223 100-1,105,108,109, 110-1,118
VMF-224 105,108,110-1, 113,118
VMF-253 108
VMO-251 97,118-9
VMSB-131 118
VMSB-132 118
VMSB-141 108,110-1
VMSB-142 118
VMSB-231 105,113
VMSB-232 100,105,111
United States Navy Order of Battles 1942 115 Order of Battle, June 44 194 Squadron Victory totals June-Aug 44 205
US 5th Fleet 193
Task Force 58 193-4,200,203
TG 58.1 193,195-6,200,203-5
TG 58.2 193,195,200,203
TG 58.3 193,195,198, 200,202-3
TG 58.4 193,195-6,200,203
TG 58.7 193,199-200
Task Force 16 114
Task Force 17 114
Task Force 61 97
Task Force 62 97
Task Force 64 114
Pat Wing 10 67,73,75
Air Group 10 115,119-20
Air Group 15 197,200,201
Air Group 16 198
VB-6 99,116
VB-8 114
VB-10 202
VB-16 202
VC-5 205
VC-33 205
VC-41 205
VF-1 196,200,202-5
VF-2 195-6,199-205
VF-5 98-101,103,105,108, 110-1,118
VF-6 98-100,103,118,201
VF-8 199,202,205
VF-10 114-5,118-20,195,199, 201-2,205
VF-13 204-5
VF-14 200,202,204-5
VF-15 195-6,199-202,205
VF-16 189-91,200-2,205
VF-24 195,198-9,202,205
VF-25 199,201,205
VF-27 199-200,205
VF-28 195,198-9,205
VF-31 195,199,204-5
VF-32 205
VF-50 200,202,204-5
VF-51 195,198-9,205
VF-71 110,113,118
VF-72 114,118
VF(N)-76 201,204-5
VF(N)-77A 202,204-5
VF(N)-101 198,202
VS-3 108,110-11,113
VS-5 99
VS-10 114
VS-71 99,108,111,113,116
VT-3 103
VT-8 108,110-1,117,119
VT-10 114,119-20,195,202
VT-16 189-91,195,200,202
'Flight 300' 105,108
Unwin, F/Sgt GC 57
Upton, Plt Off HC 57
Urbanowicz, Sqn Ldr W 49,57
Uto, NAP 2/C Kazushi Tainan Ku 98,108,119

Vandergrift, Gen Archie 97
Van Haren, Lt Arthur, Jnr 205
Vatutin, Gen, Russian, 150
Vechta, Germany,163
Vegesack, Germany,174
Vejtasa, Lt Stanley 114, 118
Ventnor, Isle of Wight, England, 46
Velenikhino, Soviet Union, 147
Verben, Germany 177
Verkhopenye, Soviet Union 147
Vickers Aircraft Co, 51
Vickers "S" 40mm gun, 134
Victoria, USS cruiser, 100
Victoria Cross 36,47,51,168
Victorious HMS aircraft carrier 82,86
Vienna, Austria, 186
Vigan, Philippines, 71,72,73,75,76
Vigorous, Operation, army, 90
Villa, Fg Off J W 57
Villamor, Cap Jesus 74
Vincennes USS cruiser,100
Vineyard, Lt (jg) M W 203,205
Vinke, Ofw Heinz 165
Vistula, River, Poland, 19,25,26,27
Vollbracht, Oberstlt Friedrich 58
Voris, lt (jg) Albert 203,205
Voronezh, Soviet Union, 142
Vorozheikin. Arsenii V, Profile 147
Vose, Lt James E 115
Vought V-156F, 144
Vraciu, Lt Cdr Alex 200, Profile 201,202,205
V-1, Fieseler Fi 103 flying bomb, 161,168
V-2, A-4 rocket 161

Wagner, Lt Boyd D, Profile 74,75
Wake Island, 193
Wakoo, Lt Tainan Ku 73
Walker, F/Sgt 163
Wallens, Plt Off RW, 45
Wallis, Barnes, 168
Warburton, Wg Cdr A 88
Warmwell, England, 36
Warsaw, Poland, 19,20,22,24,25,26,28,52
Washington, USS, battleship, 119,120
Wasp, USS aircraft carrier, 86,88,89,90,97,105,108,110
Wasp USS, (New), 200,201
Watchtower, Operation, Guadalcanal 97
Weaver, Fg Off C, III 88,91
Webb, Ens Wilbur B 201,205
Webster, Fl Lt JT 45,51,57
Weir, Plt Off A N C, 46
Wellington, Vickers 81,83,88,90,127,157
Welshman British tanker,89
Welter, Ofw Kurt, 162,163
Werra, Oblt Franz von 48
Wesendorf, Germany, 163
Weslowski, Ens John 108,118
Westerland, Germany, 162
Western Desert Air Force, see Desert Air Force
Westland Aircraft Co, 55
Weymouth, Dorset, England 34
Whitley, Armstrong-Whitworth 47,157
Wicht, Polish D D, 23
Wick, Major Helmut, 46,48
Widhelm, Lt Cdr Gus, Hornet, 114,115
Widzew, Poland, 24
Wiegand, FW Gerd,181
Wehrmacht 33,141,152,158
Army Group Centre 142,152,193
Army Group South 26,141-2,144-5
2nd Army 142
3rd Army 19
4th Army 19
6th Army 136,141
8th Army 19,26
9th Army 142,151
10th Army 19,20,21,24,26
14th Army 19,21
4th Panzer Army 142,145,148,150
Army Detachment Kempf 142,145,148,150,152
For individual Korps, Divisions and Regiments 19,21-26,126-30,136, 145-150,152
Wielun, Poland, 20,21
Wiener Neustadt, Austria 175
Wiese, Hpt Johannes 145, Profile 146
Wight, Isle of, England 45,46,56
Wilcke, Oberst Wolf-Dietrich, JG 3, 185
'Wilde Sau', 162,163,165
Wilhelmshaven, Germany, 157,173
Wilhelmstor, Germany 176
Williams Plt Off JW 249 Sqn, 88,91
Willius, Oblt Karl 182,187
Wilson, Brg General Russell 185
Winchester HMS, destroyer,58
'Window' 160,162,164,167,200
Wirth, Lt(jg) John L VF31 205
Wlodowa, Poland, 27
Wolf, Lt (jg) John T 195,205
Woltersdorf, Oblt Helmut 26
Woods, Gen Louis, USMC 117
Woods-Scawen, Plt Off A, 51
Woods-Scawen Flg Off P P 51,57
Woolaston, England, 53
Wooldridge, Wg Cdr J De L 158
Worthy Down, England, 47
Wrenn, Ens George L, 114,118

'X-Gerat', navigation aid 56

Yakovlev Yak 7B, 147
Yakovlev Yak 9 142,143
Specification 148,152,152
Yakovlevo, Soviet Union, 147
Yamada, Rear Adm Sadoyoshi 97
Yamaguchi, Ens Sadao 110,204
Yamamoto, Cdr 110
Yamamoto, Lt Shigehira 119
Yamato, Japanese battleship, 195
Yamashita, Sahei 98,99
Yarra, Flg Off J W 88,91
Yates, Fg Off, 163
Yawata, Japan 196
Yeovil, England 55
Yevstigneyev, Gds Col, Kirill A, 240th IAP Profile 147
Yokosuka D4Y, 196
Specification 197,198, 199,200,203
Yorktown USS, aircraft carrier 204
Yoshida, NAP 1/c Motosuma 99,119
Yoshimura Pty Off 3/c Keisuka 113,119
Yugira Japanese destroyer, 105
Yugoslavia, 82,181
Yura Japanese cruiser 113
YB-40 Beoing Fortress gunship 174
Y Service, 34

Zarniskiye Dvory, Soviet Union 146
Zaytsev, Col VA 146
Zechlin, Hpt Ernst 165
Zemke, Col Hubert 184,185
Zigzaou, Wadi, Tunisia 135
'Zitadel' (Citadel) Operation, Kursk 141-2,150-2
Zorner, Hpt Paul 163
Zuara, Tunisia 129
Zuiho, Japanese aircraft carrier 114-5
Zuikaku, Japanese aircraft carrier 103,114-6,189-91, 200,203
Zuyder Zee, Holland 164

Picture credits

John Batchelor 134 (bottom), 168
Jerzy Czynk 24,25,26-27
John Foreman 21,46,48,89, 134,146,158-59,162,163, 179,185,186
D Gillam 49
Imperial War Museum 38,44, 49,90,92,128,132,161
Yasuho Izawa 67,70-71,72-73, 76,98-99,106-107,112,196, 198,199,201,204
Malcolm Passingham 144,145, 147,150, 150-151,152
I Primmer 88
Royal Canadian Air Force 89
Jerry Scutts 25 (bottom), 34-35, 45,51,53,56,60,84,101,109, 111
Christopher Shores 89,126, 134 (top),149,193
General Sikorski Institute 49
State Maggiore 85
Ray Toliver 74,102,104, 108,135, 184,201,203
USAF 70,175, 176,177
US Marine Corps 200